2 KINGS

DALE RALPH DAVIS

2 KINGS

THE POWER AND THE FURY

'Excellent, crisp, lively exposition.'
Bibliotheca Sacra*

DALE RALPH DAVIS

CHRISTIAN FOCUS

Dale Ralph Davis is pastor of Woodlands Presbyterian Church, Hattiesburg, Mississippi. Previously he taught Old Testament at Reformed Theological Seminary, Jackson Mississippi. He has previously written commentaries on *Joshua*(ISBN 1-85792-602-1), *Judges*(1-85792-578-5), *1 Samuel*(1-85792-516-5), *2 Samuel*(1-85792-598-X) and *1 Kings*(185792-703-6)

© Dale Ralph Davis 2005

ISBN 1-84550-096-2

10 9 8 7 6 5 4 3 2 1

Published in 2005
Reprinted 2006
by
Christian Focus Publications Ltd.,
Geanies House, Fearn, Ross-shire,
IV20 1TW, Great Britain

www.christianfocus.com

Edited by Malcolm Maclean
Cover design by Alister MacInnes

Printed and bound by
CPD, Wales

Contents

The Torn Kingdom (continued)
2 Kings 1–17

The Last Days
2 Kings 18–25

Abbreviations

ABD	*Anchor Bible Dictionary*
ANET	*Ancient Near Eastern Texts*, 3rd ed.
BDB	Brown, Driver, and Briggs, *Hebrew and English Lexicon*
DCH	*Dictionary of Classical Hebrew* (ed. D. J. A. Clines)
ESV	English Standard Version
IDB	*Interpreter's Dictionary of the Bible*
IDBS	*Interpreter's Dictionary of the Bible/Supplementary Volume*
ISBE	*International Standard Bible Encyclopedia*
JB	Jerusalem Bible
K-B	Koehler & Baumgartner, *Hebrew and Aramaic Lexicon*
LXX	The Septuagint
NASB	New American Standard Bible (updated ed.)
NBD	*New Bible Dictionary*
NBV	New Berkley Version
NEB	New English Bible
NIDOTTE	*New International Dictionary of Old Testament Theology & Exegesis*
NIV	New International Version
NJB	New Jerusalem Bible
NJPS	Tanakh: A New Translation of the Holy Scritures according to the Traditional Hebrew Text (1985)
NKJV	New King James Version
NLT	New Living Translation
NRSV	New Revised Standard Version
REB	Revised English Bible
RSV	Revised Standard Version
TEV	Today's English Version
TWOT	*Theological Wordbook of the Old Testament*

Preface

When I taught in seminary I was always glad when I had a class on November 10, Martin Luther's birthday. We would do a 'Luther' cheer to begin class that day. I would holler, 'Give me an "L"!' and they would shout it back, and so on through Brother Martin's surname until I could yell, 'What does it spell?' and they would thunder back 'Luther!' It was a rousing way to begin class and forty or so, mostly male, voices easily rose to the invitation for mounting bedlam. I've far fewer opportunities for rowdiness now that I'm serving a congregation again, but I was especially delighted over Luther's birthday this year because it was the very day I finished the rough draft of this 2 Kings commentary. Twenty years ago I began writing, hoping to produce expositional commentaries on the 'Former Prophets' (Joshua–2 Kings minus Ruth) and it is gratifying to finish that course.

I am especially thankful to the kind folks at Christian Focus, who picked up an 'orphaned' series halfway through. I have never forgotten Malcolm Maclean's visit one March day and his willingness to take a rejected 2 Samuel manuscript back to Scotland with him. And I owe a huge debt to the elders at Woodland Presbyterian where I now serve. Any number of times they have asked me if I was 'getting enough time to work on the commentary.' They even offered to relieve me of preaching the evening services for a while in order to free up time to write. (Actually, there may have been more behind that offer than I'm willing to admit.) I get to serve with such generous and encouraging men.

This book goes out as a tribute to Derek and Rosemary Thomas and to David and Andrea Jussely, former and esteemed colleagues while at Reformed Seminary, Jackson, Mississippi, and special friends always. David did me (and others) the immense favor of pastoring Woodland Presbyterian some years before I arrived here. Because he poured some ten years of his sweat and prayers into this congregation, my work is so much easier now. One of the privileges I now miss is having an office door fifteen feet from Derek's, where I could find sense, hilarity, and helpfulness, usually all at one time. Not that I didn't help him. I still remember the days he would arrive at the seminary very early but forget his keys and wait, woebegone-like, until I arrived to let him in. It is my delight to send off *Power and Fury* in honor of these dear brothers and elect ladies.

Advent 2004

Introduction

When I was serving in theological academia we would occasionally have a student who couldn't begin studies at the start of the term. He might arrive, say, three weeks into the semester. Such students drop into the middle of things and that is a hard place to begin; they have to play catch-up and get their academic sea legs quickly. Generally, we don't like to begin in the middle of things. We want to see the whole play or read the whole novel.

2 Kings, however, makes us begin in the middle of things. It opens with the paramedics inspecting mangled King Ahaziah after a brutal second-storey fall. Rather abrupt.

Actually, this undesirable situation was not always the case because 2 Kings has not always been 2 Kings! Originally our 1 and 2 Kings were simply the single book of Kings. However, Greek translations of the Old Testament (after ca. 200 bc) divided the book into two segments, probably because of its length. This division then appeared in printed editions of the Hebrew text (1500s) and continues in, among others, our English Bible tradition.

So we must go back, at least momentarily, to pull 1 Kings into the picture and to see 1–2 Kings as one overall document. In a previous volume,[1] I laid out the major divisions of 1–2 Kings like this:

---

[1] *The Wisdom and the Folly: An Exposition of the Book of First Kings* (Ross-shire: Christian Focus, 2002), 11.

I.   The Golden Age, 1 Kings 1–11
II.   The Torn Kingdom, 1 Kings 12–2 Kings 17
III.   The Last Days, 2 Kings 18–25

The first segment focuses on the splendor of Solomon's reign, the second on the 'divided' kingdom(s) (north and south, Israel and Judah) with far more attention to the northern kingdom and its apostasy, and the third on Judah (the southern kingdom) by itself as it slides, only slightly hindered, into divine judgment and Babylonian exile.

Now that is the big view of the 'book' of Kings. And yet, in spite of the artificial division of Kings, one can almost say that 1 Kings and 2 Kings each carries its own distinct emphasis; in fact, they follow a similar pattern, moving from generally positive to terribly negative. 1 Kings begins with the blessing and wisdom of Solomon's kingship (1 Kings 1–10) only to continue with the folly of both Solomon and of the northern kings—especially Jeroboam I in his slick syncretism and Ahab in his raw paganism (1 Kings 11–22). 2 Kings moves similarly, beginning with an interlude of grace under the ministry of Elisha, through whom Yahweh displays the power he would lavish on Israel (2 Kings 1–8); with grace despised, however, the process of judgment presses on until Yahweh consigns his people to the tender mercies of the Assyrians and Babylonians (2 Kings 9–25). Hence I dub this study of 2 Kings, *The Power and the Fury.*

The Torn Kingdom
(continued)

2 Kings 1–17

1

The Fire This Time
(2 Kings 1)

Second Kings begins on a positive note: Ahab is dead.
You may think that is a nasty sentiment, but you must
remember that Ahab was a conduit that allowed pagan sewage
to engulf Israel (1 Kings 16:29-34), one who tolerated injustice
(1 Kings 21), and who hated God's word (e.g., 1 Kings 22). But
the Ahabs always die—that is good news. The bad news is that
Ahab, Jr., follows him. Ahaziah is a chip off the old, dead block.
Welcome to Israel, 852 BC.

One could develop this exposition under various schemes
but since Old Testament historical narrative is 'a declaration
from God about God' (Alec Motyer) I far prefer highlighting
how Yahweh reveals himself in this passage.

The God who detests our idols (vv. 1-8)
Who knows exactly how it happened? Ahaziah fell from the
second floor when some screen-work gave way. Apparently
a serious injury since his inquiry implies he was uncertain of
recovery. We needn't debate whether Ekron's god was Baal-
zebub or Baalzebul. The Baal-prefix says it all: he walks in
the religious rut of his father as goaded by Jezebel (1 Kings
16:29-34). The king in Samaria thinks his hope for years to come
squats in a temple forty-five miles (seventy-two kilometers)
away in Philistia.

'But the angel of Yahweh spoke to Elijah the Tishbite…' (v. 3a). God doesn't twiddle when apostasy is afoot. There were Ahaziah's messengers (v. 2) and now there is Yahweh's messenger sent to intercept them. Elijah's message is both question and judgment:

Is it because there is no God in Israel that you are going to inquire from Baal-zebub god of Ekron? Now therefore, here's what Yahweh says: 'The bed to which you have gone up—you will not come down from it, but you will surely die' (vv. 3-4).

So Elijah went off per instructions (v. 4b).

The next thing we know, Ahaziah's lackeys are reporting back to him (v. 5). The writer assumes that we are intelligent readers, so he omits details of the actual encounter between Ahaziah's men and Elijah. Assuming it took place as directed, he focuses the king's surprise at their swift return (v. 5b). Ahaziah knows they've aborted their mission. Why? They tell the king of the man who met them, the orders he gave, the message he announced (v. 6). They obeyed his orders; the stranger's authority trumped the king's authority.[1] The king presses for a description of the culprit (v. 7). Hearing that he was a 'hairy man wearing a leather belt around his waist' (v. 8, NKJV), he knew—probably with a mix of despair and rage—that it was Elijah.[2]

What do we meet in this section of the story? Above all, *an intolerant God.* The suave, self-appointed connoisseurs of religious taste in our time will be aghast if ever they happen on to this story. How can Yahweh in his wild, untamed holiness sentence a man to death simply for exercising his religious preferences in a critical hour of his life? Yahweh here is not the democratic sort of God people crave, according to the polls. Our times would prefer the mythology of the Ancient Near East, where gods and goddesses were permissive and casual and never insisted upon exclusive loyalty. None of these deities thought it a mortal sin should one of his/her devotees want to

---

[1] Ahaziah's messengers must have been impressed by Elijah's authority. They do not question him at all and willingly risk the royal wrath by returning with the king's orders unfulfilled. Cf. K. D. Fricke, *Das zweite Buch von den Königen*, Die Botschaft des alten Testaments (Stuttgart: Calwer, 1972), 19-20.

[2] NKJV is correct in v. 8: 'hairy' describes Elijah himself, not his clothing.

be ecumenical in his devotion. But in the Bible we meet Yahweh and keep bashing ourselves against his first commandment (Exod. 20:3).[3] Nor is it any better in the New Testament. Jesus goes around insisting folks must smash idols if they would follow as disciples (Mark 10:21-22). He is as obnoxious as Yahweh. Who does he think he is?

We also meet *a trenchant idolatry* here. We must not think Ahaziah's resort to Baal-zebub was simply a sudden act of desperation in a moment of weakness. Flip back your Bible page to 1 Kings 22:52-53, where the writer summarizes the *policy* of Ahaziah's reign. 'He served Baal and bowed down to him' (v. 53). In verse 2 (of the present text) Ahaziah only displays the *consistency* of his 'faith'. His appeal to Baal was not a knee-jerk reaction in a sudden emergency. Baal has always been Ahaziah's deity of choice; he has had no place for Yahweh. His idolatry was due to preference, not to ignorance or weakness.

In one of his books Carl Henry discusses the view of Hoyle and Wickramasinghe that life arrived on earth from outer space. Hoyle and Wickramasinghe 'project a supraterrestrial principle of intelligence, one somewhat more than human yet less than ultimate and absolute and hence not a personal God.' Looking beyond the earth to the whole universe for an explanation of life has, according to these theorists, distinct advantages. 'For one thing,' they say, 'it offers the possibility of high intelligence within the universe that is not God.'[4] That is a most revealing statement. Whom are they trying to avoid? Looks like they have a vested interest in positing something, anything, so long as 'it' is not the personal, omnipotent God. Their idolatry seems light-years away from Ahaziah's but at root it is the same: a *commitment* has already been made that wants no truck with Yahweh. For the king the idol was Baal; for the scientists a nebulous, non-divine super-intelligence afoot somewhere in the universe.

---

[3] I like the way the Scots Confession (1560) puts this matter front and center. The very first lines of the confession are: 'We confess and acknowledge one God alone, to whom alone we must cleave, whom alone we must serve, whom only we must worship, and in whom alone we put our trust.' It goes on to describe and identify the triune God, but this *demand* comes first.

[4] Quotations from C. F. H. Henry, *God, Revelation and Authority*, 6 vols. (Waco: Word, 1983), 6:178-79.

Yet Ahaziah's was also *a foolish idolatry*.[5] For a believer in Yahweh there is such a sadness about it all. Here is the king, perhaps near life's end—at least his request (v. 2) suggests Ahaziah knew it could be his 'last illness'. And in this desperate moment we hear, 'Go, inquire of Baal-zebub.' The moment so crucial; the recourse so asinine. The spectre of death does not necessarily produce good sense.

In one of his novels Walker Percy has his lead character, Will Barrett, writing a letter in which he lampoons both Christians and unbelievers—particularly the latter. According to Barrett, an unbeliever is crazy partly because

> he takes comfort and ease, plays along with the game, watches TV, drinks his drink, laughs, curses politicians, and now and again to relieve the boredom and the farce (of which he is dimly aware) goes off to war to shoot other people—for all the world as if his prostate were not growing cancerous, his arteries turning to chalk, his brain cells dying off by the millions, as if the worms were not going to have him in no time at all.[6]

Staring our end in the face, whether slowly or suddenly, ought to drive us to sobriety and truth. But it doesn't necessarily drive us to sobriety; that was Will Barrett's point. And sometimes it makes us sober (as, apparently, in Ahaziah's case) but not smart (seeking Baal, not Yahweh). Death is no time to be playing with dead-end religious options. We must have the One who has the words of eternal life (cf. John 6:68). But here is Ahaziah about to step off the edge of life with nothing but Baal, or, I should say, with nothing.

We also run into *a kind severity* in this passage. No doubt about the severity—Yahweh's wrath glows at white heat, his disdain oozes out of his question, 'Is it because there is no God in Israel that you are going to inquire of Baal-zebub?' (v. 3). His judgment is unsparing: Ahaziah will be bed-ridden and death-stricken (v. 4).

---

[5] I owe the bulk of this point to my friend and former colleague Derek Thomas. I simply had not thought of it until I heard him preach on this text at First Presbyterian, Jackson, Mississippi.

[6] Walker Percy, *The Second Coming* (New York: Farrar, Straus, Giroux, 1980), 189-90.

Yahweh's words are repeated three times (vv. 3, 6, 16)—clearly they highlight the central concern of the narrative. When Ahaziah sends to Philistia he implies Israel has no God; when he appeals to Baal-zebub he is implying that Yahweh is either non-existent or irrelevant and inadequate. (Is this not, in principle, the essence of all our idolatry? By taking first recourse to other helps and supports we subtly confess the inadequacy and insufficiency of Yahweh to handle our dilemmas.) So Yahweh's intrusion is anything but affable and courteous. He sends Elijah to cut off and stifle the king's godless expedition. The command Elijah hears is very similar to one he received in 1 Kings 21:17-18. There Ahab had allowed Jezebel to shove Naboth and his sons through her meat-grinder so that Ahab might obtain Naboth's vineyard. Then 'the word of Yahweh came to Elijah the Tishbite, saying, "Rise, go down to meet Ahab king of Israel, who is in Samaria..."' And here in 2 Kings 1 we find the same idiom: 'But the angel of Yahweh spoke to Elijah the Tishbite, "Rise, go up to meet the messengers of the king of Samaria..."' (v. 3). Rise, go down to meet; rise, go up to meet. But the import is the same: nail him in his tracks.

If, however, Yahweh is severe, he is at the same moment merciful. His nasty interruption of Ahaziah's mission is, if the king could only see, a last opportunity. Yahweh did not allow Ahaziah's idolatry to proceed in peace but invaded his space and rubbed his face in the first commandment again. Again we see our uncomfortable God: Yahweh is furious, not tolerant; holy, not reassuring; loving, not nice. But there *is* love in his fury. He won't let you walk the path to idolatry easily; his mercy litters the way with roadblocks. That is a wonder considering he so detests our idols.

The God who defends his witness (vv. 9-12)

Some commentators are quite clear that this section is *not* one of their favorite Bible stories. John Gray, for example, writes:

> There may well be a nucleus of historical fact in Elijah's protest against Ahaziah's appeal to the oracle of Baal of Ekron (vv. 2-8, 17), but in the annihilation of the king's innocent emissaries by fire (vv. 9-16) there is a moral pointlessness, which relegates the tradition to the same category as Elisha's baneful curse upon the rude boys of Bethel (2.23f.).[7]

Another writes of the 'preposterousness of the miraculous element' in the story and laments 'its inhumanity with the destruction of the innocent fifties'.[8] Now some difficulties cannot be alleviated. Some scholars and readers will always find the miraculous preposterous, and no story of 102 troops turned to toast can meet the standards of middle-class refinement. But 'moral pointlessness'? Has anyone who holds that really read the story? So we must dive in.

Let's begin with *blame*. Why did Elijah do that? Answer: he didn't. The first two captains come strutting onto the scene each with his own brand of arrogance. The first emphasizes royal authority: '*The king* has ordered, "Come down"' (v. 9b); the second demands speed: 'O man of God, here's what the king says: "Come down—quick!"' (v. 11b). In each case Elijah replies, 'If I am a man of God, let fire come down from heaven and consume you and your fifty men' (vv. 10a, 12a).[9] When we are told that fire 'came down from heaven' (vv. 10b, 12b) we are to understand that God answered Elijah's call affirmatively. If Elijah's request was wrong-headed or reprehensible or perverse, God would not and should not have assented. The account shows that Yahweh approved Elijah's call for fire.[10] So let's quit beating up on Elijah. Blame Yahweh—he did it.[11]

---

[7] John Gray, *I & II Kings*, Old Testament Library, 2nd ed. (Philadelphia: Westminster, 1970), 459. The story is not morally pointless in my view, but, supposing it were, I fail to see how moral pointlessness in itself is a valid argument against historicity.

[8] J. A. Montgomery, *A Critical and Exegetical Commentary on the Books of Kings*, International Critical Commentary (New York: Charles Scribner's Sons, 1951), 348.

[9] When Elijah picks up their term of address, he seems almost to be saying, '"Man of God," hmm…do you really understand what that may mean? "God" isn't a mere three-letter word, you know. If I am a man *of God*, then where I am God is likely to be acting.' Indeed this last is what Elijah calls for, because when he says 'Let fire come down *from heaven*,' he means 'Let Yahweh send it.'

[10] In his earlier work (*Elijah and Elisha* [1957], 77-78) R. S. Wallace holds that as God's servants we are 'often as mistaken, self-centred and stupid as Elijah was in his behaviour on that mountain.' He proposes an anti-Elijah, pro-God explanation: 'Elijah may have given a most unworthy representation of the true nature of God and yet God protected him and used him. In this conflict between the vicious and rebellious king and the foolish and unworthy prophet God took the side of the prophet. He did not withdraw His help from Elijah because Elijah made a callous and dramatic fool of himself. He did not wait until one side was prepared to behave in a perfectly holy manner before He chose which side He was to be on.' Granted, God may give his help to his servants even in their wrong-headedness—one may find that in other texts. But for 2 Kings 1 I think Wallace's explanation suffers from hermeneutical schizophrenia, for Yahweh's response implies that Elijah's request was proper in these circumstances.

[11] Occasionally Jesus' rebuke of James and John in Luke 9:54-55 is taken as his implicit disapproval of Elijah's actions in 2 Kings 1. It is no such thing. Jesus rebukes

Now we must consider *intent*: What was the king trying to do by sending two military contingents to apprehend the prophet? This question mystifies some commentators: '[I]t is unclear why Ahaziah, who had already received Elijah's word through messengers (v. 6), should now wish to consult him through military personnel.'[12] Unclear? Ahaziah wished to 'consult' Elijah? Do you send a fifty-man posse to procure a consultant? Some interpreters never understand this passage because they never consider Ahaziah's intention. Ellison is right: 'The fifty men were not intended to be a guard of honour! It was an open declaration of hostilities, and Elijah treated it as such.'[13] Ahaziah planned to silence the word of God through Elijah—probably by liquidating Elijah (cf. the implied danger to Elijah's life in the angel of Yahweh's words in v. 15). The king was not inviting Elijah to dinner. Why is this so hard to see? Here is an undefended prophet accosted by royal military muscle. The palace intends to use its police in order to dispose of the prophet.

We are ready then to consider the *function*. That is, why the fire (vv. 10b, 12b)? What was Yahweh's objective in sending his judgment in this form?

One cannot understand 2 Kings 1 unless one remembers 1 Kings 18. The latter passage relates the 'god contest' on Mount Carmel, Yahweh versus Baal. Fire was the burning issue of the day: the God who answered by fire would show himself to be the real God (1 Kings 18:21, 23-24, 36-39). It was a matter of *proof*. That is the function of the fire in 2 Kings 1 as well. Oh, it should have been unnecessary. King Ahaziah surely knew what had taken place just a few years before at Mt. Carmel. It was a public, prime-time affair covered (if one may be anachronistic) by all the major news networks. It was not done in a corner. It scared the liver out of the folks who saw it and they never

---

James and John for misreading the present situation (a Samaritan village refusing him hospitality) - such judgment is not yet called for since 'his present mission is not as judge but as saviour' (E. Earle Ellis, *The Gospel of Luke*, New Century Bible Commentary [London: Oliphants, 1974], 152).

[12] G. H. Jones, *1 and 2 Kings*, New Century Bible Commentary, 2 vols. (Grand Rapids: Eerdmans, 1984), 2:376.

[13] H. L. Ellison, *The Prophets of Israel* (Grand Rapids: Eerdmans, 1969), 34. Cf. also Walter Brueggemann, *1 and 2 Kings*, Smyth & Helwys, 2000), 285.

stopped talking about it. Carmel Day made the point: Yahweh is the real God, Baal a sorry non-entity. But Ahaziah didn't get the point. When he has an urgent need for health care, he appeals to Baal (v. 2)—Baal the loser (1 Kings 18). What do you do when someone is so dense, so 'thick,' that he doesn't grasp what fire (1 Kings 18:38) means? You send more fire (2 Kings 1:10b, 12b)! The point is the same, i.e., Yahweh is the only God, but the fire is not only demonstrative (as at Carmel in 1 Kings 18) but destructive (102 seared remains, thanks to Ahaziah). The first commandment really matters to Yahweh, and Ahaziah just doesn't get it.[14]

The fire, however, also functions as *protection*. Here it is Yahweh's means of defending the bearer of his word, his undefended prophet. God does not always provide such protection, as 1 Kings 18:4, 13 show. Even in Elijah's own time Yahweh did not grant all prophets immunity from Jezebel's bloody pogroms. Yet in this instance Elijah *is* protected from Ahaziah's clutches. What is the significance (i.e., the sign-value) of this? Does not Ahaziah represent the power of any kingdom, any throne, any ruler, any government that tries to stifle Yahweh's word and silence his witnesses? And does not this little scenario testify that no king, no despot, no tyrant will ever be able totally to extinguish the witness of the word of God in this world?

Perhaps Cornelius Martens is another case in point. Martens, a Baptist preacher in the 1920s in the Soviet Union, was once taken to the office of the local Communist Party boss, apparently for interrogation. The Party boss ordered two men to strip Martens of his clothes, but Martens told them not to trouble themselves, that he would undress, adding, 'I don't fear to die, for I shall be going home to the Lord. If He has decided my hour hasn't come, you can't do me any harm here.' This last remark drove the Party boss into a rage: 'I'll prove to you that your God will not deliver you out of my hands!' He lifted his revolver to drop Martens in his tracks, but his finger

---

[14] This episode should keep us from hankering after miracles. The miracle in this text (sending fire) is not a compliment to faith but a judgment on unbelief. If God must go to that extreme to get your attention then you, like Ahaziah, must be in nigh-hopeless unbelief. Miracles may be a sign of our perversity rather than a mark of God's pleasure.

froze on the trigger. Three times he tried to fire and failed. His face grew red, his body began to shake, and he looked ready for a coronary episode. At last he lowered the gun and asked a lesser official what Martens was condemned for. The official answered, 'He is a Baptist. Can't you see God is fighting for him?' The boss ordered Martens to get out and stay away.[15]

Did that usually happen? No, the blood of God's servants ran deep in the Soviet Gulag where they were mashed without pity. But sometimes, in the midst of it all, the Lord of the church gives the power-grubbers of this age a sign of how abysmally helpless they are. That fuels the holy defiance of God's servants, for it shows them again that the word of God *will* have free course and none of the puny, piddly, royal Ahaziahs of this age can stop it!

The God who deflates our pride (vv. 13-15)

What if there had been cable television news coverage in 850 BC? Here is this officer sitting in the barracks with a few of his men, eyes glued on the monitor, watching the live report of the recent tragedy, with shots of emergency vehicles rushing to the scene and clips of some arriving at hospital emergency rooms. Then a dispatch arrives from the palace for our captain. His face drops as he reads the first line: 'Take fifty men...'

This third captain does not spout the previous arrogance (vv. 9, 11). He is different in his posture ('and knelt on his knees before Elijah,' v. 13b), in his purpose ('and he made a plea for grace to him,' v. 13c), and in his petition ('O man of God, let my life and the life of these fifty servants of yours be valued in your eyes,' v. 13d). The man was clearly terrified, for he fully knew what had happened to the former two contingents. In verse 14 he so much as says, 'I know I am within a centimeter of destruction—please spare me.' He knelt, he pled, he trembled—he lived.

In my previous studies of this passage I have usually ignored the response of this third captain. I think that was patently wrong. His response stands in dead opposition to that of the first two officers. Surely the writer wants us to note that. Perhaps the writer even wants to suggest that here, in this

---

[15] James and Marti Hefley, *By Their Blood: Christian Martyrs of the Twentieth Century*, 2nd ed. (Grand Rapids: Baker, 1996), 233-34.

third captain's words, Israel has a model response to Yahweh's wrath. Here Israel can see the way to life.

There are always some who will object. They will say that our motives should be more positive, that we should not be driven to repentance by something so servile or negative as the simple terror that drove this captain. But this captain *is* walking down the hill alive at Elijah's side (v. 15) and he knows such sentimentality is nonsense. There is nothing wrong with terror, so long as it is a *true* terror for that can become—as it did for him—a *saving* terror. Better to be trembling and alive than a puddle of carbon.

It must have been a similar fear that gripped hearers that August day in 1756 when George Whitefield preached in William Grimshaw's Yorkshire parish. Grimshaw had had an elevated pulpit constructed outside the south wall of the parish church—the number of hearers would not then be restricted to the capacity of the church building. Whitefield stood there as he addressed a massive throng. After prayer he solemnly announced his text. It was Hebrews 9:27. 'It is appointed unto men once to die and after this the judgment.' He paused, was about to proceed but was cut off by a wild, curdling shriek from the middle of the congregation. Pastor Grimshaw hurried to investigate and, after some minutes, returned to tell Whitefield that 'an immortal soul has been called into eternity.' This news was announced to the people. After a few moments Whitefield again announced his text: 'It is appointed unto men once to die...'

Another piercing shriek rose from another part of the crowd. Horror settled over the assembly when they heard a *second* person had fallen dead. After the turmoil had subsided somewhat, Mr. Whitefield indicated his intention of proceeding with the service. He did so, doubtless announcing his text again to an assembly as still as death.[16] Do you suppose they listened to Whitefield that day on that text? And why did they do so? Fear. Indeed, terror. It was unnerving but not unhealthy. Not if it humbled them to hear. If we ever get past the first stanza of Newton's hymn we understand that: 'Twas *grace* that taught my heart to *fear*.'

---

[16] Faith Cook, *William Grimshaw of Haworth* (Edinburgh: Banner of Truth, 1997), 192-94 (citing, in part, A. C. H. Seymour).

The God who delivers on his threats (vv. 17-18)

There was no interview. Elijah simply announced to Ahaziah, eyeball to eyeball, the same word the king had already heard (vv. 3, 6) and rejected, ending with 'You will surely die' (v. 16). 'So he died according to the word of Yahweh' (v. 17a). The writer's comment is both immediate and almost laconic. As if to say, 'What do you expect? If Yahweh speaks, it happens.'

We haven't time nor space to punch rewind or fast forward buttons on the text of 1–2 Kings. So permit me to dogmatize: the fulfillment of Yahweh's word is a major theme of 1–2 Kings. Here is another case in point. The writer wants you to see it again in verses 16-17a: what Yahweh says, Yahweh does. He is the God who delivers on his threats. 'So he died according to the word of Yahweh.'

This point cuts both ways, however, for this text implies that if Yahweh so certainly fulfills his threats he will just as certainly fulfill his promises. What Yahweh declares can be counted on—that is the point. Hence his assurances are as reliable as his judgments. Christ's flock needs to know that when they look at John 6:37 or 14:3. King Ahaziah experienced one side of the certainty of God's word, but that sure word can shield as well as shatter you, can support you as well as smash you.

The writer cleans up Ahaziah's reign, using his semi-conventional formulas (vv. 17b-18).[17] B. O. Long draws attention to the peculiar nature of the account:

> Aside from the brief notice about Moab's rebellion, v. 1, this narrative is the only incident reported for the reign. Curiously, the writer recounts not how the king ruled but how he died![18]

There's something haunting then about this record of Ahaziah's brief tenure. In the supreme need of his life he did not seek the real God—that's all we know about him. That's both sad and stupid. Yet Ahaziah is not the focus of the story. God is. I've tried to stress this in the way I have stated the main points. You ought to deal with him. Of course, you can do what you

---

[17] The chronological problem of verse 17b will be addressed in our treatment of 2 Kings 3.

[18] Burke O. Long, *2 Kings*, The Forms of the Old Testament Literature (Grand Rapids: Eerdmans, 1991), 17.

want with this strange story. You can call it legend; you can aver that it deals with a primitive level of religion; you can claim it is morally offensive; or you can face the God of whom it speaks.

2

Seismic Shift in the Kingdom of God[1]
(2 Kings 2)

Theodore Roosevelt must have been an unforgettable figure. He was so full of gusto and gumption, of dynamism and vigor, that one can get tired reading about it all. On October 14, 1912, he was to deliver a speech on the New Nationalism in Milwaukee. As he was getting into his car to leave for the auditorium, a man came up and shot him in the chest. Roosevelt's doctors pled with him to go to the hospital, but he was headed for the auditorium and insisted on going there. Upon arrival, he told the people he'd been shot, asked them to be quiet and to excuse him from making a long speech. He then pulled a blood-soaked manuscript from his coat pocket and proceeded to speak for ninety minutes![2] When TR died in 1919, his youngest son cabled his brothers on Europe's battlefields with the news: 'The Lion is dead!' It was as if TR was an epoch in himself, as if with his death an era had passed.

Apprehension
Now that seems to be the mood in 2 Kings 2. As verse 1a indicates, this is the story of Yahweh's taking Elijah heavenward

---

[1] Much of the material in this chapter appeared in my earlier article 'The Kingdom of God in Transition: Interpreting 2 Kings 2,' *Westminster Theological Journal* 46 (1984): 384-95. Though the form has been recast, I am grateful to WTJ's editors for permitting me to recycle much of the substance. Let me also mention here a very stimulating article by Graham Beynon, 'Chariots, Whirlwinds and Jesus—2 Kings 2v1-25,' 12 pp., available via www.beginningwithmoses.org. Beynon seeks to place 2 Kings 2 in the larger context of biblical theology and works out its witness to Christ.

[2] Paul F. Boller, Jr., *Presidential Campaigns* (New York: Oxford, 1985), 195.

in a storm wind. Everybody concerned seems to know of it — Elijah (v. 9), Elisha (vv. 3b, 5b), and the sons of the prophets (vv. 3a, 5a). But nobody talks about it — openly. There is an air of suppressed tension in the story (vv. 1-6). Everyone in the remnant church seems on edge. With Elijah's departure an era is passing. Elisha's cry in verse 12 indicates the esteem in which Elijah was held. By the 'chariotry of Israel and its horsemen' Elisha is probably referring to Elijah himself. Chariots and horses were military materiel. To have Elijah was like having the army of God.[3] He was the true defense system of Israel. As someone has said, Elijah was 'worth divisions'.

So now Israel's defense system was gone. Or so it seemed. For in the midst of a Baal-kissing regime and a prophet-killing oppression Elijah stood in the gap. Now Elijah is to be 'taken'. Hence the remnant's dread of what comes next. How to go on? An epoch is ending. It's transition time in the kingdom of God and it feels like a seismic shift. What are we to do when 'the Lion' is taken?

Vexation

We turn aside momentarily to deal with the 'problem' of this chapter. If one has an allergy to miracles — and many biblical critics do — this narrative poses some difficulties. One has put it quite candidly:

> The world of these narratives is certainly not the world of the modern reader. Water parts miraculously. Bears come out of the woods at the prophet's command. Magic ritual purifies a polluted spring. Chariots and horses of fire appear, and a whirlwind takes Elijah "up" to God.[4]

We may dispute details of this comment but its main thrust seems accurate. And my response is: Welcome to the world of the Bible. If such matters bother us in 2 Kings 2, we shall have repeated trouble with the Scriptures. This chapter, however,

---

[3] Raymond B. Dillard, *Faith in the Face of Apostasy* (Phillipsburg, NJ: Presbyterian & Reformed, 1999), 85. Note, by the way, that the chariot and horses of fire were *not* Elijah's transportation. These merely *separated* Elijah and Elisha; Elijah went up in the storm wind (v. 11).

[4] Richard D. Nelson, *First and Second Kings*, Interpretation (Louisville: John Knox, 1987), 157.

seems especially to vex some scholars, for its episodes seem so outlandish or brutal or both. Hence John Gray, for example, assures us the episode at Bethel (vv. 23-25) is 'in every respect a puerile tale' and that 'there is no serious point in this incident'.[5]

There are, however, ways of dealing with this difficulty via the mantra of 'genre'. In all interpretation, we are rightly told, it is important to identify the type of literature (genre) we are seeking to interpret. The material in 2 Kings 2 is dubbed 'legend', which refers to stories highlighting the wonderful and miraculous but not bound to recount real events as they happened.[6] Hence readers can now be counseled not to interpret these texts in 'a narrowly historical way' but to think of them as 'symbolic narrative'.[7] To be crass but truthful, in much scholarship miracle signifies legend. Granted, a prophetic legend may have had a kernel of truth, but the prophet's admirers have souped it up with such fantastic 'memories' (in 2:23-25, with up-with-Elisha hype) that the original reality is now invisible.

There are at least two problems with this approach. One is literary. It would help a great deal if we had similar stories, i.e., prophetic legends, in other ancient Near Eastern literature. Then we could tell that the stories in 2 Kings 2, for example, were similar to a number of other samples. But there are no 'prophetic legends' in other ancient Near Eastern materials. How do we know then that a snip in 2 Kings 2 is a legend? Because a scholar says so? But we have no comparative literary material for such identification.

The second problem is presuppositional. The 'miraculous' accounts in 2 Kings are written in the same narrative style as Bible writers use in relating historical material. One senses then that the problem some scholars have is not literary but

---

[5] John Gray, *I & II Kings*, Old Testament Library, 2nd ed. (Philadelphia: Westminster, 1970), 479. Gray minces no words: 'The supposition that Elisha invoked the name of Yahweh to curse the boys, with such terrible consequences, is derogatory to the great public figure, and borders on blasphemy' (p. 480). It is curious that the latter consideration did not prevent Gray from stating some of his conclusions in his commentary.

[6] Burke O. Long, *2 Kings*, The Forms of the Old Testament Literature (Grand Rapids: Eerdmans, 1991), 29, 34-35, 304.

[7] Terence E. Fretheim, *First and Second Kings*, Westminster Bible Companion (Louisville: Westminster/John Knox, 1999), 139.

philosophical. It's a matter of world view. Many still seem to
suffer from a nineteenth-century hangover that comes to the
Bible presupposing that the universe is a closed system. I have
enough unbelief already (cf. Mark 9:24) without swallowing
that camel. Hence I label these accounts prophetic narrative
and acknowledge that in them the God of Israel has dirtied his
hands in doing mighty things in the affairs of his people.[8]

Observation

Before coming to exposition, there are two literary matters
we should consider since they will underscore the unity and
importance of this chapter.

First, note the structure. Geography shapes the chapter.
The original starting-point is Gilgal (v. 1—probably not the
one near Jericho and the Jordan) and the ultimate destination
is Samaria via Mt. Carmel (v. 25). But between these points we
find a distinct geographical pattern:

Elijah and Elisha }	Bethel, v. 2
	Jericho, v. 4
	Jordan, v. 6
Elisha alone }	Jordan, v. 13
	Jericho, v. 19 (cf. v. 18)
	Bethel, v. 23

Now if you read through 2 Kings 2 you will realize that the
writer could well have concluded his narrative with verse 18.
But he didn't—he included another Jericho and Bethel episode.
I think this geographical pattern is quite deliberate and hardly
accidental. First, it shows that the water (vv. 19-22) and bear
(vv. 23-25) episodes are integral parts of the narrative and not
rootless tales floating around looking for a literary home. Take
these sections out and one destroys a conscious geographical-
literary pattern. Hence we have an argument for the unity of the
chapter. Further, this pattern shows that Elisha really did receive
the first-born share (cf. Deut. 21:17) of Elijah's spirit (v. 9), because
Elisha *retraces* Elijah's very steps doing his mighty works.

---

[8] I have found Paul R. House's discussion of these matters very helpful; see his *1, 2 Kings*,
New American Commentary (Nashville: Broadman & Holman, 1995), 50-58.

Second, observe the position of this chapter. It stands between the concluding formula for Ahaziah in 1:17-18 and the introductory formula for Jehoram/Joram in 3:1-3.[9] One could slide 2 Kings 2 out of its place and never miss it, for the end of chapter 1 would flow right into the beginning of chapter 3.[10] Some see this as evidence that 2 Kings 2 was a later addition shoved into place at this point. I think there's a better explanation: the writer/editor, assuming he was endowed with a modicum of intelligence and skill, deliberately interrupted the predictable flow of his narrative and injected this Elijah-to-Elisha story at this point because he considered it to be of particular importance. Important it was. Just as Joshua 1 addresses the question, How shall we go on now that Moses has died?, so 2 Kings 2 raises—and answers—the question, How can we go on when Elijah is going to be taken from us?

Exposition
There is, then, this anxiety over Elijah's departure. A quiet dread and uncertainty seems to hover over Israel's remnant (vv. 1-6). And yet the chapter suggests that there are anchors that remain in the shifting circumstances of the people of God.

God's power still reaches us (vv. 7-15)
The two notes about the sons of the prophets (vv. 7 and 15) wrap this section. I assume that they observed what occurred at the Jordan but did not likely witness Elijah's departure. They saw Elijah wrap his mantle and strike the Jordan with it; they saw the Jordan divide this way and that and the two men walk over to the other side (v. 8). Then they see Elisha return alone with the mantle that had once been thrown over him (1 Kings 19:19).

> And he took Elijah's mantle which had fallen from him and struck the waters; and he said, 'Where is Yahweh, the God of Elijah—even he?' So he struck the waters and they divided this way and that; and Elisha crossed over (v. 14).[11]

---

[9] The date given in 1:17-18 seems to conflict with that in 3:1. We will touch on this difficulty in our treatment of 2 Kings 3.

[10] The same can be said of Joshua 2. See my discussion in *Joshua: No Falling Words* (Ross-shire: Christian Focus, 2000), 29.

[11] I follow Keil in taking *àp-hû'* as an emphatic phrase ('even he').

What Elijah had done, Elisha now does. And the sons of the prophets get the point: 'The spirit of Elijah rests upon Elisha' (v. 15). Yahweh's power is still available through Elisha. Let's flesh this out a bit more.

Verse 14 implies that *God's power is not tied to a particular era*. The events of verses 8 and 14 clearly re-enact the events of Joshua 3–4, when Yahweh cut off the waters of the Jordan and Israel entered Canaan. Here in 2 Kings 2, however, the Jordan parting is not so public. Only a group of the remnant views it here. But what is the text saying when Elijah and Elisha duplicate the dividing of the Jordan? Simply that the God of 1400 BC is just as mighty in 850 BC. His arm has not atrophied. Imagine how folks in Elisha's day might claim that they lived in a different time—it was, after all, the Iron Age. Perhaps they could say that they faced different cultural problems, that the world political configurations had changed drastically. But the text says it doesn't matter, because the God of the Bronze Age (Joshua 3–4) is the same in the Iron Age—no matter how avant-garde it may seem. Nor should this point be wasted on us. God is still saving and sanctifying his people, still keeping them from the evil one, and the Holy Spirit is still leading wandering Christians to repent and to renew their obedience. These works are not limited to Pentecost or to the Reformation or to the 18th century revivals. The historical God is also the contemporary God. Even as I write I think of two former students, now pastors, who are seeing clear signs of God's work in their congregations. This is not happening in exciting new church plants in bustling cities but in traditional churches in obscure towns too small even to have a decent grocery store.

Verse 14 also demonstrates that *God's power is not limited to a certain instrument*. The sons of the prophets saw this: 'The spirit of Elijah rests upon Elisha' (v. 15). Elisha, by Yahweh's power, can do the same works as Elijah (vv. 8, 13-14). Realizing this should prevent us from idolizing certain servants of God. The prophets likely wondered, What will we do now that Elijah is no longer with us? And if we think that, we must, like Elisha himself (v. 14), look for the *God* of Elijah to be with us. Our help is in the name of the Lord not in the charisma of his servants. God's leaders change, God's power persists. Perhaps sometimes God removes his most illustrious servants so that we will not make idols of them, as though they are the only conduits of God's help. Perhaps God deliberately displays his might through 'lesser' instruments so that we will not be transfixed on the pizzazz of God's servants but on the strength of God's arm.

This point reminds me of Emanuel Stickelberger's description of Calvin's funeral:

> Calvin had given definite instructions for his funeral. Nothing must distinguish it from that of any other citizen. His body was to be sewed into a white shroud and laid in a simple pine coffin. At the grave there were to be neither words nor song.
>
> The wishes of the deceased were scrupulously carried out. But although in accordance with his will all pomp was avoided, an unnumbered multitude followed the coffin to the cemetery Plainpalais with deep respect and silent grief.
>
> He who was averse to all ambition did not even want a tombstone. Just a few months later when foreign students desired to visit the place where the Reformer's earthly remains rest, the place could no longer be pointed out among fresh mounds.[12]

Very appropriate. Why do we need a Calvin grotto when we have the God he served?

God's wisdom still settles us (vv. 15b-18)

The text says that wisdom matters and Elisha has it. The sons of the prophets, however, do not recognize this. They submit to Elisha (v. 15b) because they observed the obvious: recrossing the Jordan (v. 14) authenticates Elisha as the bearer of Yahweh's power. They submit and yet they don't submit. After Elisha refuses their request to send a party in quest of Elijah's remains (v. 16), they pressure him so relentlessly that he relents (v. 17a). The search is fruitless. They catch up to him at Jericho to hear his 'Told you so' (v. 18). This little episode shows the sons of the prophets that Elisha knows what he's talking about. Elisha is not only the bearer of God's power but of God's wisdom.

---

[12] Emanuel Stickelberger, *John Calvin* (Cambridge: James Clarke, 1959), 151.

Wisdom is important. A few months ago I noticed a picture and brief explanation on the front page of our local newspaper. Two men had stolen a car; the Jackson city police were in pursuit. The chase came to an end when the thieves crashed into a concrete utility pole while attempting to make a turn at an intersection. One suspect was flat on his back on the ground, handcuffed, receiving attention from a paramedic. The story had an unusual twist: the suspects were using a pair of pliers to control the car because the steering wheel was missing. (Someone has told me that thieves remove the whole steering wheel if it has been secured by a 'club' or locking device.) Please understand. I am not condoning auto thievery. I am only pointing out the obvious: it is very difficult to control an automobile with a pair of pliers in a high-speed chase. Should one decide to steal an auto, one should always steal one *with* a steering wheel. It's only wisdom. Otherwise, one is both criminal and stupid.

The church is a good bit like car thieves and the sons of the prophets. She doesn't value wisdom very highly. The sons of the prophets could see power all right in Elisha's jaunt through Jordan. That impressed them. But they weren't looking for wisdom. Wisdom is not one of God's flashier gifts. It is mundane, ordinary, quiet. God's power often makes waves, but God's wisdom is more sedate. Wisdom is available (James 1:5—note it is the wisdom that has the savvy to negotiate trial with endurance, vv. 2-4), but we ignore it.

A congregation may be earnestly praying for one of its number. Then the medical tests come back: no sign of cancer. The saints are overjoyed—as they should be. Even Presbyterians get ecstatic over such things. But what if they hear of another believer who has decided to cut up and throw away his credit cards (because they tempted him to overbuy) and to pay up his debts? Who thinks much about that? It's only wisdom. Or a pastor may see the Spirit use the steady teaching of the word to transform a husband and father in the parish. And, of course, he thrills to see it. The same pastor, however, may make a practice of divulging confidential information to his wife, information she has no right to know. But he attaches little importance to the matter. After all, it's only a matter of wisdom. And who in the church prizes that?

God's grace still thrills us (vv. 19-22)

Elisha is at Jericho, just west of the Jordan River and a bit above the northern end of the Dead Sea. Jericho has a problem with its water supply, so that, according to NIV and NASB respectively, the land is 'unproductive' or 'unfruitful' (v. 19). But I think these versions give a wrong impression. In my judgment the New Jerusalem Bible has captured the sense better:

> The people of the city said to Elisha, 'The city is pleasant to live in, as my lord indeed can see, but the water is foul and the country suffers from miscarriages.'

'Suffers from miscarriages' better picks up the sense of the verb *šākal* (see K-B, 4:1491-92). Moreover, when Elisha announces Yahweh's 'healing' of the waters, he assures townsfolk that the water supply will no longer cause death or miscarriage (v. 21). The problem is far more serious than unproductive land (cf. NIV). There was something lethal in the water supply, causing fatalities in livestock and humans. Hence when verse 19 says, 'the land miscarries,' I take 'land' as a cipher for its occupants, i.e., livestock and people.

Elisha demands a new bowl[13] with salt in it. He takes these props to the water source, throws the salt in, and declares: 'Here's what Yahweh says: "I have healed these waters—neither death nor miscarriage will come from them anymore"' (v. 21). And the writer adds: 'So the waters were healed unto this day, in line with the word of Elisha which he spoke' (v. 22).[14]

What are we to make of this? I suggest that we not choke on the salt. It sounds strange to us, a new bowl with salt, but in many of these miracles we meet some sort of visible action that accompanies the mighty work.[15] The salt is the external sign, the word is the essential component: 'Here's what Yahweh

---

[13] The word is *ṣĕlōḥît*, used only here in the Old Testament. Best guess is bowl or small container (cf. K-B, 3:1027).

[14] The Marah story of Exodus 15:22-26 furnishes a fascinating parallel to our passage. In that instance there was also a problem with water (bitter, Exod. 15:23), into which Moses, upon Yahweh's instruction, threw (Exod. 15:25, same verb as in v. 21 here) a tree or piece of wood, and the water became sweet. Then follows a promise that in covenant fidelity Israel would continue to experience Yahweh as her 'healer' (a participle of *rāpā'*, Exod. 15:26, the verb used in vv. 21 and 22 of our passage here).

[15] Some would press the significance of the salt, e.g., H. L. Ellison, *The Prophets of Israel* (Grand Rapids: Eerdmans, 1969), 46.

says: "I have healed these waters"' (v. 21). Hence in this episode, the use of visible sign and spoken word shows that *God's word through God's prophet brings God's grace to God's people.* And this episode stresses the *transforming* impact of that grace.

Let us back up and explain. The location is important—Jericho. Here one must pull previous texts into the picture.[16] After Israel's conquest of Jericho Joshua uttered a curse upon any man who would dare to rebuild this condemned place:

> So Joshua swore an oath at that time: 'Cursed be the man before Yahweh who rises up and shall rebuild this city—Jericho; at the cost of his firstborn he will lay its foundations and at the cost of his youngest he will set up its doors' (Josh. 6:26).

And, typically, in the dark days of Ahab when few gave a rip about the word of God, a contractor decided he was up to the challenge:

> In his [Ahab's] days Hiel the Bethelite (re)built Jericho; at the cost of Abiram his firstborn he laid the foundation, and at the cost of Segub his youngest he set up its doors, in line with the word of Yahweh which he spoke by the hand of Joshua son of Nun (1 Kings 16:34).

Hiel had at least two graves as monuments to his achievement. Jericho was the place where a curse was both uttered and inflicted. Jericho is a place under a curse.

Isn't this backdrop significant for verses 19-22? The city under a curse now receives a blessing of grace. The place where Yahweh inflicted his destructive word now enjoys his healing word. Long ago at Marah (Exod. 15:22-26) Yahweh had shown he would rather heal than destroy—and he has not changed. Here in 2 Kings 2 Curseville has become Graceburgh. Is this incident not a cameo of Yahweh's own character? See how he delights to turn the most curse-ridden, sin-laden, judgment-bearing situations into episodes of his grace in living color? It seems too good to be true and too

---

[16] Here I am much indebted to the (now) Rev. Ed Hurley, who, when a student in my Bible Interpretation class, first pointed out to me the importance of Joshua 6 and 1 Kings 16 for understanding the present passage.

much for sane sinners to hope for. But it is the testimony of this text: God's word through God's prophet brings God's grace—even to Jericho.

Is this not a needed word in our church assemblies? If you are a pastor, don't you thrill to preach such a word? Isn't there hope here for that woman in the third row from the front who has had two abortions in her past? Does this text not address the man who still despairs as he looks back to that sin-twisted, knowingly rebellious decision he made, and, though he has long since repented in tears and sincerity, a cloud seems to hover over his life—he fears he can never enjoy the sunlight of God's smile again. Or perhaps it was that immoral act, years ago, that has infected your marriage and infested your conscience; and, though finally confessed, you are convinced that, though God may tolerate you, he can never welcome you or delight in you. Sometimes pastors and preachers must grab such folks by the scruff of the neck, and when they ask, 'Hey, where are you taking me?', we must say: 'I'm carting you off to Jericho, and when we get there, I'm going to shout to you, "Here is your God!"' Is there anything as thrilling as that—as meeting the Lord who 'binds up the brokenness of his people, and heals the wounds inflicted by his blow' (Isa. 30:26, ESV)?

God's judgment still frightens us (vv. 23-25)

Well, in any case, it *should* frighten us. This little passage has all sorts of naysayers. Some seem aghast at how humorless and/or savage Elisha seems to be. Perhaps if Elisha had had *decaffeinated* coffee, he wouldn't have been so edgy? A closer look should help.

Let us pick apart the situation. First, the group. The Hebrew phrase in verse 23 is *ne'ārîm qĕtannîm*, which I would translate 'young lads'.[17] I agree then with H. L. Ellison: 'If we think of them as between ten and twelve, we shall probably not be far out.'[18] Next, the place. Bethel was a center of Jeroboam's bull worship (1 Kings 12:25-33), had been for eighty years, and its loyalists probably felt little affection for Yahweh's true prophet.

---

[17] See my article (pp. 392-93) cited in footnote 1 for the support for this rendering.
[18] Ellison, *Prophets of Israel*, 47. In any case, they are not five-year-olds who escaped from kindergarten and didn't realize what they were saying.

One might infer that the lads' mockery reflected their parents' hostility.

Third, note that these lads acted with deliberate intent. The text reads: 'He was going up on the road, but young lads went forth from the town and mocked him' (v. 23b). Their action was calculated; Elisha was going up on the road that went by Bethel, and these fellows 'went forth' from the walled town, out the town gate, in order to accost Elisha. The text gives no support to the usual assumption that Elisha was ambling through town and these lads, who were casually hanging out in front of the Bethel Billiards Barn, spontaneously joked about the prophet's higher anatomy. It was no such 'accidental' meeting. The prophet did not go through town but was going up on the road outside of town and these fellows 'went forth'. Theirs was a deliberate and malicious intent.

Fourth, a word about the mockery. 'They mocked him, and they said, "Go up, Baldy; go up, Baldy"' (v. 23c). Here 'Baldy' is a term of contempt. It was not suggested to the lads by immediate observation, for—in line with common practice—Elisha would have had his head covered as he traveled.[19] So they must have already known that he was in fact bald and used the term now in mockery. And they tell him to 'go up'. Their jeer uses the verb *'ālah*, the same verb used of Elijah's going up in the storm wind in verse 11. Conceivably, the juveniles could have that in mind, as if to say, 'Why don't you do an ascension-act too, Baldy?' But I think it better to connect it with the two uses of *'ālah* earlier in verse 23: 'and he *went up* from there to Bethel, and he was *going up* on the road...' So when the mockers tell him to 'go up,' they mean 'Keep on going up—right out of town.' In short, make yourself scarce.

Finally, mark the number of fatalities. The bears 'tore up of them forty-two lads' (v. 24b). The 'of them' is important. The bears mauled forty-two; the 'of them' implies a number got away. That's a small mob in any case.

In verses 23-24, then, *responsible young lads were expressing abuse, contempt, and hostility toward Yahweh's representative—and knew they were doing so.*

---

[19] Gray, *I & II Kings*, 480.

That summarizes the situation; let us move on to the result: 'And he turned round and saw them, and he cursed them in the name of Yahweh; and two female bears came out of the woods and tore to pieces of them forty-two lads' (v. 24). The word Elisha spoke here was a curse 'in the name of Yahweh'. And then there were the bears. We must size up these bears correctly. They were covenant bears. The covenant curse of Leviticus 26:22 ('I will let loose the wild beasts among you, which shall rob you of your children') explains the episode. Covenant infidelity (hatred of Yahweh's representative and, perhaps, persisting in Bethel's perverse worship) has brought the covenant curse. Had Elisha been wrong to curse, one would assume Yahweh would not have fulfilled the curse. That Yahweh did so validates Elisha's curse. Here is not an irritable prophet but a judging God.

What then is the significance of this episode? A proper answer takes in the whole chapter. Elisha is Yahweh's appointed successor to Elijah, endowed with both his power (vv. 7-15) and his wisdom (vv. 16-18) and who speaks Yahweh's word in either grace (vv. 19-22) or judgment (vv. 23-24). It is important to keep verses 23-25 with its companion piece, verses 19-22. The two go together: Yahweh's word can bring both healing (v. 21) and harm (v. 24), either deliverance (vv. 19-22) or disaster (vv. 23-24). In these two vignettes one sees the double-edged word of God at work in both grace (Jericho) and judgment (Bethel) among his people.

That is the overall significance. What is the particular import of the Bethel disaster? Does it not tell us that Yahweh's curse finds those in Israel who despise him? They may be among the official, card-carrying covenant people of God but the radar of Yahweh's curse will find those who show they detest him by despising his servants. Should this text not stir in us a humble fear? Scholarly arrogance will often dismiss this clip as an outlandish tale, but Matthew Henry long ago pointed us to the right attitude and response: 'Let the hideous shrieks and groans of this wicked, wretched brood make our flesh tremble for fear of God.'[20] That message, however, runs cross-grained to our Western culture's view of God, who, to put it crassly,

---

[20] Matthew Henry, *Commentary on the Whole Bible*, 6 vols. (New York: Fleming H. Revell, n.d.), 2:718.

should prove at all times to be a nice sort of chap. Nor does the current evangelical church 'ethos' care to hear such negativism, such scare theology. But apparently no one has informed Jesus, who has the gall to tell us:

> But I have this against you, that you have abandoned the love you had at first. Remember then from what you have fallen; repent, and do the works you did at first. If not, I will come to you and remove your lampstand from its place, unless you repent (Rev. 2:4-5, NRSV).

There is a holy fright the church needs to recover.

So Elijah has been 'taken'. But it's all left—power and wisdom, grace and judgment. Elisha asked the right question: Where is the *God* of Elijah? Answer: Right here, with his struggling, suffering servants. Elijah is gone, Yahweh remains.

3

We Three Kings
(2 Kings 3)

We were visiting my oldest brother in Arizona. My dear sister-in-law had packed us a mammoth lunch which we were slated to enjoy at noon, high up in the mountains where my brother was taking us. Someone managed to bring along a few carrot sticks but the sad fact was that we had forgotten the lunch. It was not, as expected, in the trunk of the car but reposed in all its substantial splendor at my brother's house. One can barge off into something without the one essential item one needs most. That is the situation in 2 Kings 3. These three kings are going to be, as we say, dead meat without the word of God (cf. v. 13). In their desperation they seek what they may have 'forgotten'. A fascinating story, is it not, whenever you find three politicians turning to religion? They turn to Elisha, the servant of the word. So the text is telling us: *Our only hope is in the word of God.* We will develop our exposition around that theme.

The Totalitarian Claim of the Word of God (vv. 1-3)
Here we are, about 850 BC, with Jehoram king of Israel.[1] The writer assesses him immediately on the most crucial issue—his

---

[1] Don't get confused: we have double Jehorams. Our focus here is the northern Jehoram (some versions, like NIV, have 'Joram'), son of Ahab, brother of Ahaziah (2 Kings 1). The alert reader will notice the chronological conundrum in 1:17b and 3:1. The former says that northern Jehoram began to reign in the second year of southern 'Jehoram son of Jehoshaphat king of Judah'; the latter says that northern Jehoram began reigning in the eighteenth year of Jehoshaphat of Judah. LXX smoothes out the problem by dropping 1:17b and 'expanding' 1:18 (so that it looks a lot like 3:1-3), giving the eighteenth

religious policy (vv. 2-3). His assessment uses the Hebrew particle *raq* ('only') twice. Jehoram did evil *only* not like his father and mother (v. 2a); *only* he clung to the sins of Jeroboam (v. 3). That is, he was not as wicked as he could have been, yet he was not righteous as he should have been. The writer makes the same emphasis in his double use of the verb *sûr* (turn away). Jehoram *turned* (=took) *away* the pillar of Baal (v. 2), but he himself did not *turn away* from the sins of Jeroboam (v. 3b).

Do you feel the bristling impatience in this text? You see the dual point the text is making? On the one hand, the text recognizes degrees of evil. Jehoram suppressed at least some of the raw paganism of Baal worship; admittedly, it's better to have someone ruling whose wickedness is not as lurid as Ahab and Jezebel's. It's not good, but, in a relative sense, it's better. Yet Jehoram clung (note the strong verb, *dābaq*, used in Genesis 2:24 of the man clinging to his wife) to the refined paganism of Jeroboam's cult (see 1 Kings 12:25-33). English translations rightly render the *raq* ('only') that begins verse 3 as 'nevertheless'. 'Nevertheless he clung to the sins of Jeroboam.' For all the qualification of verse 2, don't you sense the impatience of the Bible's 'Nevertheless' here? The Bible is never satisfied with anything less than total submission. It's as if our writer throws his pen down in disgust and hollers, 'That's not enough! It won't do to go around saying it's not as bad as it could be. Anything less than thorough-going, faithful first-and-second-commandment worship just won't cut it!'

Once in a seminary class John Gerstner told of preaching in a church in Baltimore. Apparently his sermon had been on our depravity, our utter wretchedness in sin and our total inability to commend ourselves in any way to God outside of Christ. After the service a woman told Dr. Gerstner—as she held up her thumb and forefinger with a miniscule space in between, 'That sermon made me feel this big,' to which Gerstner retorted, 'That's too big!' Apparently she had missed something about

---

year of Jehoshaphat as Jehoram's inaugural year (as 3:1 does). But there needn't be any conflict between southern Jehoram's second (1:17) and Jehoshaphat's eighteenth (3:1) years if they shared a co-regency. The text of 8:16 (as it stands) indicates they did so. This is not conservative wish-fulfillment; even John Gray supports the co-regency (*I & II Kings*, Old Testament Library, 2nd ed. [Philadelphia: Westminster, 1970], 481). See especially, Walter C. Kaiser, Jr., *A History of Israel from the Bronze Age through the Jewish Wars* (Nashville: Broadman & Holman, 1998), 297.

the totality of sin. In any case, in Dr. Gerstner's view, her sense of her sinfulness had not gone far enough.

That is the point in verses 2-3. One may relinquish greater evils (a passion for Baal worship) yet cling to evil nonetheless (Jeroboam's syncretism).[2] Because we give up a more depraved form of idolatry does not mean we are free (note again the verb *dābaq*, to cling). That principle is single but its applications are multiple. This impatience of the Bible that refuses to accept anything less than total fidelity is only a reflection of the intolerant God of the Bible who insists on having all your affections.

The Alarming Danger of the Word of God (vv. 4-14)
Mesha king of Moab had been a vassal of Ahab; sheepbreeder that he was, he paid his tribute in lambs and wool (v. 4). But Mesha grew restive and revolted from Israel's authority (v. 5).[3] Jehoram preferred a docile to a defiant Mesha, perhaps because Moabite wool helped his Israelite economy. So Jehoram began building a coalition (vv. 6-7) 'to whip Mesha back into line'.[4] Jehoshaphat, king of Judah, appears to be his usual compliant self (cf. 1 Kings 22:4). Jehoram and Jehoshaphat, along with the 'king' of Edom (probably a vassal of Judah), make their way south through Judah, turn east below the Dead Sea, and approach Moab from the south.[5] Troops and pack animals plod right into disaster; they've exhausted their supply of water and

[2]Kaiser (*A History of Israel*, 333), however, questions whether Jehoram decisively left Baal worship: 'Jehoram's attitude towards the Baal cult of his father and mother is difficult to determine. At first he removed the image of Baal that his father had made (2 Kings 3:2), leaving the impression that he was not sympathetic to Baal worship. But that could hardly be the case, since he was ironically urged by the prophet Elisha to seek help from the prophets of his father and mother, an obvious reference to Baal prophets. Did this not signify that such was his normal practice anyway (2 Kings 3:13)? In fact, when Jehoram's successor—the usurper Jehu—came to the throne of Israel, it was necessary for him to slay the prophets of Baal...' This last refers to 10:18-30.
[3]Read all about it on the so-called Moabite Stone; see D. Winton Thomas, ed., *Documents from Old Testament Times* (New York: Harper & Row, 1958), 195-98. Ahab likely lost control of Moab during the Aramaean wars of his later years (cf. 1 Kings 22) but the revolt was surely full-steam upon Ahab's death and the nearly immediate demise of Ahaziah (2 Kings 1). See, handily, J. A. Thompson, 'Moabite Stone,' NBD, 3rd ed., 777.
[4]Eugene H. Merrill, *Kingdom of Priests* (Grand Rapids: Baker, 1987), 350.
[5]See *The Macmillan Bible Atlas*, 3rd ed., 97-98, and Y. Aharoni, *The Land of the Bible*, rev. & enl. ed. (Philadelphia: Westminster, 1979), 336-40. According to his claims on the Moabite Stone, Mesha now controlled fortified points in northern Moab (north of the Arnon River). The allies may have chosen to attack from the south in order to avoid Mesha's line of fortifications in the north.

there is none to be had on site (v. 9b).[6] Jehoram ascribes the
whole mess to Yahweh's sovereignty (v. 10)—as many like to
do when caught in their follies. To hear him tell it Moab will
certainly clean up on the allies. Jehoshaphat of Judah, though
dull in some respects, does not so easily despair: 'Is there no
prophet of Yahweh here for us to consult Yahweh through
him?' (v. 11a, NJB).[7] When perplexed Jehoshaphat turns to the
word of God. One of Jehoram's servants pipes up with the
news that 'Elisha, son of Shaphat, is here'.[8] Interestingly, the
southern king knows of the northern prophet (v. 12a) and all
three politicos troop off in search of Elisha (v. 12b).

What was Elisha doing there? Why was he traveling with
the troops? The Bible doesn't satisfy our curiosity about details
that don't matter. Elisha engages in no opening pleasantries. In
fact, the writer completely omits any introductory statement or
inquiry by the kings, which makes Elisha's first words all the
more stark and brutal: 'What business have you with me? Go
to your father's and your mother's prophets' (v. 13, NJB). Why
this sudden interest, Elisha seems to say, in Yahweh's word?
Go to the Baal prophets your mother fed (1 Kings 18:19) or
to the bootlickers your father kept at court (1 Kings 22:6-8).
Apparently there was no seeking of Yahweh's guidance before
this military venture, but, now that Jehoram is in a jam, he
seeks Yahweh. And all of a sudden Jehoram has this belief in
the sovereignty of Yahweh (expressed again in v. 13b). (Always
beware of folks who cite the sovereignty of God in order to
excuse or accuse but not to worship and adore.)

Elisha will not back down. His response is both carefully
solemn (note the oath formula in 14a) and painfully blunt:

---

[6]In 2 Kings 2 the parting and crossing of the Jordan (vv. 8, 14) recalled Yahweh's
cutting off the Jordan at the conquest in Joshua 3–4, indicating that Yahweh's might
for his people remained undiminished. Does the lack of water here in 2 Kings 3 mean
to recall the post-exodus situations in which Yahweh provided water? Cf. Exodus
15:22-27; 17:1-7; Numbers 20:1-13; 21:4-5.

[7]NJB's 'consult' is *dāraš*, to seek, inquire. Ahaziah did not *dāraš* Yahweh's word
(1:16) but Baal-zebub's (1:3, 6, 16) and was judged for it. Here Jehoshaphat models
a proper response.

[8]'[Jehoshaphat's] request for a prophetic inquiry elicits the news, not from the king
of Israel but his servant, that Elisha is in the vicinity. By putting this information in the
mouth of a servant rather than in that of the king of Israel himself, the writer subtly
denigrates the king whose first reaction is despair' (Robert Cohn, *2 Kings*, Berit Olam
[Collegeville, MN: Liturgical, 2000], 21).

'Were it not that I accept the face of Jehoshaphat king of
Judah, I would pay no attention to you—I would not look
at you' (v. 14b). There goes the stereotype of the 'kind and
gracious' Elisha.

Now chew a bit on Elisha's words. Do you hear him? He
is saying that Jehoram is *beyond the help of Yahweh's word*—if
it weren't for Jehoshaphat. That is a frightening implication:
*you can place yourself beyond the point of receiving direction or
help from God.* How might you know if you are in danger of
doing that? Well, if your pattern is to seek God, like Jehoram,
only for your convenience, so that you are trifling with God.
You may be interested only in escape from trouble not in
the path of discipleship. That was Jehoram. He wanted to
use the word of God in the moment but not to submit to it
long-term. Jehoramites view the word of God as something
for emergency only, but not for normal days. God is simply
the airbag in the disasters of life—which you hope you
never have to use. If that is your pattern, you may be placing
yourself beyond the help of God's word. That is the alarming
danger of the word of God.

The Typical Tendency of the Word of God (vv. 15-25)
Elisha wanted to hear some music. During that time Yahweh's
hand came upon him and he prophesied (v. 15). Yahweh's
word was a double promise of water (vv. 16-17) and victory
(vv. 18-19). Yahweh will turn the dry wadi (stream bed) into
pools of water (v. 16), and, though the army will see no wind
or rain, there would be an abundance of water for both troops
and livestock (v. 17).[9] And Yahweh will put Moab into their
power, so thoroughly that

---

[9]Verse 16 is a bit difficult, reflected in English versions. Literally it reads: 'Making
this wadi full of pools.' The word for 'pools' (*gēb*) occurs only two or three times in
the Old Testament and refers to a pit, cistern, or, possibly, a trench. (With water any
of these can be a 'pool'!). But is Yahweh making the pools (e.g., ESV, RSV) or are the
troops commanded to dig pits or trenches to retain the promised water (e.g., NASB,
NIV)? Waltke and O'Connor take it both ways at different points (*An Introduction to
Biblical Hebrew Syntax* [Winona Lake, IN: Eisenbrauns, 1990], 119, 594)! I think it is
describing Yahweh's action; see, e.g., G. H. Jones, *1 and 2 Kings*, New Century Bible
Commentary, 2 vols. (Grand Rapids: Eerdmans, 1984), 2:396-97, and M. Cogan and
H. Tadmor, *II Kings*, Anchor Bible (Garden City, NY: Doubleday, 1988), 45.

you shall strike down every fortified town,
and every choice town,
and every fine tree you will fell,
and every spring of water you will stop up,
and every good portion of ground you will mar with stones (v. 19).[10]

Then the writer sketches the double fulfillment of this double promise: in the morning the water was there (v. 20) and in the morning the victory began (vv. 22-25). But verses 20-25 tell of a wrinkle we would not have guessed simply from Elisha's prophecy in verses 16-19: water and winning are connected. Israel's water brings Moab's defeat. Moab's troops saw the reddish cast the morning sun gave to the water and inferred it was blood; Israel's coalition must have fallen to internal fighting and bleeding (vv. 22-23a).[11] Jubilantly they dash for the spoil and run into swords (vv. 23b-24a). They run from the swords with coalition troops in hot pursuit, going on and striking down Moabites (v. 24b; the text is difficult but not unclear). Their victory (v. 25) takes the shape of Elisha's prediction (v. 19). Moab seems at its last gasp (v. 25b).

But where is this 'typical tendency' of the word of God? In verse 18: 'This is too trivial a matter in Yahweh's eyes—so he will give Moab into your hand.' 'This' refers to Yahweh's supplying water for the whole famished army. Elisha is saying that rehydrating Israel's parched troops and pack animals is a 'piece of cake' for Yahweh, or, more accurately, 'small potatoes.' So Yahweh will not limit himself to such trivial work but

---

[10]Some (e.g., Seow, *New Interpreter's Bible*, 3:183) think the tree-chopping and devastation here contravenes the law of Deuteronomy 20:19-20. But it does not. That text only forbids whacking down food-producing trees as lumber for siege works. 'The prohibition of cutting down trees, found in Deut. 20:19-20, does not apply here. The law in Deuteronomy is designed to ensure that the army's food supply would not be cut off since non-fruit bearing trees are excluded' (T. R. Hobbs, *2 Kings*, Word Biblical Commentary [Waco: Word, 1985], 37). The severity here might be retribution for the severity Mesha boasts of inflicting on Israel on the 'Moabite Stone' (see H. L. Ellison, *The Prophets of Israel* [Grand Rapids: Eerdmans, 1969], 49).

[11]John Gray makes a good case for the initial battle occurring much further to the east than usually supposed (beyond the head of the Zered or Wadi Hasa). He nicely meshes the details of the narrative with this geographical proposal/supposition. See especially his comments on verses 8 and 17; *I & II Kings*, 485, 487. Some, however, hold the invasion route was much further to the west—partly in light of known weather conditions; see Bruce R. Crew, 'Did Edom's Original Territories Extend West of Wadi Arabah?,' *Bible and Spade* 15/1 (Winter 2002): esp. 7-8.

also hand Moab over as well.[12] This is the typical tendency. Yahweh not only addresses the immediate dilemma but has the penchant to do far more than was asked. This is vintage Yahweh. You come to him seeking grace and you receive 'grace on top of grace' (John 1:16). Yahweh's goodness tends toward extravagance—even for the likes of Jehoram (vv. 13-14). Water plus Moab is an equation highlighting both the generosity and omnipotence of God. Watering a languishing army? That's simply not grand nor lavish enough for Yahweh!

During the 1950s a company hired a consultant to assist in marketing ice cream. The consultant checked current ice cream ads. They were hardly moving, plugging as they did superior quality and flavor. So he put some interviewers to work, talking to people about what ice cream meant to them. They discovered that most, especially those beyond their teen years, had emotionally loaded feelings about ice cream. They had vivid childhood memories of ice cream. 'We used to sit on the porch every night at the farm and eat ice cream out of soup plates. You could almost drown in the stuff.' They associated ice cream with abundance. They spoke of wanting to 'sink your mouth right into it'. Such were the comments. Armed with such psychological ammunition the consultant urged his ice cream maker to show ice cream in his ads not in a neat, trim dip on a plate or cone, but in lavish portions overflowing the cone or bowl.[13]

I do not intend to put theology into a marketing mode. But isn't that what we find so attractive about Yahweh? We easily conjure up memories of his overflowing generosity. Single requests have been met with triple blessing. We have found him to be good—opulently good. He just tends to be that way.

Before we leave this section, however, we must deal with a problem, for some of you are upset. Some have been muttering

---

[12]One meets the same idiom and argument in Isaiah 49:5-6. Yahweh's Servant is to 'raise up the tribes of Jacob and to restore the preserved ones of Israel'. But that is too 'light', i.e., too trivial or inconsequential (comparatively speaking). Hence Yahweh says, 'I shall appoint you a light of *nations*—you will be my salvation to *the end of the earth*' (emphasis mine). I do not speak without reverence—but it is a playful idiom; it's as if Yahweh says, 'The full and complete restoration of Israel is such a paltry affair—let's make this salvation world-wide and pull the gentiles in. That will be more worthy of me.'

[13]Vance Packard, *The Hidden Persuaders* (New York: Pocket books, 1958), 85–86.

that this idolatrous rascal Jehoram doesn't *deserve* such benefits. Of course he doesn't. But notice *why* he received them—because of Jehoshaphat, the king of David's line (see Elisha's clear explanation in v. 14). Jehoram received these benefits because of another. And it is the same with you. If you receive any benefit from God it is because you stand next to the Davidic king—Jesus, the descendant of David and Jehoshaphat. You are in exactly the same position as Jehoram. You don't deserve heaven's crumbs but receive massive mercies only because Jesus, the Davidic king, stands beside you.

The Easy Yoke of the Word of God (vv. 26-27)
It looks like Moab's last stand at Kir-hareseth (v. 25), a fortified town in southern Moab. Mesha has two moves left, both desperate. In the first he attempts to break through the Edomite segment of the enemy lines with a crack unit of 700 swordsmen (v. 26). He fails. Hence his second recourse. He takes his firstborn son, the king designate, and offers him up as a burnt-offering on the town wall (v. 27). He succeeds. The Israelite coalition leaves the field.

The tricky part is figuring out why Mesha's human sacrifice brought him the relief he desired. The explanation lies in the clause that follows the report of his sacrifice: 'And great wrath/indignation was upon Israel.' Whose wrath? Or whose indignation? Our dilemma is how to explain the explanation.

Fortunately (?), we can resort to a cliché: there are four views. View one points out that qeṣep usually refers to Yahweh's wrath. Moreover, whenever one meets the phrase 'great wrath' (qeṣep gādôl, used here) elsewhere, it refers to Yahweh's wrath.[14] If the text refers to Yahweh's anger, why is he angry? Seow suggests divine anger is 'for the violation of the deuteronomic prohibition of the scorched-earth policy in war'.[15] But we have already rejected the view of verse 19 on which his suggestion is based (see fn. 10 above).

[14] One finds it elsewhere five times (Deut. 29:28; Jer. 21:5; 32:37; Zech. 1:15; 7:12). In each case the context explicitly identifies the 'great wrath' as Yahweh's. This is not clear, however, in our text. The other usages are helpful in weighing our decision, but they do not constitute overwhelming weight. However, qeṣep appears 28 times in the Old Testament and, with only two exceptions, always refers to God's wrath. The cognate verb, on the other hand, takes both divine and human subjects.
[15] *New Interpreter's Bible*, 3:185.

View two agrees with view one that the wrath is divine but assigns it to a different divinity. In this view, the wrath belongs to Chemosh, the god of Moab. Mesha sacrifices, Chemosh becomes angry and causes Israel to flee in panic from the land.[16] A little polytheism anyone? Did a crypto-Chemoshite sneak in and doctor a biblical text? Are such scholars serious? Yes, they are. But this view is untenable even on the suppositions many Old Testament critics have about the books of Kings. They hold that Kings was edited (probably more than once) by 'Deuteronomists', vigilant theologians who shaped the Kings material in line with their point of view. They were death on paganism, abominated syncretism, and pressed exclusive Yahwism. If 3:27 refers to Chemosh's wrath and 'activity', one cannot explain how that could ever have gotten past the alleged Deuteronomic censors. They would have nailed it. A gremlin would have had to have broken into the redaction factory and given tranquilizers to all the Deuteronomists working there for such a text with such a meaning to survive. Of course I don't buy this Deuteronomistic theory, so I am content to say that no convinced Yahwist would have allowed Chemosh even one square inch of Yahweh's sovereignty.

View three holds that the wrath or fury is that of the Moabites themselves, so that Mesha's troops 'respond to this desperate act with a superhuman fury that carried them to victory'.[17] Seeing how their king was driven to such an extreme measure so enraged the Moabite army that they drove Israel from the field.

View four agrees with view three that the 'wrath' is human but assigns it to Israel rather than Moab. This view takes the preposition 'al as 'upon' rather than 'against' (it can mean either depending on the context). If the indignation is 'upon' Israel, it can mean that Israel has or manifests the indignation.[18] The text then refers to the indignation, horror, or repugnance

[16]See G. H. Jones, *1 and 2 Kings*, New Century Bible Commentary, 2 vols. (Grand Rapids: Eerdmans, 1984), 2:400, and K. D. Fricke, *Das zweite Buch von den Königen*, Die Botschaft des alten Testaments (Stuttgart: Calwer, 1972), 48-49.

[17]Iain W. Provan, *1 and 2 Kings*, New International Bible Commentary (Peabody, MA: Hendrickson, 1995), 186.

[18]K. C. W. F. Bähr, *The Books of the Kings*, Lange's Commentary on the Holy Scriptures, in vol. 3, *Samuel-Kings* (1868; reprint ed.,, Grand Rapids: Zondervan, 1960), 33.

Israel felt at Mesha's act. Hence they quit the field without total victory.[19]

All that over, 'great wrath/indignation was upon Israel.' On balance, I follow view four. The wrath or indignation is not explicitly said to be God's. If it were, one would expect some indication of its basis (which is absent). Moreover, the clause comes immediately after the report of Mesha's sacrifice and so likely depicts a reaction to that gruesome event.

So what? Our chapter paints a contrast. Three kings and their armies are at the end of their tether (vv. 9-10). Led by Jehoshaphat, they trudge off to 'inquire' of Yahweh through Elisha his prophet (vv. 11-12). Through Elisha they receive clarity and assurance (vv. 16-19). Eradication is closing its clutches around the king of Moab. His next-to-final desperate option fails (v. 26). What can one do to get one's god to pay attention? Sacrifice your firstborn son and the people's crown prince on the city wall. Maybe the reek of frying human flesh will rouse Chemosh to care.

Verse 27 is a picture of 'seeking god' in paganism. You have to coerce and manipulate—perhaps in the most costly way (cf. Micah 6:6-7). Even not very faithful Israelites are repulsed and horrified. Do you see the message for Israel here? It's as if Yahweh says: 'See where pagans go in their desperation? See where paganism leads? Do you savvy at all the matchless gift you have in a God who lives and hears and speaks and delivers without bribery?' It's as if the writer is pleading: 'O Israel, do you realize the treasure that you have in Yahweh? You never need to resort to stuff like this.' In Moab you can bash your head against the wall or sacrifice your son on it. Both are equally futile. But to Israel Yahweh has given prophets through whom one can receive the light and help one needs (see Deut. 18:15-22 in light of 18:9-14). Here is the easy yoke of the word of God. What a relief biblical religion is! If you don't believe it, try paganism.

---

[19]See Walter C. Kaiser, Jr., *A History of Israel*, 333-34. Kaiser cites a possible parallel from Ugarit; see B. Margalit, 'Why King Mesha of Moab Sacrificed His Oldest Son,' *Biblical Archaeology Review* 12.6 (1986): 62-63, 67. Incidentally, if one looks at all of 2 Kings 3 through the eyes of Jehoram one sees a pattern of *repeated frustration* for him. He comes to the throne (vv. 1-3) but Moab rebels (vv. 4-5); he plans retaliation (vv. 6-8) but the army becomes waterless (vv. 9-10); he, with others, has access to the prophet (vv. 11-12) but is severely rebuffed (vv. 13-14); he receives double promise and provision (vv. 16-25) but had to withdraw rather than occupy (vv. 26-27).

When Don McClure was serving as a missionary to the Anuaks in Sudan, one of the Anuak believers brought his son to McClure for medical attention. The lad had been fishing and had been bitten by a very poisonous puff adder. The father was calm and told the missionary, 'If the medicine will not help him, then our prayers will. And if he dies, our lives are in God's hands.' McClure teased the father by saying, 'Why didn't you kill a sheep and pour the blood on your son as you would have done three years ago?' The father lifted his hands above his head in horror: 'That was in other days. Now we believe only in the blood of Jesus.'[20] Sacrifice a child or seek a prophet. Sheep's blood or the cross. There really is a difference. 'What great nation has its gods as near as Yahweh our God is to us whenever we call to him?' (Deut. 4:7, NJB).

---

[20]Charles Partee, *Adventure in Africa* (Grand Rapids: Zondervan, 1990), 282-83. The boy recovered.

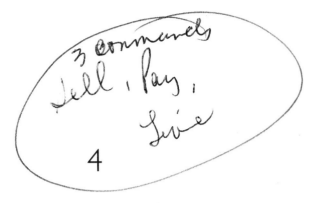

3 commands
Sell, Pay,
Live

4

Help of the Helpless and Nameless
(2 Kings 4:1-7)

Now we enter a segment of Elisha's ministry in which he shows that Yahweh's power is triumphant over debt (4:1-7), death (4:8-37), drought (4:38-44; two episodes), disease (5:1-27), and difficulty (6:1-7). It is, in its own way, quite a sustained argument. One might compare the section to the battery of Jesus' miracles in Mark's Gospel (4:35-5:43). Some of these Elisha stories are extended narratives (e.g., ch. 5), while others are very brief clips that are stingy with extras. Our current text, 4:1-7, is one of the latter.

Sometimes it is difficult to know what to make of such a sparse text. What practical use can we find in such a succinct story? Walter Kaiser tells of once hearing a message on 4:1-7 that drew special attention to the *empty* vessels and the oil. The point was that 'to the degree that we are in a condition of being empty of self, the Holy Spirit is accordingly enabled to fill us with Himself'[1]—after all, oil is always a symbol of the Holy Spirit. (Note: it is *usually* precarious to include 'always' in hermeneutical assumptions.) Is that what we must do with a terse text like this to make it 'useful'? Must we make some slick move or juice it up some way? Or can we take it straight? If we can, what does 4:1-7 teach? Originally (when the event occurred,

---

[1]Walter C. Kaiser, Jr., *Toward an Exegetical Theology* (Grand Rapids: Baker, 1981), 198. Kaiser also says he overheard some hearers flaunting their skepticism after the message. Their point was that if oil always connotes the Holy Spirit, then in verse 7 the woman was told to go out and sell the Holy Spirit and pay her debts.

ca. 840 BC, and later in the written form of it), it was a revelation to the remnant in Israel that *Yahweh, Israel's God and our God, is the help of the helpless and of the nameless*. That is the anchor point; let us approach the text via some glimpses it provides.

God's Desperate People (v. 1)

Here was a woman in double desperation. She had lost her husband by death and, as if that grief weren't enough, she is going to lose her sons by insolvency. Now that she is a widow her sons are her means of support, her lifeline; but they can be nothing of the kind when they are hauled off into debt slavery. We cannot say that the creditor was necessarily harsh—we do not know.[2] Possibly he was simply operating within his rights.[3] The lads would have to work off the debt, which must have been substantial.

This widow, however, is dealing with more than death and destitution. There is an *aggravation* in her desperation. Note her words: 'And you know that your servant was fearing Yahweh, but the creditor is coming…' Her husband had been faithful to Yahweh and to his true worship in a time when such fidelity could cost something.[4] It may have been during the regime of Ahab, when Jezebel liquidated Yahweh loyalists with such gusto (cf. 1 Kings 16:29-34; 18:4, 13). If not, there was always the religious 'status quo' in the northern kingdom—the perverted state-sponsored worship at Bethel (1 Kings 12:25-33). But this disciple of Elisha and servant of Yahweh had bucked the religious trends of the day; he swam against the stream of his culture and government. And yet his loved ones face disaster. Do you feel the rub she expresses? Don't we meet this

---

[2]We have no grounds for making him into an ogre, much as has been done with the alleged Bethlehem innkeeper in our Christmas-time mythology. Still, one can wonder why the creditor did not cut the woman a break in view of her recent grief.

[3]On debt and debt slavery, see Ze'ev W. Falk, *Hebrew Law in Biblical Times*, 2nd ed. (Provo, UT: BYU, 2001), 93-97. We do not know if the creditor charged interest. Israelites were not to exact interest of fellow Israelites (Exod. 22:25; Lev. 25:35-38). But Israelites, like Anglicans and Presbyterians, were known to trample on the law. 'This law is in marked contrast to the customs of nations surrounding Israel where interest exacted ranged from 20 percent to 50 percent. A higher rate was charged on grain than on precious metal; e.g., in the Old Babylonian era the interest on barley was 33 1/3 and on silver 20 percent' (J. E. Hartley, 'Debt,' ISBE, 1:905, citing Saggs in part).

[4]Cf. M. Cogan and H. Tadmor, *II Kings*, Anchor Bible (Garden City, NY: Doubleday, 1988), 56.

in a hundred different ways? Here is a Christian woman who has served Christ sacrificially and now her cancer has returned. Here is a farmer in the Mississippi Delta who confesses Christ openly and yet his crops have failed two years running and he is going to lose his farm. Or here is an earnest Christian husband and father who is raising and teaching his children in the fear of the Lord, and a drunk driver smashes into his wife and children when they were returning from a school basketball game and kills them all. 'Your servant was fearing Yahweh, but the creditor is coming.' This woman faces this perennial mystery and seems to be asking if Yahweh has any provision for them in this fix.

Yet hers is a *faithful* desperation. Where do we see faith? In the fact that she 'cried out to Elisha', Yahweh's servant. Note that her faith simply clings, simply informs. It does not speculate. She lays the problem before him—she doesn't suggest a solution or raise possible options. It was the way of Mary and Martha: 'Lord, the one you love is sick' (John 11:3, niv). No recommendations, no outline of procedures. Jesus can be trusted to know what to do—just tell him the situation. It was the recourse of Jehoshaphat, facing an invading horde and turning to Yahweh in transparent candor: 'We do not know what to do, but our eyes are on you' (2 Chron. 20:12, esv). At wits' end and telling Yahweh about it. Insofar as this woman appeals to Elisha, Yahweh's servant, she appeals to Yahweh; as she casts her burden on Elisha she casts it on Yahweh. And so we see a familiar combination: she is in trouble and she believes.

Yet there is more than faith here; there is *privilege* in her desperation. Verse 1 tells us she 'cried out to Elisha'. Then notice what follows in verse 2: 'Elisha said to her, "What can I do for you? Tell me—what do you have in the house?"' Do you hear that? Do you hear how eager Elisha is to help? Now compare this to the previous story of the three kings. Flip back to 3:13-14 and hear Elisha's scathing repulse of King Jehoram. He would not pay attention to him or see him—except that Jehoshaphat was with him. Other things being equal, the king had put himself beyond Elisha's concern and God's help. But how different it is with this nameless widow! She brings her troubles to Elisha, the man of God, and Elisha only thinks of

how he might help. Do you see the difference? She has *access*
to God in her troubles. You may have no particular status, but
have you thought of what you *have*, if, through Jesus, you have
the privilege of access and can bring your troubles to God?
What a mercy Psalm 142:2 describes!

God's Typical Tendencies (vv. 2-6)
Even in little snips of stories we must rivet our attention on
God—what he is doing, what he is revealing about himself,
how he is acting. And Yahweh seems to leave the fingerprints
of his ways on this story. I suggest that the story highlights the
ways God tends to work—not absolute procedures but typical
patterns. I will discuss these patterns, though more at the level
of broad principle than of specific application.

First, note *where God begins* (v. 2). 'What do you have in the
house?' 'Your maidservant has nothing at all in the house,
except a flask of oil' (v. 2b). Obviously her reply is meant to
indicate an absence of resources not the possibility of such.
We are not to think of this woman as finishing her statement,
pausing momentarily, and then, with a flash of light in her
eye, exclaiming to the prophet, 'Oh, I see! A flask of oil—*there's*
a possibility; a Widow's Helper Starter Kit!' No, she had no clue.
The flask of oil is a sign of her destitution. By mentioning it she
stresses the meagerness of anything she has or can offer.[5] How
often God begins his work at the point of our inadequacies.
He makes us recognize how hopeless the whole situation is
('Your maidservant has nothing at all…except…'). And then
he may begin, as here, with the very item that symbolizes our
helplessness and make it the means of his help.

That sort of thing happened once in southeast Alabama.
The boll weevil arrived in that area about 1910 and wreaked
havoc on cotton, the area's main cash crop. Cotton production
dropped from 38,000 bales in 1914 to 7,000 bales in 1917.
Farmers tried everything to kill weevils—carbolic acid, ashes,
insecticides, whiskey, among others. So some farmers turned
to raising peanuts, others tried corn, hay, and livestock. With
this diversification the economy stabilized and the community

---

[5]The text suggests an interesting contrast: the single mention of the flask of oil (v. 2)
followed by six references to multiple 'containers' or 'vessels' in verses 3-6.

prospered. Hence in 1919 one of the merchants suggested that a monument was called for. So if you drive to Enterprise, Alabama, today, you can view such a memorial—a woman in flowing robes holding aloft a football-size, seventeen and a half pound iron likeness of the boll weevil. It was both the symbol of their destitution *and* the beginning of their recovery.

Jesus operates in an Elisha-mode in Mark 6. He asks the disciples, 'How many loaves do you have?' (v. 38). He did not ask, 'Do you have enough?' What they had was utterly insufficient, but he began his work with those five loaves and two fish. 'What do you have in the house?' Next to nothing. And God often begins with that.

Second, observe *how God conceals* (vv. 3-5a). The episode, per Elisha's instructions (v. 4), was to occur behind closed doors, a directive the widow was careful to fulfill (v. 5a). Is there any significance to this? Why the secrecy (cf. 4:33)?

Now it was not a total secrecy. Neighbors knew something was afoot, what with borrowing all their extra pottery. Perhaps one can imagine the woman or her lads going round to today's fast food establishments asking if they had empty five-gallon pickle buckets to give away. Curiosity would surely be roused. But the door was to be closed on the mighty work of God. This suggests that sometimes God's mighty acts in our behalf are not to be the object of public gaze or report. Sometimes God works quietly, in a hidden way, perhaps precisely because he does not want hullabaloo or fanfare or religious rah-rah over his marvelous provision.

Might this sample of God's pattern here in 2 Kings 4 imply that there are times when a Christian is *not* to testify of some bounty Yahweh has given? This is not always the case to be sure—see, e.g., Psalms 34:4-6; 40:9-10; 66:16-19. But *sometimes* it may be that God's staggering goodness is to be kept to oneself and not made the subject of a testimony at a Christian Women's Club luncheon. Why might that be? (Here we must go beyond the edge of the text to answer.) Because it can become an occasion of pride and Christian posturing (cf. Matt. 6:1-18). Oh, we'll still load our stories with clichés about how all the glory belongs to God. But isn't there something gratifying in God's marvelous work when we can say he did it *for me*?

Maybe the most faithful thing you can do is to keep your mouth shut about God's amazing goodness to you! At any rate, some of God's work is not for public consumption, not for the Christian tabloids, and we need to ask ourselves, with our various Christian testimonies, if we are magnifying God or stroking ourselves.

Third, we can see *what God stimulates* (vv. 5-6). Verse 5 assumes the widow's complete obedience: 'So she went from him, and she shut the door behind her and behind her sons; they kept bringing to her and she kept pouring.'[6] The story does not repeat the requests she made to the neighbors, the explanations, the conversations. The text assumes that. 'She went from him'; then we see the door closing.

We need to head off at the pass one way of looking at this episode. Sometimes one hears expositors beating up on this widow because of the limitations of her faith. They pick up on the end of verse 6, 'and the oil stopped.' Alas—so goes the lament—the oil stopped. Had the woman only gotten more vessels there would have been more oil. Of course, this approach 'preaches', for who of us has enough faith? But the text depicts her clear obedience to Elisha's instructions not the defects of any expectancy on her part. In verses 3-4 we hear the prophet's instructions; verses 5-6 report the woman's obedience. There was no deficiency in her obedience.

But Yahweh's provision did require her obedience. The answer came, the miracle occurred as she acted.[7] I do not want to press this too far. But does this teach us that it is God's way, in meeting the multicolored needs of his people, to exercise and build our faith rather than to circumvent it? He tends to pull us into the process in such a way as our trust in him must become visible.

It was New Year's Day 1954. I was a small lad and my father took me along to visit my uncle. Uncle Bade (long 'a'—don't ask me how he got the nickname or what it meant) was listening to the 'Bowl' games—American football all day—on radio. I still remember one of those games. Rice University was playing

---

[6]The verb forms in verse 5b are participles, indicating continuing action. The reader has a vivid picture of the miracle in process: 'they kept bringing...she kept pouring.'

[7]No one can say prophetic magic is at work, for Elisha is not even present when the marvel takes place.

Alabama. Rice had the ball. One of Rice's running backs got loose and was pounding down the field with nothing between him and the goal. The sportscaster said he was going to go 'all the way,' or something of that ilk. A sure score. Then a strange thing happened. An Alabama player charged off the bench and tackled the Rice runner! Of course it was illegal. The player was not properly in the game. So they awarded Rice the touchdown. Yet there's something wonderful in the illegality. The fellow simply couldn't help himself; he couldn't bear to see Rice score; and, willy-nilly, he was sucked right into the game.

The God of the Bible often pulls us into and catches us up in the process of supplying his people's needs. He usually, it seems, makes us participants rather than spectators. When Yahweh provides, whether amazingly or routinely, he frequently designs not merely to supply your need but to build your faith and spark your obedience in the process.

God's Overflowing Kindness (v. 7)
The widow gets all her cues from 'the man of God.'[8] He gives her three commands: sell, pay, live. Sell the oil, pay the debts, live on the leftovers. Yahweh grants an abundance far beyond the immediate need: 'and you and your sons can live on the rest.' Yahweh had his eye on both the immediate emergency (debt) and the ongoing need (sustenance). We shouldn't be surprised. It is Yahweh's way to do more than we ask, to meet not only present need but continuing need.

God in his generosity often gives 'more'. But some of this 'more' may not appear in the form we prefer. I think of Romans 5:1-5. Paul itemizes some of God's gifts (peace with God, v. 1; access into the realm of grace, v. 2a; the hope of enjoying God's glory, v. 2b); then he writes, 'And not only this, but…' (v. 3a). That is, not only all of that—there's more! And what is it? 'Boast(ing) in our afflictions.' But the principle is the same: it is God's practice to make his goodness overflow! Christians then have to be very careful. Watch your cup—God

---

[8]This is the first time Elisha is called 'the man of God' (here by the narrator). According to V. P. Hamilton, the phrase occurs 76 times in the Old Testament, of which 55 are in 1–2 Kings. The term is used of Elisha (29 times) far more than of anyone else (NIDOTTE, 1:390). Perhaps the term refers particularly to those through whom Yahweh uniquely speaks and acts. Note how Elijah seems to assume that a genuine man of God can exercise heavenly power (2 Kings 1:10, 12).

tends to make it overflow and then you have a mess of blessing on your hands.

I want you to take a good look at this widow again. This obscure, nameless woman. Do you know that our writer in 1 Kings 16:23-28 describes the reign of one of the most important figures in Israelite politics and history—King Omri?[9] Omri, for all his apparent importance, gets six verses from our writer. This Yahweh-fearing widow gets more press than Omri. Which shows that *God's desperate people matter to him.*

---

[9]1 Kings 16:21-22 mention Omri when giving the political situation before he became king; but the actual entry for Omri himself is 1 Kings 16:23-28.

5

The Sad and the Glad of God
(2 Kings 4:8-37)

I remember getting my first car. I no longer had to ask my father for the family car. I could go and come whenever I wanted. Freedom had come. But I also remember the radiator hose that blew out on the interstate, the wheel alignment, and the two new tires I had to buy. That car was both fresh freedom and dull responsibility. It was the same when our boys got their first dog. They had a live toy. Then the novelty wore off. They always had to see Sarah had food and water. She was crazy to run and play, but they weren't in the mood. They had to scour the back yard and clean up her messes. She was fun and she was trouble. A mixed bag.

Our narrative fits this pattern. As I noted before, 2 Kings 2–8 depicts Elisha as a prophet of grace, at least to the believing remnant in Israel. Yet sometimes God's grace and gifts appear to be a mixed bag, as in this story. There's a lot of the sad along with the glad. *God's gifts to his people may contain both the sad and the glad of God.* I will develop the exposition via a series of observations.

The Simplicity of God's Goodness (focus on vv. 14-17)
Elisha passes through Shunem (about fifteen miles southwest of the southern tip of the Sea of Galilee). A 'great woman' (lit., i.e., a woman of some standing and probably wealth) constrains him to eat at her place (v. 8a). This begins a regular practice:

whenever Elisha travels through Shunem, he enjoys this woman's hospitality (v. 8b). She urges her husband to erect an addition to their house—a small, closed-in roof room that could be furnished with the necessities. Then Elisha could have both board and room with them (vv. 9-10). She wanted to do this simply because she was sure Elisha was a 'holy man of God' (v. 9a). Jesus would have been proud of her (Matt. 10:41-42).

Elisha, however, wanted to reward her for her kind provision. On one of his visits he had Gehazi summon the woman to see what she might like Elisha to do for her. Elisha had 'connections'—he could put in a good word for her with the king or captain of the army (v.13a). She refuses this offer. 'I dwell among my own people' (v. 13b). That is, I have everything I need right here in my own clan and community.

What to do for the woman who has everything? Gehazi has an idea. He informs Elisha of two facts: the woman has no son and her husband is old. So Elisha announces God's gift: 'At this season, about this time next year, you shall embrace a son' (v. 16, ESV). The woman thinks this incredible (v. 16b), but the Bible doesn't; it continues on in its laconic, 'of-course' style: 'So the woman became pregnant and gave birth to a son' just when and as Elisha had predicted (v. 17).

This is not the first time this sort of thing has occurred. There is a phrase in verses 16 and 17, *kā'ēt ḥayyāh* ('next year' in NASB) which only appears in one other passage—Genesis 18:10, 14. Of course, that is the story of another 'impossible' birth, impossible because Sarah had already been through menopause (18:11) and knew she couldn't have kids. It's as if the use of *kā'ēt ḥayyāh* in verses 16 and 17 is meant to give us a flashback to Sarah in Genesis 18.

And, naturally, that brings to mind a whole biblical motif—the barren woman who gives birth. Sarah's saga in Genesis 11–21 begins this pattern. Then we meet Rebekah—and if you do the math in Genesis 25:19-26 you realize that Rebekah was childless through twenty years of marriage, until Esau and Jacob were born. Then comes Rachel, Jacob's favorite, who remains childless all through the soap-opera scenario of Genesis 29:31–30:24, where, at last, she bears Joseph. In Judges 13 we meet the childless Mrs. Manoah, who becomes

Samson's mother; then comes Hannah in 1 Samuel 1 out of whose tears and prayers comes Samuel; next our Shunammite lady appears in 2 Kings 4. Then we walk into the New Testament and find Elizabeth (Luke 1:7).

However, 2 Kings 4 is unique among all these instances of the 'barren woman' pattern. In all other cases either the birth of the child is essential for continuing a covenant people or the child becomes a significant leader in a time of crisis for Israel. Had Isaac and Jacob not been born, the slender line of the covenant people would have gone extinct. Without Joseph, Jacob's family would have perished in famine. Samson was at least a wild boar in the Philistines' vineyard that kept them from ever relaxing. Samuel proved to be the glue that held Israel together during the turbulent transition to monarchy. And John the Baptist (of Elizabeth) prepared a people for the long-expected Jesus. None of this applies in 2 Kings 4. Obviously, the birth of this child is not essential to national continuity; there are plenty of Israelite kids floating around. Nor does he become an outstanding leader or prominent figure in Israel's life. He probably farmed the home place and died again. We don't even have his name. What's the point? That sometimes Yahweh gives such a gift not because he will fulfill some grand redemptive-historical function but simply because he wants to make a woman happy with a child. Sometimes it's far simpler than we imagine.

One of Charles Schulz's *Peanuts* cartoon strips shows Charlie Brown examining some of Linus' art work. Linus has drawn a picture of a man, and Charlie is very complimentary, although he observes that Linus drew the man with the man's hands behind his back. Charlie is apparently in a therapeutic mood and proceeds to interpret Linus' behind-the-back technique. 'You did that,' Charlie intones, 'because you yourself have feelings of insecurity,' to which Linus heatedly retorts, 'I did that because I myself can't draw hands!' It's that simple.

Sometimes that's how it is with God's ways. He delights to give you good gifts not because you're so prominent (note: we don't know the Shunammite's name either) or useful (neither she nor her son made any 'outstanding contribution' to the kingdom of God, so far as we know) but simply because he's that kind of God ('who richly supplies us with all things to enjoy,' 1 Tim. 6:17b, NASB). The Belgic Confession strikes this note when it calls God 'the overflowing fountain of all good' (Article 1). Frequently God gives his gifts to his servants simply to make them happy with his gifts. Don't let any sourpuss version of Christianity rob you of this point. Only the gospel according to the serpent makes God out to be stingy (Gen. 3:1-2) and manipulative (note 'for…' in Gen. 3:5).

The Inconsistency of God's Ways (vv. 18-30)[1]
We have a mini-biography of this lad in verses 18-20. It begins with 'And the child grew' (18a) and ends with 'and he died' (20). Terribly abrupt: he grew…he died. All in three verses. The writer only relates the fatal scenario in the field. You remember her words in verse 13? She had no needs. You see her in verse 28? Very needy. *It was Yahweh's gift that made her needy.* The poor widow of verses 1-7 faced desperate need; now the wealthy woman of verse 8-37 knows the same. The creditor was going to take the widow's sons; death has already taken the Shunammite's. Social position is no prophylactic from catastrophe.

But do you see the real problem? God had given a gift (vv. 16-17) only to take it away (vv. 18-20). She plopped her dead son on the man of God's bed—it was, she thought, Elisha's responsibility. Read ahead to see her intensity (v. 27) and hear her anguish (v. 28). What are we to make of God here?

When our boys were in elementary school they once were discussing a certain substitute teacher one of them had endured. This sub was supposedly not as gracious, kind, or—perhaps—forbearing as the regular teacher. At last Seth charitably and bluntly summed up the matter: 'She's a Christian, but she's a *mean* Christian.'

This text nudges us to ponder a similar dilemma. Is that true of Yahweh? Must we say he is God but that he's a mean God? God's promise brought a son and yet here is the death of the one promised. Does Yahweh make glad only to increase the pain? Does he lift us up in order to drop us all the harder?

---

[1] Some readers may prefer to place quote marks around 'inconsistency', but I'm trying to depict God's ways as the woman would have perceived them—and as we perceive them when walking in the muck.

Note, by the way, that this problem is not recent. God's servants
and maidservants have been asking it for ages (as in this text).
Many saints have sobbed 'in bitter distress' (v. 27) because
they do not know why God has crushed them. The fact that
Scripture features such narratives as this shows that the Bible
itself presses us to think about this problem.

But what to do? The Shunammite is going to ride off to the
'man of God' (v. 22). She must have withheld from her husband
any word of the lad's death; hence his perplexity over her
travel plans (v. 23).[2] Off she goes the fifteen to eighteen miles
to Mt. Carmel, brushing aside Gehazi's authorized inquiries (v.
26), until she reaches Elisha, grabs his feet, and pours out her
bitter complaint (vv. 27-28). Nor will she leave him (v. 30).[3]

But there is faith oozing out of verses 28 and 30. After all,
clinging to the man of God (used six times of Elisha in vv. 21-30:
vv. 21, 22, 25 [twice], 27 [twice]) is in some measure clinging to
Yahweh. Not that Elisha is divine, but he is Yahweh's authorized
representative, and so when she has recourse to him it is as if she
has recourse to Yahweh. So where does she turn? Where can she
go? Only to the same God who has perplexed her—there is no one
else to whom she can go. What can you do when God's mercy has
turned to malice? Take the bitter distress and in it keep clutching
at the God you don't understand. We have a word for that: faith.
(Which tells us, by the way, that faith is not serenity.)

The Limitations of God's Servant (vv. 27-33)

So she came to the man of God, to the mountain, and grabbed
hold of his feet. Then Gehazi came near to push her away, and the

---

[2]Her husband asks, 'Why are you going to him today—it's not new moon or Sabbath?'
(v. 23). 'From these words,' Keil (*The Books of the Kings*, Biblical Commentary on
the Old Testament [1876; reprint ed.,, Grand Rapids: Eerdmans, 1965], 311) writes,
a number of scholars 'have drawn the correct conclusion, that the pious in Israel were
accustomed to meet together at the prophets' houses for worship and edification, on
those days which were appointed in the law (Lev. xxiii.3; Num. xxviii.11 sqq.) for the
worship of God; and from this Hertz and Hengstenberg have still further inferred, that
in the kingdom of the ten tribes not only were the Sabbath and new moons kept, as
is evident from Amos viii.5 also, but the prophets supplied the pious in that kingdom
with a substitute for the missing Levitical priesthood.' In this way Elijah and Elisha
nurtured a believing remnant while the nation at large was pro-Baal (1 Kings 16:29-34)
or pro-bull (1 Kings 12:25-33).
[3]She uses the very same oath formula that Elisha himself had used in 2:2, 4, 6,
when Elijah seemingly tried to dump Elisha at various locales.

man of God said, 'Leave her alone, for she is in bitter distress, and
Yahweh [emphatic] has hidden it from me and has not informed
me (v. 27).

Some scholars assure us that these Elisha stories are prophetic
legends, not historical narrative. Elisha's ministry is allegedly
'shrouded by the veils of pious legends and miracle narratives'.
We are told Elisha's followers, enamored as they were with the
memory of their beloved master, padded their stories of him.
Indeed, they are 'overloaded with legendary elements', because
the storyteller wanted 'to enhance the fame of the prophet'.[4]

If that is the case, Elisha's devotees did a lousy job here. The
last thing you do if you want to enhance a prophet's fame is
to depict him shrugging his shoulders, as if to say 'Beats me!,'
and admitting that Yahweh has hidden the whole affair from
him. That hardly polishes the prophetic image, and makes for
poor legends.

The text shows the man of God (the term occurs eight times
in vv. 8-37) limited in *knowledge* (because Yahweh withheld it,
v. 27; contrast 2:16-18) and limited in *power* (vv. 29-31, the staff
episode),[5] and so he can only come in *earnest prayer* (v. 33). True,
one might say that means are used in verse 34, but the stress
is not on Elisha's ingenuity but on his utter dependence. One
might even say that Elisha's action in verse 34 is an *expression*
or *extension* of his prayer of verse 33.[6] The power then is wholly
Yahweh's, for which Elisha can only pray. The text suggests the
limitations of all God's servants.

---

[4]For this approach, see S. Szikszai, 'Elisha,' IDB, 2:91-92; also Claus Westermann,
A Thousand Years and a Day (Philadelphia: Muhlenberg, 1962), 148-50.

[5]When Gehazi placed Elisha's staff on the corpse, verse 31 says, literally, 'there
was no voice and no attentiveness.' Compare 1 Kings 18:29, where similar language
highlights the powerlessness of Baal.

[6]John Gray takes the mouth, eye, hand contact as a form of contactual magic
'whereby the properties of one party were transferred to another', an indication of
popular belief and practice at that time (*I & II Kings*, Old Testament Library, 2nd ed.
[Westminster: Philadelphia, 1970], 498-99). I think, however, that Simon DeVries has
better understood such prophetic actions. His comments regarding Elijah's similar
action in 1 Kings 17:21 apply equally well here: 'Then Elijah stretches himself three
times "out over" or "upon" the lad; it is not magic, but a typical symbolic act familiar to
the prophetic movement in Israel. It is an "acted out" way of saying, "Let his lifeless
body be as my lively body…"' (*1 Kings*, Word Biblical Commentary [Waco: Word, 1985],
222). In verses 34 and 35 we twice read that Elisha 'bent over him [the lad].' The verb
is *gāhar* and occurs only once elsewhere, in 1 Kings 18:42, where it depicts Elijah's
posture as he pleads with Yahweh for rain.

This includes those servants we admire the most. Some will think of a particular Bible teacher or pastor whose influence has been immense in shaping one's thinking and faith. Others will think of a mentor who has 'discipled' them and proved to be a light at the dark and treacherous turns of the Christian walk. Still others recall a friend who seems to radiate the likeness of Christ, one whose intercessory prayers and steady companionship have proven the ballast needed during uncertain times. These are all the Lord's gifts. But it is crucial to remember that none of Christ's servants are as adequate as he is. So however much we may prize their help and admire their walk, we must not make idols of them. We dare not make them pale substitutes for Jesus, for they will certainly disappoint us if we do.

Perhaps this text is also a call to us to recognize our own limitations as servants of Christ—and to enjoy the freedom that comes from that. Elisha shows much wisdom in dealing with this distress. 'Yahweh has hidden it from me and has not informed me' (v. 27). He didn't have an answer. Nor do we always need to give an 'answer'.[7] Some Christians assume they have a gift for knowing the solution to the distresses of other Christians, and they would do well to catch Elisha's humility and keep their mouths shut. Often we don't have a clue about what God is up to in some believer's trouble. How liberating to be able to confess: 'Yahweh has hidden it from me and has not informed me.'

The Witness to God's Power (vv. 32-37)
Yahweh's ear heard Elisha's cry (cf. v. 33) and the lad's nose recovered before his eyes did (v. 35b). Sneezes never sounded so healthy! Yahweh restored the lad to life.

Now this is a 'clue' episode. That is, this restoration is a specimen, a sign, a pledge, a preview of the victory God can

---

[7] This may go cross-grained with some who make much of biblical truth as sufficient for all the needs of God's people. I would agree in principle. But there are some who have a high view of the Bible and a low degree of wisdom, who are quick to slap a biblical text on someone without real discernment of the circumstances of their 'victim'. At the same time (and I hope it's obvious) I am not implying we should never give biblical direction to people. Some of us have had to recover from 'pastoral theology' courses that propagated such a view. It was all right to grunt intelligently, but one was never to direct someone what to do.

and will grant his people at the last. Sometimes the question comes up: Why doesn't God do this now? For the same reason that most dead folks stayed dead in Jesus' time—it's not time yet for all to be raised. Did Jesus restore people to life? Certainly (Matt. 11:4-5; Mark 5:35-43; Luke 7:11-17; John 11:38-44), but apparently not all that many. He didn't empty the cemeteries during his earthly ministry. It wasn't time yet. His people will be raised on Resurrection Day at his second coming (cf. 1 Thess. 4:13-18). But until then the Lord gives his people 'previews' to assure them that death will not have the last word with them. I take 2 Kings 4 as one of those. After all, how were believing Israelites to understand this story? Were they not to infer that *the God of Israel can deliver his people even from death?*

Take a little trip with me—forward in the text but not far from Shunem. Go to Luke 7:11-17 and stand outside the village of Nain. Now New Testament Nain was not far from Old Testament Shunem, for both were located on the Hill of Moreh at the east end of the Plain of Esdraelon. Shunem was on the south side of the hill and Nain was a couple of miles away on the north side of the hill. And all this is easy to remember, for both Shunem and south begin with 's' and Nain and north begin with 'n.'

Jesus cancelled the funeral at Nain. Don't you suppose that the folks in Luke 7 remembered something very similar that had happened around 800 BC just over the hill in Shunem? Well, it was recorded in their Scriptures and it happened so nearby. Yet there are differences between 2 Kings 4 and Luke 7. Elisha could only acknowledge the woman's bitter distress; Jesus tells the widow of Nain not to weep (Luke 7:13). That is one of the most absurd and calloused things to say, unless one has power to deal with the cause of her weeping. Moreover, Elisha prays, but Jesus *speaks* to the young dead man and he sits up (Luke 7:14-15).

While here we should notice the context in Luke 7. In 7:2 a centurion's slave is 'at the point of death', and the centurion sends for Jesus to heal him before death takes him away. But verse 12 presents a far different case. This man had already died, and with him his mother's future. Can the Lord work with power here? Can he merely keep people from dying or can he, as it were, enter the very realm of death itself and plunder its prey at will? You see what Luke 7 teaches you: *Not even death can put you beyond the reach of Jesus' power or beyond the sound of his voice.* What an anchor this should be for us!

Dr. John 'Rabbi' Duncan seemed to have this anchor. About 1839 his wife died after the birth of their second daughter. He took a friend with him to look at the dead body. He stood over her motionless form, and, without uttering anything else, repeated 'with thrilling solemnity' the answer to Shorter Catechism No. 37: 'The souls of believers are at their death made perfect in holiness, and do immediately pass into glory; and their bodies, being still united to Christ, do rest in their graves till the resurrection.'[8]

How God's people need the assurance he gives them in their 'preview' texts like 2 Kings 4 and Luke 7. That is what such texts want to give us. And I can see them now…that wealthy lady leaving Shunem and making her way up the south side of the Hill of Moreh, and—yes, there is the widow of Nain, not dressed quite so smartly, walking up the north slope to meet her. And there they are, shouting to the servants of God from the top of the Hill of Moreh: 'Death shall not have dominion over you!'

So why this story? So you'll know about the Shunammite and Elisha? Hear of an instance of Iron Age home remodeling? No, the story is here to reveal your God—the God who delights to amaze his 'ordinary' people with his good gifts; who sometimes baffles us with the mysterious sorrow he brings; who places limitations upon his servants so that we will never esteem them *too* highly; and who gives us a sneak preview in 800 BC that not even death will be able to separate us from the love of God in Christ Jesus our Lord.

---

[8]A. Moody Stuart, *The Life of John Duncan* (1872; reprint ed.,, Edinburgh: Banner of Truth, 1991), 62-63.

6

The Peril of Church Suppers
(2 Kings 4:38-41)

Once my brother drove up to the main intersection in our small, western Pennsylvania town. It was the only intersection with a traffic light, and the light was red. At the corner where my brother stopped was a service/petrol station. A sign heralding its brand of oil and gasoline sat high atop a pole at that corner. Somehow a truck smashed into that pole; the pole gave way and came crashing down across the front of my brother's car. He's waiting for a green light and he gets a gasoline sign. Who would expect that? Who drives up to an intersection, thinking, 'A sign from a service station will fall on my car'? It's completely unexpected.

That is the way the sons of the prophets must have remembered this incident of the stew. Who knows how many meals they may have shared before, but, probably, they'd had 'large pot stew' before, and it had proved as uneventful as waiting for a green light. But now one gagged, another choked, one more screamed. The stuff was either utterly unpalatable or highly lethal.

So what had happened? After Elisha had placed the order for stew, one of the men went out looking for herbs, found some wild gourds, collected a bunch, and sliced them into the pot (v. 39). The word for 'gourd' is only used here but is usually identified with the *citrullus colcynthus*, which produces a small yellow melon that acts as a strong laxative. A large quantity can be fatal.[1]

What are we to make of this terse episode? What is its point? Are we being warned never to eat a meal with our church fellowship group? Or, if we do, to stay away from the vegetables and squash? What does this little clip teach?

The Situation of God's People (v. 38a)

This story instructs us about the situation of God's people. 'But Elisha returned to Gilgal,[2] and there was a famine in the land' (v. 38a). This famine was likely an evidence of Yahweh's judgment on Israel. Is famine always and necessarily a divine judgment? No. But Yahweh had given to Israel a detailed covenantal interpretation of life in what we call the covenant blessings and curses (see especially Leviticus 26 and Deuteronomy 28). In the covenant curses, famine was one manifestation of Yahweh's judgment upon Israel's infidelity (Lev. 26:20, 26; Deut. 28:38-40, 53-57; Amos 4:6).[3] So I think the famine noted here implies that Israel in Elisha's time is enduring a degree of Yahweh's wrath.

And so is the believing remnant. These sons of the prophets under Elisha's tutelage were part of the 'true church' within the apostate nation. But they were not exempted from suffering the famine that all Israel suffered. A special exception would be wonderful. Once several of the famed Brooklyn Dodgers baseball team of the 1950s were caught speeding. One of them,

[1]Cf. M. Cogan and H. Tadmor, *II Kings*, Anchor Bible (Garden City, NY: Doubleday, 1988), 58. The story is short but has its puzzles. For example, when the men holler, 'Death is in the pot!', are they via exaggeration complaining that the stew is grossly inedible or do they really mean this could be their last supper? Perhaps both? In any case, the vittles are vicious; somehow the meal is harmful (cf. v. 41c). And the last clause of v. 39 poses a second puzzle. Some versions construe the verb as singular, referring to the man who collected and chopped up the gourds—he did not know what they were (ESV, RSV). The verb is actually plural—'they did not know,' referring to the whole group. In that case, all the men did not know what these gourds were or their malicious properties (so NASB, NIV), perhaps, as some suggest, because they were strangers to the area. The text, however, can also be translated, 'But they did not know.' What they didn't know is not expressed—it must be supplied. The text may be saying that the rest of the group did not know that this one fellow had dumped the gourds into the stew. Had they known that, they might have prevented anyone from sampling it.

[2]We don't know if this Gilgal was the one near Jericho and the Jordan River (cf. Josh. 5:9) or one located in the territory of Ephraim.

[3]For details of covenant curses and blessings, see Douglas Stuart, *Hosea-Jonah*, Word Biblical Commentary (Waco: Word, 1987), xxxii-xlii.

Pee Wee Reese, had shown himself adept at talking policemen out of traffic tickets. But this time centerfielder Duke Snider (who wore No. 4) was driving. When the officer approached the car, Snider said, 'Hi, officer, I'm Duke Snider of the Dodgers and this is...' The officer growls, 'I hate baseball.'[4] Baseball players are no exception; even Dodgers get traffic tickets. And there is no special provision for Yahweh's disciples here.

This may be a piece of realism some of us need. In this famine, Yahweh's remnant also suffered the effects of the nation's sins. When some disaster strikes a nation today, we may not be completely certain it is a divine judgment. (Sometimes it seems primarily a work of wicked human oppression.) But God's people in that nation are not usually evacuated beforehand. They suffer with the rest. If an invader wreaks havoc and decimates a nation, the church in that nation shares in its woes and sufferings. There is no safety button Christ's people can press, no form they can submit to claim an exemption. We need to know this, lest we expect of God something he's never promised to give. This realization might also nudge us to intercessory prayer for Jesus' flock in nations now ravaged by war and suffering.

The Earthiness of God's Interests (vv. 38, 40)
In this exposition I am treating verses 38-41 and verses 42-44 separately. However, if we combine them momentarily we notice that these two episodes use the verb 'ākal (to eat) eight times. Without becoming Marxists, we can see a very important point here: Yahweh is very earthy; daily bread matters to him. How close the God of the Bible is to where you live!

The fact that there is a famine (v. 38) tells us that food dare not be wasted. In such circumstances it is tragic when the stew is ruined and/or harmful (v. 40). There is a certain necessity here. The miracle is not superfluous or ridiculous. It is a work of necessity as well as of mercy. And if Christians in the West view this incident as trivial, they only reveal a lack of sympathetic understanding. Ray Dillard helps us here:

It is striking how many of the stories about Elijah and Elisha have to do with food. It is difficult for modern Western readers

[4]Duke Snider and Bill Gilbert, *The Duke of Flatbush* (New York: Zebra, 1988), 117.

to understand what life in an agrarian society of basically subsistence levels meant for the average individual in ancient Israel. Starvation and hard times were never far away... In modern Western countries, food is a far smaller part of a household budget than it has ever been; the time invested in gathering it is ordinarily limited to how long one spends in a supermarket or convenience store and perhaps a small family garden. Life was very different in ancient Israel. In subsistence or marginal economies, providing daily bread may represent the largest expenditure one makes and may also consume almost every waking moment.[5]

So needs that may appear frivolous to some are quite real and legitimate when we know the facts. Perhaps you've sometimes heard some believer talk of praying for a parking place when going to a store or office. And you may think that is trivializing prayer and making the Lord into a genie to meet our convenience. But when you see that sister has a brace on her leg or hear that that brother has a severe heart condition you understand. Isn't it wonderful to know Yahweh, a God who is not above trafficking in the nuts and bolts of life? Have you noticed that daily bread comes first in the petition-section of the Lord's Prayer, before the forgiveness of sins? Is Jesus implying that he understands us?

The Sign of God's Work (v. 41)

> So he said, 'Then take flour.' And he threw it into the pot. Then he said, 'Pour it out for the people, and let them eat.' And there was nothing harmfull in the pot (v. 41).

This was the hour of flour! Perhaps it seems a tad bizarre to us, but we should be getting used to this by now. Remember the use of salt at the healing of Jericho's water supply (2:20-21)? A *visible sign* or some overt action sometimes accompanies biblical miracles. Jesus was never above using outward signs—note his treatment of the deaf and mute man in Mark 7:31-37: he thrusts his fingers into the fellow's ears, then spits, and touches his tongue with the saliva.[6] We may make the arrogant mistake

---

[5]Raymond B. Dillard, *Faith in the Face of Apostasy* (Phillipsburg, NJ: Presbyterian and Reformed, 1999), 106.

of thinking that we are beyond this level, that we in the 'New Testament era' have no need of such elementary props. If so, why has Christ given us water for baptism and bread and wine to eat and drink?

Why does the Lord insist on using visible signs, even for sophisticated believers in this advanced 'post-modern' era? In part, I surmise, to give us pegs on which to hang the memory of his works.

Leland Ryken has written of the Puritans' knack for seeing God in the ordinary events of life. He notes how Walter Pringle told his children the exact places where certain things happened to him. His first exercise of prayer came 'at the north-east of Stitchel Hall'. Much later he committed his new-born son to God 'at the plum tree on the north side of the garden door'.[7] That plum tree becomes a non-technical sacrament conjuring up the memory of Pringle's intercession for his infant lad. One might say that plum tree would never be the same. That earthly artifact would always recall that prayerful hour.

So why does God mix visible signs in with his mighty works? So that God's work may *grip* you and hold your memory captive. Not that God always uses visible signs (see, e.g., vv. 42-44). But our wise Creator knows that sometimes the best way to our mind is through our imagination, and so he may use pictures instead of arguments. Can you picture attending a reunion of the sons of the prophets years later? 'There was that time,' one of them says, 'when Uzziah chopped up those weird gourds into the stew and nearly killed us.' And then another pipes up. Does he quote Elisha's command to pour out the stew (v. 41b)? No, he exclaims, 'And remember how Elisha grabbed all that flour and heaved it into the pot?' Visible signs are God's defense against spiritual amnesia.

However, not only does a visible sign accompany this miracle, but the miracle itself constitutes a *prophetic sign*, a preview of what is yet to come. The miracle certainly involves the removal of harm, and yet that may also be considered as

---

[6]On some of the background, see R. T. France, *The Gospel of Mark*, New International Greek Testament Commentary (Grand Rapids: Eerdmans, 2002), 302-03. France notes that 'physical contact is clearly more appropriate in the case of a man who would be unable to hear spoken words'.

[7]Leland Ryken, *Worldly Saints: The Puritans as They Really Were* (Grand Rapids: Zondervan, 1986), 209.

a precursor of the final reversal of the curse (à la Isaiah 11:6-9 and 65:17-25),[8] a small sign of what is coming.

In the last days of the Third Reich, allied bombers came in another wave near Berlin. Rudolf Reschke's mother grabbed her fourteen-year-old son and dragged him into the cellar where his nine-year-old sister sat shivering and crying. The shelter was shaking; plaster fell; the lights flickered and went out. Mother and sister began to pray, and soon Rudolf joined them in the Lord's Prayer. The bombing grew worse; the shelter shuddered. They had been through many raids, but not like this one. Rudolf's mother, with her arms around both children, began sobbing. He knew she was worried—his father was at the front fighting in the German army and then there were these bombs. Rudolf was angry at the planes for frightening his mother. Before his mother could restrain him, he dashed out of the shelter. He ran up to their ground-floor apartment, went straight to his room and his collection of toy soldiers. He chose the most impressive-looking 'soldier' with particular features painted on its china face. He took it into the kitchen, hefted down his mother's heavy meat cleaver, and, in the middle of the air raid, went out into the apartment house courtyard. He put the doll on the ground. With one stroke he severed its head. 'There!,' he cried, as tears stained his face. He looked down unrepentantly on the loose head of Adolf Hitler.[9]

It was only a piece of violence against a toy soldier, and yet it was a vignette of what would actually occur the afternoon of April 30, 1945, when Hitler would pick up a Walther pistol, put it in his mouth, and blow his brains out. One might say Rudolf's blow was a preliminary picture of that.

I suggest that the principle is the same in our text, but the reality signified is not tragic. It's only a pot of stew rendered harmless, but it's a small sketch of the day when 'they shall not hurt or destroy in all my holy mountain' (Isa. 11:9a). We must be grateful to a Lord who's not ashamed to stoop to picture-language if it will sustain the faith of his servants.

---

[8] I owe this point to two of my former students, Jeff Voorhees and Alonzo Ramirez.
[9] Cornelius Ryan, *The Last Battle* (New York: Simon and Schuster, 1966), 263.

The Fallibility of God's Servants (v. 39)

The text may intend this herb-collecting, gourd-slicing prophet to be a testimony to the grace of God. Dillard thought that in this story 'we see our God redeeming the labor of his servants, so that it would not be done in vain'.[10] Here is this fellow, then, with the best of intentions, who nearly sent all his colleagues gagging to the emergency room to get their stomachs pumped. He doubtless meant well, was utterly sincere and without malice, but committed a major gaffe.

Once when I was about six years old I decided our old 1940 Chevrolet needed to be washed. I retrieved a bucket, squirted it a third full of water, found me an old rag that was slouching around the garage, and proceeded to 'wash' the car—all I could reach. I'd dip the rag in the bucket and swipe it across fenders and doors, dipping and swiping until finished. But what a tragic surprise when later we discovered Pop's black Chevy covered with chocolate mud swirls. I knew nothing about using the hose and clean water to rinse off what I had so dutifully rubbed. I simply kept dipping an already dirty rag into increasingly dirty water. But I still recall how sincere I was. My intentions were good. And it was a mess.

And there are times when we do the same in the service of Christ. Perhaps we sported an undisciplined zeal that repelled rather than drew friends to Christ. Or we gave someone counsel which we were sure was well-considered, but it turned out to be wrong-headed or even harmful. Or we dealt in a certain way with one of our children and now, with hindsight, we realize what we imposed or allowed proved detrimental rather than helpful. About as foolish as a guy cutting up a vicious laxative into a pot of stew.

But the power of God overcame this cook's foible. What an assurance and encouragement this text should be for Christ's fallible servants. Too often we are the stars in episodes of 'Christ and our mistakes'. But what relief when we see—as in this text—that the Lord does not allow our errors to derail his kingdom or destroy his people. How many times Christ

---

[10]Raymond B. Dillard, *Faith in the Face of Apostasy*, 108. See also Ronald S. Wallace, *Elijah and Elisha* (Grand Rapids: Eerdmans, 1957), 120-23 ('Christ and our mistakes').

cushions our folly, redeems our errors, neutralizes our stupidity. What a consolation to have such a Lord.

You can probably resume going to church suppers—just be careful. And be careful to learn what this near disaster is telling you about your God.

7
Christ and Our Deficiencies
(2 Kings 4:42-44)

They summoned Jefferson Davis to Montgomery, Alabama, to assume the presidency of the Confederate States. In mid-February 1861, Davis left Jackson, Mississippi, by rail and traveled north, then east across Tennessee, arriving in Chattanooga. He made something like twenty-five speeches during the two-day journey. From Chattanooga, he angled southward to Atlanta and from there to Montgomery. Some think this trip may have been unnerving for Jeff Davis. After all, he was going from Jackson to Montgomery, the latter less than 300 miles east of Jackson. But by rail he must travel north into Tennessee, east to Chattanooga, then south to Atlanta and Montgomery, a roundabout of 850 miles — on half a dozen different railroads using three different gauges of track. It was an ill omen. How could the south expect to move men and supplies rapidly with such a grossly inadequate system?[1]

Elisha's servant had a similar problem: How could he set this utterly inadequate supply of food before a hundred men? (see v. 43). It simply wasn't enough. No slap on the donor. But so much bread and grain only go so far. One didn't need a calculator to figure it out. The provision in the previous story

[1]See Paul Johnson, *A History of the American People* (New York: HarperCollins, 1997), 457-58; and William C. Davis, *Jefferson Davis: The Man and His Hour* (New York: Harper Perennial, 1992), 304-305. Incidentally, I am sure the title for this chapter owes a subconscious debt to Ronald Wallace's treatment of this section in his *Elijah and Elisha* (p. 123) under 'Christ and our inadequacies'.

(vv. 38-41) was dangerous; here it is inadequate. This story is concise and straightforward, so we rush to trace its significance for us.[2] What may we rightly see in this little vignette?

The faith that still lives in a faithless land (v. 42a)

The man's address was Baal-shalishah, which was somewhere in the hill country of Ephraim.[3] He 'brought to the man of God bread of the first-fruits, twenty barley loaves and fresh grain in his sack.' Mention of the first-fruits drives us back to the Pentateuch (Exod. 23:19; Lev. 23:20; Num. 18:13; and Deut. 18:4-5). The last two references specify that the first-fruits were to go to the priests. But this citizen of Baal-shalishah brings his first-fruits to Elisha. How does one explain that? I think H. L. Ellison was right:

> The man was recognizing Elisha as the one true representative of God in the land; he did not wish to bring the first-fruits to the priests who had been contaminated by the Baalized worship of Jehovah, or even with Baal worship itself. By a gesture reminiscent of Mk. 3:31-35 Elisha, by sharing the *bikkurim* [first-fruits] with his hearers, proclaimed that they too shared in his relationship to God.[4]

The priests, then, in the northern kingdom—whether Ahab's Baal enthusiasts (cf. 1 Kings 18:20-22) or Jeroboam's appointed cronies at Bethel (1 Kings 12:31)—had, by their infidelity, excommunicated themselves from the functions and privileges of Yahweh's priesthood. What then was someone with remnant-faith to do if he wanted properly to dispense his offering of first-fruits? Bring it to the leader of Yahweh's remnant.

This text is so encouraging because we find here this citizen of Baal-shalishah who is still serving Yahweh in the midst of an apostate nation. 1 Kings 19:18 is true. Yahweh was right.

---

[2] The word *ṣiqlōn* (v. 42), used only here, is a puzzle. 'Sack' or 'bag' is a guess—perhaps a good one.

[3] M. Cogan and H. Tadmor, *II Kings*, Anchor Bible (Garden City, NY: Doubleday, 1988), 59, and Carl G. Rasmussen, *Zondervan NIV Atlas of the Bible* (Grand Rapids: Zondervan, 1989), 228, propose Khirbet Marjame, sixteen miles NE of Jerusalem.

[4] H. L. Ellison, *The Prophets of Israel* (Grand Rapids, MI: Eerdmans, 1969), 51. Cf. Paul House (*1, 2 Kings*, New American Commentary [Nashville, TN.: Broadman & Holman, 1995], 269): 'Not all Israelites adopted the religion of Jeroboam and Ahab. Faithful individuals supported the separatist Yahwist prophets (cf. 1 Kings 18:1-15). The Lord did indeed reserve "seven thousand" who refused to worship Baal (cf. 1 Kings 19:18).'

There *will* be a remnant of faithful believers in this corrupt and hardened nation. God does preserve a people in the thick and thin of evil society. Who knows where you'll find them? Maybe in Baal-shalishah.

I remember reading a story about Eric Liddell. He was traveling in China during the Japanese occupation. He was waiting at an inn when the Japanese military came in to inspect all luggage. Liddell opened his and the man's eyes fell on the New Testament nestled there. In slow, broken English, he said, 'Bible—you Christian?' He held out his hand and shook Liddell's, then turned and went off. Who would have guessed that Jesus had a servant in the Japanese army?

I like that stanza (not in many editions) of 'The Church's One Foundation' that begins: 'The church shall never perish...' Hardly surprising, since Christ is preserving a people from the rot and decay around them. That's why all over the planet we run into faith that still lives in faithless lands. And no Ahab or Jeroboam can snuff it out.

The word that still supplies a needy people (vv. 43-44)

The emphasis falls upon the bare word of Yahweh in this episode. There is no visible sign this time around, no throwing in salt or flour, no stretching oneself on top of a corpse. To his servant's objection Elisha simply orders, 'Give to the people and let them eat,' and then explains, 'for here is what Yahweh says, "Eating and leaving"' (v. 43b). That is, they'll eat and have so much there will be leftovers.[5] And that's what happened, 'in line with the word of Yahweh' (v. 44). Yahweh will feed a hundred men with a few measly barley loaves if that's what he says he will do.

Perhaps Deuteronomy 8:2-3 is the classic passage for this teaching on Yahweh's word and Israel's provision. God afflicted and tested Israel those forty years in the wilderness (v. 2). He reduced them to the point that they were dependent upon his supply of this unprecedented manna; he intended them to see that 'man does not live by bread alone but that man lives by all that comes out of the mouth of Yahweh' (v. 3). The Israelites

---

[5]The verb for 'be left over' is *yātar*, also used in verse 7, where Elisha tells the widow that she and her sons can live on 'what is left over' from the sale of the oil.

must understand that they go on living not because they masticate bread, even if it's manna; rather they live because Yahweh has decreed (the decision has come out of his mouth) that he would sustain them, whether by manna or some other means. When a wilderness Israelite went out of camp on a Wednesday morning and saw the manna on the ground he should have said, 'Well, I see that Yahweh has decided that we should live another day.' He should look behind the sustenance to the repeated daily decision that supplies the sustenance. Yahweh's word may decide to feed his people with daily manna or with hopelessly few barley loaves—or via well-stocked grocery shelves. But if I live where we have this last privilege, I must never make an idol of the stocked shelf but confess that it is stocked because Yahweh has determined to feed me in that way for now.

Back to 2 Kings 4. The impossibility of verse 43 is met by the word of Yahweh. Verses 43-44 teach us that Yahweh's word is more certain than empirical appearance. If it's a choice between what you can see with your eyes and what Yahweh promises, take Yahweh's word.

We must take care, however, what inferences we draw from this account. We are liable simply to say that this story shows that God will *always* supply his people with daily bread; believers will never lack it.[6] But the 'obvious' inference is not necessarily the only or proper one.

There is a story about a man who went round giving talks on temperance. Once he placed a beaker of alcohol in front of his audience. Then he dropped a worm into it. Not surprisingly the creature succumbed. The lethal effect of alcohol was clear. But it helps to have someone else express the point, so he asked the audience what his demonstration taught. One fellow piped up: 'If you have worms, you should drink alcohol!' The speaker had probably not considered that alternative.

Verses 42-44 are not a promise that Yahweh will without exception supply believers with daily bread in all circumstances,

---

[6] I am not disputing that God does give us daily bread and that, in fact, this is his usual, consistent practice. Else why would Jesus instruct us to pray to the Father for it? Does this mean, however, that no Christians will ever starve? Can we infer that from God's multiplying food for Elisha's crew? We wouldn't draw that conclusion from the feedings of the 5000 and 4000 in the Gospels, would we?

natural as such a generalization may seem. Rather the text is simply teaching that whatever Yahweh promises will be so. Food is brought, but it is not enough, but Yahweh says it will be more than enough. If Yahweh says that what is deficient will be sufficient, even abundant, then it will be so. Second Kings 4 puts me back in the Deuteronomy 8:3 situation. It doesn't guarantee me immunity from need or even starvation. Rather it means that I stand beside that manna-seeking Israelite that Wednesday morning and say, 'I will eat today, if I eat, because Yahweh has decided that I will have enough.' That's not bad — and it begets praise.

The story that still points to an adequate Savior
This story also points forward and can't help but bring to mind Jesus' feeding miracles. We recall the feedings of the 5000 (e.g., Mark 6:30-44) and of the 4000 (e.g., Mark 8:1-10). The former appears in all four Gospels. In John's account of that, Andrew plays an interesting role. He has come upon a boy who was willing to part with his lunch, so that Andrew could say semi-hopelessly, 'There is a lad here who has five barley loaves and two fish; but what are they among so many?' (John 6:9, RSV). It is, in another but more respectful form, the same question of deficiency that Elisha's servant had raised (2 Kings 4:43a).

We are not to understand Elisha's and Jesus' miracles as straight parallels. Jesus' works are in the how-much-more category. He feeds not 100 but 5,000 and 4,000. In both cases he has fewer loaves than Elisha (Mark 6:38 and 8:5). Jesus' provision is also of the 'eating and leaving' variety (2 Kings 4:43b), but one guesses that the 'leavings' were far greater (Mark 6:43 and 8:8). Jesus' feeding miracles have other Old Testament links than with this obscure episode buried in 2 Kings 4. But surely those who had minds to remember were meant to recall Elisha's deed and to realize that 'a greater than Elisha is here'.

Here then is a Savior who is not stymied or frustrated either by our own deficiencies or those we bring before him. We go around mumbling, 'How can I?' or 'What are these among so many?' But our deficiency is no crisis for Jesus' adequacy. 'Our own powers and talents and resources always seem ridiculously and depressingly short of what is needed for the task God has set us.'[7] But Jesus is there and somehow makes it enough—or far more than that. Our 'deficiency syndrome,' however, is an absolute necessity. If it were not so, we'd be the proudest cocks, strutting the stuff of our Christian success before a Savior we don't desperately need.

We have now finished 2 Kings 4 and need to sum up. You may think that four chapters on the fourth chapter is a bit of overkill. But that's the way I wanted to do it and, after all, I'm writing the book! If you go back over 2 Kings 4 you might notice that there's no chronological scheme, so that we don't know, for example, that the raising of the Shunammite's son occurred *after* the widow got out of debt. It is related in that sequence, but we don't know that it is a chronological sequence. Apparently the writer is following a topical arrangement here, piling up story after story in order to make a point. What point? Is it not to show the supremacy of Yahweh and his power over debt (vv. 1-7), death (vv. 8-37), danger (vv. 38-41), and deficiency (vv. 42-44)?[8] Isn't he showing us our omnicompetent God?

---

[7]Ronald S. Wallace, *Readings in 2 Kings* (Eugene, OR: Wipf & Stock, 1997), 57.

[8]Cf. Richard D. Nelson, *First and Second Kings*, Interpretation (Louisville: John Knox, 1987), 175: 'These four stories share a common theme of life rescued from death, hope from hopelessness. In each case life is threatened: by economic tragedy and slavery, by the death of an only child, by famine and poison, by a shortage of food. In each case the power of God through the prophet Elisha breaks into this hopelessness and shatters it with a word of life.'

8

Grace Goes International
(2 Kings 5)

Here was the man who had everything: position, esteem, adulation, success, bravado—and leprosy. Of course, many Bible handbooks or footnotes in Bible translations hasten to assure us that this was not necessarily Hansen's disease, i.e., modern leprosy, but may have been some form of psoriasis or scabies or other skin disease. This seems to be the case with Naaman, for when Gehazi received Naaman's 'leprosy' he was 'as snow' (v. 27) and the lesions of Hansen's disease are never white.[1] However, Naaman's condition was severe enough to elicit sympathy (v. 3) and to stir an eagerness for healing (vv. 4-5).

We can discuss this text in either a neat or sloppy way. We could package it up around a single theme so as to make it more digestible. But in this case I prefer the 'sloppy' approach, that is, I simply want to underscore the various theological keynotes as I work through the text.

God's sovereignty is total (vv. 1-4)
Naaman's leprosy comes like a thud at the end of verse 1. But that is not the most shocking note in the text. Well, it shouldn't surprise us if we have our biblical theology working properly. Anyway, there it is; the reason why Naaman had such a nationwide reputation: 'For by him Yahweh had given

---

[1]See the very balanced article by R. K. Harrison, 'Leper, Leprosy,' ISBE, 3:103-06.

victory [lit., salvation, deliverance] to Aram.' Here is God's sovereignty in what we would call *the big events*. Yahweh is Israel's God and yet Yahweh directs what happens to, in, and for Aram. Yahweh is the God who grants success to the Aramaean military. Yahweh, the text implies, controls Syrian politics and foreign affairs. He is no small-time director of an Israelite ghetto, not some mascot of a little Jewish club. Here is the God of Psalm 24:1. Yahweh is both God of the church and Lord of the world. Yahweh draws near to his people but that does not mean he allows pagans to run around unsupervised.

Verse 2 is the other side of the coin. Yahweh is sovereign not only in the big events (v. 1) but in *the small circumstances*, in one single, young life. It's heart-rending even if reported matter-of-factly: 'Now Aram went out as raiding parties and took captive from the land of Israel a little girl, and she was serving Naaman's wife' (v. 2). The writer draws a contrast between Naaman as 'a great man' (v. 1) and 'a little girl' (v. 2); Naaman was a great man 'before his master' and this girl was serving 'before the wife of Naaman'.

Now the whole story hangs on this little lass and yet we don't even know her name. As she went about her housework one day she mentioned how burdened at heart she was over her poor master's condition. There was a prophet in Samaria who could bring healing to him (v. 3)! Naaman, apparently desperate, decided it was worth a try (v. 4). The rest is history.

But chip away at verse 2 and sense the personal tragedy in it. Were the girl's parents killed in the Aramaeans' raid? She was spirited off by raiders, never to return home again, never to see loved ones again, living the rest of her life in servitude in a foreign country (though one could have drawn a worse lot than working for Mrs. Naaman). What was it like when she was wrenched away that Thursday morning? Was she not scared out of her wits? When Israelites received their electric bills there would be no enclosure with a picture of this lass with the legend, 'Have you seen this girl?,' along with the date of her disappearance. No, she was gone for good—after probably the worst trauma of her young life. Whatever dreams she had of personal fulfillment or simply of life among her family and village had been smashed. And, apparently, she was from a godly home, from a remnant family, for she knew of Elisha and had confidence that God's power operated through the prophet (v. 3).

And yet, in Yahweh's providence, in this story everything hangs on this little girl, on her tragic servitude. Without her Naaman would never have been healed. *People are often brought into the kingdom of God at great cost to other people.*

Sometimes the means God uses to bring people to himself seem...well, so incidental. A little captive girl. Or a discarded book. Arno C. Gaebelein sent a free copy of his first book, *Studies in Zechariah*, to every rabbi in greater New York City and never received an acknowledgement from any of them. After a while, however, a young Hebrew Christian began to attend one of Gaebelein's meetings. He had been secretary to a well-known rabbi. The rabbi had tossed *Studies in Zechariah* into the waste basket, but the secretary had fished it out, read it, and trusted Christ![2] Yahweh's sovereignty is so fascinating.

And total. Do you see how in two verses this text teaches you that both international politics (v. 1) and individual circumstances (v. 2), both world affairs (v. 1) and personal dilemmas (v. 2) are under Yahweh's sway? Both the big picture and the minor details belong to him. His sway extends from parliaments and war departments to the doorknobs and phone calls and parking places of life. For Yahweh there is no tension between Isaiah 66:1 and Matthew 10:29.

God's 'servants' can be pathetic (vv. 5-8)

Naaman comes into Israel bearing official correspondence[3] and sufficient funds to buy his way through government red tape and to reward any successful faith-healer.[4] Probably the king of Aram thought that any prophet worth his salt in Israel would be connected to the king's court—hence his letter to the king. But Israel's king is devastated, immobilized, alarmed.[5]

---

[2] Warren W. Wiersbe, *Living with the Giants* (Grand Rapids: Baker, 1993), 176.

[3] International correspondence over medical matters was not unusual. See Donald J. Wiseman, *1 and 2 Kings*, Tyndale Old Testament Commentaries (Leicester: Inter-Varsity, 1993), 207, and G. H. Jones, *1 and 2 Kings*, New Century Bible Commentary, 2 vols. (Grand Rapids: Eerdmans, 1984), 2:415.

[4] T. R. Hobbs points out that Naaman's gift (v. 5b) would amount to 340 kilograms of silver and 90 kilograms of gold, an enormous amount (*2 Kings*, Word Biblical Commentary [Waco: Word, 1985], 63-64).

[5] The king of Israel is not named. We might guess it was Jehoram (cf. 2 Kings 3).

He's sure Aram is only looking for grounds to pick a fight (v. 7). We face quite a contrast here when we view verses 5-8 up next to verses 1-4. The faith of the little girl stands out against the despair of Israel's king (v. 7). This would be a good place to lay out the structure of the whole chapter:

Structure of 2 Kings 5[6]

A leper, v. 1

Contrast: a believing maid, vv. 2-4
a frightened king, vv. 5-8

Prophet & captain, vv. 9-14
{
Elisha's word, vv. 9-10
Naaman's rage, vv. 11-12

Servants' argument, v. 13
Naaman's obedience, v. 14
}

Contrast: a converted pagan, vv. 15-18
a perverted Israelite, vv. 20-26

A leper, v. 27

We are, of course, interested in the first contrast here. Mrs. Naaman's girl is full of expectation and confidence; Israel's king is full of dread and dismay. Elisha has to take the initiative with the king; the king doesn't even seek out the prophet.

The king then does not know the power of God (cf. Matt. 22:29). Well, theoretically, he does; he exclaims, 'Am I God to kill and to make alive?' (v. 7). Apparently he knew God could do such things. But for him it was only a formula. He can see nothing beyond politics.[7] One might say that the king is the epitome of the unbelieving, unseeking attitude of Israel. He, as no other, should set the tone for the people of God. Probably, however, he reflects their attitude. He lives life without recourse to

---

[6]I am indebted to Ronald Wallace for suggesting the second contrast between Naaman and Gehazi; in his *Elijah and Elisha*, p. 135, his heading was: 'Naaman the Israelite and Gehazi the Syrian.'

[7]On the idolatry of politics, see Jacques Ellul, *The Politics of God and the Politics of Man* (Grand Rapids: Eerdmans, 1972), 29.

God. He is king of a people who have been at least part of the covenant nation; he should therefore be seeking God in such dilemmas. He, like the nation, has the name of Israel but not the faith of Israel.

In my country the early movie industry was fascinated with 'westerns'. The 'west' pictured in the films was that beyond the Mississippi River from about 1860-1890. One of the first westerns was Edwin S. Porter's popular little movie *The Great Train Robbery* (1903); it depicted the far west, where train robberies were still taking place. However, there is one problem with the movie. It was filmed in New Jersey![8] So one could say it was inauthentic.

That is the problem with Israel's king and, likely, with Israel. You can be part of—or over—the people of the covenant and not have the faith of the covenant. Is this king not a warning to you? You may be numbered among God's outward people and yet live life without God. Your name may be on a church roll and yet you do not seek for him, long for him, or thirst for him. You do not cast your anxieties upon him. You may be a long-standing Presbyterian (or some other variety) and have no faith in the Lord Jesus Christ at all. We may profess God and yet live life without him.

God's ways are offensive (vv. 9-14)

The king is frantically pacing round his private chamber, muttering about the 'international incident' Syria is trying to stir up (v. 7b). Several advisors stand by in mute stupor. A message from Elisha arrives, offering relief to the distraught king; the king can send the foreign general to Elisha's address (v. 8). Which must have been amusing. I doubt Elisha's abode was very pretentious, and yet there is this whole diplomatic entourage pulling up outside his door. Neighbors probably gawked in bewilderment. Perhaps they were a bit upset that Syrian chariots were parking on their front lawns. But how are God's ways so offensive here?

God's ways humble our pride. Perhaps Elisha simply lacked 'people skills'. In any event, he began his relation with Naaman in a manner guaranteed to insult him. Elisha did not even

---

[8] Paul F. Boller, Jr. and Ronald L. Davis, *Hollywood Anecdotes* (New York: William Morrow, 1987), 280.

grant Naaman the dignity of a personal greeting. He 'sent a messenger' out to Naaman with the good news (v. 10). A king might send a messenger, but why would a prophet? Elisha seemed to be acting royally. Naaman is probably thinking, Who does this two-bit, dirt prophet think he is that he sends his toady out to me? Naaman's grammar in verse 11 shows that Elisha had aggravated him. After going off in a huff Naaman exclaimed, 'Look, I thought [lit., said], "He will certainly come out *to me*…"' The last two words are emphatic in the Hebrew text.[9] Naaman is somebody and he knows it—and he expects others to recognize it. But all he gets is a bare word (v. 10b) from the prophet's nameless lackey. Elisha treated Naaman like a leper who needed to be healed. And Naaman didn't like that. So you just as well brace yourself: God may not make a fuss over you.

God's ways reverse our expectations. It all comes out in verse 11: 'Naaman was incensed and went off; and he said, "Look, I thought: he will certainly come out *to me,* and he shall stand and call on the name of Yahweh his God and wave his hand over the place and recover the leper."' Naaman had already written God's script for him. He expected a regular piece of ancient Near Eastern faith-healing complete with all the shouting and razzle-dazzle.[10] He wanted something more entertaining than a mere word of promise. We are not so far from Naaman. How often we already have our idea of how God ought to operate. When he doesn't mesh with our expectations, we become 'disappointed' with God.

---

[9] John Gray, *I & II Kings*, Old Testament Library, 2nd ed. (Philadelphia: Westminster, 1970), 506; and Rick Dale Moore, *God Saves: Lessons from the Elisha Stories*, JSOT Supplement Series (Sheffield: JSOT, 1990), 75.

[10] Dillard puts it well: 'Naaman expected Israel's God and prophet to be just like what he had known at home: itching palms and magic shows. He had brought plenty of money, and so he expected the prophet to deliver on the magic. Naaman wanted "vending machine grace"—put your money in and take your blessing. The prophet was expected to appear, accept the pay, and "wave his hand over the spot and cure me of my leprosy"' (Raymond B. Dillard, *Faith in the Face of Apostasy* [Phillipsburg, NJ: Presbyterian and Reformed, 1999], 116). As Fricke points out, Elisha wanted to show how different he was from any professed wonder-workers Naaman may have known. Hence the healing was to take place at the Jordan, far from Samaria where the prophet was. In this way the miracle would be recognized as God's work done in faithfulness to his word and not in any way determined by the presence or personality of the prophet (K. D. Fricke, *Das zweite Buch von den Königen*, Die Botschaft des alten Testaments [Stuttgart: Calwer, 1972], 72).

At such times J. B. Phillips charges we are worshiping a false god, one he calls the 'perennial grievance'. Here, folks allege, is the God I trusted and he let me down—with the prayer that went unanswered or the disaster that was undeserved. Such people usually 'set up in their minds what they think God ought or ought not to do, and when he apparently fails to toe their particular line they feel a sense of grievance.'[11] Naaman fits this mold; perhaps we do as well. We not only want God's benefit but want to specify the way in which he must bring it. So the sovereign God has become our errand boy.

God's ways trample our broadmindedness. Elisha's word reeked with dogmatism. 'Go and wash seven times in the Jordan' (v. 10). Why did it have to be the Jordan? Why must it be this way and no other? Why this 'scandal of particularity'? Why can not there be several viable approaches to the matter? Why couldn't he wash in the Abana or Pharpar and get the same results (v. 12)?[12]

In 1948 when the Jews in Jerusalem were slowly being strangled by the Arabs, some of the ultra-orthodox rabbis spoke to Dov Joseph, the Canadian lawyer in charge of supplying the remaining Jews, wanting to surrender their own quarter or at least work out their own deal with the Arabs. Their quarter had been hard hit by the Arab Legion's shelling. At least their women and children would be spared. Joseph knew such a recourse would infect the whole city with panic. He told the rabbis, 'You do what you believe to be right, and I shall do what I believe to be right.' Long silence. Finally, the spokesman asked what Dov Joseph believed was right. He retorted, 'I think that if anyone attempts to raise the white flag, he will be shot.'[13] There was no room for negotiation. It was an either-or. No tolerance. Do it my way or die. Do it this way—or stay a leper.

Of course this is what we find in the gospel. Paul didn't have to do a demographic survey in Corinth to know that Jews demand power and Greeks seek polish, yet in the teeth of these expectations he declares, 'But *we* preach Christ as the crucified

[11] J. B. Phillips, *Your God Is Too Small* (New York: Macmillan, 1963), 51.
[12] Abana is usually identified with the present-day Barada, while the Pharpar may be the river el-Auwaj, south of Damascus; see M. Cogan and H. Tadmor, *II Kings*, Anchor Bible (Garden City, NY: Doubleday, 1988), 64.
[13] Larry Collins and Dominique La Pierre, *O Jerusalem!* (New York: Simon and Schuster, 1972), 499.

one, a scandal to Jews and foolishness to gentiles' (1 Cor. 1:23). An appalling absence of seeker-sensitivity.

I don't think I am 'spiritualizing' to point out how Naaman's complaints are the very objections many people make to the gospel. Naaman (and perhaps you?) didn't like the *humiliation* of the gospel (vv. 9-11a), nor the *simplicity* of the gospel (vv. 10, 11b; 'wash and be clean'), nor the *narrowness* of the gospel (v. 12). It was too much for a man who thought he was somebody. Ray Dillard sums it up well:

> 'Wash in the Jordan and be cured of leprosy.' What a preposterous idea! I can't think of anything more ridiculous!

> Well, maybe one thing is more ridiculous—the idea that putting your trust and faith in a man executed on a cross almost two thousand years ago can give you a renewed life now, forgiveness from sin, resurrection from the dead, and eternal life. Now that beats all![14]

God's work is unmistakable (vv. 15-19)

Naaman is not the same. This is obvious in his *attitude*: five times in verses 15-18, while speaking to Elisha, he calls himself 'your servant'.[15] Quite a shift from the arrogant ranting of verses 11-12 against the two-bit prophet of Samaria. It is clear from his *confession*: 'Look, now I know that there is no God in all the earth except in Israel' (v. 15b). Would that Elisha could have gotten more Israelites to believe that! King Ahaziah (2 Kings 1:3, 6, 16) never could get it into his head. But here is an Aramaean who declares the only true God exists in Israel.[16] It is clear from his *resolution*: 'Let there be given to your servant a two-mules' load

---

[14]Dillard, *Faith in the Face of Apostasy*, 118. Note that the anonymous again (cf. vv. 2-3) prove significant in the story. Naaman's rage (v. 12b) would have taken him straight back to Aram. But his batch of nameless servants, by appealing in part to his vanity (v. 13), successfully woo him to the Jordan. The sovereignty of God dresses itself in such natural duds.

[15]Rick Dale Moore, *God Saves*, 78.

[16]'The way the cure has been wrought, however, has made it clear to him that Elisha's God is not simply a convenient metaphor for unnatural prophetic powers but a living person. Healing has not come via a semi-magical wave of the prophetic hand (v. 11). It has been delivered by the living Lord, at a distance from the prophet. It is the directness of God's action that has convinced Naaman of God's reality—and it was necessary to take him to the Jordan if he was to experience that directness. Ambiguity would have remained, had Elisha been involved' (Iain W. Provan, *1 and 2 Kings*, New International Biblical Commentary [Peabody, MA: Hendrickson, 1995], 193).

of soil, for your servant will no longer make burnt-offering or sacrifice to other gods but only to Yahweh' (v. 17b). Don't be so mesmerized by the soil sample[17] that you are deaf to Naaman's commitment: he is going back to Aram where he will worship Yahweh exclusively. And his transformation is clear from his *sensitivity* (v. 18). This last may seem a bit of a problem; let me comment on it in more detail.

Some readers may be disappointed at verse 18. Naaman has just professed he will only worship Yahweh and now he seems to fudge, to enter this proviso, this exception: 'In this matter may Yahweh pardon your servant: when my master goes into the temple of Rimmon to bow down there, and he leans upon my hand, and I bow myself in the temple of Rimmon—when I bow myself in the temple of Rimmon, may Yahweh pardon your servant in this matter.' Naaman says that as part of his job description he must escort the king when the latter goes to worship Rimmon. Naaman seems to say that he himself will not be worshiping Rimmon when he goes through this formality but that it goes with his position (as we say, it 'goes with the territory') and he can scarcely avoid it. Naaman will, of course, be worshiping on Israelite dirt somewhere close to his house. But for this cultic irregularity Naaman seems to be pleading for pardon in advance.

Superficially Naaman's request might give ground to some to rag on Naaman's incomplete commitment. One might hold forth here on 'the peril of small compromise' or harangue folks about the disappointment of 90 percent commitment. But the fact is that Elisha sent Naaman off in peace (v. 19a) and didn't seem overly concerned about the matter, perhaps because Naaman was miles ahead of scores of Israelites. Note, positively,

---

[17]It is too easy for Christians with a superficial knowledge of John 4 to patronize Naaman. Doesn't he know, after all, that the worship of God is not tied to particular turf? But Naaman may have been more perceptive than some realize. T. E. Fretheim suggests that he 'desires that such worship take place at an altar built on the soil that he takes back with him. A *material* tie is thus provided to the community of faith, which Elisha represents. A solely spiritual relationship across the miles with the community is seen to be insufficient; there is need for those ties which are tangible, for the life of faith is not lived out in spiritual terms alone' (*Deuteronomic History* [Nashville: Abingdon, 1983], 155). Others have engaged in soil transport. After the American Revolution, Lafayette 'carried home with him a quantity of American soil sufficient for a grave, and was buried in it when he died in 1834' (Barbara Tuchman, *The First Salute* [New York: Alfred A. Knopf, 1988], 292).

what verse 18 shows. It shows a sensitive conscience. Here is a man who feels the rub between his exclusive allegiance to Yahweh and the expectations of his work place. And it *bothers* him. Would that Bethel-visiting or Baal-kissing Israelites were bothered like this! Would that they could have the uneasy conscience of this gentile! Would that apparent inconsistencies drove them to seek pardon. More on this momentarily; for now we emphasize how God had simply transformed Naaman.

Yahweh's grace didn't only heal Naaman of his leprosy but made him a faithful, fearful worshiper. We have here an Old Testament version of 1 Thessalonians 1:9-10. Naaman not only lost his leprosy that day at the Jordan—he lost his paganism as well. And this is clear (to recap) from his attitude, confession, resolution, and sensitivity. God's work leaves clear evidence.

It's like the lad near Sandfields (Dr. Lloyd-Jones' first pastorate) who told his teacher about the dinner his family had enjoyed one noon—gravy, potatoes, meat, cabbage, even rice pudding. Then he explained it all: 'My father has been converted.' What he had spent on Friday night to booze himself silly he now brought home to feed his family.[18] Or there was a domestic servant who wanted to join the Metropolitan Tabernacle and Spurgeon was quizzing her about her faith. When he pressed her for *evidence* that Christ had changed her, she blushed, and admitted, 'Well, I sweep *under* the mats now.' In one case it may be cabbage and rice pudding, in another a broom under mats, but God's transforming work leaves traces in its wake.

There is nevertheless a dark side to this transformation of Naaman. Before I press that, however, I want to argue via the structure of 2 Kings 2–8 that our writer thinks the story of Naaman holds special importance. If that is so, perhaps Israel was meant to sit up and pay attention.

We can plot out the overall structure of 2 Kings 2:1-8:6 as follows:

---

[18]Iain H. Murray, *David Martyn Lloyd-Jones: The First Forty Years 1899-1939* (Edinburgh: Banner of Truth, 1982), 220-21.

^A Introduction: A true man of God ministering grace & judgment, ch. 2

   ^B Grace to Israel, ch. 3 (King Jehoram)

      ^C Grace to the remnant, ch. 4 (3-4 episodes)

         ^D Grace to the gentile, ch. 5 (Naaman)

      ^{C'} Grace to the remnant, 6:1-7

   ^{B'} Grace to Israel, 6:8-23; 6:24–7:20

^{A'} Conclusion: What shall we say to these things?, 8:1-6

Chapter 2 (section A) is a proper introduction to this segment, introducing, as it does, Elisha as a prophet authenticated by both the power (vv. 9-14) and the wisdom of God (vv. 15-18) and who will bring both grace (vv. 19-22) and judgment (vv. 23-25) to Israel. And 8:1-6 (=A') is a fitting conclusion. The writer has clearly thrown chronology to the winds, because in 8:1-6 the king is visiting with Gehazi—obviously the episode of 5:20-27 happened after this royal interview even though reported before it. But the king begs Gehazi to tell him 'all the great deeds Elisha has done' (8:4). For the writer this would be a fitting caption for all that precedes from chapter 2 on. Elisha's deeds here are primarily deeds of grace—grace to the whole apostate nation (B, B'), grace to the believing remnant (C, C'), and, in the heart of it all, grace to a foreigner (D). Placing the Naaman story in the center of his structural sandwich suggests the writer thought it carried particular weight.

You may or may not be impressed by this structural argument for the special importance of the Naaman story. But even if it's not *specially* important, it is still important and makes an important point: this story is bad news for Israel. Now how is that? Well, everything that Naaman says in verses 15-18 condemns Israel. Where in Israel will you hear a confession like Naaman's (v. 15)? Who in Israel, aside from the remnant, is determined to worship only Yahweh (v. 17)? Where in Israel can you find a conscience that intuits the either-or of Yahweh's demand for exclusive worship (v. 18)? Naaman's faith far outstrips anything one can find in syncretistic Israel. This Aramaean implicitly condemns Israel; he receives the blessings of Israel's God while Israel is passed by.

That's what Jesus said—and it almost got him killed. 'And there were many lepers in Israel in the time of Elisha the prophet, and not one of them was cleansed—only Naaman the Syrian' (Luke 4:27). This threw the fine folks in the Nazareth synagogue into a rage. They weren't upset because Jesus said God showed mercy to a gentile but because Jesus said that God cleansed Naaman while bypassing Israel. Israelite lepers stayed lepers; God cleansed a pagan one. God *turned away* from Israel when he extended grace to Naaman. That captures Jesus' argument and explains Nazareth's anger.

But isn't it a needed word, especially to privileged Christians who have long enjoyed the word of God? What is happening when a first-year college student, with no church background, an alcoholic father and a mother with a live-in boyfriend embraces Christ when a campus minister explains the gospel to him, while another student who has been raised in a Bible-preaching church and known the gospel nearly all her life stands aloof from it and seems to be unmoved by it? Is God again bypassing Israel while cleansing an Aramaean? It should be enough to make the evangelical church tremble among her privileges.

God's grace can be dangerous (vv. 20-27)

Now we will see the other major contrast of the chapter, between Naaman, the converted pagan (vv. 15-19), and Gehazi, the perverted Israelite (vv. 20-27). In order to assess Gehazi's act we must go back to Naaman's post-Jordan interchange with Elisha.[19] Why was Elisha so adamant (note his oath) about refusing Naaman's gift (v. 16)? Doubtless because he wanted to impress on Naaman that Yahweh is a God of grace. One doesn't bribe, manipulate, or cajole Yahweh like pagans do their gods. Yahweh doesn't forever have his hand out looking for a pay-off. Yahweh is simply a 'gifty' God.

---

[19]As Fricke points out (*Das zweite Buch von den Königen*, 73), the high point of the narrative is not Naaman's healing, reported in a mere half-verse (v. 14b), but his personal encounter with the prophet in verses 15-19.

Perhaps now we can begin to understand Gehazi's offense. Of course, there were other—one is tempted to say, lesser—offenses. It's ironic to see him break the third commandment in verse 20. He's apparently irked that Elisha took no loot from 'this Aramaean', surely an ethnic dig. So Gehazi swears by Yahweh's name ('By the life of Yahweh') that he would certainly relieve Naaman of some of his assets. His barefaced lie (v. 22) tramples on the ninth commandment, and his covetousness (tenth commandment) drives him from the start (cf. Elisha's comment, v. 26). But Gehazi's most lurid offense was his *distorting the truth about Yahweh*. Gehazi destroyed in a moment all that Elisha had tried to teach Naaman in verse 16. His whopper about the two unexpected guests twists not only the truth but the truth about God and does so by obscuring God's grace.

It doesn't take much to distort. Recently, one of our elders while teaching adult Sunday School referred to the story about a woman traveling in Europe and who found a stole or some piece of jewelry she craved for herself. The price was outrageous. She wired her husband, telling him of her desire—and the price. Her husband wired her back: 'No, price too high.' Well, that wasn't quite the case. That was the message her husband gave the telegraph operator, but it seems the telegraph clerk omitted the comma. The woman received 'No price too high' and there was jubilation in Europe! And it was only the lack of a comma.

In Gehazi's case it was only, as it turned out, two talents of silver and two suits of clothes (vv. 22-23). But the damage was done. H. L. Ellison could well be right:

> Oriental etiquette demanded apparent reluctance in accepting a gift. Naaman took for granted that Elisha was carrying the matter rather further than usual, and that Gehazi's story (22) was merely polite invention.[20]

At any rate, Gehazi's greed implied that Yahweh was a 'taker' like all the other deities that littered the Near East. So Gehazi's offense is no trifle. This explains why Gehazi's punishment

---

[20]H. L. Ellison, 'I and II Kings,' *The New Bible Commentary*, 2nd ed. (Grand Rapids: Eerdmans, 1954), 320.

(v. 27) is so severe, why God deals so harshly with him. As Dillard says,

> it was because Gehazi was undoing what God had done: God wanted Naaman to know his free grace, but Gehazi was trying to put a price on the goodness of God. The God of Israel did not accept bribes; he would not be manipulated by money or make room for human pride. His grace was free. Gehazi was implying otherwise, and it would be at great cost to him.[21]

Grace is just as frightening in the New Testament. Paul's statement in Galatians 1:8-9 ought to shock the liver out of us:

> Yet I say that if I, or an angel from Heaven, were to preach to you any other gospel than the one you have heard, may he be damned! You have heard me say it before and now I put it down in black and white—may anybody who preaches any other gospel than the one you have already heard be a damned soul! (Phillips)

The battle Paul was fighting in Galatians was for the gospel of grace. There were those claiming or implying that Jesus was not enough, that Jesus' death alone was insufficient to win salvation. So Jesus had to be supplemented. One had to tack on something to God's grace in Christ. And so in Galatia there was this Jesus-plus movement: Jesus plus circumcision, or Jesus plus my good works. In my country today we have a whole 'denomination' that teaches that baptism is essential to salvation. Jesus plus baptism.

Some groups flat out reject grace. The end of a Masonic funeral prayer asks that 'after our departure' we may be 'received into thine everlasting kingdom, to enjoy, in union with the souls of departed friends, *the just reward of a pious and virtuous life*.'[22] But others will seem to esteem Christ's work and declare it inadequate in the same breath. A Mormon publication assures us that the 'atonement of Jesus Christ does not answer for our individual, personal sins, which are forgiven only on the condition of repentance, baptism, and a good life by each of us'.[23] Apparently

[21]Dillard, *Faith in the Face of Apostasy*, 115.
[22]Cited in *Masonry in Light of the Bible* (St. Louis: Concordia, 1954), 20.
[23]Cited in Edgar P. Kaiser, *How to Respond to...The Latter Day Saints* (St. Louis: Concordia, 1977), 18-19.

Christ made atonement but it needs to be supplemented big time. Jesus plus. And the 'plus' obscures Jesus.

Even the evangelical church may fall into this heresy. Let me put it this way. Sometimes movements arise within or alongside of the church which prove of immense help either in understanding or living the gospel. But at times Christians can be so caught up in this or that movement that one wonders if it doesn't become Jesus' alter ego to them. Please understand. These are often good and helpful groups providing useful ministries. But we can make them such icons that we end up in the Jesus-plus mode—in my country, Jesus-plus-Promise-Keepers, Jesus-plus-Focus on the Family, Jesus-plus-Bill Gothard, or—dare we admit it?—Jesus-plus-Reformed theology.[24]

Grace is both marvelous and dangerous, dangerous when it is obscured. Ask Gehazi, standing there with leprosy. He was fortunate. It could be worse (Gal. 1:8-9).

---

[24]This application may make some folks livid—but only if they are blind to their own penchant toward idolatry.

9

When God Gave a Preacher the Axe
(2 Kings 6:1-7)

D r. John 'Rabbi' Duncan had agreed to preach on
a sacramental fast-day in a village seven miles from
Aberdeen. He had gone a good way on foot when he wanted
to take a pinch of snuff. But the wind was against him so he
turned round to indulge himself and, having done so, went
straight ahead without bothering to turn round and head off in
his previous direction. Duncan was brought to his senses when
he met a man coming out of Aberdeen who thought Duncan
might be the preacher he was on his way to hear! Fortunately,
he got Dr. D turned in his pre-snuff direction.[1]

Now you can do that with this passage. You can go off in
the wrong direction with this text. In one sense, it's easy to do
because this little incident is such a teaser. You ask yourself:
Why is this story about the aquatic axe in Scripture? Answer:
It shows the power of Yahweh working through the prophet.
True, but...it seems so trivial, so senseless, so unnecessary, so
outlandish. Besides, what substantial teaching can we get from
it? So there are various approaches—that go off with Rabbi
Duncan in the wrong direction.

Some *rationalize* the episode. What really must have happened,
buried as it is under all manner of inevitable accretions and
well-meant embellishments, is that Elisha poked around with
that branch he hacked down in the place indicated until he

---

[1]David Brown, *The Life of Rabbi Duncan* (1872; reprint ed.,, Glasgow: Free Presbyterian, 1986), 178.

successfully inserted it into the socket of the axe-head and lifted it to the seminarian's waiting hands. Or it could be that the prophet simply scooted the axe-head with his branch into shallower water where the fellow could retrieve it.[2] Never mind that the text does not read this way. Others do not bother to rationalize the story but simply declare it 'clearly legendary', an event blown out of proportion by the admirers/disciples of Elisha.[3]

Still others, perhaps with more reverence for Scripture, will *allegorize* this text; that is, they hold that the text means something other than what it says. For example, the iron axe-head is man's soul, the Jordan stands for judgment. So man's soul is hopelessly lost beneath the waters of judgment. The stick or branch is wood, of course—and so is the cross. When the cross of Jesus enters the situation man's soul is rescued. Nevertheless, faith is necessary—the man had to 'reach out his hand' and take it.[4]

The problem with allegory is that it seldom works. A husband wouldn't dare allegorize his wife's grocery list. She has noodles written down. He says to himself that we have the expression 'use your noodle', meaning 'use your head'. So he flips a head of lettuce into the grocery cart. She has marshmallows on the list. Marshmallows are soft. She wants something soft, so he gets a four-pack of Charmin (in our stores this is, in my opinion, the softest toilet tissue). Chicken is on the list. He recalls that sometimes we call people 'chicken' if they seem to lack courage. Sometimes we accuse such folks of being 'yellow'. Immediately he has his clue—she wants something yellow. But is it butter or cheese? Now you can interpret your wife's grocery list like that if you want, but I suggest that upon leaving the grocery store you simply keep on driving out into the sunset and not bother to go home. There is no warrant for allegory here. The axe-head is a real hunk of iron, not a human soul; the stick is a tree limb not the cross, the river is simply the Jordan.

---

[2]See the commentaries of John Gray and G. H. Jones for this proposal.

[3]See Claus Westermann, *A Thousand Years and a Day* (Philadelphia: Muhlenberg, 1962), 148-50.

[4]See Raymond Calkins, 'II Kings: Exposition,' *The Interpreter's Bible*, 12 vols. (New York: Abingdon, 1954), 3:215-16. Calkins himself thought the miracle reported in this passage trivial and incredible, like some other Old Testament miracles. However, he included an allegorical interpretation (similar to the one I rehearsed) which he ascribed to evangelist J. Wilbur Chapman.

Others *moralize* the text, that is, they find in it some lesson they fancy it teaches. Imagination can run riot here. The story is a rebuke for borrowing other folks' property. Or maybe we could couch it in proverb-form: Don't cut wood near a river. If you think about it, that proverb has multiple applications. Maybe it's a tract against building programs. Or does it suggest we should license axes and/or ban the lending of them? Some of this is clearly ridiculous; but if moralizing is the way, it can be difficult to isolate the more excellent moralizings.[5]

Can we take it straight? And, if so, what does this text intend to teach us?[6]

God's concern for a simple need (v. 5a)

As this one fellow was felling his rafter or whatever he hoped it would be, 'the iron—it fell into the water.' And that axe-head seems to be the weightiest item in the story. But before we dismiss it as below our attention we must put this submerged axe in context.

Here in 6:1-7 we have both a simple and an individual need. If we drift back to chapter 5 we rediscover Naaman with an individual need, but his need had huge political ramifications (ask the king of Israel), for, after all, Naaman was somebody (as he himself well knew, 5:11). After this axe-head story we run into stories of military engagements with Aram (Syria) in 6:8-23 and of the Aramaean siege of Samaria in 6:24-7:20. So here are scenes of international politics, foreign affairs, military strategy and national crises—and in the middle of all that God

---

[5] I think Alexander Stewart gets mired in moralizing here. The fact that the prophets' meeting place is 'too confined' (v. 1) points out that 'growth is the normal condition of a healthy religious life'. The secret of this group's prosperity is 'every man a beam' (v. 2), i.e., everyone bearing his part of the load, with no one shirking responsibility. (See his *A Prophet of Grace* [Edinburgh: Knox, 1980], 185-94). These matters may be true and/or be taught elsewhere in Scripture, but one may question whether this text intends to make these points.

[6] Our passage has some verbal ties with previous stories: 'cry out' (*ṣāʿaq*) in 6:5 appears also in the widow's cry of 4:1 and when the men taste the lethal stew (4:40); Elisha 'throws' (*šālak*) a stick into the Jordan in 6:6 as he threw salt into Jericho's spring (2:21) and flour into the ruined stew (4:41); Elisha's question in 6:6a parallels his queries to the widow in 4:2; and in both 6:7 and 4:7 Elisha instructs what is to be done after the miracle has occurred. The widow in 4:3 borrows ('asks,' *šāʾal*) containers just as our tool-less friend had done in 6:5 (lit., 'it was asked'). It is somewhat interesting to see who talks the most in 6:1-7. The sons of the prophets log 25 Hebrew words in vv. 1-2, while Elisha only uses seven (one in 2b, two in 3b, two in 6a, and two in 7a).

cares about a measly axe-head? So in the midst of Middle East chaos, the threat of world-wide terrorism, economic collapse in Argentina, civil disorder in Colombia, and starvation in Zambia and Zimbabwe, can God have an interest in the details that perplex me? Isn't his agenda full?

But the greatness of God in large measure consists in the fact that he is 'faithful in little'. We make a mistake when we confuse God's greatness with 'bigness' or when we associate his greatness only with bigness. Then we begin to carve out for ourselves a graven image of the living God which shapes him in our image: he is so busy, so preoccupied and distracted, pressured under time constraints. This CEO-type God can have no time for Joe or Jane Peon. Ah, but that is not our God. Part of his greatness appears in the fact that he does attend to the small problems, the dinky details, the individual needs, the mundane and ordinary affairs of the believer's life. The hairs of your head *are* numbered; God does care about your axe-head.

A few years ago I noted an anecdote about William Gladstone in *The Presbyterian Journal*.[7] During Gladstone's days as prime minister of Great Britain, there was a rather unnotable man, a street cleaner, who used to sweep the streets near the Parliament building. He was familiar to those whose business brought them into that area. One day he was missing from his customary work. A Christian worker inquired after him and found him, eventually, in a little attic room, furnished only with the barest necessities. The Christian worker asked the man if he didn't get lonely, if anybody ever visited him. Yes, he was assured, he had had a visitor. 'Mr. Gladstone visited me.' The city missionary was amazed and inquired if he meant *the* Mr. Gladstone, the prime minister. 'Yes, Mr. Gladstone visited me. He sat right there on that stool, and read the Bible to me.' So here is William Gladstone, prime minister of Great Britain, who probably had more than forty-eight things to do that day, sitting in the garret of an ailing street cleaner. This is, of course, only an anemic and pale analogy of the constant and intense attention of our Father to what seem like our tiny needs.

If we don't believe correctly here, then the little problems, the small details, the insignificant matters will pile up and we won't

---

[7] I have not been able to verify the story but have no reason to doubt it.

cast them on our Father because surely he can't be bothered, so we will think on them, brood on them, fear over them—all because we're too proud to say, 'My axe-head's in the water!' Do you see the God you have? Heaven is his throne and earth is his footstool (Isa. 66:1)—and your axe-head matters to him.

God's power for a genuine need (v. 5b)

What a plaintive cry: 'Oh no, my master—it was borrowed!' (v. 5b). The text clearly reflects the straits in which some of these men lived. This fellow didn't even own an axe, so he had to borrow one. Hence his despair when it sank—meals, tools, and pennies could not be taken for granted. Such an iron tool would be relatively expensive, and this fellow probably realized he was in for some sweat equity in coming weeks or months.[8] How far we are from understanding him! Our knee-jerk reaction is to say, 'Why, just go down to the hardware store and buy yourself a new one.' And, of course, this young prophet would retort, almost angrily, 'With what?'[9] This miracle therefore was no piece of unnecessary razzle-dazzle. God doesn't do miracles for kicks. There was a genuine need for God's help, and when there is a genuine need for it we needn't be surprised if he brings it in a mighty way.

The text seems to say that you can expect God's supply for a genuine need. We may often need divine wisdom to make clear what our real need is. This is especially true for Christians in the west, where we have inflated 'need' to cover so much. And we must understand that God may supply need in either a marvelous or a mundane way. However, this text (as the rest of the Bible) testifies that our destitution is the arena for Yahweh's help and that our emergencies are the props for his finest acts.

---

[8] Cf. Ray Dillard's comment: '[W]e are worlds away from Israel in the ninth century BC. We usually date the beginning of the Iron Age to around 1200 BC. We know that for at least a time Israel lagged behind her neighbors in developing the technology to exploit this metal (1 Sam. 13:20-21). Iron implements would have been tremendously expensive. Many hours of labor would have been required to gather the wood for fires, to refine the ore, and then to shape and sharpen the tool. There was not much "discretionary income" in ancient Israel. Losing a borrowed axhead then would be comparable to wrecking a borrowed car today' (*Faith in the Face of Apostasy* [Phillipsburg, NJ: Presbyterian and Reformed, 1999], 125).

[9] I think the reason some scholars think this story/miracle trivial is because they have never put themselves in this prophet's sandals to look on his problem as he saw it.

God's providence for a future need (vv. 3-4a)

By 'providence' I simply mean God's fascinating and unguessable way of working out matters for the good of his people. You see it in this text, though not obviously. Notice something basic. The presence of Elisha, the man of God (as he is called in v. 6), turns out to be a very crucial factor. What if he'd never been asked? Or what if he'd refused to go?[10] What if he hadn't been there? Then the Jordan wins, the axe-head loses. Cheers for that son of the prophets who specifically asked Elisha to go along. 'Please go with your servants'—what weighty words those turn out to be! How important such scrawny little details can become. They make all the difference.

Now there is no way that either this prophetic student or Elisha could have guessed that their request and response would be so critical. And so do we not need to divine from this text that there are circumstances God often arranges before we ever know we'll need them? Looking back over the story, must we not say that God's providence was already at work when no one could know it? The request (v. 3a) and consent (v. 3b) seem like such a routine piece of courtesy that we think nothing of it, and yet in that bit of trivia God was already at work providing for a need that was yet unseen and unknown.

Dennis Le Blanc recalls how close President Reagan came to losing his life when John Hinckley shot him. One of the areas the bullet hit was around his stomach muscles. Reagan had worked

---

[10]We can pick apart the whole passage like this:

Problem, v. 1
Proposal, v. 2a
Consent, v. 2b

         Request, v. 3a
         Consent, v. 3b
         Presence, v. 4a

                Work, v. 4b
                Accident, v. 5a
                Distress, v. 5b

                        Question & location, v. 6ab
                        Sign & miracle, v. 6c
                        Instruction & recovery, v. 7

However, the very center of the passage in terms of word count is the 'consent' segment in the second section above. Interestingly, as things turn out everything hinges on Elisha's word of consent in the exact middle of the story.

out so often that doctors had told him years before to ease off
because his chest and stomach muscles were so developed they
were afraid this would contribute to a hernia eventually. But
those overdeveloped stomach muscles helped slow down the
bullet—and it stopped an inch from his heart.[11] A 'provision'
had been in place long before a need came along.

Some of my readers can doubtless tell their own stories of
a similar ilk. There was some jot-and-tittle type of occurrence
that never fazed your mind. And later you recognize that it
was the hinge of Yahweh's immense goodness to you. Here
is God's hilarious way of being for his people in the puniest
circumstances for their good and deliverance. What should we
do but adore and worship?

God's appeal to a spiritual need

Here I want to focus on the possible message of this little story
as a whole. I admit this procedure can be somewhat speculative
but the exercise is, I think, worth our time. I want us to consider
how Israel might have heard this little narrative—or how they
should have heard it. We know that 1–2 Kings wasn't completed
until after Judah was captive in Babylon (see 2 Kings 24–25). So
we might ask: how would the exiles in Babylon hear this story
some 300 years after Elisha?

In order to answer this question we must link up 6:1-7 with
the four stories in 4:1-44. Those stories, along with 6:1-7, show
Yahweh delivering and helping the believing remnant in Israel.
Here among the faithful minority were various folks, each
with his/her own version of desperation, to whom Yahweh
brings his grace and help. The combined testimony of 4:1-44
and 6:1-7 reminds me of the final line in J. Wilbur Chapman's
hymn: 'Saving, helping, keeping, loving, he is with me to the
end.'[12] That is precisely what Yahweh is doing for his faithful
servants in their emergencies, large or small.

Now how might such a testimony strike the people of Judah,
years later, who had lost their land and kingdom and had been
carted off to Babylon? Could we not understand these stories
(6:1-7 among them) as an *appeal* to this people who had lost
their way and had preferred apostasy to fidelity? Are they not

[11]Told in Peggy Noonan, *When Character Was King* (New York: Viking, 2001), 116.
[12]'Jesus! What a Friend for Sinners!'

saying, 'Israel, here is the God available to you'? 'See,' so they imply, 'how Yahweh's arm works for those who fear him, how near he is to the broken-hearted, to the poor and needy. Turn and seek this God who offers himself to you.'

In one day Stonewall (as he was later known) Jackson's world caved in. His infant son had been born dead and then his dear Ellie hemorrhaged and died that Sunday evening. He wrote his sister Laura the sad news:

> My Dearest Ellie breathed her last on Sunday evening, the same day on which the child was born dead. Oh! the consolations of religion! I can willingly submit to anything if God strengthens me. Oh! my Sister would that you could have Him for your God! Though all nature to me is eclipsed, yet I have joy in knowing that God withholds no good things from them that love and keep his commandments.[13]

There is more than a little pathos in that note, especially in that appeal: Would that you could have Him for your God! That, I suggest, may well be the message of 6:1-7 (and 4:1-44) to Israel marooned in Babylon. 'Here is a God who is present and mighty in every sort of emergency. Would that you could have him for your God!'

Perhaps 2 Kings 6:1-7 is not a massive compendium of theology, but it may nevertheless be precisely the word of God you need just now. So don't despise this little word of God. Aren't you *glad* that—at least this once—God gave a preacher the axe?

---

[13]James I. Robertson, Jr., *Stonewall Jackson: The Man, the Soldier, the Legend* (New York: Macmillan, 1997), 158.

10

Safe in the Shadow of the Lord
(2 Kings 6:8-23)

Advertising thrives on its appeal to security. You don't want your loved ones bereft of resources, do you, should you die? Hence life insurance. One ad for automobile tires features a baby sitting inside x-brand of tires conjuring up images of absolute safety. Denture adhesive makes the same appeal: use it and 'go have yourself an apple' (in public). Though this appeal to security can be manipulated, twisted, and corrupted, the fact remains that one of the appealing elements of biblical religion is its testimony that *no one is so safe as the people of the Lord even when they live in the most frightening of times.* That is the testimony of this fascinating and comic narrative.

There is so much we don't know about this narrative. We don't know if it stands in chronological order with what precedes. We don't know how Elisha knows all the plans and moves of the king of Aram (vv. 9, 12). We don't know the names of the kings of Aram and Israel. I would guess Ben-hadad II and Jehoram, but we can't know for sure, since the narratives in this section are not necessarily in chronological order. In any case, all the characters but Elisha are anonymous; he is the only one with a personal name. Nor do we know how the Aramaean/Syrian lieutenant knows what he knows about what Elisha knows (v. 12). So we may guess that we have a story that took place somewhere around 845 BC—with a good many unanswered questions.

Our story is very artfully written, as the following structure should indicate.

Structure of 2 Kings 6:8-23

Sparing Israel, vv. 8-10
    Frustration and disclosure, vv. 11-12
        The right place, vv. 13-14
            Crisis of fear, v. 15
            Prayer for sight, vv. 16-17a
            Answer to prayer, v. 17b

            Crisis of 'attack,' v. 18a
            Prayer for blindness, v. 18b
            Answer to prayer, v. 18c
        The wrong place, v. 19
    Disclosure and danger, vv. 20-21
Sparing Aram, vv. 22-23

This structure may also serve as a map for the text. I will not, however, give much attention to literary matters in the exposition. We will focus on its main testimony: The Lord surrounds his people from this time forth and forever (Ps. 125:2).

The kingdoms of earth meet His uncanny protection (vv. 8-13)
Well, it *was* uncanny. The king of Aram would plan his strategy (v. 8) but Israel seemed wise to it (v. 10)—repeatedly so (v. 10b). When an enemy regularly eludes your schemes and ambushes one can't help but become suspicious. There must be a mole, a traitor, in the inner circle who is supplying military leaks to Israel. One day at a council of war the king's frustration explodes: 'Will you not tell me who among us is for the king of Israel?' (v. 11b).[1] Only then do his underlings tell him what

---

[1] I am following the usual interpretation of the king's question. Max Rogland, 'Pro or Contra? 2 Kings 6:11,' *Presbyterion* 27/1 (Spring 2001): 56-58, reads the preposition *'el* as 'against' rather than 'for'. That is, the king sarcastically attributes their failures to 'mind-boggling ineptitude on the part of his servants' (p. 58). Hence he means: Is anyone (except myself) actually *against* Israel? The king's question is sarcastic in either case.

they seem to have known all along: 'Elisha the prophet, who is in Israel, tells the king of Israel the words you speak in your bedroom' (v. 12; see also v. 9). Naturally the king wants to know where Elisha is so he can take him out of the way (v. 13a). (Did he not think that this plan also might be known to Elisha?)

One can appreciate the royal frustration. It was like the scourge of Rocky Mountain locusts in the American west in the nineteenth century. They would stop trains in their tracks because the oil from their millions of crushed bodies made the locomotives' wheels spin.[2] All that power and no traction. And that was the king of Aram here. All his plans, his tricks and strategies, and no success.

But this is a continuing pattern. God still frustrates the plans of the enemies of his people in the most uncanny, ironic ways. In the 1970s many Christians in China were worshiping (as they still do) in house churches. Their meeting places were constantly being changed in order to avoid crackdowns. Leaders would be arrested and sent to labor camps. At one particular meeting those present had a very strong sense of Christ's love and the Spirit's presence. At the end of the meeting five visitors stood and announced they had been sent to make arrests. Now they too wanted to believe.[3] The Protector of the church had disarmed the enemy.

God does not always intervene that way. Often Christ's people who are 'hated by all' (Mark 13:13) are ruined and crushed by Christ's enemies. And yet biblical narrative, church history, and Christian biography are literally littered with instances of God's strange—and often amusing—protection of his own. We may chuckle as this Syrian king slams his fist down on the maps on the conference table and seethes over the Judas in his ranks, but we catch the serious point: No one can touch or harm God's people unless their Defender allows. There are gobs of times that Yahweh's people, like believing Israel in Psalm 124, have to praise him for what he has *not* allowed the kingdoms of this world to inflict on his people.

<hr>

[2]Otto L. Bettman, *The Good Old Days—They Were Terrible!* (New York: Random House, 1974), 60.
[3]James and Marti Hefley, *By Their Blood*, 2nd ed. (Grand Rapids: Baker, 1996), 77.

The servants of God enjoy His unseen protection (vv. 14-17)
Our fears prevail when we don't see the unseen. At least that was the case for Elisha's aide. He didn't expect such a shock as he stumbled out early that morning to pick up the *Dothan Dispatch* from the sidewalk—'an army surrounding the town, with horses and chariots' (v. 15a). He bolts back through the screen door, crying, 'Alas, my master! How can we manage?' (v. 15b). Elisha in response states the big fact (v. 16) and prays for the servant's perception of that fact (v. 17). It is one thing to hear 'Don't be afraid, for those who are with us are more than those who are with them' (v. 16); it is another to be strongly, consciously, and vividly impressed by that reality (v. 17). Elisha prayed that Yahweh would show his servant the forces ranged in Elisha's defense, 'and Yahweh opened the eyes of the lad and he saw—and indeed, the hill was full of horses and chariots of fire all around Elisha' (v. 17b). As throughout the book of Exodus, the fire here signals Yahweh's presence, and so, as in 2:11 (where Elijah was 'taken'), these are the Lord's legions.[4] They surround Elisha—and his servant. It is good to hear this truth (v. 16) but so much more consoling to be *held* by this truth (v. 17).[5]

---

[4]Cf. the comments of Iain W. Provan, *1 and 2 Kings,* New International Biblical Commentary (Peabody, MA: Hendrickson, 1995), 176.

[5]For some reason Hobbs seems to identify the fire forces with the Syrian army. 'But in spite of Elisha's reassurance and prayer, all that the young man can see is the enemy surrounding them and about to attack' (T. R. Hobbs, *2 Kings,* Word Biblical Commentary [Waco: Word, 1985], 74). He adds that the 'chariots and "fire horses" which fill the hills can hardly have been Israelite [of course!]. They are the same ones that move down to attack Elisha' (p. 78). I don't know what drives Hobbs' explanation; it is simply tortuous. John Gray (*I & II Kings,* Old Testament Library, 2nd ed. [Philadelphia: Westminster, 1970], 512-13), of course, is rather sure that no vision of horses and chariots of fire can fit the category of history and so he tells us what may have *really* happened:

> The apparent vision of the horses and chariots of fire (v. 17) and the blinding of the Aramaeans (v. 18, cf. Gen. 19.11) certainly suggests saga rather than sober history, but the historical basis of the tradition of the vision of the horses and chariots and the bringing of the enemy into Samaria may have been an ambush in the hills which ring the Plain of Dothan, in which the chariot-force of Israel closed the exit from the plain and shadowed the Aramaeans, while Elisha guided them southwards into another ambush where the main force of Israel awaited them in the vicinity of Samaria, perhaps in the natural amphitheatre to the north of the city. Elisha's disclosure to his lad may refer to the ambush at Dothan, and his prayer that the Syrians should be blinded may be the hope that not until the final disclosure near Samaria should they be aware that they were being shadowed. This and his organization of an efficient intelligence service, through his general mobility and many local contacts, and the diplomatic advice to spare the prisoners, may have been the actual role of Elisha in an actual Aramaean raid.

This text reminds me of Bunyan's description of Christian's approach to the Palace Beautiful in *Pilgrim's Progress*. A short distance away from the porter's lodge Christian entered a very narrow passage and then spied up ahead two lions in the way. Then Bunyan adds, 'The lions were chained; but he saw not the chains.' How it would help us sometimes to see the chains!

How might this revelation of Yahweh's unseen protection have come across to Israel in later years? Remember that this is not simply an incident that occurred in the ninth century BC; but this account is part of 1–2 Kings, which, as a book, was originally directed at Israel in exile, after the Babylonians had decimated Jerusalem and Judah (see 2 Kings 24-25). How would such exiles in Babylon 300 years after the event read 6:8-23? Especially the repentant remnant? Cut off from their homeland, under a pagan superpower, were they to be swallowed up as a chunk of ethnic trivia and be flushed down the stool of history? No, for 'those who are with us are more than those who are with them' (v. 16). But they probably didn't see the horses and chariots of fire.

Of course, the experience of Jesus instructs us that the unseen protection is present even if it is not 'activated'. Jesus rebuked Peter in Gethsemane with 'Or do you think I cannot appeal to My Father, and He will at once put at My disposal more than twelve legions of angels?' (Matt. 26:53, NASB). Imagine—there were 72,000 mighty spirits chomping at the bit to intervene in Jesus' defense. But the legions were idle because the cross was the will of God. But in Gethsemane it was as if Jesus turns and says quietly, 'Peter, I don't lack resources.' Which means that Jesus knew and lived under the unseen protection of 2 Kings 6:8-23.

What if God doesn't show you the horses and chariots of fire? Then you must go on, leaning on the fact of verse 16 if the sight of verse 17 is denied you. How we need those unseen legions. You walk through the heartbreak of family breakdown, perhaps crushed by marital infidelity; you wait for your appointment

This is a sample of rationalism, a fancy term for unbelief. And Gray's revised version requires a near miracle itself. If his reconstruction is what really happened, the biblical writers (note the plural—there must never be just one) must have been creative literary geniuses indeed to take Gray's prosaic event and 'retell' it in the form of the extant biblical text.

in the oncology unit; or you wade into one of those hated but recurring periods of deep depression. It's all right to ask him to show you a glimpse of the horses and chariots of fire.

The enemies of God receive His unexpected protection (vv. 18-23)
Here is an account of humor and grace. Elisha does a bit of praying throughout this story. His second prayer is in verse 18 and his third in verse 20. In verse 18, as the Syrians close in, Elisha prays that Yahweh strike them with 'blindness' ('blinding light,' njps). The word is *sanwērîm*, used only here and in Genesis 19:11 when the Sodomites were near Lot's door. The 'blindness'—certainly here and probably in Genesis 19—is not an absence of sight but some sort of visionary befuddlement or visual confusion. Elisha, after all (after assuring them he would take them to the fellow they were *really* looking for), was able to lead them on a ten-mile jaunt to Samaria (v. 19). Another prayer, the third (v. 20), and…Guess where, fellows?! The king of Israel needs a little restraint; he was thinking of a bloodbath rather than a banquet (v. 21). But Elisha directs him to the latter (v. 22). So it was. Israel feasted the enemy and sent them home (v. 23).

Now we see that this is also an account of grace and hope. What was this strange twist of events meant to display, especially to the Syrians? They had fallen into the hands of Yahweh's prophet and Yahweh (through his prophet) had spared them. Who would have guessed? Spared by the enemy.[6] It is unheard of. It's not supposed to happen.

In the Market Garden offensive in Holland during World War II, Lieutenant Michael Long of the Glider Pilot Regiment was leading a fighting patrol through some heavy undergrowth. Suddenly he came face to face with a young German. Long opened fire with his revolver, but the German's sub-machine gun dropped Long with a shot in his thigh. Long had only grazed the German's right ear. The German calmly sat on the disabled Long's chest and sprayed the area with his sub-machine gun. As he did so, the hot shell cases would drop into the neck of Long's clothes. An infuriated Long nudged the

---

[6]It may be that the sparing of the Syrians is bad news for Israel. Yahweh is preserving those who will soon scourge his people (cf. 8:12-13).

German, pointed to the shell cases, and hollered, 'Sehr warm.' The German obligingly replied, 'Oh, ja!' and shifted his position so his shells didn't scorch Long. After the German ceased firing, he searched his captive and was on the verge of tossing away Long's first-aid kit. Long, however, pointed to his thigh—and the German pointed to his ear. With the firing continuing all around them, the two men bandaged each other's wounds before Long became a POW.[7]

That is not the sort of 'care' one expects between enemies. It is rather exceptional. And the Syrians knew this all too well. One can almost hear their hearts thud when Yahweh opened their eyes after Elisha's prayer: 'they looked and—ah!—in the middle of Samaria!' (v. 20b). They knew it was 'curtains'. And yet they were spared. If then the Syrians really had eyes to see they would understand that they had come under Yahweh's protection; it was offered to the likes of them. For here Yahweh not only protected Elisha and Israel by disabling the Syrians but protected the Syrians by restraining Israel's king. Not only Israel but unwashed gentiles can have Yahweh as sun and shield. What an opportunity this was for these Syrians if they had had eyes to see it. This text is joyful news we can bring to all: it's not just for churchy folks—the shelter of the Lord is open to you. One is tempted to tamper with Joseph Hart's marvelous hymn—'Come, ye Syrians, poor and wretched, weak and wounded, sick and sore.'

---

[7]Cornelius Ryan, *A Bridge Too Far* (New York: Simon and Schuster, 1974), 513-14.

11

A Sure and Severe Deliverance
(2 Kings 6:24–7:20)

March 1865, Richmond, Virginia. The signs in store windows told a story of war: Bacon, $20 a pound; live hens, $50 each; beef, $15 a pound; fresh shad, $50 a pair; butter, $20 a pound.[1] So it was during the War between the States. Cities can be reduced to desperate conditions in wartime. Ask Samaria.

So in the text we are in Samaria, royal capital of the northern kingdom, forty miles north of Jerusalem. Ben-hadad II[2] of Syria/Aram with a massive force has penetrated to Samaria and placed it under siege.[3] In this situation *Yahweh shows grace to his desperate people by granting them deliverance.* Our exposition will try to unpack that deliverance.[4]

---

[1]Burke Davis, *To Appomattox* (New York: Rinehart, 1959), 9.

[2]Others identify him as Ben-hadad III and some place the narrative in the time of Jehoahaz (ca. 814-798) or Jehoash (ca. 798-782). But, although the king of Israel is not named in this narrative, I think it more natural to assume it is still Jehoram (ca. 852-841) and that the Syrian king is Ben-hadad II. Note too the difference between this assault with the whole mustered army (6:24) and the previous forays and raids in 6:8-23. This distinction shows there is no contradiction between 6:23 and 6:24.

[3]'Samaria was built on a hill rising over 300 feet above the valleys on the N, W, and S, with a commanding vista of a long, sloping ridge to the E' (ABD, 5:915). 'With the exception of the east it is surrounded by hills on all sides, like a rounded cone in a huge saucer. It has no natural defenses like Jerusalem or Tyre, but its location, elevation, and distance from the surrounding hills, when joined with defensive walls, made it almost impregnable' (George A. Turner, *Historical Geography of the Holy Land* [Grand Rapids: Baker, 1973], 212). For a description of Samaria's defenses, see ABD, 5:917.

[4]In literary terms we have six scenes: 6:24-25 (severity of siege), 6:26-31 (the king and the woman—cannibalism), 6:32–7:2 (Elisha under attack), 7:3-11 (four lepers), 7:12-15 (apprehensive king and the logic of what's-his-name), and 7:16-20 (fulfillment of Elisha's word and death of the king's man). Exposition, however, need not be tied to this literary scheme.

117

The Desperate Need for Deliverance (6:24-33)

We cannot tell if the Syrians ravaged the Israelite countryside. It may be they blitzed to Samaria and invested it in the hope that reducing the center of government would bring the capitulation of the whole nation. But larger questions of Syrian strategy are of little concern to Samarians simply trying to stay alive. Here in Samaria we see a picture of *human desperation.*

Food expense reflects part of that desperation: 'So the famine was so severe in Samaria…until a donkey's head sold for 80-weight of silver and a fourth of a kab of dove's dung for five-weight of silver' (6:25).[5] Who knows how many calories in a donkey's head—but it is probably not nutritious and certainly not kosher.[6] If the standard wage was about one shekel per month[7] (and if the shekel is the weight understood in 6:25), then eighty shekels for donkey garbage shows someone is frantic for food. 'Dove's dung' may be pigeon manure, though some, drawing on Akkadian evidence, think it's a popular name for carob pods.[8] Whether ingested as food or burned as fuel, a half-pint for five shekels is out of sight.

But the human expense eclipses even the panic for food. As the king passes along on the wall, perhaps doing a little personal reconnaissance, a woman hollers at him (v. 26). She wants his help. After a cynical rebuff (v. 27), he asks her of her trouble (v. 28a). She complains of injustice: this woman had agreed with a fellow mother to eat her son on one day and that woman's son on the next. The complainant had dutifully surrendered her son to the cooking pot, but next day, when the other mother had vowed her son for the meal—no son. She'd hid him. It simply wasn't right (vv. 28b-29). Perhaps the king

---

[5]I assume that the weight specified is the shekel (cf. 7:1, 18), although the term is not explicitly used in this verse.

[6]Cf. Lev. 11:3-8: The donkey has a single (not split) hoof and is not a ruminant. Hence its meat is unclean for Israel.

[7]John H. Walton, Victor H. Matthews, and Mark W. Chavalas, *The IVP Bible Background Commentary: Old Testament* (Downers Grove: InterVarsity, 2000), 393.

[8]Compare college and university students today who may call their school's food service 'Poison Palace.' They don't mean it literally; it's simply their name for—and perhaps estimate of—the institutional food. So 'dove's dung' could have been a popular name for something else. Cf. M. Cogan and H. Tadmor, *II Kings,* Anchor Bible (Garden City, NY: Doubleday, 1988), 79.

never rendered judgment—he simply gave way to anguish
(v. 30) over the horror of what this siege was bringing about.[9]

Now Yahweh had said there might be days like this. Hence
we face here not only human desperation but *divine judgment*.
In the covenant curses Yahweh had graphically threatened
Israel with just this disaster should she cling to her infidelity
(Lev. 26:27-29; Deut. 28:52-57; see also Lam. 2:20; 4:10). What
we witness in the text then is not Syrian atrocity but divine
punishment.

In addition, we see *exhausted patience* in the king's reaction
(vv. 30-33). Hearing that woman's story (vv. 28b-29) drove the
king over the edge. When he tore his clothes everybody saw
the sackcloth he wore underneath (v. 30). But the king was now
in a mood for murder rather than repentance (v. 31). It is time
for Elisha's head to come off.

Elisha is aware that the king has plans for his head (v. 32). If
Elisha knows the military plans of the king of Syria (6:12), surely
he will know the murderous designs of the king of Israel. The
king had sent off one of his henchmen, but before the fellow
arrived Elisha told the elders sitting in his living room what
the murdering king had in mind and ordered them to bar the
door to prevent the fellow's entrance. Not gaining entrance, the
lackey could at least holler in the king's message: 'Look here,
this disaster is from Yahweh. Why should I wait for Yahweh
any longer?' (v. 33b).[10]

It may be that Elisha had counseled the king to repent—
hence the sackcloth (v. 30). It is quite probable that the king's
exasperation in verse 33 shows he is rejecting Elisha's direction.
Elisha had likely told the king to wait in faith for Yahweh's

[9]Ashurbanipal's (Assyrian, ca. 669-633 BC) sieges apparently brought on such cannibalism (ANET, 298, 300), as did the Romans' siege of Jerusalem (cf. Josephus, *War*, 6:201-13). Clarence Macartney recalls a ninteenth-century episode: 'At the time of the gold rush to California, the Donner party, made up of high-class religious people from Illinois and other Midwest states, was overtaken by the snows in the Sierras at what is now Donner Lake, where most of them perished. It is a matter of record that the stronger waited eagerly for the weaker to die that they might devour their bodies. Even murder was committed so the survivors could devour the corpses' (*Chariots of Fire and Other Sermons on Bible Characters* [New York: Abingdon-Cokesbury, 1951], 115-16).

[10]See Bruce K. Waltke and M. O'Connor, *An Introduction to Biblical Hebrew Syntax* (Winona Lake, IN: Eisenbrauns, 1990), 313. This is certainly the king's message. Some think he delivered it himself since they emend 'the messenger' (*hammal'āk*) to 'the king' (*hammelek*). The syntax and connections of verses 32-33 are a bit difficult but the picture is clear enough.

deliverance and help. But maternal cannibalism had soured him on this option. In 6:33 the king espouses his utilitarian view of religion: 'I've tried this repentance and faith approach but it's not working. Yahweh will only inflict disaster—he has no intent to rescue.' There's often a fine line between sackcloth and cynicism.

But surely the major impression we receive from this section is that of *political helplessness*. As James Mead says, '[T]his narrative makes an argument about *the ineffectiveness of royal power* in a situation that only Yahweh can reverse.'[11] The government simply can't find a solution. And yet aren't many of us in the West sucked into thinking that our governments are somehow a big chunk of our hope?

A few years ago I caught a clip of the NBC morning news. Deborah Norville was at the news anchor desk. They switched to an area of our country where there had been some local disaster. Norville was questioning one of the men of the area. I still remember one of her questions: What is *the government* doing to help? That is so often our hope. And, of course, if the government is not responsive, we can overthrow it and establish another. But, as Barbara Tuchman reminds us, 'Revolutions produce other men, not new men.'[12] There is no solid hope in politics. We must beware of the subtle idolatry that whispers, 'The government must cope with this.' The text implies that

---

[11]James Kirk Mead, *"Elisha Will Kill?": The Deuteronomistic Rhetoric of Life and Death in the Theology of the Elisha Narratvies* (Ann Arbor: UMI, 1999), 154 (emphasis his). Cf. also Jacques Ellul (*The Politics of God and the Politics of Man* [Grand Rapids: Eerdmans, 1972], 61):

Samaria will be saved, but to accomplish this God neither uses nor relies on the courage of the soldiers, the skill of the generals, the politics of the king, or the return of all the people to virtue and morality. God will save Samaria by a miracle. He will do it by the most ridiculous, empty, and illusory miracle, by a noise, a wind, an echo, by an illusion which makes a victorious army flee. This is an illustration of the fact that God chooses 'things that are not, to bring to nothing things that are' (1 Corinthians 1:28). But it also shows how much noise and how little weight or worth or significance there is in what man does. I think that we who take our politics and bombs and elections so seriously should take this seriously too. Here we have a victorious army, a devastating war, imperial politics, and then an echo; there is nothing left. God in heaven does indeed laugh to scorn the furious raging of the people (Psalm 2:1ff.). He laughs at our political passions and our military and revolutionary storms.

[12]Barbara W. Tuchman, *The First Salute* (New York: Knopf, 1988), 300.

governments don't cope very well. If a government insures a degree of justice and civil order, and if graft and dishonesty are not totally rampant in it, that is probably as much as we can rightly expect. We must drop anchor in Psalm 146:3-6. The first words in Calvin's Sunday morning liturgy are the constant corrective we need: 'Our help is in the name of the LORD, who made heaven and earth' (Ps. 124:8).[13]

The Astounding Promise of Deliverance (7:1-2)

Elisha has good news for the king. Yahweh had said, 'About this time tomorrow a seah of fine flour will cost a shekel and two seahs of barley will cost a shekel in the gate of Samaria' (v. 1). Just twenty-four hours. The news was too good to be true; the king's adjutant had the gift of sarcasm: 'Why, should Yahweh go making windows in the heavens, could this thing occur?' (v. 2a). So Elisha follows his promise with a threat: 'Look, you'll be seeing it with your eyes but you won't eat of it' [lit., 'from there'] (v. 2b).

Elisha was not promising cheap food but relief from the siege; he was saying that things would *begin* to return to normal. A seah of fine flour is about seven and a half quarts and still costs approximately one month's wage. According to Babylonian sources, a shekel of silver would ordinarily buy about a hundred quarts of barley, but here it buys only fifteen (= two seahs). So Elisha was not predicting cut-rate groceries in 7:1 but relative relief, which would seem substantial when compared to the situation of 6:25.[14] Simply the fact that there *was* barley instead of dove's dung is a vast improvement.

But it was still too much for the royal aide to believe. Hence he was given a word of judgment (v. 2) that excluded him from the enjoyment of the promise.[15] Note how the Old Testament expects and demands faith (just like the New). But it's crucial to note what sort of faith it demands. It requires that we believe

---

[13]Bard Thompson, *Liturgies of the Western Church* (Philadelphia: Fortress, 1961), 197.

[14]See the calculations and discussion in Walton, Matthews, and Chavalas, *Bible Background Commentary*, 394, and in Cogan and Tadmor, *II Kings*, 81.

[15]'What is possible for God cannot be measured in terms of what is conceivable to mortals. The officer will *see* the miracle happen, but he himself will not *eat*. Salvation for the people will involve judgment for this one man, for to mock the prophetic word is to mock the LORD' (Iain W. Provan, *1 and 2 Kings*, New International Biblical Commentary [Peabody, MA: Hendrickson, 1995], 201).

what Yahweh has promised. We are not called to have some general faith that God will do unheard of, bizarre, or unlikely things—as though if we only squeeze our eyes shut, clasp our hands tight, and pump up enough faith to believe, then God will do whatever we want. You may want to believe that God will drop a twelve-feet long, four-feet wide pickle on your church wiener roast, along with a twenty-gallon pot of ketchup. But I doubt he'll do it, not because God doesn't seem to flaunt pickles on steroids but because he hasn't *promised* to supply strange condiments for your church picnic. But if God *promises* deliverance, however wild it may seem, we are required to believe it. We must believe *what Yahweh says* no matter how unlikely.

We have many unlikely words of our Lord. 'Because I live, you also will live' (John 14:19; cf. 6:40). Do you believe that, as you go on through life standing at more and more graveside services? Or Philippians 2:10-11 (every knee bows at the name of Jesus). Doesn't it seem like a wild pipe-dream when history seems to consist of terror, coup, and oppression? Or we hear Romans 6:14: 'For sin will not lord it over you, for you are not under law but under grace.' I have met some who nearly deny this. They seem to think that their past—either their sin or that of others against them, or both—has so crippled them and determined their responses that they can hardly expect to live a life free from sin's grip. They seem to use victimization to deny sanctification. How do we handle Jesus' assurance in John 10:28—'And I give to them [his sheep] eternal life, and they will never, ever perish, and no one will snatch them out of my hand'? Is this not too much to believe in light of our own waywardness, weakness, and waffling? Or is it gloriously true in spite of it all?

The Unlikely Instruments of Deliverance (7:3-11, 12-15)

One wonders at first glance what verse 3 has to do with anything read so far. 'There were four men, lepers, outside the gate' (v. 3a, NJPS). There they are, but we've no idea yet what connection they have with anything in our story. The bare sequence reminds one of the 'Now...this' linkage on TV's newscasts, which Neil Postman so abominates:

The newscaster means that you have thought long enough on
the previous matter (approximately forty-five seconds), that you
must not be morbidly preoccupied with it (let us say, for ninety
seconds), and that you must now give your attention to another
fragment of news or a commercial.[16]

But biblical narrative is not so inane as contemporary television,
and it will make clear why it so abruptly introduces these
lepers.

Actually, the whole 'leper episode' has been very carefully
crafted and we must note its obvious structure if we are going
to understand it correctly.

Structure of 7:3-11

Lepers outside the gate, v. 3a
   Decision, vv. 3b-4
      Action, v. 5
         Explanation, vv. 6-7
      Action, v. 8
   Decision, v. 9
Lepers back to the gate, vv. 10-11

The center of the section is the 'explanation' (vv. 6-7) which
expresses the primary theology of the account. Why did
the Syrians skedaddle as they did? Because of divine
intervention:

Now the Lord [emphatic] caused the Syrian army to hear the noise
of chariotry, the noise of horses, the noise of a large army, and they
said, each to his brother, 'Look, the king of Israel has hired against
us the kings of the Hittites and the kings of Egypt to attack us.'
So they rose and fled in the twilight and abandoned their tents,
their horses, and their donkeys—the camp as it was—and fled
for their lives (vv. 6-7).

This is the Lord's doing, and it is marvelous in our eyes
(cf. Ps. 118:23). The praise is his and the writer underscores this
by placing Yahweh's role at the heart of the story.

But deliverance needs evangelists to proclaim it. That's where the lepers come in. It began in their little piece of logic (vv. 3b-4). If they enter the city—famine, death.[17] If they remain outside the gate, the same. If they desert to the Syrians, they could either be executed or spared. It's a no-brainer. Off to find the Syrians.

Not a Syrian soul to be seen (v. 5). The timing is dramatic. The lepers 'rose' (*qûm*) at twilight (*nešep*) to defect (v. 5a) and the Syrians 'rose' at twilight (same terms) to flee (v. 7a). As the lepers plod off to Syria's camp, the Syrians fly out of their camp in panic. Then it's party time: eating and drinking and socking away for their retirement accounts and wardrobes (v. 8). Next tent, same routine. Then it was conscience time; they became uneasy. 'We're not doing what is right; this day is a day of good news and we are keeping quiet; and should we wait till morning light, we shall be guilty' (v. 9a). They needed to tell (*nāgad*) the king's household (v. 9b). Off they go, tell the gatekeeper (v. 10a) and some tell the king's household (v. 11; *nāgad* two more times in vv. 10-11). Here then the instruments of deliverance are *unclean lepers*.

They are not alone, however, for a *nameless servant* also plays a crucial role (vv. 12-15). The scene occurs in the king's quarters. One can almost see Jehoram pulling on his trousers with a deep scowl on his face. He at least is not naïve; he's studied military tactics; he knows what's happening. He has his own spin on it all: 'I will tell [*nāgad*] you what the Syrians are doing...' (v. 12). The king has it figured out. Of course the camp is deserted—the Syrians are hiding, for crying out loud. It's called strategy. Only a fool would fall for it. The king doesn't seem to consider the possibility of an alternative scenario, in spite of Elisha's previous promise.[18] So one can have God's miracle (vv. 6-7) and the report of good news via the lepers (vv. 10-11), but if no one goes out from the doomed city to see, to risk, all will be of no use.

Huzzahs and cheers then for this nameless servant who has the audacity to talk sense. The text of verse 13 is a bit rough but not really unclear:

---

[17] Of course, lepers were to be segregated from people (Lev. 13:45-46), but in this siege who would care?

[18] 'Having heard Elisha's prophecy the day before, he is not yet able to give Yahweh credit for a strange and miraculous departure' (Mead, *Elisha Will Kill?*, 157).

Then one of his servants answered and said, 'Now please let them take five of the remaining horses which are left in it [the city]; indeed, they are like all the multitude of Israel which are left in it; indeed, they are like all the multitude of Israel who are finished off; and let us send and see.'

What possible peril can there be? Since Israel is 'finished off,' there isn't much to risk, you know. Off they go to see (v. 14). The Syrians are gone (v. 15a). They tell (*nāgad*) the king (v. 15b).

All this is vintage Yahweh—using unclean lepers and nameless servants. Ellul grasps this nicely:

> Here again we see God's freedom in the choice of means. God chooses some men among others. He associates men secondarily with himself in the doing of his work. But what men? Not the most qualified, the most informed, the most worthy, the most alert. We see God choose lepers to discover the miracle just as it is women coming to the tomb with their own material concerns who discover the great miracle. The lepers are rejects. They are unclean.[19]

The discovery of God's work is placed in the hands of the unclean and the unnamed. Surely we feel this text grabbing us by the lapels and pulling us down to kneel and praise. Here Yahweh uses neither the healthy nor the prominent. Doesn't God deserve high praise for the lowly servants he uses?

George Collins tells of an esteemed elder in his home church. Much of the leadership in the congregation fell to Duncan MacRae because their church was without a pastor. Duncan would not presume to preach but he would read sermons of others. So on any given Sunday, Thomas Boston or Robert Murray M'Cheyne might be 'preaching'. The care of the church often weighted this elder down and discouraged him. He had been praying a good bit about it. Now one Lord's Day morning when Duncan MacRae was on his way to church he was overtaken by a fellow Collins calls 'a local halfling—a poor man with scarcely the intellect of a little child.' He could not receive instruction nor could he even dress himself, even though his clothes only consisted of a long kilt and a loose jacket to match. But he always made his way to church. MacRae was downcast

[19]Ellul, *The Politics of God and the Politics of Man*, 62.

that morning as he walked along and when this fellow overtook him, he said to him—simply to greet and talk to somebody, 'I wish you had a good word for a poor man, Murdo.' 'I have that,' came the surprising response! MacRae was likely a bit non-plussed, but asked, 'What is it then?' The answer came back in Gaelic but in English it would be: 'The prayer of the destitute, He surely will regard.' He was quoting Psalm 102:17.[20] How does the Lord encourage one of his downcast servants? Through a fellow who apparently couldn't learn, who couldn't even dress himself. Yahweh reruns these episodes again and again.

And so my obscure status does not prevent me from serving this delightful God; my mundane circumstances are no hindrance to being used by him. My daily calling then is not useless. And, in any case, we can pass on news of a greater deliverance than that of Samaria.

The Haunting Tragedy of Deliverance (7:16-20)

So the people plundered the Syrian camp (v. 16a) and 'a seah of fine flour went for a shekel and two seahs of barley for a shekel' (v. 16b). That was the clear part of Elisha's word (7:1). But there was a mysterious part as well—the threat he'd aimed at the king's officer: 'You are going to see it with your eyes but you will not eat of it' (7:2b). That became clear. The king appointed this officer to be in charge of the gate but the mad mob wasn't about to be controlled, and 'the people trampled him down in the gate, and he died'. We read that twice (vv. 17, 20). So that's what Elisha's threat meant.

These verses hammer home the veracity of Yahweh's word through the prophet. Three times we are told: the new prices in the gate came about 'according to the word of Yahweh' (v. 16); the officer died 'as the man of God had spoken' (v. 17); so 'it came about according to the word of the man of God' (v. 18). True, that word had contradicted all appearances and stood opposed to the most likely human projections. But it would prove true because *Yahweh* had spoken it.

But it's tragic—in the midst of deliverance this fellow is destroyed. Cornelius Ryan tells how in the 1945 push toward

---

[20]G. N. M. Collins, *The Days of the Years of My Pilgrimage* (Edinburgh: Knox Press, 1991), 30-31.

Berlin a platoon of American tanks entered the village of Tangermünde. All was quiet until they entered the town square and then mayhem broke loose. Germans opened fire. In the ensuing battle and chaos an American soldier jumped up on Lt. Robert Nicodemus' tank and identified himself as a POW being held by the Germans. He said about 500 prisoners were being held in town in two compounds. Lt. Nicodemus was about to call for artillery support but didn't want to shell a town full of American prisoners. He decided to try to liberate one of the compounds to get those men out of the line of fire. The POW led Nicodemus to the one compound. When the POWs saw the American officer, they jumped their guards and soon disarmed them. Nicodemus led the prisoners out. As the group drew near the last enemy-held street and saw the American tanks in view, one GI turned to Nicodemus and exclaimed, 'I'm a free man now. They can't kill me.' Then this poor fellow walked into the middle of the street and a German sniper shot him through the head.[21] In the moment of deliverance there was disaster.

That is the situation in this text, only here it is not a simple tragedy but a tragedy brought on by the officer's own unbelief. By his unbelief he did not falsify God's word but forfeited his own benefit from that word. The story should drive us straight to Hebrews: 'See to it that you do not refuse Him who is speaking' (Heb. 12:25, NASB). How perilous the word of God is! How precarious to think God can't possibly be all that upset over a certain degree of unbelief.

---

[21]Cornelius Ryan, *The Last Battle* (New York: Simon and Schuster, 1966), 312-13.

12

The Lord Who Revives and Slays
(2 Kings 8:1-15)

Why should you care about a woman who emigrates from her homestead? About a rap session between a prophet's servant and the king? About another coup in a Near Eastern kingdom? Because they all reveal your God to you. This is the business of Scripture, and we must always come to the word of God with these theocentric spectacles on. Four times in verses 1-6 a form of the verb ḥāyāh (here = restore to life) is used (vv. 1 and 5 [3 times]) in reference to Elisha's restoring the Shunammite's son to life (see 4:8-37). The same verb is used in another form at least four times in verses 7-15 (vv. 8, 9, 10, 14) when Ben-hadad asks if he will 'recover' from his illness. In verses 7-15, however, the focus is not on any recovery this king makes but on the ruin and suffering his successor will bring. So one might say that this passage reveals *Yahweh as the life-giver (vv. 1-2 and 3-6) and the death-bringer (vv. 7-15).* Let us look at the text piece by piece.

Small Kindness (vv. 1-2)

It is all background but the writer makes it the foreground of his story—something Elisha had spoken to the woman whose son he'd restored to life. This is the woman of 4:8-37. Elisha gives her a tip about the hard times coming: 'Yahweh has called for a famine, and, what's more, it is coming on the land for seven years' (v. 1c)—with advice about what to do: 'Rise, go, you and your household, and sojourn wherever you can sojourn' (v. 1b). She follows the prophet's counsel, apparently to her advantage, and stays in Philistia seven years (v. 2).

Why this help? Does it not go back to 4:9-10, when this woman proposed a little house remodeling project to her husband? She sensed that Elisha was a 'holy man of God', i.e., Yahweh's prophet, and wanted to make this accommodation for him. Simply because he was the Lord's servant. It is an Old Testament case of Matthew 10:41-42 (cf. Heb. 6:10).[1] God doesn't miss cups of cold water (Matt. 10:42), and he remembers this woman's kindness to his servant by granting kindness to her.

So here was God's kindness in his famine warning system. Think what it must have meant to her. Admittedly, these two verses are not the main focus of the story, but what an encouragement Elisha's tip must have been to her, assuring her that the Keeper of Israel had by no means forgotten her.[2] A small kindness carries a massive encouragement.

Pastor Martin Niemoller was a leader in the Confessing Church in Germany during the Nazi terror. One day he was taken away by the secret police. Mrs. Niemoller was now by herself, having no idea if or when her husband would return. In a little bit she heard some singing and gingerly walked over to the window. There below she saw the women's choir of her church. They'd heard of their pastor's arrest and had come to sing to her.[3] It didn't release her husband but it was a small kindness that said she was not forgotten. The Lord's tokens are often like that; they give us just enough to keep us on our feet.

Huge Responsibility (vv. 3-6)
The seven years pass. The famine is over. The Shunammite returns from Philistia. Apparently, someone has grabbed her homestead or else the crown had appropriated it. She goes to the king to plead for redress (v. 3). The writer depicts a vivid scene in verse 4: the king is in the process of visiting with Gehazi.

---

[1] Of course, the object of such kindness need not be a prophet; Matthew 25:40 teaches that it may be the most obscure of Christ's people ('one of the least of these brothers of mine').

[2] Some assume that the woman's husband had died by this time since he is not mentioned here. This is likely (cf. 4:14, where he is 'old') but unprovable.

[3] James and Marti Hefley, *By Their Blood: Christian Martyrs of the Twentieth Century*, 2nd ed. (Grand Rapids: Baker, 1996), 208-09.

Wait a minute, someone says. What's Gehazi doing here, when he was stricken with leprosy in 5:27? Wouldn't he be excluded from general society? Probably so. But I think the writer expects you to use your noodle and to understand that his narratives are not necessarily in chronological order. Hence the Naaman episode actually occurred after this one in 8:4-6. If you refer to my treatment of 2 Kings 5, and especially to the position of that chapter in the structure of 2 Kings 2–8, you will note that topical or theological considerations governed the writer's placement of 2 Kings 5; chronology was not crucial there.

So back to verse 4. The king (apparently Jehoram) asks Gehazi, 'Tell me all the great things that Elisha has done' (v. 4b). 'Tell' (*sāphar*) is the key word here; it appears three times in verses 4-6. What does the king want to be told? He wants to hear about Elisha's deeds that weren't so public. Some of Elisha's work was well known to the king (see ch. 3; 6:8-23; 6:24-7:20), but he'd doubtless heard rumors about astounding things Elisha had done among the remnant or his inner circle and he wanted to hear about those deeds. Those would include all the matters in chapter 4 plus 6:1-7—and perhaps others not recorded in the 2 Kings text.

So the king is getting an ear-full from Gehazi. The latter testifies that Elisha restored the dead to life and launches into the story of the Shunammite woman and her dead lad (4:8-37). Gehazi must've choked on his dentures. While he was telling the Shunammite story in came that very woman, with her son, crying out to the king about her house and land (v. 5b). Gehazi is nearly beside himself: This is the woman, he tells the king. And this is the kid (v. 5c). He was dead as dirt—I know. This is the kid Elisha brought back to life!

What timing! Once while I was pastoring in Baltimore I was talking with one of our deacons in my study. It was late afternoon. Both of us needed to be going and both of us said, nearly at the same time, 'I have to go pick up Joel.' It was nearly spooky. His oldest son was Joel and my youngest son was Joel, and we both said at the same time that we needed to go to their schools and pick up our Joels. It was a small but striking occurrence.

How much more striking when this woman and her son walk in during Gehazi's replay of 4:8-37. So the king inquired, first-hand, of the woman and she rehearsed (*sāphar*, v. 6a) the same story, confirming Gehazi's report. This so impressed the king that he designated an officer to handle her case and to see that not only her land and house were restored but even her losses from her farm's produce (v. 6b).

Why is this text placed here? The king (presumably Jehoram) hears this testimony of 'all the great deeds' Elisha had done (for us this would = chapters 2–7, for Jehoram the parts of that record of which he had no personal knowledge). He knew not only mercies that had been extended to him (chapters 3 and 6:8–7:20) but mighty acts of deliverance, even from death. All this makes the king terribly accountable. How will he respond to this massive testimony of the grace of God?[4] Elisha had once scored him for false allegiance (3:13-14). Has he changed? Will he change? According to the summary in 3:1-3 (especially 3b), Jehoram made no single-minded commitment to Yahweh.

But he was very impressed with the testimony of Yahweh's power through Elisha. Impressed enough to give the Shunammite justice (v. 6b). Clearly he's interested in the stories, is apparently fascinated with the testimony, but remains unchanged (3:1-3). So we have a king who was curious but not committed, attracted to Elisha's works but not submissive to Elisha's Lord; it was fascination not faith.

This is a sad but common reaction. During Easter vacation of 1941 InterVarsity Fellowship held its annual conference at Trinity College, Cambridge. Martyn Lloyd-Jones gave the presidential address on the raising of Jairus' daughter (Luke 8:41-56). He stressed the limitations of human knowledge and the power of Christ (focusing on v. 53). The Master of Trinity College, the historian G. M. Trevelyan, was there. He was not a believer but afterwards greeted and complimented Lloyd-Jones: 'Sir,' he said, 'it has been given to you to speak with great power.'[5] That

---

[4] I think the account of 8:1-6 is deliberately placed after chapters 2–7 to force the reader into the same dilemma as the king. After we read of Yahweh's multiplied grace and power through the prophet for six chapters we too are in a Jehoram-situation. You have heard the testimony—what sort of response will you make?

[5] Timothy Dudley-Smith, *John Stott: The Making of a Leader* (Downers Grove: InterVarsity, 1999), 123, citing Oliver Barclay.

is the Jehoram syndrome. One can recognize something of the power and pull of the gospel without embracing that gospel. There is, it seems, a vast gulf between being charmed by the truth and being converted to the truth. The men of Nineveh will likely stand up at the judgment and condemn Jehoram and his heirs for they repented when they had only a simple word of judgment but no catalog of grace (cf. Luke 11:32).

Sad Necessity (vv. 7-15)

All sorts of questions arise as we follow Elisha to Damascus (v. 7a). Why was he going to Damascus? And what are we to make of Ben-hadad/Hazael's forty camels' load gift (v. 9a)? Is that intended literally or is it hyperbole for a humongous clergy fee? The big question, however, comes from the interview, after Hazael had passed on Ben-hadad's inquiry about whether he would recover from his illness. The dilemma centers around Elisha's response in verse 10 and involves a textual problem.

Well, maybe it does. Most versions don't think so; only the NIV among recent versions notes an alternative reading. The first part of Elisha's message in verse 10 is usually read positively: 'Go, tell him, "You will certainly recover," but Yahweh has shown me that he will surely die.' But, of course, he doesn't recover but (apparently) Hazael snuffs out his life (v. 15). Patterson and Austel explain:

> Elisha's reply to Hazael was an enigmatic one: the answer to the king's question was both yes and no (v. 10). Yes: if left to normal circumstances of healing, the king would recover; and no: Elisha, who was at that moment anointing [?] Hazael as king, knew that this treacherous man would use the king's illness to effect his coup d'état. Accordingly Hazael could testify truthfully to the king. The illness was not a fatal one of itself.[6]

Elisha's word about Ben-hadad's recovery then carries an implicit 'other things being equal' with it; that is, he would recover provided Hazael keeps his mitts off of him.

The other possibility follows the traditional written text in verse 10 and translates: 'Go, say, "You will certainly not

---

[6]R. D. Patterson and Hermann J. Austel, '1 and 2 Kings,' *The Expositor's Bible Commentary*, 12 vols. (Grand Rapids: Zondervan, 1988), 4:200.

recover," and Yahweh has shown me that he will surely die.' On this reading, Hazael lied to Ben-hadad in verse 14 and decided to help Elisha's prophecy (and information, v. 13b) come to pass. The difference arises from a little form, pronounced in either case 'low', but spelled differently. In one case it is a prepositional phrase, 'to him,' in the other a negative, 'no/not.'

The usual line on this problem is that copyists probably changed 'to him' to 'not' in order to prevent Elisha from appearing as a devious prophet.[7] But such explanations can cut both ways. It is also conceivable that 'not' was changed to 'to him', because if 'not' remained, there was then a contradiction between Elisha's word and Hazael's report in verse 14 (perhaps not considering that Syrian pretenders are terrible liars). Suffice it to say that there are more noses on the side of 'to him' (see Patterson and Austel above), but I am not completely convinced.[8] In any case, the two 'Yahweh-has-shown-me' clauses (vv. 10, 13) carry the primary freight. The upshot is: 'He'll die, you'll be king' (vv. 10b, 13b).

This moment marks a turning-point in the ministry of Elisha. As one eavesdrops here on his conversation with Hazael, one can't help but remember what Yahweh had told Elijah at Mt. Horeb (1 Kings 19:15-17). Elijah was to anoint three instruments of judgment to scourge unfaithful Israel: Hazael, Jehu, and Elisha. He did claim Elisha for Yahweh's service (1 Kings 19:19-21) but we hear nothing of Hazael and Jehu. Whatever we make of this, it appears the writer intends us to see Elisha now setting apart Hazael as Yahweh's instrument to bring judgment on Israel (see v. 12). In chapters 2–7 Elisha had served primarily as a minister of the grace of God, but in chapters 8–10 he will appear as a minister of the judgment of God.[9] Israel is sinning away her day of grace.

The emphasis in this section then is in verses 11-12. Elisha seems to stare down Hazael (v. 11 is difficult) and then breaks down and weeps. Military men are not used to being around

---

[7]This apparent deviousness comes out sharply in TEV: 'The LORD has revealed to me that he will die; but go to him and tell him that he will recover.'

[8]For a defense of 'not' in the text, see C. F. Keil, *The Books of the Kings*, Biblical Commentary on the Old Testament (1876; reprint ed.,, Grand Rapids: Eerdmans, 1965), 334-35.

[9]For a good discussion of this, see K. D. Fricke, *Das zweite Buch von den Königen*, Die Botschaft des alten Testaments (Stuttgart: Calwer, 1972), 101.

crying prophets. This disturbs Hazael. He asks the reason for the tears (v. 12a). 'Because I know,' Elisha replies, 'what disaster you will do to the sons of Israel; their fortified cities you will send up in fire, their young men you will kill with the sword, their children you will dash in pieces, and their pregnant women you will rip open' (v. 12b). The usual atrocities of war. Hazael is both puzzled and ecstatic. He thinks such horror would look marvelous on his resume but cannot understand how he'd be in a position to accomplish such feats (v. 13a). Until Elisha tells him he will be king over Syria (v. 13b). That means curtains for Ben-hadad, because Hazael decided to assist the prophetic vision (v. 15).[10]

We can allow Hazael to dash off and plan his political future, but we need to stay a moment and watch Elisha weeping. For in Elisha's attitude in verses 11-12 we see Yahweh's attitude (Ezek. 33:11) and Jesus' attitude (Luke 19:41-44). Yahweh is just and righteous and so will and must judge an apostate people, but he is so slow to anger and full of mercy that there is an element of divine sadness in his judgment. Andrew Bonar captured this point in his own vivid way: 'I think He will weep over the lost as He did over Jerusalem. It will be something to be said for ever in heaven, "Jesus wept as He said, Depart, ye cursed." But then it was absolutely necessary to say it.' Or, again, vintage Bonar: 'I think that the shower of fire and brimstone was wet with the tears of God as it fell, for God has "no pleasure in the death of him that dieth".'[11]

Hazael is enthusiastic over the fine future before him, a future in which he will batter and crush Israel. But Elisha is depressed. He knows there must be a Hazael as Yahweh's instrument to judge his faithless people. But, for Elisha, judgment is both necessary and sad. Elisha's tears are sent from above, for that is how Yahweh views it. There is no fiendish delight in Yahweh's judgment. Here is your God and you should prize him for his *nature*, the God who mingles his tears with the fire and brimstone.

---

[10]The details of verse 15 are a bit difficult to reconstruct. For example, we don't know exactly what the *makbēr* (covering) was. It appears Hazael suffocated the king.

[11]Marjory Bonar, ed., *Andrew A. Bonar: Diary and Life* (1893; reprint ed.,, Edinburgh: Banner of Truth, 1960), 511.

You may think this is not the most spellbinding narrative in the Bible, but it is instructive nonetheless. In one kindness the woman received you see a kindness that should hearten you; in the truth the king received you see a responsibility that should alarm you; in the tears the prophet shed you see a judgment that should sadden you. You have seen here the Lord who revives and now slays.

13

One, Big Evil Family
(2 Kings 8:16-29)

Marriage has such consequences. I once had a great aunt who, as I understand, was not wed till she was in her fifties. Nothing wrong with that, mind you, but there may have been a reason. Her husband was hard-working, gentle and congenial. No one in our family could figure out what could have tempted him. No one ever heard much complaint from him. But my aunt was always dirty and often crabby and how my uncle could live in the filth and stench of that woman's house both amazed and puzzled us. After about thirty years death mercifully took him, for my aunt lived to be ninety-nine. One would rather live three lives as a bachelor than part of one with her. A marriage packs such consequences.

That was the case in Judah anyway. Now you may think, 'Judah—where have I heard of that before?' Actually, you haven't heard of it in 2 Kings—at least not directly. The last time our writer specifically focused on the kingdom in Judah was in 1 Kings 22:41-50 (the reign of Jehoshaphat). Now, after nearly eight chapters with the camera on the northern kingdom, he introduces Jehoram as Jehoshaphat's successor, beginning to reign on his own ca. 848 BC.[1] Jehoram's marriage carried

---

[1] I do not spill much ink on the problems of the chronology of the kings of Israel and Judah. For the present case, Jehoram of Judah, see Edwin R. Thiele, *The Mysterious Numbers of the Hebrew Kings*, rev. ed. (Grand Rapids: Eerdmans, 1965), 32, 34-35, 65-71. On the royal chronologies overall, see Leslie McFall, 'Has the chronology of the Hebrew kings finally been settled?,' *Themelios* 17:1 (1991): 6-11.

consequences—it produced one, big evil family. Let's develop this further as we ooze into the teaching.

Infidelity is contagious (vv. 16-18, 25-27)

It's all very simple: Jehoram 'followed the practices of the kings of Israel—whatever the House of Ahab did, for he had married a daughter of Ahab—and he did what was displeasing to the LORD' (v. 18, NJPS). That daughter of Ahab was Athaliah (see v. 26).[2] If you have Ahab's daughter you begin to imbibe Ahab's mindset, you follow Ahab's ways. That is the point of verse 18. The cancer from Israel has metastasized to Judah. It's likely only a matter of time now.

Our writer makes his point more emphatically when he describes Ahaziah's reign. Of course, this son of Jehoram has Athaliah, 'daughter of Omri, king of Israel' (v. 26) for his mother. 'So he walked in the way of the house of Ahab, and he did evil in Yahweh's eyes like the house of Ahab, for he was related by marriage to the house of Ahab' (v. 27). The 'house of Ahab'—three times in one verse. No doubt about what is the dominant force in the policies of Judah. The house of David is goose-stepping to the bark of Ahab's daughter.

One wonders why Jehoshaphat cemented an alliance with Israel (1 Kings 22:44) by marrying his son (Jehoram) to Ahab's daughter (2 Kings 8:18; 2 Chron. 18:1). Perhaps he thought it a suave move in face of the resurging Assyrian menace under Ashurnasirpal II and Shalmaneser III.[3] But it was a spiritual, moral, national disaster. Jehoshaphat seemed to be long on piety and short on sense.

When John G. Paton was serving as missionary on Tanna in the New Hebrides, white traders came round the island and put ashore, at different ports, four young men who were ill with measles. Their plan was to infect the natives with this plague, wipe out of bulk of them, and then take their land. The epidemic spread, many died, and mission work was set back because natives did not distinguish between traders and missionaries—both were white.[4] Paton's enemies operated out

---

[2]In verse 26 she is called the daughter of Omri (Ahab's father), but 'daughter' is also used as = 'female descendant,' so there is no big problem here.

[3]Cf. J. Barton Payne, '1, 2 Chronicles,' *The Expositor's Bible Commentary*, 12 vols. (Grand Rapids: Zondervan, 1988), 4:498.

[4]James Paton, ed., *John G. Paton: Missionary to the New Hebrides* (1889; reprint ed.,, London: Banner of Truth, 1965), 150-52.

of intentional malice. Jehoshaphat, on the other hand, acted out of deficient discernment. But the contagion spreads either way. Now northern infidelity reigns in the southern kingdom—and apostasy never dies a natural death.

Covenant is tenacious (v. 19)

After hearing that the Ahab-ian virus had infected Judah (v. 18), one might expect to at least catch a whiff of coming brimstone. Instead, we get an explanation of why Yahweh did *not* exterminate Judah in spite of Jehoram's aping Ahab:

> But Yahweh was not willing to destroy Judah on account of David, his servant, since he had promised him to give him a lamp, with regard to his sons, all the days (v. 19).

The verse refers to the Davidic covenant (2 Sam. 7:12-16) under the figure of the lamp. Originally David was the 'lamp' (*nēr*) of Israel (2 Sam. 21:17), as though he himself embodied Israel's life and prosperity. But the ongoing line of Davidic kings constituted a 'lamp' (*nîr*) to David (1 Kings 11:36; 15:4; and here, 2 Kings 8:19). In Psalm 132:17 the lamp (*nēr*), in my view, refers to the coming messianic king who climaxes the Davidic line.[5] Our verse here is simply saying that Yahweh's 'Davidic plan' is still in force and the wickedness of some two-bit Ahab-clone in Judah isn't going to overthrow it.

Imagine a man who opens a restaurant in the town where he lives, population 5,000. He is committed to his community and determines that he is going to keep his restaurant there and serve superb food at reasonable price. All goes well for several years and then the landlord demands a precipitous rise in building rent. Our friend cannot handle the increase and make necessary profits so he moves across the street to another location. The next year fire guts part of that building and he is forced to relocate again. Several of his workers leave at nearly the same time; he cannot obtain reliable help and so his wife, a son, and a daughter go to work with him. A new restaurant opens up in town, featuring more ambience in atmosphere

---

[5]See W. A. VanGemeren, 'Psalms,' *The Expositor's Bible Commentary*, 12 vols. (Grand Rapids: Zondervan, 1991), 5:809. For the possibility that 'fief' or 'dominion' rather than 'lamp' is the preferred rendering, see Richard L. Pratt, Jr., *1 & 2 Chronicles* (Ross-shire: Christian Focus, 1998), 352. However, the theology remains the same.

and a more ornate and expensive menu. He loses some of his
well-heeled customers. Then a woman slips and falls on the
wet sidewalk outside his place, waxes litigious and sues. The
case doesn't stick but costs our man a bundle in attorney's fees.
As time goes on, it becomes clear that none of his immediate
family cares to inherit and run the business and he is thinking
that it will close upon his retirement. Fortunately, one of his
nephews is interested, moves to the area, and clearly 'takes' to
the people and to his uncle's fine restaurant tradition. During
this transition time, our man also notices a significant increase
in his overhead and realizes he would have to nudge up his
prices a bit. Mixed in with all of this are the 'usual'—e.g.,
discovering one of his cashiers is helping herself to a little extra
money. And yet for all his setbacks he has made good on his
determination to stay there and to provide excellent food at
reasonable cost.

One might refer to this last as the man's policy. He persevered
in making his policy a reality. Circumstances repeatedly
seemed to sabotage his policy, but his policy triumphed over
circumstances. Now that is the point of verse 19. Yahweh's
policy is called his covenant. In this case, his covenant with
David, which is simply his plan for how he will bring his
kingdom into—and over—this world. But there are myriads of
circumstances that seem bound to thwart Yahweh's covenant
policy. Like Jehoram, who takes Athaliah to his bed, the
northern kingdom as his platform, and who bathes his own
royal house in blood (2 Chron. 21:4). Jehoram will lose his
own guts (2 Chron. 21:15, 18-19) but Yahweh will not lose his
kingdom. The breaking of the covenant cannot prevent the
coming of the covenant. Why is this so? Because 'Yahweh was
not willing' (v. 19a). Here is the bastion of hope for the saints
of the Lord.

Losses are disturbing (vv. 20-22)
The text is a bit sticky here. What is clear is that Edom revolted
against Jehoram's rule (v. 20). What is not so clear is what exactly
happens in verse 21. Taking the text as it stands I look at it this
way: Jehoram crossed over to Zair (location disputed; no one
knows with certainty) along with all his chariot force. Then

in a night attack Jehoram struck down Edomites who were surrounding him and his army—including the captains of Edom's chariot force. Then the troops of Judah (lit., 'the people') fled for home. I surmise from this that when Jehoram went to put down Edom's revolt he found himself trapped and closed in by Edomite forces. So, in a desperate night attack, he was able to break through part of the line held by Edom's troops and chariotry and make a way for Judah's army to escape sure disaster. However, Edom's rebellion succeeded, as verse 22a makes clear. So Jehoram saves his skin but loses Edom.[6]

'Then Libnah revolted at that time' (v. 22b). Now we don't know the exact location of Libnah. It was somewhere in the low hills of west Judah, possibly a site twenty miles southwest of Jerusalem.[7] But it was a town of Judah. What on earth is happening when one of his own cities secedes from Jehoram's authority? Perhaps Philistine pressure (cf. 2 Chron. 21:16-17) forced a change in local government in Libnah. In any case, it was lost to Jehoram. And these losses are disturbing.

I think the writer wants us to look on Edom and Libnah as Yahweh's initial scourges upon Jehoram. However, I must admit this point is not as clear as it is in Solomon's case in 1 Kings 11. There the writer specified that Solomon's troubles were God's judgments (see 1 Kings 11:9-13, 14, 23). (And we must always beware of donning the robes of Job's friends and thinking just because there is trouble there must have been some particular sin.) Here in 2 Kings 8 the writer makes his point more subtly than in 1 Kings 11: he simply describes Jehoram's wicked reign and then goes on to rehearse his substantial losses. And we are to see Yahweh's hand behind, in, and under them. We are to understand there is a connection between the two.

Sometime ago I was fascinated with Paul Johnson's account of the life of Karl Marx. Marx engaged in little physical exercise, smoked heavily, drank much, and consumed large amounts of highly spiced foods. Then Johnson says that he rarely took baths

---

[6]'Edom's revolt, at all events, was a heavy blow to Judah's economy. Not only the mines and the shipyards, but the entire caravan trade with Arabia was lost' (Claus Schedl, *History of the Old Testament*, 5 vols. [Staten Island: Alba House, 1972], 4:97).

[7]Libnah was a town originally allotted to the tribe of Judah (Josh. 15:42) and to the Levitical priests (Josh. 21:13). Cf. Carl G. Rasmussen, *Zondervan NIV Atlas of the Bible* (Grand Rapids: Zondervan, 1989), 128, 243.

or washed much at all. He suffered from a 'veritable plague of boils' for a quarter of a century, which naturally enhanced his irritability. These boils varied in size and nastiness but 'at one time or another they appeared on all parts of his body'. Johnson naturally suggests a connection between Marx's general filthiness and his scourge of boils.[8] Ever think of keeping yourself clean, Karl? The one problem almost inevitably flows from the other.

That is the way it is in this text. Jehoram institutes a 'northern' type regime and preliminary judgments begin. I think, however, we must be careful when applying this point on the individual level. There are gobs of Christians who, upon meeting reverses and troubles, wonder if God is chastening or judging them for some sin. Such self-examination in itself is not wrong. But so often in such cases one has to direct these folks to texts like Psalm 103:10 and tell them to run a yellow highlighter over the verse and then to circle it with an orange one. If we think in individual terms qua Jehoram, what the text depicts is the trouble God brings when a man departs from his covenant commitment to Yahweh. It's not a matter of dredging up this or that sin, this failure or that bit of unfaithfulness. It has to do with having a sacred obligation to serve Yahweh alone and turning your back on him. If you have pledged yourself to Christ and have turned away from him, then don't be surprised if you meet a Jehoram treatment.

Circumstances are prepared (vv. 28-29)

The text is a bit of a puzzle. Verse 28 says that Ahaziah (son of Jehoram of Judah) 'went with Joram[9] son of Ahab to battle with Hazael king of Syria (Aram) at Ramoth-gilead.' In that fracas Joram apparently received severe wounds, for he returned to Jezreel, west of the Jordan, to 'get himself healed' (v. 29a). While Joram was taking his 'R and R' Ahaziah 'went down to see Joram son of Ahab in Jezreel' (v. 29b).[10] This last line suggests that Ahaziah had not been at Ramoth-gilead with Joram. So

---

[8]Paul Johnson, *Intellectuals* (New York: Harper Perennial, 1990), 73.

[9]The Hebrew text uses this spelling here; sometimes it uses 'Jehoram' (e.g., 1:17; 3:1). Confusion is especially easy when one has an almost exactly contemporary Jehoram in Judah (v. 16).

[10]Presumably, Ahaziah 'went down' from Jerusalem, for—elevation-wise—one always 'went down' from Jerusalem, even when going, as some of us say, 'up north.'

when verse 28 says that Ahaziah had gone with Joram to battle it probably means that Ahaziah sent troops from Judah to support the effort, not that he necessarily graced the battlefield with his personal presence. In any case, Ahaziah came to make a sick call on Joram—little did he dream it was the last sick call he would ever make.

These last two verses of 2 Kings 8 set the stage (with all props in place) for what is to come in chapter 9. It seems like a perfect set-up. It's like the time when Uncle Joe Cannon, Speaker of the U.S. House of Representatives (1903-1911), announced that he was taking a group of friends on a summer excursion through Yellowstone National Park. The builder of the park's road system had been waiting for this. He arranged for four stagecoaches to take the group around and made sure that Joe Cannon was in the last one. The driver was instructed to keep Cannon's coach as close to the one ahead as reasonable safety permitted. During the sightseeing Joe Cannon received a tremendous powdering from the volcanic ash on the roads. When he returned he was fuming over the condition of the park roads. The road man then reminded Cannon that there *were* plans for improving the roads but no money available. In the next Congress a generous appropriation was made for redoing the roads.[11] Joe Cannon had unknowingly provided the perfect set-up for the shrewd road superintendent.

That is the case at the end of 2 Kings 8: Joram on leave in Jezreel; Ahaziah visiting the royal convalescent. Little did they know what was planned for them. From their comfy surroundings in Jezreel they will walk right into the judgment of God.

Maybe you need to read on into 2 Kings 9 to appreciate this moment at the end of chapter 8. The stage is set. The characters are in place. Judgment is ready. All that's needed is a little anointing oil.

---

[11]Paul F. Boller, Jr., *Congressional Anecdotes* (New York: Oxford, 1991), 246.

14

Terrible Swift Word
(2 Kings 9)

At 3:00 a.m. on June 22, 1941, three million German troops surged into Russia in a massive attack. Joe Stalin, having been adequately and repeatedly warned, refused to believe Germany would attack. After all, there was a non-aggression pact between them. But it should have come as no surprise, for fifteen years earlier near the end of his second volume of *Mein Kampf* Hitler had indicated that Germany must find her *Lebensraum* to the east.[1] Hitler's policy was in *Mein Kampf*; the execution of the policy began in June 1941.

Now I am not comparing Hitler's perfidy with the Lord's ways, but the situational principle is similar to what we find in 1–2 Kings. To Elijah at Mt. Horeb Yahweh had outlined his policy and ordained the instruments of his judgment upon Israel: Hazael, Jehu, and Elisha (1 Kings 19:15-17).[2] Elisha had begun his work in 1 Kings 19:19-21, and Hazael begins his work in 2 Kings 8—so now there is no reason to be surprised that Jehu begins his in chapter 9. Yahweh announces his policy in 1 Kings 19:15-17 and later—in 2 Kings 8 and 9—we see its execution. Indeed, we've been expecting chapter 9-like events

[1]John Toland, *Adolf Hitler* (New York: Ballantine Books, 1976), 221, 623.
[2]There is debate over how literally Yahweh's instructions in 1 Kings 19:15-17 were meant to be carried out. Was Elijah himself to anoint all three men? He actually called only Elisha (19:19-21). Was Elijah only partially obedient? Some think so. All three were to be 'anointed,' but only Jehu is explicitly said to have felt the oil (2 Kings 9:6). All three are, in any case, set apart, either by Elijah (1 Kings 19:19-21), or by Elisha (2 Kings 8:7-15), or by an Elishan assistant (2 Kings 9:6-10).

to happen, for we've remembered that Elijah's prophecy of
1 Kings 21:20-24 was put on 'delay status' until the days of
Ahab's son (21:29)—and Joram is Ahab's second son to reign
over Israel (1 Kings 22:51; 2 Kings 1:17). Ever since 1 Kings 21
we've been expecting this. 2 Kings 2–8 sort of daddles along
through Joram's reign showing much grace and mercy, but
soon, we know, disaster will fall.

2 Kings 9 is a fascinating story, and, since it is lengthy, a sort
of narrative map may be useful:

The Pattern of 2 Kings 9

Instructions and obedience, vv. 1-10
Coronation and conspiracy, vv. 11-16
Riding and retribution, vv. 17-37
A cloud of dust, vv.17-20
A series of deaths, vv. 21-37

I will cast the exposition, however, into two major divisions.[3]

The Madness of Yahweh's Word (vv. 1-16)

Well, it *did* seem a bit mad. Here are the alleged brass of Israel's
army sitting around outside at Ramoth-gilead, where they
are holding the place against the Syrians.[4] A young prophet
appears, wants to speak privately with the head commander.
Jehu and prophet disappear inside for maybe two to three
minutes. Suddenly the door opens and the young prophet

---

[3]For the morass of critical speculations (about sources and traditions) on 2 Kings 9, see Burke O. Long, *2 Kings*, The Forms of the Old Testament Literature (Grand Rapids: Eerdmans, 1991), 114-16. Long himself admits that the narrative came together 'through a process we can only dimly perceive' (p. 116), an admission far ahead of much furrow-browed guesswork. For historical background, see, briefly, Claus Schedl, *History of the Old Testament*, 5 vols. (Staten Island: Alba House, 1972), 4:98-99, and Alfred J. Hoerth, *Archaeology and the Old Testament* (Grand Rapids: Baker, 1998), 321-22; for post-Jehu developments, see John Bright, *A History of Israel*, 3rd ed. (Philadelphia: Westminster, 1981), 253-55.

[4]Let me quote myself: 'Ramoth-gilead (probably = Tell Ramîth) stood twenty-five to thirty miles east of the Jordan, astride the north-south King's Highway leading to Damascus in the north. A road also ran westward from Ramoth-gilead to Beth-shan and other points west of the Jordan. Incense and spice caravans trucked through Ramoth-gilead. That meant whoever controlled the site collected "caravan transit revenues" ' (*The Wisdom and the Folly (1 Kings)* [Ross-shire: Christian Focus, 2002], 319). Hence Israel's interest in the place, à la 1 Kings 22 and here.

dashes off without even a banal 'Have a nice day' (vv. 4-10). Who wouldn't be curious? 'Why did this mad guy come to you?' (v. 11). The term seems to have been used as a derogatory slam upon prophets (Jer. 29:26; Hos. 9:7).[5] But the prophet had no corner on madness, for later, when the watchman could make things out, he cried that the one leading the pack might be Jehu son of Nimshi, because he drove the chariot like Jehu always did—madly (v. 20). But let's get out of that chariot and go back and listen to what the prophet told Jehu:

(6b) Here's what Yahweh the God of Israel has said: 'I have anointed you king over Yahweh's people, over Israel, (7) and you shall strike down the house of Ahab, your master, and I shall avenge the blood of my servants the prophets and the blood of all Yahweh's servants shed by the hand of Jezebel, (8) and the whole house of Ahab shall perish, and I shall cut off those belonging to Ahab, the one urinating against the wall and those shut up or at large[6] in Israel; (9) and I shall make the house of Ahab like the house of Jeroboam son of Nebat and like the house of Baasha son of Ahijah. (10a) And Jezebel—the dogs will eat her in the portion of Jezreel and there will be no one burying her.

There is a two-beat emphasis in this announcement: the house of Ahab (7a) and then Jezebel (7b); then, again, the house of Ahab (8-9), and Jezebel (10). And though, according to the prophecy, Jehu is the instigator (v. 7a, 'you shall strike down'), Yahweh himself is the primary actor: 'I shall avenge' (v. 7b), 'I shall cut off' (v. 8b), 'I shall make' (v. 9a).

---

[5]On the latter text see Duane A. Garrett, *Hosea, Joel*, New American Commentary (Nashville: Broadman & Holman, 1997), 196. On the root *šg'*, be mad, see V. P. Hamilton, TWOT, 2:905. For 2 Kings 9, T. R. Hobbs holds that the 'term is used here simply as a demeaning and derogatory reference to one who was already known to be somewhat crazy. Jehu's comment reveals that the man was well known by the group of officers' (*2 Kings*, Word Biblical Commentary [Waco: Word, 1985], 115).

[6]"Shut up or at large' reflects the traditional understanding of the phrase (= 'both bond and free'). The phrase occurs five times in the Old Testament but we are not sure of its precise meaning. Hobbs proposes 'those locked up and forsaken', indicating that not even prisoners will be safe in the coming purge. Cogan and Tadmor render it 'even the restricted and abandoned' here and, drawing on its use in Deuteronomy 32:36, suggest that incapable or incapacitated persons are being spoken of. Hence the phrase here 'is an expression of the finality of destruction; the house of Omri will be cut off to the very last person, not even the sick and feeble will escape' (*II Kings*, Anchor Bible [Garden City, NY: Doubleday, 1988], 107). This suggestion is attractive but we have no certainty on the matter.

Now some have problems with Elisha's understudy in this story. They point out that Elisha's instructions in verses 1-3 only give the fellow a one-liner to speak (v. 3a) when he anoints Jehu, but when he actually carries out his commission he adds four more verses' worth (vv. 7-10) to what Elisha had told him to say. (Substantially, he reasserts Elijah's prophecy against Ahab in 1 Kings 21:21-24.) Some wonder about such 'disobedience'.[7]

But the young fellow is not disobedient but only a 'victim' of Hebrew narrative. Sometimes, apparently to avoid unneeded repetition, a narrative gives only a snatch of—for example—what someone is to say, and then, when they actually say it, it will quote the person in full.[8] One sees the same pattern in 1 Kings 21: there Yahweh gives Elijah a one-verse speech to make to Ahab (v. 19) which grows to four-plus verses when Elijah delivers it (vv. 20b-24). Was Elijah disobedient? I don't think so—it's just this summary-then-expansion literary pattern that doesn't want to ruin a perfectly good story with undue repetition.

Jehu's associates, of course, are incurably curious—what did this whacko want with him (v. 11a)? Jehu seems to dismiss the matter. But, unless Jehu had quick access to a shower and shampoo, it would be difficult to hide both the sight and the fragrance of the anointing oil on his head. When Jehu comes clean there is a spontaneous coronation (vv. 12-13). One infers that Joram was hardly the poster-boy of the army. So the conspiracy is on (v. 14a), all furloughs are cancelled (v. 15b), and the mad ride to unseat the king begins (v. 16).

Now I want to draw some inferences, especially from the young prophet's speech (vv. 6-10). If the army command called him mad, the implications of his prophecy might seem

---

[7]See, e.g., Ronald S. Wallace, *Readings in 2 Kings* (Eugene, OR: Wipf and Stock, 1997), 106; and for more thorough discussion, see James K. Mead, *"Elisha Will Kill?" The Deuteronomistic Rhetoric of Life and Death in the Theology of the Elisha Narratives* (Ann Arbor: University Microfilms, 1999), 123-27.

[8]You note I said 'sometimes', because sometimes a passage will repeat rather fully and exactly. Check the record of the tribal leaders' gifts in Numbers 7—the twelve gifts are exactly the same but the whole inventory of each one is repeated in exact detail twelve times. However, here in 2 Kings 9 there is another instance of narrative 'economy'. When Jehu relented and told his army cronies what the prophet told him, he said, literally, 'According to this and according to this he said to me, saying, "Here's what Yahweh says..."' (v. 12b). 'According to this,' etc., is literary shorthand, used in order to avoid exact repetition of the prophet's speech (see Cogan and Tadmor, *II Kings*, 108).

equally mad, but then Yahweh's word never deals in boring commonplaces. What then do we see here?

1. *The word of God is the catalyst of history.* I write this on Christmas Day 2002 when my own country is straddled with a 'sluggish' economy. At such times one sometimes hears economists or politicians talk of 'stimulating' the economy with various measures, which may make up a 'stimulus package'. And sometimes in Scripture Yahweh seems to jump start or stimulate history's course with his word. One sees it here. No sooner does the prophet throw open the door and bolt off, no sooner does Jehu report his words to his comrades than a revolt is under way. What stirred it up? What was the catalyst? The word of God. Likely Jehu and Co. were only too happy to rebel; nevertheless, it was Yahweh's word that incited them to it.

We just saw the same sort of thing in 8:7-15. Elisha itemized all the disaster Hazael would inflict on Israel: firing her fortresses, killing her young draftees in war, bashing her infants to death, and slicing open her pregnant women (v. 12). Elisha wept, Hazael smiled. But how could he, a mere underling, pull off such newsworthy work? Elisha informs him that the Lord has shown him that Hazael is to be king of Syria (v. 13b). That seemed to give Hazael an idea—he administered the last rites to the king and took the throne (vv. 14-15). It was Hazael's own decision to do that, but Elisha's word was the catalyst behind it.[9]

The word of God incited Jesus, but to submission instead of rebellion. What else can we make of Matthew 26:53-54? Jesus has just demanded that Peter put his sword away for two reasons. First, Jesus has all the defense he could need: one request to the Father and twelve legions of angels would be dispatched. But, second, if that option were taken, 'how then would the Scriptures be fulfilled that say it must happen in this way?' (v. 54, NIV). What does he mean—'this way'? He means that the Scriptures have said that the Messiah's work will be accomplished through the weakness of the cross not by the power of the sword. And so the Scriptures move him to

---

[9]We may have another instance of this in the rise of Jeroboam I in 1 Kings 11:40. Why would Solomon have tried to eliminate Jeroboam unless he had, stirred by Ahijah's prophecy (1 Kings 11:29-39), raised the standard of rebellion? See Bright, *A History of Israel*, 228.

choose the path of humiliation and suffering in order to fulfill the Scriptures![10]

We are accustomed to saying that the word of God controls history but our text implies more: it is as though the word of God *drives* history.

2. Politics, the realm of the bleak and the boring, stands under the judgment of God. You may doubt that claim but it's true so far as this text goes. Yahweh says, 'I will make the dynasty of Ahab like the dynasty of Jeroboam son of Nebat and like the dynasty of Baasha son of Ahijah' (v. 9), that is, defunct. Jeroboam had been the first king of the northern kingdom; Nadab, his son, had succeeded him and was knocked off by Baasha (1 Kings 14:14; 15:25-31). One dynasty, only in its second king, down the hole. After Baasha, his son Elah reigned and was assassinated by Zimri when Elah was too soused to know any better (1 Kings 16:1-14). So here are the also-rans piled in the trash can of history, where they were consigned by Yahweh's word (1 Kings 14:14; 16:1-4). And now with Joram's coming demise the dynasty of Omri/Ahab will join its predecessors in the royal landfill of Yahweh's rejects.

I think verse 9 is a political statement. Not that there can never be rulers or leaders cut from different cloth, but verse 9 seems to reflect the general and boring pattern of politics as a realm in revolt against God's word and in which his judgment is repeatedly necessary. And it goes on in this dull tedium.

I had never read anything by the American writer F. Scott Fitzgerald. Recently, however, I read *The Beautiful and the Damned*. The story is of one Anthony Patch, who never works but lives off some bonds, waiting for the blessed death of his grandfather so that he can inherit his fortune. He finally marries Gloria, whose immaculate beauty he idolizes. There is no gripping plot; one only follows the downward descent of their lives, a tedious saga filled with beauty, uselessness, and booze. I am not a literary critic. I can only speak of my impression as a reader—there was just such a *weariness* about it all. That is the

---

[10]'This divine "must" [Matt. 26:54]...is not for Jesus sheer inevitability, since he still believes it possible to gain instant aid from the Father. Instead, it is the commingling of divine sovereignty and Jesus' unflagging determination to obey his Father's will' (D. A. Carson, 'Matthew,' *The Expositor's Bible Commentary*, 12 vols. [Grand Rapids: Zondervan, 1984], 8:548).

sense verse 9 gives about the political realm. It's the theatre of history where we're doomed to watch the most dismal reruns. Not that there can't be exceptions. But if we put our hope there we are below stupid.

3. *Yahweh is vigilant to avenge his suffering people (vv. 7, 10).* Jehu will strike down Ahab's house (v. 7a) and in doing so Yahweh 'will avenge the blood of my servants the prophets and the blood of all Yahweh's servants shed by the hand of Jezebel' (v. 7b). Whether they were prophets who spoke out against her or simply Yahweh loyalists who stood in her way (e.g., Naboth, 1 Kings 21), Jezebel brutally eliminated them. And Yahweh had the tally of every prophet silenced and of every servant butchered. And so with heaven's knack for propriety the dogs will eat Jezebel (her name stands in emphatic position in verse 10) in the portion of Jezreel and there will be no one burying her.

Yahweh remembers every last one of his servants who was done to death by this godless sow. This is not surprising for the Bible is clear that the vindication of his people is at the top of Yahweh's agenda and their welfare the constant anxiety of his heart (see, e.g., Matt. 25:31-46, esp. v. 40; Luke 18:7-8; Rev. 6:9-11). Jesus indicates that if someone brings ruin to one of his disciples it is better for that person to have a millstone (in Matt. 18:6 he meant a huge, donkey-pulled millstone) hung round his neck and be dropped into the sea. The imagery is deliberately absurd—Jesus is saying that the most horrendous death would be preferable for a disciple-destroyer than what he/she will actually receive. Sometimes it seems that throughout their blood-red history Yahweh's worshipers have been bludgeoned into oblivion, but the text says that there is an eye that sees and a Judge who takes note.

In late September 1938 there was a conference in Munich in which, it seems, Chamberlain (Britain) and Daladier (France) were determined to pacify Hitler and grease his way into Czechoslovakia. Naturally, there were great hopes war could be averted. But some in London were not so elated. Winston Churchill muttered, 'And what about Czechoslovakia? Does no one think of asking their opinion?'[11] Sometimes it seems

like that in the history of God's people—like there is but one
voice raised in protest; but it's a mighty voice (Psalm 29) and
it simply says, 'I will avenge the blood of my servants.'

If our prophet is mad (v. 11), the madness he speaks is
utterly sane.

The Path of Yahweh's Justice (vv. 17-37)

Perhaps it stirred the watchman no end. He'd always been told
in his civil defense training just how crucial his work was, how
the safety of all citizens rested on his vigilance. But long periods
might go by with no excitement and it's hard to stay on edge
without a crisis. So a thrill may have shot through him when
he spied the cloud of dust and a crowd of riders! Here was
real work. And not only excitement but mystery—the first two
riders the king had dispatched were not returning (vv. 17-19).
Then he got to display his expertise, for he could tell who was
coming by the wild way he drove (v. 20).

Joram, of course, had no idea what it all meant: that's why
he dispatched horsemen to ask, literally, 'Is it peace?' (vv. 18,
19). I think this is meant, as some translations (e.g., NJB, NJPS)
have it, in the sense of 'Is all well?'[12] Joram had no idea of what
might have happened at Ramoth-gilead. Conceivably Jehu
may be bringing word of a victory, or, more likely, of disaster.
Some commentators wonder why, after both horsemen did
not return, Joram (and Ahaziah) drove out to meet Jehu (v. 21)
without protection. But the text does not say he was without
support—he may well have had a bodyguard.[13] Joram's
suspicions were likely raised when his two emissaries did not
return, but what choice did he have? He had to find out what

---

[11]Toland, *Adolf Hitler*, 488.

[12]TEV translates, 'The king wants to know if you come as a friend?' That is the
sense of those versions that translate 'Is it peace?', i.e., as opposed to hostile intent.
D. J. Wiseman looks at *šālôm*/peace here through the lens of its use in ancient Near
Eastern diplomacy and holds Joram is seeking negotiation with Jehu, which the latter
rejects (' "Is it peace?"—Covenant and Diplomacy,' *Vetus Testamentum* 32 [1982],
esp. 321). See the helpful discussion in K-B, 4:1506-10, whose view I follow. Cf. further,
Saul Olyan, '*hăšālôm*: Some Literary Considerations of 2 Kings 9,' *Catholic Biblical
Quarterly* 46 (1984): 652-68.

[13]So rightly, I think, Walter Brueggemann, *1 & 2 Kings*, Smyth & Helwys Bible
Commentary (Macon, GA: Smyth & Helwys, 2000), 386. Joram would not have a
large contingent with him; one presumes most of the troops were stationed at Ramoth-
gilead.

was going on. If one is to be alarmed he must know what to be alarmed about!

If we hitch a ride in Jehu's chariot we can trace the path of Yahweh's justice, which strikes Joram first (vv. 21-26). Joram knew it was revolt when Jehu answered his 'Is all well?' with 'How can all be well as long as your mother Jezebel carries on her countless harlotries and sorceries?' (v. 22, NJPS). Joram turned and began to hightail it out of there but Jehu's arrow plunged between his shoulder blades and penetrated his heart (v. 24).

Irony is the trademark on Joram's judgment. The writer hints of this when he reports that Joram met Jehu 'at the plot of Naboth the Jezreelite' (v. 21d). This jogged Jehu's memory and he told Bidqar his aide to heave Joram's body into 'the field-plot of Naboth the Jezreelite' (v. 25a). He recalls the heavy word Yahweh had laid on Ahab when they had been in the king's entourage (v. 25b) and quotes chapter and verse: ' "As surely as I have seen the shedding of Naboth's blood and that of his sons yesterday," says Yahweh, "I shall pay you back in this plot," says Yahweh' (v. 26a).[14] Hence Jehu bids Bidqar to fulfill prophecy and chuck Joram's carcass on Naboth's land (v. 26b).[15]

If we can believe Jehu—and there is little reason not to—we learn something in verse 26 that 1 Kings 21 had not told us: Jezebel had Naboth's sons liquidated as well. Of course this was necessary in order to 'free up' Naboth's inheritance. But Jehu picks up the watch-word of the God of the exodus when he quotes Yahweh: 'I have seen the shedding of Naboth's blood and that of his sons,' which conjures up Exodus 3:7: 'I have

---

[14]On the text see R. J. Williams, *Hebrew Syntax: An Outline*, 2nd ed. (Toronto: University of Toronto Press, 1976), sect. 456 (p. 74).

[15]Just what prophecy is fulfilled is a bit of a puzzle. One thinks most naturally of 1 Kings 21:19, although there are two difficulties with that. First, 1 Kings 22:38 seems to fulfill 21:19 (though that need not exclude another fulfillment here); and second, 21:19 may have no stress on 'place' at all. On this latter point, cf. Iain Provan's rendering of 21:19, 'Instead of dogs licking up Naboth's blood, dogs will lick up your blood—yes, yours!' See his argument and the texts he cites in *1 and 2 Kings*, New International Biblical Commentary (Peabody, MA: Hendrickson, 1995), 160; cf. also DCH, 5:460-61, esp. item 16. Here in 2 Kings 9 Jehu may be referring to another prophecy (unrecorded in Kings) and/or another incident (cf. Provan, 213). This hints at authenticity, for had some devious Deuteronomist put his spin on Jehu's words he would have made them match up exactly with former prophecies. In any case, the irony of Joram's being dumped on Naboth's land is unavoidable.

surely seen the affliction of my people who are in Egypt' (cf. Ps. 10:11, 14). The exodus God always sees when, where, and by whom his servants are crushed and prepares the 'pay back' (cf. 2 Thess. 1:6-8). Naboth may be dirt to Ahab and Jezebel but Yahweh knows his name.[16]

If Joram's end highlights the irony of God's judgment, Jezebel's displays the *horror* of that judgment. Jehu enters Jezreel.[17] Jezebel in the meantime has been briefed on what has occurred (v. 30a) and apparently divines what is coming. She is hardly unnerved. Out come the cosmetics; she gets on her mascara, teases and fixes her hair, and, looking like the queen, peers through the window as Jehu comes through the gate (v. 30b). Her sarcasm is in top form: she asks Jehu, 'Is all well, Zimri, murderer of his master?' (v. 31b). There are some who think Jezebel here holds out an offer of negotiation (lit., 'Is it peace?') to Jehu and that she dolls herself up in order to allure or seduce him to take over the harem and thereby rule by being united to Ahab's dynasty.[18] But, as Cohn notes, 'the parallel between Jehu's treason and Zimri's [on whom see 1 Kings 16:8-20] is too strong to be ignored and the epithet "murderer of his master" is hardly designed to flame Jehu's desire.'[19] Instead Jezebel gussies herself up in her full regalia as an act of defiance to Jehu. She will go out in style—or so she thinks.

Jehu hollers up for help. Who is for him? Several eunuchs pop their heads out (v. 32). He orders them to throw Jezebel down. They give her a lift and down she goes. Some of her blood splatters on the walls and on the horses. And Jehu tramples her (v. 33). Jehu goes in lunch. After cooling down a bit he gives

[16]Ahaziah receives short shrift—just enough space to show Jehu disposes of him (vv. 27-29). Being an ally of Joram was enough to seal his doom—why waste a prophetic quote on him? This report features its own problems: (1) The text of v. 27 is a bit damaged, and (2) it is difficult to mesh the geography of vv. 27-28 with the Chronicler's statement in 2 Chronicles 22:9 about Ahaziah hiding in Samaria. There are no direct contradictions between the two reports but I am not smart enough to reconcile them satisfactorily. See Paul R. House, *1, 2 Kings*, New American Commentary (Nashville: Broadman & Holman, 1995), 290.

[17]I wonder if Jehu may have allowed his servants to pursue Ahaziah after he was wounded at Ibleam, while Jehu himself returned to Jezreel.

[18]See, e.g., John H. Walton, Victor H. Matthews, and Mark W. Chavalas, *The IVP Bible Background Commentary: Old Testament* (Downers Grove: InterVarsity, 2000), 397; cf. also B. O. Long's description of Parker's view in *2 Kings*, 129-30.

[19]Robert L. Cohn, *2 Kings*, Berit Olam (Collegeville, MN: Liturgical, 2000), 70.

orders to bury Jezebel—after all, she's a blue blood (v. 34). But Jehu's crew has a problem—nothing to bury. While Jehu was at his sandwich the scavenger dogs were busy with their own untended cuisine. Nothing left but some spare parts (v. 35).[20] When they inform Jehu, he's ready with another prophetic fulfillment:

> It is the word of Yahweh which he spoke by the hand of his servant Elijah the Tishbite, saying, 'In the portion of Jezreel dogs will eat Jezebel's flesh, and Jezebel's corpse shall be as dung on the surface of the field in the portion of Jezreel, so that they cannot say, "This is Jezebel"' (vv. 36-37).

Jehu's citation picks up Elijah's prophecy in 1 Kings 21:23.[21] There is no real disparity between Elijah there and Jehu here except that Jehu quotes more than 1 Kings 21:23 reports Elijah as saying. We must consider that Jehu may not have picked up the Bible Memory Award in Sunday School and that he may be 'tweaking' the prophecy for political mileage, but it could well be that 1 Kings 21:23 reports Elijah's anti-Jezebel prophecy only in summary and that he may actually have said more, which Jehu remembers here. Again, if a fabricator was at work, he would be sure to have Elijah's prophecy and Jehu's memory match up exactly. Yahweh's word had predicted the dogs—and they came during Jehu's lunch. In this case the grossness of the judgment fits the wickedness of the offender.

We can make a couple of observations from this account of Jezebel's end. First, *wicked people can meet their deaths with great flair.* She was godless but gutsy. With Max Factor on her face and sarcasm on her lips she faced Jehu head on. Some of the children of this age can do that. They can be dashing even in death. Go out in style. Leave their loved ones (did Jezebel have any?) stories to tell about the brash way they walked into the Grim Reaper's field. But one's boldness in face of death does not exempt from judgment after death. Someone may put on a memorable piece of drama at death and still be damned.

Secondly, *the demise of the wicked should be the joy of the*

---

[20] 'The narrative is at pains to exhibit the humiliation of Jezebel, in an instant transformed from a narcissistic queen to a piece of rubbish in the street' (Brueggemann, *1 & 2 Kings*, 388).

[21] And, please note, the young prophet's word here in v. 10.

righteous. It may sound crude to put it that way but that's only because the church has stopped living in, for example, Psalms 83 and 94 and has been sucking up the bland milk of tolerance from the breasts of an anemic culture for far too long. There is no biblical spine in our theology.

Admittedly sometimes we're a bit shocked by the biblical attitude in these matters. I recall a time when our boys were young and I would read them Bible stories before bedtime. After the story we would pray. One evening the story was about Elijah and Jezebel, and it told about how Jezebel was flipped out of the window to her death. I put aside the little book and we went to prayer. Our oldest boy usually tried to reflect what we'd read in our story in his prayer. And it was so this night. Luke prayed: 'Dear God, thank you for letting Jezebel die.' I remember being somewhat jolted by the straightforward gratitude but, thankfully, said nothing. Later I realized that Luke was exactly on target. It is always good news for the saints when their oppressors are judged and removed. That's the word of 2 Kings 9: 'Joy to the church—the queen is dead!'

15

When Heads Roll
(2 Kings 10)

On one December day in 1937 Joe Stalin and Molotov approved 3,167 death sentences—and then attended the cinema. In 1937 and 1938 alone Stalin approved execution lists containing some 40,000 names. Welcome to Stalin's Soviet Union. The terror of 1936-38 was especially severe. Over a million-odd executions; millions sent to die in Arctic camps. The Communist party itself was devastated, with half its membership arrested; over a million died, either executed or 'working' in camps. Seventy percent of the Central Committee perished.[1] Stalin seemed to have a contract to populate Sheol. Gaining and keeping power can be a bloody business. But revolutions and/or dictators can be like that. Take Jehu's revolt, for instance. Blood drips from the story of 2 Kings 10—though Jehu son of Nimshi is a rank amateur beside butcher Joe Stalin. But in Jehu's case, well, Yahweh had said it would be like that.

Since 2 Kings 10 is a long chapter it may be useful to chart its development before jumping into exposition:

Head heaps, vv. 1-10
[Summary, v. 11]
Double meeting, vv. 12-16
[Summary, v. 17]
Always wear your vestments, vv. 18-27
[Summary, v. 28]

[1]Robert Conquest, *Stalin: Breaker of Nations* (New York: Viking, 1991), 199-207.

Vv. 29-36:
> Qualification, vv. 29, 31
> New word, v. 30
> Old word, vv. 32-33
> Exit Jehu, vv. 34-36

The writer includes summary statements (vv. 11, 17, 28) at the end of the major sections, while verses 29-33 supply the true assessment of Jehu.

Fulfillment of Yahweh's word is sometimes unsanitary (vv. 1-11, 12-17)

The emphasis in these two sections falls on verses 10 (Jehu's theology) and 17 (the writer's theological comment), both of which highlight the fulfillment of Yahweh's word. However, we need to get the facts before we rush to fulfillment, to know what has occurred before we ask why it is significant.

In verses 1-11, verses 1-6 seem to form a prelude unit:

Ahab's seventy sons, v. 1a
> Jehu's first letter: challenging their spunk, vv. 1b-3
>> Fear and submission, vv. 4-5
> Jehu's second letter: challenging their loyalty, v. 6a
Ahab's seventy sons, v. 6b

After this the episode concludes with a slaughter (v. 7), spectacle (v. 8), and speech (vv. 9-10).

So Jehu wrote letters to Ahab's supporters in Samaria.[2] They had everything they needed to fight for their regime—they could pick one of Ahab's line for the throne (v. 3) and put to use all their military resources (v. 2b). But they were totally intimidated (v. 4) and sent word of their complete capitulation to Jehu (v. 5). For which there was a price—or a test. If you are for me, if you are listening to my voice, that is, if you are as subservient as you claim, you will see that the heads of your

---

[2]Jehu sent the letters to 'Samaria, to the leaders of Jezreel, i.e., the elders, and to those supporting Ahab' (v. 1). Some wonder what the leaders of Jezreel would be doing in Samaria and so think there must be some glitch in the text. But they may well have fled to Samaria when they saw what Jehu was doing in Jezreel. See T. R. Hobbs, *2 Kings*, Word Biblical Commentary (Waco: Word, 1985), 126.

master's sons arrive in Jezreel tomorrow (v. 6a). They are as docile as the elders of Naboth's town (1 Kings 21:9-14), slaughter the seventy men (v. 7) and ship their heads off to Jezreel.

One marvels at the writer's matter-of-fact style in verse 8. One can nearly imagine an English butler in an old movie announcing in his unflappable way, 'Sir, the heads you ordered have arrived.' Jehu has them placed on overnight display (v. 8b)[3] and then uses them as visual aids for his next morning's speech (vv. 9f.): 'You are innocent [lit., righteous]. See, I am the one who conspired against my master, and killed him; but who has struck down all these?' If I might paraphrase Jehu, I understand him to say: 'Sure, I knocked off Joram. But this can't be my work—these heads arrived via the postal service. Someone else did this. There is widespread support for me. These are royal heads—I have the loyalty of the folks at the highest levels.'

In verse 11, the summary note, the writer assures us that Jehu has 'secured' Jezreel; he 'dispensed with' all Ahab's relatives there, his nobles, court favorites, and religious functionaries. No survivors.

Samaria is the other royal stronghold and Jehu sets out for the capital (v. 12a); most of verses 12-17, however, has to do with two encounters on the way to Samaria:[4]

On the way to Samaria, v. 12a
    Jehu meets Judeans, vv. 12b-13
      Slaughter, v. 14
    Jehu meets Jehonadab, v. 15a
      Support, vv. 15b-16
Samaria..., v. 17

Jehu's encounter with Ahaziah's kinsmen (vv. 12-14) bristles with questions. We don't know, for example, where Beth-eked of the shepherds (v. 12) was located. Somewhere between Jezreel and Samaria. And if these Judeans had gone by Samaria, surely they knew of the slaughter of Ahab's seventy descendants; why then were they continuing on to Jezreel? But we don't know that they came via Samaria; in fact, their

---

[3]The Assyrians had a real knack for stacking heads. See D. D. Luckenbill, *Ancient Records of Assyria and Babylonia*, 2 vols. (London: Histories & Mysteries of Man, 1926/1989), 1:143, 147-48 for Assur-nasir-pal, and 1:213, 215, 219 for Shalmaneser III.

[4]T. R. Hobbs' discussion of vv. 12-17 led me to see its structure (*2 Kings*, 125).

answer in v. 13b assumes they knew of no threat at all against
the king's sons.[5] Some may also wonder why they were not at
least wary when they encountered Jehu. But why should they
be? They likely wouldn't have recognized Jehu—there were no
tabloids or newspapers making newsmakers' faces immediately
recognizable throughout Israel and Judah. Finally, one may
wonder why Jehu wiped out the king of Judah's relatives since
they were not a part of Israel. But the royal houses of Israel and
Judah had intermarried (2 Kings 8:18, 26) and so Jehu probably
assumed that, having the golden opportunity, he must decimate
the pro-Ahab contingent in Judah as well.

Jehu also meets Jehonadab son of Rechab on the way to
Samaria. Jehonadab seems to be on his way to meet up with Jehu
(v. 15a). Jehonadab expresses enthusiastic support in response to
Jehu's inquiries (v. 15c).[6] We don't know exactly what to make
of Jehonadab. His descendants appear in Jeremiah 35, and they
tell Jeremiah that Jonadab (alternate spelling), their ancestor,
commanded them never to drink wine, build houses, sow seed,
plant vineyards, but always to live in tents (Jer. 35:6-7). From
this it is easy for some to infer that this 'group represented
fanatical support for what they considered to be the old ways of
Yahwism, symbolized by a return to an idealized nomadism'.[7]
Others, however, think Jehu may have had his eye on Jehonadab's
military support. 'Rechab' is from the same root as *rekeb*, chariotry
or chariot. Some think that 'son of *rkb*' may refer to a member of
a metal-workers' group that produced chariots.[8] Whatever we
make of the 'Rechabites,' Jehonadab was apparently a Yahweh

---

[5]Hobbs, *2 Kings*, 128, wants to repoint the (Hebrew) preposition and noun 'for the peace of' (lit.; usually, 'to greet') to an infinitive, which would mean 'to avenge, pay back'. These then would be a southern unit sent north to avenge the deaths of Ahab's sons. But if this is so, why were they apparently unarmed, for Jehu gave orders to take them alive (v. 14a)? Not a likely command if they had come equipped for conflict. As for the geography and communications, Richard Nelson suggests these Judeans may have been coming in the 'back door' to Jezreel via the Jordan Valley and Beth-shan, 'which would explain their being out of touch with the current crisis' (*First and Second Kings*, Interpretation [Louisville: John Knox, 1987], 204).

[6]Here I follow Cogan and Tadmor, who take *yēš wāyēš* as an emphatic expression, 'It is indeed!' (*II Kings*, Anchor Bible [Garden City, NY: Doubleday, 1988], 115). That is, 'Yes, I support you with all my heart.'

[7]Nelson, *First and Second Kings*, 204; cf. also Cogan and Tadmor, *II Kings*, 114.

[8]This view is too involved to sketch here; those interested can see B. K. Waltke, 'Reckab, Rechabites,' *Zondervan Pictorial Encyclopedia of the Bible*, 5 vols., 5:42-44, and Frank S. Frick, 'Rechab,' ABD, 5:630-32.

loyalist or Jehu wouldn't have professed his 'zeal for Yahweh' (v. 16) as he did. Likely Jehu was wanting to secure the support of the 'conservative' elements in Israel. And half a verse (17a) tells us that Jehu exterminated all the remaining Ahab-ians in Samaria.

Now that is what happened. And the point of the text is that all this is the fulfillment of Yahweh's word. Jehu said as much as he delivered his speech between those two stacks of heads: 'Know then that not a bit of Yahweh's word which Yahweh spoke against the house of Ahab has fallen, but Yahweh has done what he had spoken by the hand of his servant Elijah' (v. 10). But we're a bit queasy about this. We're not sure that Jehu should be our theologian-in-residence or our interpreter of (for him) contemporary history. After all, Yahweh's word against Ahab was all too convenient for Jehu. But the writer will not allow us to question Jehu's theology, for he himself so much as supports it in verse 17. There our writer confirms that the eradication of Ahab loyalists in Samaria was 'in line with the word of Yahweh which he had spoken to Elijah'.[9]

If we cannot dispute Jehu we may be tempted to question Yahweh. Why does he work like this? Why does he allow the gore of man to carry out the will of God? Couldn't he operate in a cleaner way? Perhaps. But we must remember two points. First, the Bible shows that God frequently works, we might say, indirectly—through human instruments, and, unlike surgeons, God has no sterilized instruments; all of them are flawed and many of them opportunistic, self-serving Jehus. So God uses wicked people to carry out his divine design. Second, this is a situation involving the judgment of God, and it is very difficult to make judgment pleasant.

A couple of weeks ago both my wife and I were out of town on separate trips, she to Tennessee and Virginia to see friends and family, and I to Colorado for a conference. I arrived home several days before she did, and, naturally, I had amassed a pile of dirty laundry. Since I would soon run out of some articles, I knew I must wash clothes. Fortunately there is a setting on our washer for an 'extra large load'. I promptly selected that

---

[9]Cogan and Tadmor, *II Kings*, 118, recognize that this is 'the basic theme which unifies all aspects of the narrative: Jehu's deeds against the House of Ahab fulfill YHWH's word delivered through his prophets. Indeed, Jehu himself is permitted to voice this rationale no less than three times (9:25-26, 36-37; 10:19 [sic; they mean 10:10].'

and threw in my whites, mediums, and darks in the same batch (there were no new clothes whose colors might run). They all made a nice full load. I had almost all my clothes done in one easy batch. But that is college-boy technique. It appalls Barbara. It isn't proper. Her loads are sorted according to color and sometimes, I think, fabric, and supplemented with softener. So washing can be done in a refined or a barbaric way. Either way, the wash gets done. And I suppose that's how Yahweh works. He can fulfill his word in a direct, pollution-free way if he chooses, but often he does it in an unrefined way through tainted instruments. Either way, the word gets fulfilled. And the fulfillment of Yahweh's word is sometimes unsanitary.

Zeal for Yahweh's cause is frequently deficient (vv. 16, 18-31)
Jehu promised Jehonadab 'zeal for Yahweh' (v. 16). But that's not what it looked like when Jehu announced his religious policy. 'Ahab served Baal a little; Jehu will serve him much' (v. 18). And the summons went out to the prophets, servants, and priests of Baal to be present, upon pain of death, at an inauguration service where Jehu would make a 'great sacrifice' to Baal (v. 19a). Then the writer enlightens you with a little aside—Jehu was acting deceptively in order to wipe out the worshipers of Baal (v. 19b). All Baalists are notified and arrive to fill the house of Baal from wall to wall (v. 21). How can Baal fail? It looks like Baal's day, with even greater government gusto behind him. Even the writer subtly hints at the 'dominance' of Baal, referring to Baal seventeen times in verse 18-28.

Jehu makes sure all Baalists don vestments (v. 22), which will make them easy to identify for his execution squad. He also makes sure no servants of Yahweh will be there—this is no ecumenical service (v. 23). Jehu goes in for the sacrificial procedures but has eighty commandos under orders outside (v. 24). When he leaves the liturgy he sends in his men to cut them all down (v. 25). This they do, wiping out worshipers and leveling temple and its pagan paraphernalia, making it all a part of Jehu's temples-to-toilets program (vv. 26-27). Then verse 28—that frugal summary: 'Thus Jehu wiped out Baal from Israel.'

Time was when one wondered if anyone would ever be able to write words like verse 28. Under Ahab it looked like Baal was in the saddle for the duration (1 Kings 16:29-34). What unexpected good news. But it may make some a bit nervous. After all, they might say, wiping out Baal's devotees was not a part of the prophetic mandate laid down to Jehu, unless one is going to interpret the 'house of Ahab' (9:7) very broadly. That is true, and yet if we remember Deuteronomy 13, we should hesitate to condemn Jehu.[10] That being said, I tend to think that wiping out the Baal cult had more to do with Jehu's zeal for Jehu than his zeal for Yahweh. Now I cannot support that directly from the text—it's a historical hunch. But since Ahab and Jezebel had sponsored the Baal cult, one guesses that Ahab's dynasty likely had numerous supporters in Baal circles. Jehu, then, likely purged the Baal worshipers not because he was so pro-Yahweh as that he was anti-Ahab. Eliminating Baal eliminated Ahab loyalists, dissolved support for Ahab's family, and so would consolidate Jehu's power.

But verse 28 must be taken with what follows to catch how it functions. Verses 28-31 should be kept together; they form a double two-beat pattern:

> Commendation, v. 28
> Qualification, v. 29
> Commendation, v. 30
> Qualification, v. 31

So Jehu wipes out Baal worship (v. 28), but he himself didn't turn away from Jeroboam's bull cult (v. 29); Yahweh commends and rewards Jehu for obliterating Ahab's house (v. 30), but, the writer repeats, he did not 'turn back' from Jeroboam's drivel (v. 31). Jeroboam is sort of the Pontius Pilate of the Old Testament—his name lives in infamy over the history of Israel for he, after a fashion, sealed their doom.[11] The problem with Jehu's revolution is not that it went too far, but that it did not go far enough! As Fretheim rightly says, the revolution did not go *deep* enough, that is, into Jehu's own heart (cf. v. 31).[12]

---

[10]See my discussion of 1 Kings 18:40 in *The Wisdom and the Folly: An Exposition of the Book of First Kings* (Ross-shire: Christian Focus, 2002), 243-45.

[11]See *The Wisdom and the Folly*, 164-66.

A passage like this should help us formulate some practical political theology. I've touched on this previously, so will not belabor it. It's not that we should be indifferent but that we shouldn't be naïve about politics. It is the realm of disillusionment. Jehu overthrows apostasy—but retains perversion (vv. 29, 31). One can understand why evangelicals in Russia were encouraged when they heard the reforms promised by the Communists. They seemed particularly delighted with a statement from one leader: 'Each person must have complete freedom not only to observe any faith but also to propagate any faith...None of the officials should even have a right to ask anyone of his faith; this is a matter of conscience and nobody should dare to interfere in this field.'[13] That was Vladimir Lenin. And we know where that went. In spite of what Jehu says, God's people know that 'zeal for Yahweh' is next-to-extinct in political circles. So they are not surprised when a Jehu delivers far less than he should—or, for example, when the Nebuchadnezzar of Daniel 2 turns into the Nebuchadnezzar of Daniel 3.

Instruments in Yahweh's hands are always responsible (vv. 32-33)

Yahweh promised Jehu a four-generation dynasty, because he had carried out Yahweh's will in eradicating the house of Ahab (v. 30). That seems appropriate: limited blessing for half-hearted zeal, for Jehu exterminated Ahab's paganism but retained Jeroboam's syncretism. The sequence suggests that the initial scourges of verses 32-33 are Yahweh's judgments for Jehu's lukewarmness.[14] So, literally, 'in those days Yahweh began to cut off from Israel' (v. 32a). The verb here ($q\bar{a}\d{s}\bar{a}h$) may suggest cutting off piece by piece,[15] i.e., one chunk after another of Israel's real estate being lost to her. As verse 33

---

[12]Terence E. Fretheim, *First and Second Kings*, Westminster Bible Companion (Louisville: John Knox, 1999), 173.

[13]Cited in James and Marti Hefley, *By Their Blood: Christian Martyrs of the Twentieth Century*, 2nd ed. (Grand Rapids: Baker, 1996), 227.

[14]Some point to Hosea 1:4 as evidence that Yahweh was judging Jehu's house for Jehu's nasty bloodbath in Jezreel. But that text should probably be translated, 'I will bring the bloodshed of Jezreel upon the house of Jehu,' i.e., God will bring the same violent end to Jehu's dynasty which came to Ahab's dynasty; see the discussion in Duane A. Garrett, *Hosea, Joel*, New American Commentary (Nashville: Broadman & Holman, 1997), 56-57.

[15]K-B, 3:1120.

indicates this meant the loss of Gilead and Bashan, actually all of Israel's turf east of the Jordan. Hazael, the Syrian/Aramaean king, was responsible for this: 'so Hazael struck them down throughout all the territory of Israel' (v. 32b). There it is: Yahweh began to cut off, Hazel struck them down. Hazael is Yahweh's instrument just as Jehu was. And Yahweh's word had predicted Hazael's scourge (1 Kings 19:15-17; 2 Kings 8:12-13) just as it had predicted Jehu's purge (2 Kings 9:7-10).[16]

This is a sobering summary, for it is telling us that one instrument of Yahweh's judgment (Hazael) is raised up to bring judgment on a previous instrument of Yahweh's judgment (Jehu).[17] This tale will repeat itself. Though Yahweh will use Assyria as the rod of his anger against his own people, as the axe that whacks down his own covenant nation, yet Yahweh will destroy the axe for forgetting it was merely an axe in the divine Lumberjack's hands (Isa. 10:1-19). Yahweh will give Judah and surrounding countries to his 'servant', the Babylonian Nebuchadnezzar, 'until the time of his own land comes' (Jer. 27:7). Yahweh presses kings and other reprobates into his service but such servants seldom accept servanthood and so Yahweh raises up another servant to consign his previous servant to the dumpster of history.

All this is scary, however, because it doesn't merely involve the movers and shakers and swelled heads of politics. Jehu's story testifies that one can be used by God *and* judged by God. We need go no farther than Matthew 7:21-23 to find the Jehu paradigm in the New Testament. You can be both used by Christ and rejected by Christ. Just because you have at some time in some way been the Lord's servant does not mean you are viewed with the Lord's pleasure. It is very solemn. Let Jehu haunt us—to fear and faithfulness.

---

[16]For brief descriptions of how this worked out historically, see Cogan and Tadmor, *II Kings*, 120-21, and Hobbs, *2 Kings*, 131. Assyrian king Shalmaneser III seems to have inflicted heavy losses upon Hazael (ca. 840-838 BC). Jehu submitted to Shalmaneser and paid tribute to him (see Alfred J. Hoerth, *Archaeology and the Old Testament* [Grand Rapids: Baker, 1998], 321-22, for the Black Obelisk of Shalmaneser). Later, however, Shalmaneser's attention was diverted to battles in the north and east, which eventually gave a rejuvenated Hazael opportunity to harass Israel.

[17]'When God is using rogues and brutes to do his will, he is marvellously able to limit their power and success by matching them against each other' (Ronald S. Wallace, *Readings in 2 Kings* [Eugene, OR: Wipf & Stock, 1997], 124).

16

The Lady Who Saved Christmas
(2 Kings 11)

Let's pretend that you live where I currently live, in the deep south of the United States. And let's pretend it is near the Christmas holidays. Let's go on pretending…that there is an ongoing southern tradition of having cinnamon-spiked prune juice for Yuletide. It's thought to be a delicacy. It's formulated in Nova Scotia, but it comes via an over-ground white, plastic pipeline all the way down to Mississippi. Now what if some grungy soul in New Jersey, who doesn't want nice southern folk to enjoy perfectly pruny holidays, gouges a hole in the pipeline? That pipeline is so exposed, so vulnerable.

God did something like that. He made the coming of his kingdom—and therefore of Christmas—depend on a promise he made, and he placed that promise, openly and exposed, in all the turbulence and upheaval of human history. Sometimes we call that promise the Davidic covenant, as when Yahweh assured David: 'Your house and your kingdom shall be made sure forever before me; your throne shall be established forever' (2 Sam. 7:16; or, as Psalm 89:36 has it: 'His line shall continue forever, his throne, as the sun before me' [rsv]). Hence David's line of kings, the 'Davidic pipeline', would never bite the dust, and, eventually, the future David, the messianic King, would bring this line to its awesome climax. The kingdom of Israel divided, however, and David's line reigned over a postage-stamp sized kingdom called Judah, and there the day came about 840 BC when it looked like there wouldn't ever be any Christmas and history would be Messiahless. But the text forbids us to despair, for the big truth 2 Kings 11 teaches is that *Christ will never allow his kingdom to suffer eclipse.*

The story follows a mostly symmetrical structure, and it will be well to have this in front of us before we focus on the teaching of the text.

Structure of 2 Kings 11

Death and preservation, vv. 1-3

Secret plan, vv. 4-12
    Revealing king's son, v. 4
    Priest's instructions, vv. 5-8
    Compliance, vv. 9-11
    Coronation, v. 12

Public event, vv. 13-19
    Revealing king's son, vv. 13-14
    Priest's instructions, v. 15
    Compliance, v. 16
    Covenant + destruction, vv. 17-18
    Installation, v. 19

Death and peace, v. 20

Now let us move into the teaching of the narrative.

The Utter Folly of Covenant Compromise

Here we look at the history leading up to 2 Kings 11. How did Athaliah get here in the first place? She was the daughter of Israel's Ahab and became the wife of Jehoram, son of Jehoshaphat king of Judah (8:18; 1 Kings 22:44; 2 Chron. 18:1); and she was the mother of Jehoram's son Ahaziah who fell in Jehu's northern coup (v. 1; 9:27-28).[1] So Jehoshaphat of Judah

---

[1] I shall try to avoid undue repetition. See my previous discussion in chapter 13 above (on 8:16-29); see also *The Wisdom and the Folly*, 337-38, on 1 Kings 22:41-44.

concluded a marriage alliance with Ahab of Israel, giving his son Jehoram to Ahab's daughter Athaliah.[2]

So long as Jehoshaphat lived the tone in Judah seemed very much the same. What difference did a state marriage make? But come 848 and 841 BC the story changes. One wonders if Athaliah didn't goad Jehoram to purge his brothers (2 Chron. 21:1-7). And of course Athaliah was up to her own massacre when the time came (our text, v. 1). One wonders if Jehoshaphat ever had a clue that his diplomacy would lead to such ruin.

A year ago I read a clip in our local newspaper about a two storey bungalow located about seventy miles east of San Diego along the U.S.-Mexico border. The house was on a pig farm and I suppose it looked like any normal house. But drug agents broke into a closet and found the entrance to a 1,200 foot tunnel, sporting electric lights, ventilation ducts, and wooden walls. The tunnel ended in the fireplace of a house just beyond the metal wall that separates the U.S. from Mexico. Folks smuggled billions of dollars of drugs via that 'thoroughfare'. It may look quite normal, but it hides all kinds of ruin. That was the way with the marriage alliance Jehoshaphat engineered. It looked reasonably harmless for a while—but because of it the whole Davidic covenant nearly bit the dust.

As I've said before, Jehoshaphat was personally godly but covenantally stupid. And his stupidity gives him a share in the blood dripping from Athaliah's hands. None of us are kings, few of us are even 'movers and shakers', but if we are in covenant with Yahweh and yet marry the godless we will nearly always wreak havoc and ruin among our descendants.

The Mad Fury of Yahweh's Enemies (v. 1)

We should build up to this opening verse by reviewing the *specific situation* in Judah up to Athaliah's rampage. The seed of David had already been severely decimated. First, Jehoram,

---

[2]We do not know whether Athaliah was also the daughter of Jezebel (as opposed to some other wife of Ahab). Athaliah's behavior hints at Jezebelian genes. K. D. Fricke suggests that in a marriage alliance with a foreign court it is likely that only a 'full-blooded' daughter would be offered (*Das zweite Buch von den Königen*, Die Botschaft des alten Testaments [Stuttgart: Calwer, 1972], 146). John Bright thinks chronological considerations rule out the Jezebel-Athaliah connection (*A History of Israel*, 3rd. ed. [Philadelphia: Westminster, 1981], 242, n38), but Cogan and Tadmor counter him (*II Kings*, Anchor Bible [Garden City, NY: Doubleday, 1988], 98).

Athaliah's husband, killed all his brothers when he gained sole power (2 Chron. 21:1-4). Next, Philistines and Arabs invaded Judah and carried off and killed all of Jehoram's sons except the youngest, Jehoahaz/Ahaziah (2 Chron. 21:16-17; 22:1). Then, in his one-year reign, Ahaziah is caught with Joram of Israel in Jehu's purge and is himself purged (2 Kings 9:27) along with forty-two members of Judah's royal family (10:12-14). Hence one wonders who could possibly be left for Athaliah's ministry of murder aside from her own grandchildren. But it was Athaliah's hour of power and 'she rose up and destroyed all the royal seed' (v. 1).

Now it is important to understand that this is simply the *typical trend;* it is a sample of the instinctive hatred the rulers of this age have for Christ's kingdom. It is terrible but typical. This is the sort of thing you can expect from the head knockers of this world whenever they have the power to do so. Check out Herod in Matthew 2:13-18. Reprobate rulers have a savage hostility toward Christ, his people, and his kingdom, and sometimes they are so successful that God's cause and people may seem on the verge of extinction. 'Do not be surprised, brothers, that the world hates you' (1 John 3:13, ESV). We don't have to wait until we hit a Daniel 7-, or 2 Thessalonians 2-, or Revelation 13-situation: there are all sorts of antichrists along the way. And any prophecy buff worth his salt knew how to spell antichrist in 840 BC: A-t-h-a-l-i-a-h.

Is this really so in our day? Is Athaliah's sword still dripping? Ask the two million who've perished in south Sudan over the last two decades, many of them Christians. Ask believers in Indonesia where 10,000 Christians (one report—this is probably far too low) have perished at the hands of Muslims. This is par. This is what we can expect. Don't even be surprised if you see tinges of this fury in your office or shop or school.

The Huge Significance of Unsung Servants (v. 2)

> Then Jehosheba, daughter of King Jehoram, sister of Ahaziah, took Joash, Ahaziah's son, and stole him from the midst of the king's sons who were to be massacred—him and his nurse into a room of beds; so they hid him from Athaliah and he was not put to death.

Wherever antichrist is, Christ always has faithful servants. Here her name is Jehosheba, sister of Ahaziah, daughter of Jehoram, wife of Jehoiada the priest (this last from 2 Chron. 22).[3] Somehow in this emergency she spirits away the sucking infant Joash, along with his nurse, crams them in a room marked 'Bed Supplies', and then, apparently raises him in her apartment in the temple complex for six years (v. 3a). Yahweh's promise to David was one infant away from proving false and falling to the ground. What a crucial moment! Jehosheba is the human agent responsible for preserving the kingdom of God in this world. If it weren't for Jehosheba, there wouldn't be any Christmas. The Davidic pipeline would've been broken. Here is the lady who saved Christmas. She is God's Rolaid in what sometimes seems the soap opera of history. Because of her initiative in verse 2, all of verses 4-18 can take place. You see how strategic Jehosheba's act is? Yahweh's promise hung by a frazzled thread in 840 bc and she kept it from snapping.

You see Yahweh's method, don't you? No spectacular intervention. Oh, he could have caused Athaliah's hiatal hernia to make her choke on her granola one morning before she ever started her bloodbath. But he didn't—he had his servant Jehosheba in place.

You may draw an erroneous inference at this point. You may think that your service for Yahweh is not crucial like Jehosheba's. I am, you might say, seldom or never thrust into dramatic scenarios like the one she faced. You sure? If you are a Christian parent you have responsibility over the church in your house, where you are meant to serve as prophet, priest, and king. As prophet you teach the word of God to your children, as priest you intercede and wrestle in prayer for them, and as king you rule over them with proper discipline and protection. It's because my parents understood that that I am in the kingdom of God. Don't tell me your kingdom service doesn't matter.

---

[3]Robert Cohn points out the irony: 'The second verse sets Ahaziah's sister as the savior of Ahaziah's baby son against Ahaziah's mother...' (*2 Kings*, Berit Olam [Collegeville, MN: Liturgical, 2000], 77). We find similar irony elsewhere: Pharaoh's daughter stymies Pharaoh's decree—in one case (Exod. 2:1-10), and Jonathan and Michal, Saul's children, shield David from their father's designs (1 Sam. 19).

And it's interesting, isn't it, that Jehosheba's name is not exactly a household word? Daughter of a king, wife of a priest, she had some status. But we don't hear of her again. You yourself probably didn't think of her all this week—until you happened to read this chapter. She may well have been relatively obscure in her own time. Folks, after all, were still talking about the Battle of Qarqar (853), and Shalmaneser III was *Time* magazine's 'Man of the Year'. John Bright in his *History of Israel* doesn't refer to Jehosheba by name in his narrative nor even list her in the index. But isn't this the glory of God—that he does not need powerful or prominent people? So we will be wrong if we become fixated on Jehosheba. We could too easily do that. Then we'd start marketing Jehosheba mugs, Jehosheba sweatshirts, Jehoiada-Jehosheba coffee table books (à la the Charles and Diana genre), and we'd try to get her on a Christian TV network. Sometimes the Bible doesn't say something directly because it expects you to be smart enough to pick it up. Don't you catch what verse 2 wants you to say? 'God wasn't napping, was he? He had just the servant he wanted in just the right place at that very time.' Your only response should be to stand and sing the doxology: 'Praise God from whom gutsy women come!'

The Subversive Presence of Yahweh's Kingdom (v. 3)

'So he [Joash] was with her in the house of Yahweh, hiding himself for six years; and Athaliah was ruling over the land.' Note the two kingdoms here; you have the visible reign of the illegitimate kingdom (v. 3b), and you have the secret existence of the true king (v. 3a). The usurper rules, but the chosen king as it were secretly reigns, unknown to Athaliah. The true king is there behind the scenes and the pretender doesn't have a clue. There is often a vast difference between what is apparent and what is actually the case.

That's what a neighbor said about Ethel Kennedy, Bobby Kennedy's wife. She recalled that on the same day photographers were at her Hyannis Port home snapping pictures of Ethel for a mother-of-the-year award, three of Ethel's kids were on the roof trying to lasso the chimney. The neighbor wondered why they didn't turn the camera on the fiasco on the roof.[4] So down

---

[4]Ronald Kessler, *The Sins of the Father* (New York: Warner Books, 1996), 330.

below you see the mother-of-the-year, while part way up in the sky her kids are playing cowboy with a chimney. That's the way it is in 2 Kings 11. Here is Athaliah ruling Judah and never even imagines a lad stashed away in a temple room patiently learning his A-B-Gs (well, that's Hebrew for you).

Sometimes this subversiveness of God's kingdom crops up in almost incidental ways in Scripture. I've always been intrigued by Philippians 4:22, where the apostle tells the church at Philippi that all the saints send greetings, 'especially those of Caesar's household.' That does not mean they were Caesar's sons or daughters, but more likely those employed in the imperial service—servants who cleaned imperial latrines or carried inter-office mail. Some of them came to Christ. Now they belong to Christ's household. In one sense Caesar is their lord, but actually they have begun to serve a different Lord. Caesar rules the empire but Jesus has begun to rule over (some of) Caesar's subjects. Jesus has set up his kingdom under Caesar's nose in his own civil service. There is a godly sneakiness about the gospel and the kingdom of God. You never know where the gospel will break out, who will be its next 'victim'! Perhaps some of you understand now why some of your family have gotten so very nervous after you told them you had bowed the knee to Jesus. They're secretly alarmed that they might be next, that he might have designs on *them*. Of course they should be scared!

You must see this as your anchor, not the secret reign of Joash, for there is a far greater than Joash who reigns now—David's Descendant and Joash's Descendant, Jesus the Lord. And the rulers of this age and the pagans around you don't know this secret. But you do, if you've swallowed Ephesians 1:20-22. This is what puts iron in your guts and makes you able to resist any other power that tries to control you. Knowing there is a legitimate King who secretly reigns keeps you from despair while the pretenders carry on.

The High Price of Covenant Restoration (vv. 17-20)
I will soon justify what may seem the undue attention to verses 17-18, but now we need to catch up on the story of the coup.

When Joash was seven, Jehoiada the priest convened a clandestine meeting with 'the chiefs of the hundreds of the Carites and of the guards' (v. 4a, NJPS) in the temple complex.[5] He swore them to fidelity and secrecy and showed them the king's son (v. 4b). What Jehoiada says next in verses 5-8 will vary according to what version you're reading. Verses 5-6 are especially difficult. I think it best simply to pass on the view of these verses I find most likely, rather than spending several pages discussing each difficulty in the text. NJPS provides a reasonably good translation:

> (5) He instructed them: "This is what you must do: One-third of those who are on duty for the week shall maintain guard over the royal palace; (6) another third shall be (stationed) at the Sur Gate; and the other third shall be at the gate behind the guards; you shall keep guard over the house on every side.[6] (7) The two divisions of yours who are off duty this week shall keep guard over the House of the LORD for the protection of the king." [Verse 8 is clear].

In light of this, Cogan and Tadmor provide a clear reconstruction:

> The royal guard comprises three companies, each one serving one week out of three...To insure the success of his scheme, Jehoiada summoned all the guards. Those on duty...were subdivided and positioned at three locations: one third at the royal palace; one third at the Sur Gate; one third at the gate behind the outrunners. All the rest, all those off duty..., who were two thirds of the total guard, took up positions within the temple to guard the king.[7]

The whole guard gathered in the temple to receive arms—spears and quivers (or, shields)—from Jehoiada (v. 10), and the detachments assigned to the temple and king wrapped the latter in their protection (v. 11). Looks like we're ready for a coronation (v. 12).

---

[5]The Carites, perhaps from SW Asia Minor, were foreign mercenaries serving as the royal bodyguard.

[6]We can only guess what the last word (*massāḥ*) in verse 6 means. DCH, 5:361-62 gives two options; we simply can't be sure.

[7]M. Cogan and H. Tadmor, *II Kings*, Anchor Bible (Garden City, NY: Doubleday, 1988), 127.

Jehoiada leads Joash out and places 'the crown upon him' and gives him 'the testimony' as well (v. 12). The word for 'crown' here is *nēzer*, which comes from the same root as the term Nazirite, a consecrated person (see Num. 6). This idea of consecration probably infects *nēzer* as well. It is used with reference to the high priest's headgear (Exod. 29:6; 39:30; Lev. 8:9); actually, it was an engraved plate the high priest wore over his forehead, designating him as a consecrated person. *nēzer* is also used of a royal crown as here (see also, e.g., 2 Sam. 1:10; Pss. 89:39 and 132:18). The word then appears 'not to connote "crown" in the primary sense, but crown in the sense of the sign of one's consecration'.[8] It was a sign of the king's consecration to his office and to God.

Joash also receives the 'testimony'. The word is *'ēdût*. It refers to God's testimony. Exodus refers to the 'tabernacle of the testimony' (Exod. 38:21) and calls the ark of the covenant the 'ark of the testimony' (e.g., Exod. 25:22; 26:33). This is because Moses put the testimony, the stone tablets with the law written on them, in the ark (Exod. 25:21). The testimony then refers to God's covenant law. In his coronation Joash received a copy of the testimony. This action was 'based on Deut 17:18, 19, 20' and was to 'remind the king that the law was to determine both his personal life and his rule as king'.[9] Here is the king, consecrated to God, called to live and rule by his covenant law.

Athaliah hears the cheering and charges into the temple. The sight had coronary thrombosis written all over it: 'Why, there's the king standing by the pillar, according to the custom' (v. 14a). At the sight of the partying, Athaliah tears her clothes and yells, 'Treason! Treason!' (v. 14b). One marvels that a usurper could use that word with a straight face. On Jehoiada's orders she is hauled out of the temple and disposed of on the way to the palace (vv. 15-16).

If you look at the sketch of the structure of 2 Kings 11 near the beginning of this chapter, you will note that the two major sections of the chapter (secret plan, vv. 4-12, and public event,

---

[8]See on this matter, T. E. McComiskey, TWOT, 2:567-68. Quotation is from p. 568.

[9]See the helpful discussion by Carl Schultz, TWOT, 2:649-50. Quotation from p. 650. See also R. D. Patterson and Hermann J. Austel, '1 and 2 Kings,' *The Expositor's Bible Commentary*, 12 vols. (Grand Rapids: Zondervan, 1988), 4:218.

vv. 13-19) follow the same pattern, except that the 'covenant + destruction' segment (vv. 17-18) in the second section is distinct—it has no corresponding element in verses 4-12. This may (let's not be dogmatic) point to the special significance of verses 17-18.

First, the covenant (v. 17). 'Jehoiada cut the covenant between Yahweh and the king and the people to be Yahweh's people, and between the king and the people as well.' As Paul House points out, the text refers to '*the* covenant', which 'indicates that a previous covenantal model was followed'.[10] This was a covenant renewal, the people repledging themselves to the commitment of Exodus 19:1-8 and 24:1-8. The covenant between the king and the people 'defined the king's obligation toward the nation and fulfilled the function of a modern constitution (2 Samuel 3:21; 5:3; 2 Chronicles 23:3)'.[11] This latter covenant was likely what Rehoboam was attempting to conclude with the northern tribes in 1 Kings 12, though he sabotaged it by his arrogant stupidity.

Secondly, there is the destruction (v. 18). 'Then all the people of the land entered the house of Baal.' So there was a temple to Baal in Judah! Doubtless part of Athaliah's legacy. 'And they pulled it down, its altars and its images they shattered to bits, and Mattan the priest of Baal they killed before the altars.'

The sequence between verses 17 and 18 is important: Covenant leads to destruction. If there is fidelity to Yahweh (17) all that attempts to sap and seduce that fidelity must be thrown down (18). When truth reigns the false must be eliminated.

In September 1944 Major General George Philip Roberts' British 11th Armored Division in a lightning dash (with help from other troops and the Belgian underground) cleared out the stunned German opposition and captured Antwerp's huge 1,000 acre harbor area intact. No warehouses, bridges, wharves, or equipment had been destroyed. It was one brilliant victory. However, no one ordered Roberts to make one more move—to strike eighteen miles north of Antwerp and sit astride the two-mile-wide neck at the east end of Holland's South Beveland peninsula. German forces

[10]Paul R. House, *1, 2 Kings*, New American Commentary (Nashville: Broadman & Holman, 1995), 299.

[11]See Ze'ev W. Falk, *Hebrew Law in Biblical Times*, 2nd ed. (Provo, UT and Winona Lake, IN: Brigham Young and Eisenbrauns, 2001), 31-32. Quotation from p. 32.

from Holland were retreating that way in order to join their forces further east. Had Roberts' forces been ordered there they would have served as a giant cork, bottling up the German 15th Army from escaping to the east and setting it up for an allied mop up operation. But this was not done. This meant that the 15th Army troops joined and reinforced German troops to the east and helped grind down the Allies' Market-Garden offensive. It also meant that since there had been no 'bottle and mop' some German troops still controlled the approaches to Antwerp's harbor. The Allies held the harbor but the Germans the approaches and so Antwerp was absolutely useless as a supply base for the Allies. Cornelius Ryan has referred to this as 'a momentous oversight' and as 'the great mistake'.[12]

That is what we would have if we had the covenant in verse 17 without the destruction of verse 18. You can't have a solid covenant victory unless all that sabotages the covenant is eliminated.[13] Some will find verse 18 so 'unpleasant', but for Israel it was an 'unpleasantness' commanded by Yahweh (check out Deuteronomy 13). Covenant-plus-destruction is ever the biblical way. For Israel's time, fidelity to Yahweh meant holy demolition (Deut. 7:1-6). And Jesus makes the same kind of demand upon would-be disciples (Luke 14:25-33), blind moralists (Mark 10:17-22), and lax churches (Rev. 2:14-16).

The Silent Manner of God's Power
Before leaving 2 Kings 11 I want us to cast a glance back over the chapter and think about the *style* of the narrative. I have tried to show that this episode is of immense importance in redemptive history because the covenant with David was almost dead and buried under Athaliah's rampage. She had almost succeeded in writing 'finis!' over Yahweh's kingdom plan. Yahweh is so vigilant in maintaining his king and his kingdom! I think the writer of 2 Kings 11 would agree that it was his intent to show that.[14]

---

[12]Cornelius Ryan, *A Bridge Too Far* (New York: Simon and Schuster, 1974), 59-61.
[13]Verse 20 supports this as well; it implies that the city was quiet ('had rest') because they had executed Athaliah.
[14]Cf. Terence E. Fretheim, *First and Second Kings*, Westminster Bible Companion (Louisville: John Knox, 1999), 180: 'Two faithful, resolute, and wise Yahwists save the day, Jehosheba and Jehoiada. Because of them the Davidic promise has a future. They take this issue directly into their own hands by hiding Joash and instructing him, and *not a single word* is spoken about God inspiring them or acting through them (not unlike at 25:27-30). God it seems has simply *entrusted* this most significant work to

But how does he do it? Does he explicitly state Yahweh's intervention or record any word or directive of Yahweh's? Note how the whole narrative is simply descriptive—there is no 'Yahweh said' this or 'Yahweh did' that. To be sure Yahweh is mentioned but all are 'third person' references: nine times in the phrase 'the house of Yahweh' and twice where the writer refers to him. But you see how *indirect* it is? Never does Yahweh even interject a word nor is there any reference to any explicit activity on his part. We've seen this before; here's another sample of Yahweh's hidden and roundabout work.

In the War between the States a truce had been granted during the battle at Cedar Mountain (August 1862) so that Union forces could remove their dead and wounded. One member of a Confederate artillery battery got his first glance at General Stonewall Jackson during this lull. He confided in his diary that he would never have taken him for the great Valley hero, for he was round-shouldered, wore a faded uniform, and looked at the ground when he walked as if he had lost something. One could pass him in a crowd and never pay the least attention to him. Yet he was the pride of the South and the terror of the North.[15]

Might we reverently say this of Yahweh? He goes about his work without attracting your attention. You may look for the expected trappings of deity and not find them. In one sense 2 Kings 11 is another biblical invitation to enjoy—in Scripture, history, and experience—the refreshing subtlety and mighty silence of our God.

Of course, you may not have expected to have your nose rubbed in 2 Kings 11, and you may not be much interested in baby Joash and his plucky aunt who saved him. But, please, try to see God's hand at work long before Luke 2. If Athaliah had had her way, there would've been no angels or shepherds or swaddling clothes or good news of great joy. Today you'd better thank God for the lady who saved Christmas.

---

faithful people and chosen to be dependent upon what they do. God continues to work in unobtrusive ways, to be sure, but God's decision to work through people means that what they do truly counts for something and, in this case, actually removes the danger to the Davidic dynasty and shapes the future of the promise.'

[15]See James I. Robertson, Jr., *Stonewall Jackson: The Man, the Soldier, the Legend* (New York: Macmillan, 1997), 538.

17

Repairs and Payoffs

(2 Kings 12)

Occasionally and very briefly, early in the morning, an ungrateful thought enters my head. It's during the morning routine of taking a shower, washing one's hair, brushing teeth and shaving. One thinks of the tedium of it all, of how each morning one must do the same chores that one did the previous morning; they are endlessly repeatable and the whole procedure seems plagued with futility. But a moment's reflection brings one out of it. You think of the alternative: corpses don't brush teeth or take showers. All of a sudden tedium takes on a bit of a glow. That is the way 2 Kings 12 begins.

Kingdom continuity, a gracious gift (vv. 1-3)
It all seems to follow a regular Kings formula. 'In Jehu's seventh year Joash reigned, and he reigned forty years in Jerusalem' (v. 1).[1] There's the usual assessment ('Joash did what was right in Yahweh's eyes,' v. 2) and a familiar qualification ('Only the high places they did not take away,' v. 3).[2] What seems,

---

[1] I am using 'Joash' for consistency. The Hebrew text here spells it 'Jehoash,' as it does during most of this chapter, though in verse 19 it reverts to 'Joash' (as in, e.g., 11:2).

[2] There's a bit of a debate over whether verse 2b places a qualification on 2a: i.e., does 'which [lit.] Jehoiada the priest instructed him' imply that Joash may *not* have done right *all* his days but only during those in which Jehoiada directed him? That clearly is the import of the parallel in 2 Chronicles 24:2. In 2 Kings 12:2 all depends on how one translates the term *'ăšer* ('which'). Some (e.g., NRSV) translate 'because', a use this particle does sometimes have. In that case verse 2 is a general summary indicating the righteous tone of Joash's reign. I think, however, that *'ăšer* qualifies its

however, like a routine formula is actually, in light of chapter 11, a kingdom victory, for the Davidic kingship has been stabilized again.

Perhaps this is the best place to set out the structure of 2 Kings 12, in order to see its contents and contrasts:

Structure of 2 Kings 12

Stabilizing of Davidic dynasty, vv. 1-3
Refurbishing temple, vv. 4-16
Depleting temple, vv. 17-18
Threat to Davidic dynasty, vv. 19-21

When assassins dispose of Joash (vv. 20-21a) the Davidic line is once again under attack though not with 'Athalian' intensity. The current Davidide is liquidated but the line remains intact for Amaziah, Joash's son, reigns. But the dynastic keynote is in the 'boring' refrains of verses 1-3. Hobbs is right: 'The dynasty is once again placed on a regular footing.'[3]

And that should be so thrilling! Granted, verses 1-3 may appear to be the literary regurgitation of our writer's style, the customary niceties he uses when introducing any new king. But verses 1-3 must be viewed in light of the scourge and disaster of 11:1. Some may think simple continuity tedious, but it is nothing less than the steady faithfulness of God. To read 'in such-and-such a year so-and-so began to reign' in post-Athaliah time in Judah borders on the fantastic. What a gift can be hidden in those 'dreary' formulas!

British Colonel John Frost's 2nd Battalion was getting battered by the German barrage. Frost & Co. were defending the Arnhem bridge in Holland during the 'Market Garden' offensive in World War II. Ammunition was nearly gone, casualties were high, and Frost's men had been fighting for fifty hours without let-up. During this time one of the battalion chaplains, Father Egan, met Col. Frost as the latter was coming out of a toilet.

nearest antecedent, 'all his days,' and so should be translated 'when' or 'in which': he 'did what was right all his days in which Jehoiada the priest instructed him' (see NASB). It essentially parallels 2 Chronicles 24:2. The writer of Kings clearly knows that not all was well later in Joash's tenure (vv. 17-18, 20-21a), but he does not choose to dwell on that the way Chronicles does.

[3] T. R. Hobbs, *2 Kings*, Word Biblical Commentary (Waco: Word, 1985), 159.

A smile lit up the colonel's grimy, stubble-covered face. 'Father,' he said, 'the window is shattered, there's a hole in the wall, and the roof's gone. But it has a chain and it works.'[4] Amid ruin and racket, devastation and death, there was a welcome bit of consistency: the toilet still works.

That is the testimony of verses 1-3. Out of the thick of Athaliah's regime (ch. 11), with Davidic blood dripping from her hands and tyranny reigning on her throne, there is, nevertheless, a seven-year-old Davidide (11:21) who begins to reign. What seems only statistical is glorious, what appears dull is thrilling. It's as if the writer says, 'The covenant still works.'

Saints must grasp all this lest they become ingrates. Surely we recognize that many of God's gifts come wrapped in plain brown paper packages—and yet they are gifts for all that. Mundane mercies are mercies nonetheless and prosaic provisions are still provisions. If the Lord has granted us a civil order where we can 'lead a quiet and peaceable life, godly and respectful in every way' (1 Tim. 2:2), that is no less a boon for all its apparent ordinariness. Actually, there are no petty providences.

Kingdom prosperity, a disappointing record (vv. 4-16, 17-18)

My structural outline in the previous section suggests that the bulk of 2 Kings 12 divides into two contrasting but unequal sections, (1) refurbishing the temple (vv. 4-16), and (2) depleting the temple (vv. 17-18). We first need to get a handle on what is happening in the first of these sections. Hopefully we can do this without going into detail over every disputed point.

Let's get a structural map in front of us as we track what happens in verse 4-16:

```
The king's plan, vv. 4-5
            Priests' default, v. 6
The king's revised plan, v. 7
            Priests' acquiescence, v. 8
The new building fund, vv. 9-16
            Collection, vv. 9-10
            Distribution, vv. 11-12
            Explanation, vv. 13-16
```

---

[4]Cornelius Ryan, *A Bridge Too Far* (New York: Simon and Schuster, 1974), 435-36.

We do not know in what year of his reign Joash directed the
refurbishing of the temple, but his orders to the priests were:

> Collect all the money that is brought as sacred offerings to the
> temple of the LORD—the money collected in the census, the money
> received from personal vows and the money brought voluntarily
> to the temple (v. 4, NIV).

The king specifies three categories of pecuniary 'sacred
offerings': (1) money from the tax of a half-shekel per head due
from every adult of military age (Exod. 30:11-16); (2) money
from those who vowed service to the temple but who chose to
give the value of their services in cash (see Lev. 27:1-8); and (3)
funds that come in from voluntary gifts.[5] The priests were to
take these funds from their assessors or assistants (probably
not from their 'acquaintances', as some have it) and out of this
income the priests were to see that repairs were carried out on
the temple (v. 5).

As so frequently, however, things go slowly in church.
We've no way of knowing when Joash gave his initial order
for temple repair, but at least by his twenty-third year (i.e.,
of his reign, when he was thirty years old) the priests had
had no repairs done (v. 6). The king summoned Jehoiada &
Co. to ask why they had dilly-dallied with the temple repairs
(v. 7a). Kings don't have to wait for answers. At least Joash
didn't. He simply orders Plan B which bypassed the priests
(v. 7b). The priests knuckle under—they will collect no more
money and they relinquish any responsibility for repairing
temple damage (v. 8). One would love to have the tapes
from that royal-priestly interchange! The writer's summary
in cold print may not convey the warm atmosphere of the
meeting.

Are we to charge the priests with dishonesty? Probably not.
Had they been devious the priests (v. 9) and the high priest
(v. 10) would not have retained a role in collecting repair funds.
When the monies all came to the priests, it's likely that they

---

[5]This breakdown follows C. F. Keil, *The Books of the Kings*, Biblical Commentary
on the Old Testament (1876; reprint ed.,, Grand Rapids: Eerdmans, 1965), 366-67.
On Leviticus 27 see the helpful summary by Chris Wright, 'Leviticus,' *New Bible
Commentary*, 4th ed. (Leicester: Inter-Varsity, 1994), 156-57.

simply 'never got around to it'. The priests were probably more slow than slick.[6]

They installed the box marked 'Temple Repair Project' (v. 9). That helped. 'It permitted the giver to divide his offering for the temple from the offering for the priests, and to see for himself that it was at once put where it could not be applied otherwise than as he intended.'[7] Whenever the box began to fill the royal scribe and the high priest would supervise handling these funds—they either 'bagged it up' or 'melted it down' (depending on what verb one assumes one is translating) and counted it (v. 10). From there it went to the construction supervisors who passed it on to carpenters, masons, and stone-cutters; the funds also purchased materials, wood and stone (vv. 11-12). None of these funds went to make temple utensils— it was all for external repair (vv. 13-14). And no complicated accounting system was necessary because the supervisors were totally honest (v. 15). And, lest anyone be tempted to organize a priests' sympathy march, our writer assures us that they retained their customary income (v. 16). And, of course, the temple restoration is a tribute to the king's piety.

With a simple 'Then' it all falls apart (v. 17a).[8] After thirteen verses depicting the refurbishing of the temple, two verses report the emptying of the same. Hazael, king of Syria, threatens Jerusalem after he had knocked off Gath, and Joash prefers bribery to battle:

> And Joash king of Judah took all the sacred objects, which Jehoshaphat and Jehoram and Ahaziah, his fathers, kings of Judah,

---

[6]For discussion cf. K. C. W. F. Bähr, *The Books of the Kings*, Lange's Commentary on the Holy Scriptures, in vol. 3, *Samuel-Kings* (1868; reprint ed.,, Grand Rapids: Zondervan, 1960), 135-36.

[7]Bähr, 135.

[8]Robert Cohn nicely catches the change here from a literary perspective: 'With only the loosest of transitions ("then"), the writer turns from Jehoash's major achievement to his worst disaster when King Hazael of Aram reappears. Reported to have attacked Israel at the very end of the account of the reign of Jehu, now Hazael threatens Jerusalem. Just as after the story of the elimination of the house of Ahab and the Baalists from the North, Israel's borders are threatened, so too here. After the overthrow of Athaliah and the re-establishment of the Davidic monarchy, the writer widens his horizon to report Hazael's advance on Jerusalem. In both cases the information about Hazael's incursions is reserved until after equilibrium has been restored. The effect is to upset the newly achieved balance and throw Judah's future once more into doubt. Elisha's prediction of Hazael's bloody future (8:12) continues to bear fruit' (*2 Kings*, Berit Olam [Collegeville, MN: Liturgical, 2000], 83).

had consecrated, and his own sacred objects, and all the gold found in the treasuries of the house of Yahweh and in the king's house, and sent it to Hazael king of Syria—and he went up away from Jerusalem (v. 18).[9]

The writer is not commending Joash for a smart move but bemoaning the king's disappointing recourse. Forking over temple treasures for political or military security never gets positive marks in 1–2 Kings—whether under the regimes of Rehoboam (1 Kings 14:25-26), Asa (1 Kings 15:18-19), Joash (here), Ahaz (2 Kings 16:8-9), or Hezekiah (2 Kings 18:13-16). All these are but previews of what the Babylonians will do (2 Kings 24:13; 25:13-17). In light of all these temple depletions, Burke Long argues

> it is no light thing that Joash is pressed to such an extent that he takes everything from the store of holy objects. It is not a question of strict fiscal accounting, for monetary values are never mentioned and each of the various notices creates the impression of a near total depletion of the treasury. Rather, these riches are conventional signs of a king's piety and of his kingdom's favor with God. Despite Jehoash's provision for regular repairs to the temple, a grave question mark hangs over his reign.[10]

Second Kings and 2 Chronicles differ markedly in the way they treat the last years of Joash's reign. Chronicles (2 Chron. 24) tells of Joash's major policy shift after Jehoiada's death. Judah abandoned Yahweh's house, took up fertility worship and idols, and Joash was such an ingrate that he had Jehoiada's own son, Zechariah, executed for daring to prophesy against the new approach. Kings does not relate any of that. Not that the writer of Kings thinks all was hunky-dory in Joash's reign. He reports Joash's assassination (vv. 20-21)—he knew there was discontentment over Joash's

---

[9]For the record, 2 Kings 12:17-18 and 2 Chronicles 24:23-25 are probably not identical. The Aramaeans take the offensive in both cases, but in 2 Chronicles 24 they leave Joash sick/wounded from battle, the immediate prelude to his assassination. In 2 Kings 12 Hazael leads Syria/Aram (he is not mentioned in 2 Chronicles 24). Hazael walked out of history by 801 BC, while Joash lived until ca. 796. Hazael's threat here in 2 Kings 12 must have preceded the Aramaean assault of 2 Chronicles 24 by some years. See Eugene H. Merrill, *Kingdom of Priests* (Grand Rapids: Baker, 1987), 364-65.

[10]Burke O. Long, *2 Kings*, The Forms of the Old Testament Literature (Grand Rapids: Eerdmans, 1991), 160.

rule. But he does not choose to describe his blatant defection and vicious injustice. Chronicles emphasizes the *wickedness* of Joash; Kings highlights the *disappointment* of Joash. Two verses (vv. 17-18) undo it all.

Tony Horwitz drove down to that part of Alabama next the Florida panhandle to see Alberta Martin. Mrs. Martin was the only living Confederate widow. The reason she was still living (in the late 1990s) was because she had married an 85-year-old Confederate veteran when she was in her twenties. (After he died, she married his grandson!) Some months after Horwitz had visited Mrs. Martin he noticed her picture in *USA Today,* along with an article. Then the Sons of Confederate Veterans flew her and her son up to Richmond. She was called 'a living link to the Confederacy'. The United Daughters of the Confederacy published a profile of Mrs. Martin in its magazine and related some of the heroics of her husband, William Jasper Martin. No sources were given to back up these claims, but he was wounded in a bloody battle near Richmond and had fought until the end, surrendering with Lee at Appomattox. But Horwitz went to the National Archives and found that William Martin was drafted in May of 1864, sent to Richmond, got measles, was released on a two-month furlough, went AWOL, and never went back. William's name appeared beside the word 'deserter' on his company's muster sheet for the rest of the war.[11] Somehow it takes all the punch out of the fanfare and the speeches and the articles. Oldest living Confederate widow—of a deserter. Disappointment can fall with a thud.

It looks as if God's providence has been frustrated by human failure. Joash's story began on such a thrilling note, that marvelous and gutsy preservation of the Davidic line in 11:1-3; it featured a persevering and successful renovation of Yahweh's house (12:4-16); and now ends in disappointment (12:17-18) and involuntary death (12:20-21). Joash's reign is a yellow flashing light of warning to us commoners. We may be orthodox believers in our profession but unless we are kept by God's power what will prevent our falling away? Again, the failure of Joash should only lift our eyes to the Descendant of David who does not disappoint. There is a built-in defect in all

[11] Tony Horwitz, *Confederates in the Attic* (New York: Vintage Books, 1998), 336-51.

merely human leadership (and recognizing this will save you from much anger and gnashing of teeth in the church). But the failure and folly of men should only make us crave and enjoy the fullness and faithfulness of Jesus all the more.

18

Grace and Grave Notes
(2 Kings 13)

Eric Clark, in his book on the advertising industry, tells of a Diet Coke commercial shot at Radio City Music Hall that reportedly cost one and a half million dollars. For a soft drink commercial! I'd wager that when most of us see such a commercial we rarely think about what's behind it. That is the way we sometimes read Kings as well. Because verse 1 of this chapter is less than scintillating we never stir to ask what's behind it. 'In the twenty-third year of Joash son of Ahaziah, king of Judah, Jehoahaz son of Jehu reigned over Israel in Samaria for seventeen years.' It seems like another dry-as-dust formula, nothing as racy as Diet Coke can produce. But we should stub our literary toe over 'Jehoahaz son of Jehu', for it tells us what's behind this lead-in verse. It is meant to conjure up 10:30 in our minds—Yahweh's promise to Jehu that because he had carried out Yahweh's extermination program on Ahab's dynasty, Jehu himself would have a dynasty for four generations. Here is the first leg of fulfillment—Jehoahaz follows Jehu as king of Israel. A dry formula but solid faithfulness. The underlying faithfulness of God is the stitching that holds Israel's history together during these days.[1]

---

[1] We must not, however, forget that verse 3b also reflects Yahweh's faithfulness to his word in 8:12!

Our chapter covers the reigns of Jehoahaz and Jehoash,[2] or approximately from 814 to 781 BC,[3] and fits well with what we know of Assyria and Syria during this period. Generally, all depended on whether Syria (Aram) had Assyria on its military plate. When Assyria was occupied elsewhere Syria distressed Israel, but when Assyria distressed Syria, Israel enjoyed relief. Since my focus is the text of 2 Kings 13 I refer the reader to other works for the historical backdrop.[4]

Before the exposition we should get a structural sketch under our belts so we are aware of how the chapter develops:

Development of 2 Kings 13

Jehoahaz, vv. 1-9
  Formulas, vv. 1-2
    Theology, vv. 3-7
  Formulas, vv. 8-9

Jehoash, vv. 10ff.
  Historical summary, vv. 10-13
  Crucial moment, vv. 14-19

  Resurrection sampler, vv. 20-21
  Covenant theology, vv. 22-23
  Inerrant word, vv. 24-25

The pity that should change us (vv. 1-9)

In the regnal (vv. 1-2) and summary (vv. 8-9) formulas we must take note that Jehoahaz was a devotee of the cult of Jeroboam

---

[2]Like his same-named counterpart in Judah this king is sometimes called Jehoash and sometimes Joash in the Hebrew text. I always use Jehoash when referring to this northern king.

[3]The reader will note a chronological conundrum when comparing verses 1 and 10. However, there is not a rub if one posits a two-year co-regency of Jehoash with Jehoahaz. In this book I do not want to bury myself—or you—in chronological difficulties. Permit me again to urge a careful reading of Leslie McFall's important article, 'Has the chronology of the Hebrew kings been finally settled?,' *Themelios* 17/1 (Oct/Nov 1991): 6-11.

[4]One may find succinct and lucid summaries in John Bright, *A History of Israel*, 3rd ed. (Philadelphia: Westminster, 1981), 253-57, and in M. Cogan and H. Tadmor, *II Kings*, Anchor Bible (Garden City, NY: Doubleday, 1988), 151-52.

(v. 2). This is no surprise. We are used to hearing it by now. His was a trenchant commitment—'he did not turn from it' (v. 2b).

The surprise comes in verses 3-7, a theological segment placed amidst the usual formulas.[5] We are not surprised that Yahweh's wrath ignites against Israel and that he gives them into the power of Hazael and Ben-hadad continually (v. 3). But we are surprised that 'Jehoahaz pleaded with Yahweh' (v. 4a). Naturally we are ready to shoot our Proverbs 28:9 missile at this Jeroboamist. Before we can launch it, however, we meet a more surprising surprise: 'Yahweh listened to him' (v. 4b). To a calf worshiper. Why on earth would Yahweh do that? 'For he saw the oppression of Israel—how the king of Syria oppressed them' (v. 4c). The same noun and verb (root = *lāḥaṣ*) appear in Yahweh's words in Exodus 3:9: 'And what's more I have seen the oppression with which the Egyptians keep on oppressing them.' The writer of Kings is saying that Yahweh is still the same exodus God, who sees not only Egyptians but Syrians squeezing the life out of his people, his apostasizing people. Our writer implies that sometimes Yahweh's pity over the distress of his people trumps the wickedness of the one seeking him for relief.

How did Yahweh answer Jehoahaz? He 'gave Israel a savior, and they went out from under the hand of Syria, and the sons of Israel lived in their tents as before' (v. 5). Israel enjoyed deliverance and a new time of security. But everyone wonders who the 'savior' is. Some (Alfred Hoerth, Walter Kaiser) think it is the Assyrian Adad-nirari III, who would 'save' by neutralizing Syria. Others think Elisha (John Gray, Paul House, T. R. Hobbs), while some hold the subsequent kings, Jehoash and Jeroboam II, carried out this saving work (C. F. Keil, probably Cogan and Tadmor).[6] I vote for the last option, partly because the

[5]One can set out the pattern of vv. 3-7 this way:

Scourge of Yahweh and Syria, v. 3
    Plea, v. 4
        Relief / Deliverance, v. 5
    Ingratitude, v. 6
Scourge of Syria, v. 7

[6]Cogan and Tadmor, *II Kings*, 143, have a concise listing of the diverse views. See Claus Schedl (*History of the Old Testament*, 5 vols. [Staten Island: Alba House, 1972], 4:133-37) for a detailed argument for Adad-nirari III as 'savior'.

root *yāša'* , to save, occurs both in connection with Jehoash in
verse 17 (arrow of 'salvation'/victory) and with Jeroboam II in
14:27 ('saved'). Actually, it doesn't much matter. What matters
is that Yahweh gave Israel a savior, not the precise identity of
the savior. And how Israel needed one! After Hazael and Ben-
hadad III finished with Israel they left Jehoahaz with a mere
rump army (v. 7a); they had pretty much knocked the sand
out of Israel (v. 7b).

However, we must pay close attention to verse 6: 'Only they
did not turn from the sins of the house of Jeroboam which
he made Israel to sin; they walked in them [lit., he walked in
it]—moreover, the Asherah stood in Samaria.' In the wake of
Yahweh's unguessable compassion (vv. 4-5) we meet Israel's
trenchant ingratitude (v. 6). The warmth of God's pity did not
soften the hardness of their infidelity. There was no 'memory
carryover' that claimed and won their gratitude.

There was once a poor negress on the Island of Mauritius
in the Indian Ocean. She had worked hard and saved long and
had finally amassed enough money to purchase the freedom
of her daughter, a slave like herself, from the man who owned
them both. She was happy to remain a slave herself simply
for the joy of seeing her daughter walking around free—with
shoes on her feet, the badge of freedom. No slave was allowed
to wear shoes. Not long after the transaction had occurred the
mother came into a room where her daughter was sitting. In
her usual affectionate way she sat down beside her daughter as
she had always done. In a moment or two, the daughter turned
on her in a rage and exclaimed, 'How dare you sit down in my
presence? Do you not know that I am a free woman, and you
are a slave? Rise instantly, and leave the room!'[7]

That is the way it was with Israel. Mercy does not melt them.
'Only they did not turn from the sins of the house of Jeroboam.'
How very contemporary. Israel wants relief from trouble not
relationship with God; she craves therapy not transformation.

The promise that should stir us (vv. 10-19)
We will come back to verses 10-13, but let's begin with
verses 14-19, which focus on Elisha. 'Now Elisha was sick

[7]John Whitecross, *The Shorter Catechism Illustrated from Christian Biography and History* (1828; reprint ed.,, London: Banner of Truth, 1968), 102.

with the sickness with which he would die' (v. 14a).[8] King
Jehoash comes to visit the ailing prophet, weeps over his
coming departure, and laments—as Elisha had done over Elijah
(2:12)—'My father, my father, the chariotry of Israel and its
horsemen' (v. 14b). Who knows whether Jehoash was sincere
or condescending? In any case, his words suggest that with
Elisha's death Israel will be left undefended, that the presence
of the prophet and the ministry of his word had been a shield
to the nation. One only need go back to 6:8-23 to see a sample
of this.

Elisha seeks to encourage the king. He directs him to lay
hold of bow and arrows (v. 15). Note how the prophet is in
total control throughout the episode: he gives orders, the king
obeys. What follows is an acted oracle. Elisha directs Jehoash to
draw the bow; Elisha places his hand on the king's; they shoot
the arrow out an east window (vv. 16-17a). Elisha interprets
the action: 'An arrow of victory for the LORD! An arrow of
victory over Aram! You shall rout Aram completely at Aphek'
(v. 17b, NJPS). The arrow signified the victory (lit., salvation)
Yahweh would give Israel over Syria (Aram).[9] Now that Jehoash
knows what the arrow means Elisha seeks to see how much
it means to him. Will the king appropriate this word with
gusto? The prophet orders him to take the arrows and 'strike
the ground', apparently shooting through the window into
the ground (v. 18a). Jehoash strikes three times and stops (v.
18b).[10] Elisha is furious with him—he should have shot five or
six times. Does he want to eliminate Syria or not (v. 19)? Elisha
gives Jehoash a blank check of the word of God, and the king
says, 'Thank you, I'll only cash half of it.'

Elisha seems to have qualified the promise because of the
tepid royal response. In verse 17 he told Jehoash that he would

---

[8]One is tempted to ask where the name-it-and-claim-it theologians were when Elisha
needed them. Perhaps they could have convinced him that it is never the Lord's will that
any of his children be sick and could have instructed him in the art of making a positive
confession in order to enjoy continuing health unclouded by death.

[9]On the 'acted oracle', especially in this episode, see Alec Motyer's helpful
explanation in his *Look to the Rock* (Leicester: Inter-Varsity, 1996), 104-05.

[10]'The narrator could have said that he "smote three times" if the reporting of a mere
quantity was at issue; but by adding the phrase, "and he stopped," the narrator calls
attention to the *cessation* of the striking as much as to the *amount* of striking' (James
Kirk Mead, *"Elisha Will Kill?": The Deuteronomistic Rhetoric of Life and Death in the
Theology of the Elisha Narratives* [Ann Arbor: University Microfilms, 1999], 86).

'completely destroy' (NIV) the Syrians at Aphek. However, in verse 19, because of the king's less than 'faith-full' response, Syria would not be 'completely destroyed'.

Now let us come back and look at the literary packaging of this text. It seems strange that in verses 10-13 we find the total summary of Jehoash's reign: the regnal formula (v. 10), religious evaluation (v. 11), bibliographic reference (v. 12), and obituary notice (v. 13). In four verses Jehoash, from beginning to end, is off the page. Then, after we have buried him, we read of the arrow episode between Elisha and Jehoash in verses 14-19. What is happening?

It's a lot like the way I used to eat cake when I was a child. Naturally, the icing was the best part of it. Because of that undisputed fact I would regularly and carefully cut the icing off the top of the cake and set it aside. Then I would eat the mere cake part of the cake first, after which, having saved the best till last, I would devour the icing. That is the way our writer treats Jehoash. Not much of vital importance to his reign—he can be disposed of in nothing but formulas in four verses. Sixteen years in four verses.[11] But he saves the 'best'—or important—part till last: the writer selects one episode from Jehoash's reign as of supreme moment. He will focus on that. That's what we meet in verses 14-19.

It is important, then, to see how verses 10-13 and verses 14-19 fit together. Verses 10-13 summarize Jehoash's whole reign, but verses 14-19 capture his most crucial moment—standing before the word of Yahweh. Hence this latter vignette gets more space than the king's whole 'bio' in verses 10-13. The text makes a value judgment: how a man responds to Yahweh's word is more significant than all the achievements and honors of a lifetime.

Now in Elisha's view—and his is the only view that counts here—Jehoash's response to Yahweh's word was obviously inadequate. He had Yahweh's promise (v. 17) and he should have grasped it with both hands. But Jehoash was content to be a three-victories man. Let us not destroy but only contain

---

[11]In the history of my own country Franklin Delano Roosevelt served twelve years as president—twelve years that are the focus of hefty tomes. No four-verse treatments. Perhaps this analogy gives one a feel for Jehoash's sixteen year-four verse treatment in Kings.

Syria.[12] That was enough for him. The promise of God did not stir him enough.

This can be the case when the gospel and its benefits are pressed on someone. Dr. John White was dealing with an East Indian whom the police had picked up for making obscene phone calls. Asked about the phone calls, the man said that the 'spirits make me do it'. What spirits? Well, there were three of them—had them ever since his father took him to see some holy man when he was a child. They talked to him and were kind to him, he said. Kept him from being lonely at night when he had no woman. Dr. White said, 'I can get rid of them for you.' His face clouded, he drew back from the table. 'No. No. I don't want you to do that.' White assured him the spirits would eventually destroy him. Finally, the man said, 'I know you can do it, but I don't want you to. You have the power of God in you. I can feel it. But you must not take away my spirits.' When the patient left White soon followed to tell him of 'God's concern for him and of the mercy of a loving Christ who could impart all the consolation he needed'. He thanked me, White says, 'with tears in his eyes but still shook his head.'[13] He had the promise of freedom and consolation but it did not stir him—enough. It could bring tears but not consent.

But Christian believers know something of this half-heartedness. We have the assurance, 'For sin will not lord it over you, for you are not under law but under grace' (Rom. 6:14). Our union with Christ has brought about regime change and we are now under the power of grace which will give us substantial liberty from sin (as a power). But some of us, using a degree of right theology, make our Jehoash response. We have become convinced of 'total depravity', and that that is our condition, and that we are so bound by certain habits, inabilities, behaviors, and reactions, that even though we claim to be Christ's there is no hope of change or transformation. Grace may as well be a mere word, the Holy Spirit a theory, and the gospel only propaganda for all we will expect from it. Yes, we have the promise but we

<hr>

[12]We do not know why Jehoash didn't take fire here. It may be that Jehoash did not want to annihilate Syria completely since that 'would mean that there would no longer be a buffer state between him and the menace of Assyria' (H. L. Ellison, *The Prophets of Israel* [Grand Rapids: Eerdmans, 1969], 54).

[13]John White, *The Masks of Melancholy* (Downers Grove: InterVarsity, 1982), 38-39.

cannot expect too much from it. Jehoash enjoys an afterlife, we might say, under different guises.

The provisions that will haunt us (vv. 20-25)
The remainder of the chapter specifies three provisions Yahweh gives Israel, and we will deal with each in turn.

1. Hope (vv. 20-21)

> (20) Now Elisha died and they buried him; and Moabite raiders would come into the land, at the coming of the year. (21) Now it happened that they were in the process of burying a man, and suddenly they saw the raiders! So they chucked the man into Elisha's grave, and the man went and touched the bones of Elisha and came to life and stood up on his feet![14]

This incident seems so bizarre to some that they simply can't stomach it. Raymond Calkins, for example, complains:

> The story recounted in vs. 21 is without parallel in Scripture. Nowhere else do we find even a hint of magic power in the bones of the dead. It is a relic of superstitious belief which somehow crept into the tradition concerning Elisha. But it is at least token of our awareness that in death we have dealings with eternity. To be quickened by contact with the living soul of a holy man, though he were dead, is one thing. For a man to come to life because his dead body touched the bones of a saint is something which finds no warrant elsewhere in what we are taught in the Bible of the ways of God.[15]

So, for some, this clip reeks of magic and relics.

But one should suppose the writer (or even a halfway intelligent editor) had a reason for placing this incident at this point. What might it be? Fretheim believes one gets the proper clue from verse 23. In the burial incident the fellows 'throw' (my translation used the colloquial 'chucked') the body into Elisha's grave (v. 21). Now the same verb occurs in verse 23—Yahweh

---

[14]There are a couple of uncertainties in the text but they do not affect interpretation. By the way, Elisha's grave was likely a cave with a stone over it, not an under-the-soil type.

[15]Raymond Calkins, "II Kings: Exposition," *The Interpreter's Bible*, 12 vols. (New York: Abingdon, 1954), 3:258. Joseph Hammond, long ago in BC (= Before Calkins) time, dealt with the so-called relic problem (*II Kings*, The Pulpit Commentary [London: Funk & Wagnalls, n.d.], 268-69).

'has not thrown [lit.] them [Israel] from his presence' (see also 17:20 and 24:20). Assuming that this latter refers to the exile the analogy is made: As the men threw the body into Elisha's tomb and there was new life, so whenever God throws Israel into exile there will still be hope. The graveside incident, then, is something of a 'symbolic narrative giving a hopeful testimony regarding Israel's future life'.[16]

This may be so, but I think the argument based on the catch-word 'throw' (Heb., *šālak*) is a stretch, because the verb in verse 23 is used with the negative. The emphasis in verse 23 is not that the exile is coming but that it has not yet come. I don't deny a possible corpse–Israel parallel but playing around with *šālak* here doesn't really support it.

Let's back off a bit and come at verses 20-21 again. We admit, on first glance, that these verses are strange and unexpected. But perhaps they should not be. When Elijah was taken from the scene he went with quite a splash (2 Kings 2:11-12), so why would we not expect something of similar moment at Elisha's passing? Something phenomenal seems eminently appropriate. Surely we don't expect someone of Elisha's stature simply to rot away quietly!

And it may be that we should think of verses 20-21 in close connection with verses 14-19. It seems as if these two sections may depict Elisha's legacy to Israel, for through Elisha, the servant of the word, she receives both deliverance (vv. 14-19) and life (vv. 20-21), or, both victory and vitality. Even when the prophet is about to die, or already dead, these gifts are still available to Israel. So I think Keil is right about verses 20-21: the restoration of the dead man was only 'brought about by contact with the bones of the dead prophet, because God desired thereby to show to His people that the divine energy, which had been active in Elisha had not, by his death, disappeared from Israel.'[17] And so Israel still has hope. I think Roger Ellsworth has got it right:

[16]Terence E. Fretheim, *First and Second Kings*, Westminster Bible Companion (Louisville: John Knox, 1999), 184. Fretheim implies the story may not be historically true but is meaningful in this context. Iain Provan takes a similar view without sitting as lightly on the historicity of verses 20-21 (*1 and 2 Kings*, New International Bible Commentary [Peabody, MA: Hendrickson, 1995], 230).

[17]As cited in K. C. W. F. Bähr, *The Books of the Kings*, Lange's Commentary on the Holy Scriptures, in vol. 3, *Samuel-Kings* (1868; reprint ed.,, Grand Rapids: Zondervan, 1960), 144. Bähr's citation is from the 1845 edition of Keil's commentary; this point is not found in the 1876 edition available in reprint.

We must not dismiss this account. It shows that the Word of God which Elisha had so faithfully borne was still mighty and powerful even though the prophet himself had died. What comfort there was here for the captives! They must often have thought their nation was as good as dead, but because of the powerful Word of God their nation would live again.[18]

So there is a word of hope here for Israel—or for what was left of Judah after 2 Kings 24–25.

But could the writer also have individual hope in view? James Mead makes some fascinating literary observations about our textual clip:

> [A]gainst the background of Moabite raids and the sadness of death, Elisha's corpse is seen as bringing about life, and this, not for an entire nation (where the many might be regarded as more important than one insignificant individual), but for someone nobody outside the story knows. Of course, the reader should not be surprised that Elisha's final deed helped an anonymous person, since almost all of the people blessed by Elisha are left anonymous (Naaman is the lone exception, and he is an Aramaean!).[19]

Perhaps then this aborted funeral is intended to underscore an individual benefit, typical of much of Elisha's ministry, while verses 14-19 highlight a national benefit. Ray Dillard seemed to take this view:

> There is no real question about what the author of the story intended, however. [At least some are not puzzled by this text!] The man whose corpse was tossed into Elisha's tomb was not comatose, drunk, or in a deep sleep—he was dead. Keep in mind the nature of miracle in the Bible: miracle is redemptive, and it points forward to the restoration of all things. In this little story, we have a glimpse of what redemption will ultimately mean—victory over death and restoration to life. It is a tiny vignette of a day when death itself will be destroyed, a glimpse of a city in which there 'will be no more death or mourning' (Rev. 21:4).

> It is fitting that the last two stories pertaining to Elisha report his role in the destruction of enemies—both the great national enemy

---

[18]Roger Ellsworth, *Apostasy, Destruction and Hope* (Darlington: Evangelical Press, 2002), 158.

[19]James Kirk Mead, *"Elisha Will Kill?,"* 93.

of the time, Aram (2 Kings 13:10-19), and the greatest personal enemy, death (vv. 20-21). The defeat of that great national enemy was a foretaste of the nation's renewal during the reign of Jeroboam II (14:25). Similarly, the victory over death was a foretaste of a yet greater victory over the grave.[20]

One hears then a similar testimony at the ends of both Elijah and Elisha's prophetic careers. In 2 Kings 2 Elijah does not die but is taken up by a storm-wind heavenward (2:11). That may not seem like much but it has tremendous hint-value. It says that though death holds sway it does not hold sway absolutely. God makes an exception in Elijah's case. Then at the end of Elisha's history we have a slice of the same testimony. But lest we think Yahweh's power over death is only for revered prophets he here rebukes death for Mr. Anonymous Joe-Schmoe-Israelite (13:20-21). It's as if the last word from both Elijah and Elisha is: Don't think death has dominion over you.[21]

One more matter. You should remember that the Old Testament has no corner on bizarre episodes. The New Testament quite keeps pace with its 'parallel' in Matthew 27:51b-53:

> (51b) And the earth shook, and the rocks were split, (52) and the tombs were opened; and many bodies of the saints who had fallen asleep were raised; (53) and when they came out of the tombs after his resurrection, they entered the holy city and appeared to many.

Matthew places this right after he reports Jesus' death (v. 50). Following J. W. Wenham we place a stop after 'opened'.[22] Many bodies of dead believers were raised (v. 52b) and verse 53 refers to this when it says they 'came out of the tombs' and that this occurred 'after his resurrection'. So their 'resurrection' didn't occur until after Jesus' resurrection, but the tombs were opened at Jesus' death. Naturally this raises a host of unanswered questions. I once heard a New Testament scholar say he didn't know what to do with this passage. But, if it is strange to us,

---

[20]Raymond B. Dillard, *Faith in the Face of Apostasy* (Phillipsburg, NJ: Presbyterian & Reformed, 1999), 152.

[21]I think then that verses 20-21 can be legitimately taken as encouraging both corporate and individual hope.

[22]Cf. D. A. Carson, 'Matthew,' *The Expositor's Bible Commentary*, 12 vols. (Grand Rapids: Zondervan, 1984), 8:581-82.

it is clear what Matthew intends. He wants us to understand that Jesus in his death has conquered death, that Jesus' death gives us life. Jesus died and tombs were opened.

These are strange incidents — Elisha's life-giving bones (2 Kings 13) and Jesus' life-giving cross (Matthew 27). But the bizarre and the true are often easy bedfellows. For example, I think of the Iranian hunter Ali, who tried to catch a snake alive by pressing the butt of his gun behind its head. The snake coiled around the butt of Ali's gun, pulled the trigger, and shot him in the head.[23] Snakes don't usually shoot men. It's bizarre but has been authenticated. So…'Why is it thought incredible by any of you that God raises the dead?' (Acts 26:8).

2. Covenant (vv. 22-23)

Verses 22-25 flip us back to the time of Jehoahaz and rather parallel verses 3-7. They remind us of Hazael's oppression of Israel under Jehoahaz (v. 22) and then tell us why there was still an Israel:

> Now Yahweh showed grace to them, had compassion on them, and turned to them on account of his covenant with Abraham, Isaac, and Jacob; and he was not willing to destroy them and he has not thrown them from his presence until now (v. 23).

That is a rather literal translation. The 'until now' at the end is tricky. Some take it to carry an ominous ring, i.e., Yahweh did not cast Israel out up to this point, but since then he has.[24] But this view, natural as it seems, does not mesh with the usage of the phrase elsewhere. 'Until now' ('ad-'attāh) occurs nine times in the Old Testament by my count.[25] In all eight occurrences outside of 2 Kings 13:23 the phrase always connotes 'to this point' or 'up to the point' and never packs the innuendo 'But later…' The phrase always brings us up to the current moment and cuts it off there.

Others claim that since verses 22ff. are the narrator's explanation, the 'until now' must refer to the writer's own time

---

[23]Wendy Northcutt, *The Darwin Awards* (New York: Plume, 2000), 36.
[24]Richard D. Nelson, *First and Second Kings*, Interpretation (Louisville: John Knox, 1987), 217.
[25]The curious may check Mandelkern's *Concordantiae*, 937-39. The texts are (English verse divisions): Gen. 32:4; 46:34; Exod. 9:18; Deut. 12:9; 2 Sam. 19:7; 2 Kings 8:6; 13:23; Ezek. 4:14; and Ruth 2:7.

in the exilic or post-exilic period, and that he is saying that Yahweh had not cast Israel out even then.[26] But I don't think that will wash either. All other instances of 'until now' refer to the moment described in the immediate context. One would expect the same here. In fact the context anchors this 'now' in the 'days of Jehoahaz' (v. 22) and after Hazael's death (v. 24). Hence I would translate, 'he has not cast them out from his presence up to this point'—referring to the time of Jehoahaz and Jehoash. NJPS reflects this understanding: 'He still did not cast them out from His presence.'

But why not? Why this grace, this compassion, to these ingrates of the northern kingdom? 'Because of his covenant with Abraham, Isaac, and Jacob.'

Yahweh had promised Abraham to give his descendants a home. He had wrapped up that promise in a covenant to make Abraham more sure of it (Gen. 15:18). He had reaffirmed the same to Isaac and Jacob (Gen. 26:3-4; 28:13). But this northern kingdom had begun apostasizing from day one (1 Kings 12), and, whether at any time the apostasy of choice was the polite form of Jeroboam or the gross form of Ahab, what Leviticus 26:25 calls 'the vengeance for the covenant' was long overdue. By this time Israel should have been long banished from her land (Lev. 26:33; Deut. 28:36-37, 64-68). But they're not. 'Because of the covenant.' You see, covenant combines both the firmness of promise and the warmth of grace. To be sure, there is such a thing as vengeance for the covenant. But behind the covenant stands the Giver of the covenant, and 'He loves graciousness' (Micah 7:18, NJPS). So when hope should be gone, it's not.

Barbara Tuchman has described the extravagant opulence of Leo X's papal regime in Rome (1513-21). An unforgettable banquet given by the plutocrat Agostino Chigi was typical of the time. Gold dishes were used to serve parrots' tongues and fish brought from Byzantium. After these gold plates were used, they were tossed out the window into the Tiber! Disposable gold plates? Not quite. There was a net below the water's surface for retrieving the vagrant dinnerware.[27] Now our writer wants to tell us that is what covenant is like. It looks like all

[26]Provan, *1 and 2 Kings*, 229-30; Fretheim, *First and Second Kings*, 184.
[27]Barbara W. Tuchman, *The March of Folly* (New York: Alfred A. Knopf, 1984), 106.

is lost but Yahweh's net is in place. This, however, is call for gratitude not indifference, for repentance not presumption.[28]

3. Truth (vv. 24-25)

Hazael obliges and dies; Ben-hadad, his son, follows him on Syria's throne (v. 24). Then 'Jehoash, son of Jehoahaz, took again the cities from the hand of Ben-hadad, son of Hazael, which he had taken from the hand of Jehoahaz his father in battle; three times Jehoash struck him down, and he recovered the cities of Israel' (v. 25). So the acted prophecy of verses 17-18 comes true. Elisha assured Jehoash he had the 'arrow of victory over Syria' (v. 17) and Jehoash had shot three times and stopped (v. 18). An angry prophet then declared the king would have but three victories over Syria (v. 19). And here they are (v. 25). Yahweh has been true to his word for the umpteenth time. Never mind that Jehoash is a calf-worshiping Jeroboam clone (v. 11) or that he is less than enthusiastic over Yahweh's promises (v. 18). In spite of the recipient Yahweh will deliver the goods promised (v. 25). In the middle of Israel's slide to ruin she still has a God who speaks truth to her.

If Jehoash was lukewarm toward Yahweh's truth, one wonders if contemporary believers are not as well. Perhaps we've become so used to truth that we don't prize it—unless we are without it. A year or so ago I went into a department store to purchase some trousers. The ones I selected were inexpensive, perma-press types for every day wear. I found a gray pair that carried my waist and inseam size on the label. To be sure that pair fit I ambled to the fitting room with them and tried them on. They were fine. I went back to the rack and selected a khaki and a navy pair as well with the same waist-inseam numbers on the labels. However, when I later tried to wear these two additional pairs I discovered they were an inch or more smaller in the waist than the gray pilot pair. I stood there in my study, strangling my stomach and trying to button and zip those pants. (Of course, I shan't tell you where I purchased them because I wouldn't want you to think ill of Sears-Roebuck.) Within my own trouser world I felt betrayed.

---

[28]Even when Israel would be 'thrown out' of the land, the covenant 'net' is still in place (Lev. 26:44-45) and repentance is still required (Lev. 26:40-42).

Those labels on all three pairs were the same but two of them were mislabeled, or, to be truthful, they lied. One never gives much thought about how marvelous truth is until one doesn't have it. And here is a kingdom that hasn't had one lick of royal faithfulness in some 135 years—and yet Yahweh still deals with them in his truth.

Now abide hope, covenant, and truth, these three. These are the provisions that will haunt Israel—or any of God's professing people. For as Israel plunges toward ruin Yahweh is not depriving or impoverishing her. In the midst of her infidelity he places hope, covenant, and truth. And so they—and we, if we are like her—will go to judgment weighted down with mercies.

19

A Little Bit of October
(2 Kings 14)

Currently I am living in what we call the 'deep south' of the United States. In winter it has a very temperate climate, but summers are torrid—high humidity and high temperatures. Before the advent of air conditioning I am sure people didn't die but melted. But October is different, absolutely lovely. Usually warm but no longer tropical, yet not with the chilly edge that I recall of Octobers in my native Pennsylvania. In Mississippi, October is perfect—relatively speaking, of course.

The sad thing about October is that it doesn't last. It tends to be the last loveliness before the browns and grays of winter. But while it's October, well, it's delightful. Now kingdoms and nations can go through an 'October' phase, when a bustling economy, national security, military success, and growing profits all seem to conspire to meet together and crown a nation's existence. Life could hardly be better (for some). And in 2 Kings 14 Israel in particular is living in her October.

In terms of content the chapter covers the reigns of Amaziah of Judah (vv. 1-22) and Jeroboam II of Israel (vv. 23-29). They are a study in contrast: the disintegration of Amaziah (a reasonably good start, followed by unteachable arrogance, humiliating defeat, and bloody conspiracy) is followed by the success of Jeroboam, who gives Israel her 'October'. Amaziah only gets verses 1-7 and 18-22 strictly to himself. He actually stands in the shadow of Jehoash of Israel in verses 8-14—and Jehoash's obituary appears a second time in verses 15-16/17 (cf. 13:12-13). When the Jeroboam section (vv. 23-29) is added, it looks like the writer's primary interest is still the northern kingdom.[1] Let's move to the theological concerns of the chapter.

Yahweh's assessment of his servants can easily be disregarded (vv. 1-4)

We focus on verses 3-4 in particular:

> And he did what was right in Yahweh's eyes only not like David his father; he acted in line with all Joash his father had done. Only they did not take away the high places; the people kept sacrificing and making offerings at the high places.[2]

It is remarkable how easily we as readers can 'accept' this estimate of Amaziah. We know, of course, from reading Kings so far that David is the standard for kings (1 Kings 3:3, 14; 9:4; 11:4, 6, 33, 38; 14:8; 15:11; cf. 2 Kings 16:2; 18:3; 22:2). And Amaziah only comes up to a Joash-standard, not a David-standard. But it may be the next point where we especially tend to yawn: under Amaziah they didn't take away the high places. We've heard this before (1 Kings 15:14; 22:43; 2 Kings 12:3) — Asa, Jehoshaphat, and Joash received generally favorable ratings and yet 'the high places were not taken away'.[3] We read this exception repeatedly and become deadened to it. (Who says reading Scripture isn't perilous?) But that should not be the effect. Rather, as here in Amaziah's case, we should note how Yahweh never fails to mark every negligence shy of full devotion to himself. After three or four times we respond with, 'Well, that's about all you can expect from the kings of Judah.' But that is not Yahweh's attitude. He is after total devotion; he's looking for another David; he's satisfied with nothing less.

Nor are we when our heads are screwed on right. A wife may say that her husband is an excellent provider but a non-existent companion. We usually would not understand her to imply that she is satisfied with that state of affairs — or that

---

[1]See T. R. Hobbs, *2 Kings*, Word Biblical Commentary (Waco: Word, 1985), 177.
[2]On the high places, cf. the helpful article by W. Boyd Barrick in ABD, 3:196-200.
[3]Worship of Yahweh could occur in 'high places' (1 Sam. 9:11-13; 1 Kings 3:2-4), but that did not seem to be the rule during the divided kingdom period (see 1 Kings 14:22-24 for Judah).

she felt the abundance he supplied on the one hand somehow covered the ache on the other. So with Amaziah. Why does righteousness have to be so restrained? Why must godliness be so tame? Doesn't the text imply that *mediocre orthodoxy is not covenantal obedience?*

In the 1880s a former Federal soldier rode the train into Goldsboro, North Carolina. He asked around for any former Confederate soldiers, and one older man came forward and agreed to take him to the scene of the December 1862 battle. Old enemies became new friends that afternoon as they rode over the battlefield. At last the Confederate said he had a question that had been bugging him for more than twenty years. He wanted to know why, after the Federals had set fire to the railroad bridge, General Foster had turned them round and marched away from the field of battle. The Yankee explained, 'We were entirely out of ammunition. We did not have a round to a man and all of us expected capture.' So, if the Confederates had given pursuit, had harassed the Federal flanks, they would have discovered this fact and have bagged 10,000 prisoners.[4] But they didn't. The Confederates had fought well, and they were content to watch the Feds walk away. Like Amaziah perhaps. It's enough to be like Joash. Why get exercised over high places? Why let righteousness get your blood up?

I suppose there is an analogous situation for some of us. We might call ourselves 'evangelicals' and yet there is little zeal after personal piety, little effort to teach and indoctrinate our families, not much passion to bear personal or public witness—or to raise our voice against unbelief in our church denomination. We're evangelical—no need to go bonkers over it. Maybe it's the Amaziah complex: we don't see why righteousness must be rigorous or godliness aggressive.

Yahweh's judgments may cast their shadows beforehand (vv. 5-14)

Amaziah's impressive record goes on. He wiped out the assassins of his father but did so with the restraint the law in Deuteronomy (24:16) requires (vv. 5-6). He pulled off a smashing victory in Edom, inflicting many casualties and

---

[4]Clint Johnson, *Civil War Blunders* (Winston-Salem: John F. Blair, 1997), 122-23.

conquering a strategic site (v. 7).[5] Then comes the 'Then...' (v. 8).
'Then Amaziah sent messengers to Jehoash son of Jehoahaz
son of Jehu king of Israel, saying, "Let's look each other in
the face"' (v. 8). Contemporary psychologists would call this
idiom 'confrontational'. Amaziah is not asking for a summit
but wants to stir up hostilities.[6] This is clear from the second
occurrence of the expression in verse 11 ('they looked each other
in the face') and from the way Jehoash understood Amaziah
in verses 9-10.

Jehoash tried to paint Amaziah a picture to show him how
stupid his saber-rattling was. In Jehoash's little fable there
appear a brier, a cedar, and a wild beast (v. 9) — they are each 'in
Lebanon'. The brier demands the cedar's daughter as a wife for
his son — and a wild beast passes by and tramples the brier. It's as
if Jehoash says, 'Did you hear that "squish," Amaziah, when the
beast walked over that puny thistle? That's you, Amaziah. You
keep on with this lame-brained war plan of yours and you'll get
the "squish" yourself.' Jehoash was saying that a brier ought to
know it was a brier, be content with its brier-ness and not try to
step out of its class. Jehoash's fable was really quite a put-down.
His further comment in verse 10 points to Amaziah's pride as the
major culprit: you knocked off Edom and 'your heart has lifted
you up'. Amaziah has become arrogant and cocky, according
to Jehoash, and, if he insists on stirring up trouble, Judah will
come to disaster with him (v. 10).[7]

But Amaziah was pig-headed (v. 11a), the battle was on at
Beth-shemesh (v. 11b), and Judah was whipped (v. 12). Jehoash
bags a prize few winners enjoy — he captures his opposite
number. Verse 13 makes quite a bit of this by putting the direct

---

[5]The 'Valley of Salt' is probably the area south of the Dead Sea in the northern
Arabah. Sela is likely es-Sela', 2.5 miles NW of Bozrah, near the King's Highway (see
A. F. Rainey, IDBS, 800, and D. J. Wiseman, *1 & 2 Kings*, Tyndale Old Testament
Commentaries [Leicester: Inter-Varsity, 1993], 244-45). 'Joktheel' may mean 'God
destroys'. Readers will notice that the 'Chronicler' gives far more press to Amaziah's
Edomite expedition (2 Chron. 25:5-16), including his worship of the conquered gods of
Edom. The writer of Kings mentions none of this, perhaps because his primary focus
is still on the northern kingdom. But that's only a hunch.

[6]The account in 2 Chronicles 25:6-10, 13 may explain Amaziah's hostility against
Israel, but his success against Edom explains why he was brash enough actually to go
to war against Jehoash. Only the latter consideration comes into view in Kings.

[7]Perhaps Amaziah proves Barbara Tuchman right—that folly is a child of power, that
the power to command frequently causes failure to think (*The March of Folly* [New
York: Knopf, 1984], 32).

object, Amaziah with all his heredity, first in the sentence: 'And Amaziah king of Judah, son of Joash, son of Ahaziah, Jehoash king of Israel captured...'[8] The disgrace goes on: Jehoash & Co. come to Jerusalem, break down 600 feet of the northern wall, plunder the wealth of temple and palace, and, with hostages, return to Samaria (vv. 13b-14).[9] At least seven times in 1–2 Kings treasures of temple and palace are either forcibly taken or given as bribes or tribute.

Treasures away...

1 Kings 14:26	Rehoboam to Shishak
1 Kings 15:18	Asa to Ben-hadad
2 Kings 12:17-18	Joash [J] to Hazael
2 Kings 14:13-14	Amaziah to Jehoash [I]
2 Kings 16:7-8	Ahaz to Tiglath-pileser
2 Kings 18:14-16	Hezekiah to Sennacherib
2 Kings 24:13-14 (cf. 25:9-10)	... to Nebuchadnezzar

Three times (the first, fourth, and seventh) these treasures are directly plundered by conquerors.

Iain Provan draws attention to the parallel between what are the fourth and seventh instances on my chart, between Jehoash and Nebuchadnezzar in their respective treatments of Jerusalem. 'The first account in Kings of foreign capture of Jerusalem is very reminiscent of the second (2 Kings 24:8ff.) where we also read of a king (Jehoiachin) taken captive with hostages and of temple and palace being plundered.' He reminds us that in chapter 14 Jerusalem has fallen for the first

[8]The verb ('captured,' *tāpaś*) is the same used of Amaziah's capturing Sela in verse 7.
[9]We simply don't know what Jehoash did with Amaziah at this point. Some think he left him on the throne with loss of face (Bright), while others believe he was carted off to Samaria and not released until Jehoash's death (Merrill).

time, and Judah 'has now had its first experience of an "exile".' Hence 14:13-20 may function as a foreshadowing of what takes place in the closing chapters of 2 Kings.[10]

It seems like Union General Ambrose Burnside should've seen a 'foreshadowing' in November 1862. President Lincoln had approved Burnside's plan to move Federal troops across the Rappahannock River near Fredericksburg, Virginia. All depended on speed and for once the Union forces had it. They arrived at Fredericksburg before the Confederates could muster any significant force there. However, Burnside's plan called for pontoons to be there and waiting, so that he could get his army south of the Rappahannock and beyond to attack General Lee. When Burnside's troops arrived on November 17 there were no pontoons. Hence no bridges.

What was the problem? Seems that on November 6 someone in Washington decided pontoons should be brought to Washington so they could be rushed to Virginia when needed. But some bureaucrat forgot the military had a telegraph line; instead he sent orders by mail and six days later the engineers received them, When the pontoons got to Washington the engineers' orders—who knows how?—were changed: they were not to make up a pontoon wagon train ready to leave on a moment's notice; rather they were to put the boats and wagons in a storage depot. When a wagon train was prepared the engineers needed 200 horses, which meant 200 sets of harness—these were delivered in their original boxes and had to be unpacked and fitted together on, of course, some horses that had never been harnessed before. By November 19 these wagons began creaking on their way, making only half a dozen miles before stopping for the night in a pelting rain. The rain continued, the road became bottomless mud, the speed five miles per day. At last an officer was sent back to Washington to requisition a steam boat and to haul the pontoons most of the way by water. It was November 25 before the pontoons arrived. The engineers did their best, but in all the comedy of Federal bungling no one ever told them that time and speed were vital.[11]

---

[10]Iain W. Provan, *1 and 2 Kings*, New International Biblical Commentary (Peabody, MA: Hendrickson, 1995), 236-37.

[11]Bruce Catton, *Glory Road* (New York: Doubleday, 1952), 21-28, 64-65.

It was all a major mess of lumbering incompetence. All
this was disaster enough. But now, with Lee, Jackson, and
Longstreet's troops dug in on the higher ground behind
Fredericksburg, Burnside, not noted for flexibility, still ordered
the crossing of the river and the assault on Marye's Heights
and lost 12,600 men—killed, wounded, and missing. It was as
if rain and mud and especially compounded incompetence was
a foreshadowing of sure disaster—and it needed only a man
of Burnside's temperament to guarantee it. It is like that in our
text. King Amaziah's capture, the city's wasted wall, the rifled
treasures, the helpless captives (vv. 13-14)—all this is a prelude
to more of the same.

One can find a good example of this foreshadowing pattern
in Amos 4:6-12. There the prophet mentions certain covenant
curses Yahweh inflicted on Israel in order to drive them to
repentance. Yet after each blow Yahweh's refrain is the same:
'Yet you have not returned to me' (vv. 6, 8, 9, 10, 11). Whether
Yahweh sent famine (v. 6), or drought (vv. 7-8), or crop failures
(v. 9), or military defeat (v. 10), or disasters (v. 11), it made no
difference.[12] Israel was dense; they didn't get the point. They
ignored the foreshadowings. All that remained then was to
'meet God' in terrible judgment (v. 12).

Judean kings, Civil War generals, and the Israelite nation
are not the only ones who ignore 'foreshadowings'. Don't
contemporary nations do the same? Certainly, we must be
careful here, for we don't have direct divine revelation like
Amos did when he accused Israel. But should we not raise the
questions? In my own nation we have had in recent years a rash
of school and work shootings—a student or a worker goes
into their respective school or workplace and begins mowing
down their colleagues. One of these happened two weeks ago
sixty miles from my home. We have had, off and on, a rash of
scandals in the highest levels of our government. We have been
attacked by terrorists, dramatically at home, more routinely (?)
overseas. Are these God's foreshadowings to awaken a nation
that has no knowledge of God, that by its courts and legislation
has guaranteed a culture of death for thirty years, that revels in

[12]See Gary V. Smith, *Amos* (Ross-shire: Christian Focus, 1998), 195-201, for a lucid
exposition of this text.

rampant immorality, and cuddles and caters to those who glory in their sexual perversions? Is God shouting at us and we are not hearing? Is he giving us glimpses to which we are blind?

Yahweh's promises give stability to the turmoil of history (vv. 15-22)

Here we have two obituaries. Jehoash really rates because this (= vv. 15-16) is actually his second obituary (see 13:12-13). We could add the footnote about Amaziah's life span (v. 17) to Jehoash's obituary here.

Amaziah's obituary (vv. 18-22) is a bit more troubled. Some hatched a conspiracy against him, tracked him down in Lachish (twenty-nine miles west/southwest of Jerusalem), and eliminated him (v. 19)—then gave him a kosher royal burial (v. 20). The people of Judah installed (or had previously installed) Azariah (or, Uzziah), Amaziah's son, as his successor (v. 21).[13]

I'm interested in what happens in the wake of these royal deaths. Things remain stable. In Israel, whose throne was no stranger to conspiracies and assassinations, the kingdom moved smoothly from Jehoash to Jeroboam II (v. 16b). In Judah, even with the upheaval of a conspiracy against Amaziah it never seemed to cross anyone's mind to bring on a non-Davidic king. Azariah may be the hated Amaziah's son, but he has been confirmed as king.

And of course we know that this political stability rests on divine promises. Yahweh had promised Jehu a four-generation dynasty (10:30); Jeroboam II is the fourth link in Jehu's line. But Yahweh had promised David an unending dynasty (2 Sam. 7:12-16) and, in spite of a Judean conspiracy, Azariah is the current proof that that promise holds true. Just because obituaries seem dull we should not miss the point: Yahweh's promises direct history, and, if there is order and stability in early eighth century Israel and Judah, it is because Yahweh's promises rule.

---

[13]There is debate about when Azariah/Uzziah's reign began. Some think it likely that he became co-regent either when Amaziah went to war with Jehoash or when he was captured in that battle (v. 13)—assuming Amaziah remained a captive for some time. Verse 21 does not necessarily describe what followed immediately upon Amaziah's death. It may rightly be translated as a pluperfect (with Wiseman against Hobbs): 'Now all the people of Judah *had taken* Azariah…and *had made* him king.' See Bruce K. Waltke and M. O'Connor, *An Introduction to Biblical Hebrew Syntax* (Winona Lake, IN: Eisenbrauns, 1990), 552-53, for waw + imperfect in pluperfect sense.

Now the Jehu promise was temporary, as 2 Kings 15 will show. But the David promise is abiding and still controls history. Even when the Davidic king was unseated at the exile (2 Kings 24-25), the Davidic line went on and resurfaces in Matthew 1 in Jesus who is called Messiah (1:16). He moves from ministry to crucifixion to resurrection to ascension to enthronement at the place of supreme authority and power in the universe (Eph. 1:20-22). And in its time that hidden reign will be visibly imposed and obvious to all (cf. Rev. 11:15).

Admittedly, it doesn't look like the David promise gives order and coherence to history. Looking at the way history seems to unwind now reminds me of our classrooms when I was in elementary school. We had kids six to fourteen in our building, two grades in each classroom. When kids got to fifth-sixth or seventh-eighth grades things were but a step away from chaos. That step was when the teacher had to step out of the room to consult with another teacher. Almost immediately—as many know—bedlam began. Spitballs would fly. Someone would heave chalkboard erasers at human targets. Another might get out of his seat to attack or punch another kid. Someone would sneak up to the chalkboard, scribble something nasty, and hope it would remain anonymous. We all could muster such bravado when teacherless. Then, of course, a lookout would holler 'She's coming!' and all would return to normal. Well mostly. Even when the teacher was there, notes got passed; thumb tacks were placed on vacant seats of unsuspecting fellow students, which, undetected, caused immediate stimulation; students whispered to their neighbors. Occasionally there was an outburst of direct defiance like mine, which inspired an episode of pedagogic hair-pulling, making me fear I might be bald from fourth grade on. Sometimes my brothers would give kids trash to throw in the pot-belly stove; the trash happened to conceal 22 caliber shells which subsequently exploded in the stove. Even with the teacher the order sometimes seemed precarious. And yet we always knew that when she was there things could not really go berserk; we knew that if we tried, she would certainly win.

That is, I suggest, the way history must be seen in light of the David promise. Even with the promise of that kingdom history sometimes looks like it has lunged over the edge of the abyss and is ready to choke to death in its depravity. But we know that the King is there, that he both reigns and will reign. And he will win. Strange that it's 2 Samuel 7 that keeps us from going nuts as we slog through our history.

Yahweh's manner of ordering history may mystify us (vv. 24-27)
Asthma nearly consumed Theodore Roosevelt as a small boy. Attacks varied in length but sometimes were hours or even days at a time. One night he had a four-hour attack and his father made him smoke a cigar.[14] Well, that was one of the proposed antidotes. Now we puzzle over that combination—asthma and cigars. Just as we might puzzle over verses 24 and 25. Jeroboam II did evil in Yahweh's eyes, yet this king restored the border of Israel from Lebo-hamath all the way to the Sea of the Arabah.[15] Evil and success is as strange a combination as asthma and cigars. Why is Yahweh allowing this to go on? Why doesn't Yahweh bring Jeroboam's reign down in a cataclysm of disaster? Why is it that Israel still worships calves and times were never better? There is wickedness in high places and with it military expansion and a booming economy.[16]

Why were things this way? Because of the word of Yahweh (v. 25b). He had spoken through Jonah the prophet predicting this massive military recovery of Israel. However, behind this

---

[14]H. W. Brands, *T. R.: The Last Romantic* (New York: Basic Books, 1997), 10, 23.

[15]Lebo-hamath marks the northern border of Canaan and of ideal Israel (Num. 34:7-9; Josh. 13:5), located approximately forty-five miles north of Damascus, a site Jeroboam also recovered (v. 28). Apparently Transjordan also came back into Israel's control (Amos 6:13). In the south Jeroboam's sway came to, or to the south of, the Dead Sea. See *The Macmillan Bible Atlas,* 3rd ed. (New York: Macmillan, 1993), 108. The kingdom (along with Azariah/Uzziah's in the south) approximated Solomonic proportions. Egypt was weak most of the eighth century, Assyria was preoccupied elsewhere for the first fifty years of it, and Damascus had both been softened up by Assyria and suffered a crushing defeat from Zakir of Hamath. All this makes a nice vacuum for Jeroboam in which to flex his military muscles. See Merrill F. Unger, *Israel and the Aramaeans of Damascus* (Grand Rapids: Baker, 1980), 89-95; Claus Schedl, *History of the Old Testament*, 5 vols. (Staten Island: Alba House, 1972), 4:140-44; and Eugene H. Merrill, *Kingdom of Priests* (Grand Rapids: Baker, 1987), 367-75.

[16]Cf. John Bright, *A History of Israel*, 3rd ed. (Philadelphia: Westminster, 1981), 258: 'By the mid-eighth century the dimensions of Israel and Judah together lacked but little of being as great as those of the empire of Solomon. Since full advantage seems to have been taken of the favorable position in which the country found itself, a prosperity unknown since Solomon ensued. The two states being at peace with each other, and the major trade routes—up and down Transjordan, into northern Arabia, along the coastal plain, into the hinterland from the Phoenician ports—all once more passing through Israelite-held territory, tolls from caravans, together with the free interchange of goods, poured wealth into both countries.'

mysterious word of Yahweh stands the warm compassion of Yahweh, and this compassion 'drove' his word:

> (26) For Yahweh saw the affliction of Israel—how very bitter it was, with neither bound or free, and with no helper for Israel. (27) And Yahweh had not spoken about wiping out the name of Israel from under heaven, so he saved them by the hand of Jeroboam son of Jehoash.

Yahweh is still the same exodus God who sees the affliction of his people (Exod. 3:7). One senses that Israel might be on the verge of being wiped out but that Yahweh is still loath to take them there.

Now then we see a corollary of our main point: *prosperity may be a sign of Yahweh's compassions but not of his commendation.* It is easy to misread signs. During Hitler's regime, whenever the Nazis held torchlight parades or massive displays in Berlin that were meant to impress the world, they would ship in thousands of storm troopers from Munich to beef up the crowds. They had to do that because Berliners themselves seem to have had a singular lack of enthusiasm for Hitler.[17] So the world might see newsreels of fanatical support for Hitler in Berlin, but it was not a sign of that at all. So Jeroboam's success was not an index of Yahweh's favor at all—only of his pity. This is a tad unnerving, for the text is saying to us—whether nations or individuals: do not mistake Yahweh's patience for his pleasure (Rom. 2:4). We'll realize this when we get to Zechariah (v. 29), when 'October' will come to an end.

Yahweh's word disdains the claims of human importance (vv. 23-29)

Now I want to look at the whole section depicting Jeroboam's reign. Note how it is put together:

Formulas, vv. 23-24

History, v. 25a

Theology, vv. 25b-27

Formulas, vv. 28-29[18]

---

[17]Cornelius Ryan, *The Last Battle* (New York: Simon and Schuster, 1966), 52.

Observe that conventional formulas dominate Jeroboam's entry. The only piece relating to Jeroboam's achievement is verse 25a—verses 25b-27 explain why it was Jeroboam was able to achieve what he did. It was all due to Yahweh's word and Yahweh's mercy. These verses also need to temper our all too natural secularism. It is too easy for us to say (cf. fn 15) that Jeroboam and Israel flourished because Assyria was in eclipse just then, and because Egypt was an international cipher at that time. Historicism would be happy with that but we should not be. Rather, those were the conditions in which Jeroboam prospered but the *cause* of his prosperity was the merciful, sovereign Yahweh who directs the fortunes of the Assyrias and Egypts of this age.

There is no doubt that Jeroboam II was a significant and powerful player on the Near Eastern stage in his time. There is no doubt he put Israel back on the map. The way all of 2 Kings 13–14 is packaged highlights Jeroboam's success.

Structure of 2 Kings 13–14

Severe reduction of Israel, 13:1-7 (Jehoahaz)

Double obituaries, 13:8-13

Elisha—dying and giving life, 13:14-21

The successes of Jehoash, 13:22–14:14

Double obituaries, 14:15-22

Extensive restoration of Israel, 14:23-29 (Jeroboam II)

Note the first and last sections of this structure. The contrast is deliberate: Israel reduced within a pinch of her life under Jehoahaz (13:1-7) versus Israel restored to her glory under Jeroboam (14:23-29). And yet one line brings Jeroboam down

---

[18]'He restored Damascus and Hamath to Judah in Israel' in verse 28 remains a conundrum ('to Judah' is the puzzle). I could list half a dozen bibliographic notes and yet add no clarity or certainty on the matter. Those fascinated over this could begin their search in the commentaries of Hobbs, Cogan and Tadmor, and Fricke.

to size: 'So he [Yahweh] saved them by the hand of Jeroboam son of J[eh]oash' (v. 27b).

Even verses 23-29 make the same point by themselves. Here is a heavyweight king and yet four of the seven verses reporting his reign consist of standard formulas, and, of the three verses that say something distinctive about his tenure only a half verse (25a) reports his historical achievement—the rest is theology (25b-27). The way Yahweh's word reports human greatness cuts it down to size.

Don McClure once described a church service among the Shullas in the Sudan. There were about 250 children and adults gathered in the chapel. All sat on the dirt floor. Many of the youngsters wore only their birthday suits. McClure, however, had a difficult time concentrating during this service. The reason: one of the missionary women had thrown away an old corset, and a Shulla man had pulled it out of the trash and—'with great dignity'—came to church wearing the corset on his head. In fact, that was all he wore.[19] Perhaps there *is* a fine line between trash and treasure! But, in spite of all the pomp and dignity, it was merely a used-up old girdle. And that is the way the Bible estimates all human achievement and grandeur that does not bow the knee to Yahweh. This point, of course, strikes at not only deviant kings but also at those who claim to minister and serve in Jesus' name, who too easily become engrossed with their 'record' or 'career'.

Jeroboam's legacy, however, is about to go up in smoke. October is really a rather short time.

---

[19]Charles Partee, *Adventure in Africa* (Grand Rapids: Zondervan, 1990), 100-01.

20

Fast Forward to Oblivion
(2 Kings 15)

It's a gift to the impatient. Whether one is listening to an audio cassette or watching a video cassette (both of which may soon be destined for technological-dinosaur land) one can arrive, rather quickly, at the precise spot one wants to hear or see. So, if I'm settling down to watch 'Gettysburg' and don't want to wait for all the preliminaries and read the dire warnings about copyrights and so on, I simply punch the fast-forward button and, at hyper-speed, go to the beginning of the movie. Now it seems as though the writer of 2 Kings 15 had his finger on the fast-forward all through this chapter. No sooner had all the solemn speeches been made at Jeroboam II's funeral in 753 BC but we are placed on a literary roller coaster and rushed at fast forward speed through the last thirty years of the northern kingdom. In thirty years it was all over, and Israel was all but flushed down the sewer line of history, a line then maintained by the Assyrians.

Our chapter is wrapped by two kings of Judah, Azariah/ Uzziah (vv. 1-7) and Jotham (vv. 32-38); in between the writer blitzes us through five kings of Israel (vv. 8-31). The writer then wants to run you through this period very quickly and, if I drag you through it slowly, I will ruin the impression he wants to make. Hence I cannot dally on all the problems of the chapter; I can only footnote them[1] and dash on to the exposition.

---

[1] Some of the conundrums are: (1) Verse 5 says Azariah (Uzziah) lived in 'the house of

The Certainty of the Prophetic Word (vv. 1-12)

Our writer doesn't seem too interested in Azariah (Uzziah). He gets but seven verses and all but verse 5 are the usual formulas. Azariah was generally orthodox in his religious policy but our writer treats him like Jeroboam II (14:23-29). Chronicles will give him a whole chapter (2 Chron. 26) and carefully trace his great success and his sad pride. The writer of Kings knows about Azariah's attempt to burn incense in the temple (2 Chron. 26:16ff.)—and assumes his readers know about it; but he doesn't describe it. He only mentions the stroke of Yahweh's judgment upon him (v. 5). Our writer is currently more interested in Israel than in Judah. Nevertheless he hints that Azariah's reign stands as a bastion of stability, for five Israelite kings come and mostly go through Azariah's reign (vv. 8, 13, 17, 23, 27). The contrast is clear: one, long reign in Judah versus chaos and coups in Israel.

Zechariah (v. 8) takes the throne after the death of his father, Jeroboam II—for six months. Shallum conspires and assassinates him (v. 10). End of dynasty. Explanation? Verse 12:

> It was the word of Yahweh which he had spoken to Jehu, saying, 'Your sons to the fourth generation will sit upon the throne of Israel.' And that's the way it was.

---

freedom' (lit.) after his leprosy; it may mean a place where he was 'free' from government duties, or it may refer to 'freedom' in the sense of separation from normal society. (2) Verse 10 says Shallum struck down Zechariah qābāl-'ām; some take this to mean 'in front of the people', i.e., publicly; others emend to 'Ibleam' (twelve miles southeast of Megiddo, a little more than that north of Samaria), following a LXX recension; Hobbs takes it as 'Kabal-am', name of an unknown place. No one really knows. (3) Tiphsah (v. 16; so the Hebrew text, followed by, e.g., ESV, NRSV, NIV) a ford on the west side of the big bend of the Euphrates, something like 350 miles north of Samaria (cf. 1 Kings 4:24). Many find it difficult to believe that Menahem could have attacked a site so far afield. Hence they (e.g., REB, NJB) prefer to read (with a recension of LXX) 'Tappuah', a town on the border of Ephraim and Manasseh. Cf. Hobbs' commentary. (4) Verse 25 says that Pekah 'struck down' Pekahiah 'in Samaria in the citadel of the palace, along with Argob and Arieh'. You don't need the typical 'three views'. If Argob and Arieh are taken as proper names, they are most likely officers of Pekahiah who bit the dust with him when Pekah and his fifty Gileadites pitched into them. (5) The 'twenty years' (v. 27) of Pekah's reign make for a rip-roaring chronological problem. If Pekah begins to reign in the fifty second year of Azariah (Uzziah) of Judah, i.e., ca. 740 BC, then twenty years would take Pekah's reign beyond the fall of Israel in 722 BC. Some, however, posit that Pekah actually began to reign in Gilead at the same time as Menahem, i.e., 752 BC. Of course, this latter is an hypothesis, but before it is dismissed one should pay careful attention to the discussion of John Oswalt, 'Chronology of the OT,' ISBE, 1:683-84.

The 'word of Yahweh' refers to 10:30, where Yahweh promised Jehu a four-generation dynasty. Not as though it couldn't have been more. Had Jehu's sons turned to Yahweh and had even begun to walk in his law one surmises Elijah's God would have extended the tenure (see 1 Kings 21:27-29).[2] But they didn't and he didn't. And Shallum brought it all to an end. Does that mean Yahweh approved Shallum's deed? No; Yahweh simply used Shallum's evil deed to bring his sure word to pass. Yahweh is not above using thugs for his own purposes.

It is the last clause of verse 12 that is so fascinating. 'And that's the way it was' translates *wayehî-kēn*, which occurs six times in Genesis 1 (vv. 7, 9, 11, 15, 24, 31), usually after God speaks. So the clause implies that what God spoke actually came into being and remained that way.[3] What is more natural and obvious than that when Yahweh promised Jehu a four-generation dynasty that is exactly what happened? 'And that's the way it was' because it could be no other way. Yahweh's word is that certain.

On 2 March 1546 George Wishart was burning at the stake outside St. Andrews castle. Bags of gunpowder had been tied to parts of his body and, though these exploded, Wishart was yet alive as the fire burned on. The battlements and windows of the castle's fore-tower were decked with tapestry and furnished with luxurious cushions so that Cardinal David Beaton and his fellow prelates might have a ring-side seat from which to enjoy the spectacle of Wishart's roasting. Before he expired, Wishart looked up toward the Cardinal and declared: 'He who in such state from that high place feedeth his eyes with my torments, within few days shall be hanged out at the same window, to be seen with as much ignominy as he now leaneth there in pride.' As Thomas McCrie has said, no prediction looked more unlikely to come about at that time. And yet about three months later sixteen men infiltrated St. Andrews castle, roused Cardinal Beaton from sleep and dispatched him. There was a tumult among the townsfolks—they wanted to know what

[2]See my discussion in *The Wisdom and the Folly* (Ross-shire: Christian Focus, 2002), 313-15.
[3]Cf. U. Cassuto, *A Commentary on the Book of Genesis: Part I—From Adam to Noah* (Jerusalem: Magnes, 1961), 33-34.

had become of the Cardinal. Hence the conspirators 'exposed the dead body from the same window, or over the same part of the battlements, where the Cardinal had, a short time before, reclined in haughty state, gazing on the martyrdom of Wishart.'[4]

We hear that and we think, 'What an audacious prediction, what an astounding fulfillment!' It seems as though the judgment of God was lurking in the syllables of Wishart's prophecy eager to leap upon the godless cleric. Wishart spoke and that's the way it was. And we are so impressed, we are so awed, so taken by that—by the word of a mere man proving true. Would that we were so staggered over those occasions— with which Scripture is littered—when the predictive word of *Yahweh* comes to exact fulfillment. Of which 2 Kings 10:30 and 15:12 constitute a case in point. There is something wrong when Wishart's accuracy moves us but Yahweh's sedates us. And, if our Lord's threats are so exact, so are his promises. Time will come when we'll be able to say of John 14:3 and 2 Peter 3:1-13, 'And that's the way it was.'

The Signals of the Coming Judgment (vv. 8-38)

We have both internal and external signs of the coming judgment in 2 Kings 15. We begin with the internal, and perhaps the best way to do so is to set out in somewhat tedious detail, on the following page, the content of the chapter.[5]

As noted before, primary attention goes to five Israelite kings (only Menahem manages a 'dynasty') while the reigns of two Judean kings wrap the block of northern kings. Among the latter the conspiracies jump out at us—against Zechariah (v. 10), against Shallum (v. 14), against Pekahiah (v. 25), and against Pekah (v. 30). Some of these were very short reigns: six months for Zechariah (v. 8), one month for Shallum (v. 13), and two years for Pekahiah (v. 23). Chronologically, we are probably dealing with scarcely more than twenty years (ca. 753-732 BC), in which there are five kings and four conspiracies. The prophet Hosea alludes to this yo-yo kind of political

---

[4]W. M. Hetherington, *History of the Church of Scotland* (Edinburgh: John Johnstone, 1841), 48-50.

[5]Cf. also B. O. Long, *2 Kings*, The Forms of the Old Testament Literature (Grand Rapids: Eerdmans, 1991), 170-72.

Pattern/Content of 2 Kings 15

Judah: Azariah/Uzziah, vv. 1-7

Zechariah, vv. 8-12
Time, v. 8
Evaluation, v. 9
Conspiracy, v. 10
Conclusion, v. 11
Prophecy/fulfillment, v. 12

Shallum, vv. 13-16
Time, v. 13
Conspiracy, v. 14
Conclusion, v. 15
Addition, v. 16

Menahem, vv. 17-22
Time, v. 17
Evaluation, v. 18
Intervention, vv. 19-20
Conclusion, vv. 21-22

Pekahiah, vv. 23-26
Time, v. 23
Evaluation, v. 24
Conspiracy, v. 25
Conclusion, v. 26

Pekah, vv. 27-31
Time, v. 27
Evaluation, v. 28
Invasion/exile, v. 29
Conspiracy, v. 30
Conclusion, v. 31

Judah: Jotham, vv. 32-38

turnover (see Hosea 7:5-7 and 13:10-11).[6] Israel is in a race to ruin, running pell-mell to extinction. If civil stability is a divine gift (cf. 1 Tim. 2:1-2), it has been withdrawn from Israel. Her own chaos is a sign that God is in the process of destroying her.

There are also external signs of Yahweh's coming scourge, in the form of Assyria. I do not think the appearance of Tiglath-pileser III[7] during Menahem's regime (vv. 19-20) indicates an invasion. Rather Menahem paid him a substantial wad of tribute in exchange for Assyrian muscle behind his throne.[8] But silver had lost its magic by Pekah's time (v. 29). Pekah seems to have been an anti-Assyrian agitator in cahoots with Rezin of Syria (cf. 16:5-9), and about 733 BC Tiglath-pileser began to put the squeeze on Israel—taking five northern towns in his invasion (v. 29a).[9] But it was worse than that: he 'took Gilead and Galilee, that is, all the land of Naphtali' (v. 29b). So Assyria dominated Israelite turf east of the Jordan and west and north of the Sea of Galilee—and the new lackey, Hoshea (v. 30), is left with little more than a sphere of influence around Samaria. But it was worse than that: Tiglath-pileser exiled populations from Galilee and Gilead to Assyria (v. 29c). There are gobs of suffering and heartache behind that simple verb 'exiled'.[10]

---

[6]On which see Duane Garrett, *Hosea, Joel,* New American Commentary (Nashville: Broadman & Holman, 1997), 167-69, 260-61.

[7]Pul (v. 19) is an abbreviation or nickname for Tiglath-pileser; see M. Cogan and H. Tadmor, *II Kings,* Anchor Bible (Garden City, NY: Doubleday, 1988), 171-72. For a translation of Tiglath-pileser's annals, see D. D. Luckenbill, *Ancient Records of Assyria and Babylonia,* 2 vols., 1:269-96.

[8]Cf. the discussion in T. R. Hobbs, *2 Kings,* Word Biblical Commentary (Waco: Word, 1985), 198-200. Hobbs thinks the money Menahem paid out was for hiring Assyrian mercenaries, not tribute. Most, however, assume the silver to be tribute. 'According to Galling's calculation…a talent is worth 3,000 shekels; working on a rate of 50 shekels per person, it would appear that 60,000 persons had to be liable to tax to raise a national revenue of 1000 talents' (G. H. Jones, *1 and 2 Kings,* New Century Bible Commentary, 2 vols. [Grand Rapids: Eerdmans, 1984], 2:526).

[9]Ijon was about nine miles north-northwest of Dan, and Abel-beth-maacah four miles west of Dan. Kedesh (in upper Galilee) was seventeen miles mostly north of the Sea of Galilee; Hazor was about ten miles north of the same. Janoah's location is uncertain. See Carl G. Rasmussen, *Zondervan NIV Atlas of the Bible* (Grand Rapids: Zondervan, 1989), 99, 126, and 132. The sites were on or near the major trade route.

[10]There was a new twist to Tiglath-pileser III's deportation scheme. 'Deportation became a two-way exchange: from newly organized provinces in the West, he transferred populations to Assyria proper, and resettled those areas with people brought from the East and South. This radical procedure of population exchange sought to make the uprooted totally dependent on the central government, forcefully amalgamating them so that "they became Assyrian"' (Cogan and Tadmor, *II Kings,* 177).

The presence and pressure of Assyria in Menahem's time (v. 19) should have unnerved those with eyes to see; but the invasion and deportation that occurred under Pekah (v. 29) shows Israel is one slight push away from total disaster. Yahweh's word in Hosea 13:10-11 may address this very situation. Duane Garrett translates:

> Where is your king, then, that he may save you in all your cities, and your judges, of whom you said, "Give me a king and princes!"?

> I will give you a king—in my wrath,
> and I will take (a king)—in my rage.

Garrett explains:

> The sense of Yahweh's answer…is ironic. "I will give you a king—in my wrath" means that God will indeed send them a king but not the king they expect. The king God will send is the ruler of Assyria, who comes as their conqueror. "And I will take (a king)—in my rage" means that God will remove the sitting Israelite monarch from his throne.[11]

That sums up 2 Kings 15: Yahweh has given Tiglath-pileser as Israel's 'king', and Hoshea's hands drip with Pekah's blood (v. 30). Indeed, with all the conspiracies in this chapter one could almost say Israel has more assassins than kings.

At any rate, there are plenty of internal and external signals of the judgment that is coming. In fact, these 'signals' seem to be part of that judgment.[12] Israel, however, seems to pay no heed to these preliminary signs of ruin to come.

Chancellorsville, Virginia, May 2, 1863. Part of the Union troops had captured some Confederate prisoners one of whom threatened, 'You wait until Jackson gets around your right [flank].' But this was dismissed as sour grapes. Union pickets went forward and found that lots of Rebels were moving around on the Federal right. But those in the know at headquarters called it a 'rolling reconnaissance' and ignored it.

---

[11]Garrett, *Hosea, Joel*, 260-61.

[12]Note that there were judgment signals for Judah as well; verse 37 indicates that Rezin and Pekah were Yahweh's emissaries against the southern kingdom.

Other scouting reports came in of huge masses of Confederate
infantry on the Union right; ranking officers dismissed these
reports with arrogance and contempt. Then a bit of laughter
erupted from some of the Union soldiers as they saw scads of
deer emerging from the woods to the west and hightailing it
in mad fashion to the east. That was the last sign. Stonewall
Jackson's troop smashed into the Union right with 28,000
men, attacking in a line over a mile wide and four divisions
deep, crashing through scrub and thorns thought to be
impenetrable. With that terrifying Rebel yell and the crash
of shells Jackson's soldiers made a pancake of the right flank
of Joe Hooker's army.[13]

It was not that there were no warnings but that warnings
were uniformly ignored. There were all kinds of 'signals'
of disaster but those who counted paid no heed. Perhaps if
some had joined the deer's mad dash they might have saved
themselves. And it was that way in the last days of Israel: clear
signals of God's coming judgment but no eyes to see them, no
ears to hear them. I refer readers again to Amos 4:6-12, where
Yahweh sent 'preliminary' and limited judgments on Israel to
awaken her and lead her to repentance. But the 'signals' were
ignored and so disaster would come. We have spoken of this
before in relation to nations. The same holds for the church.
If a church denomination equivocates and refuses to affirm
biblical moral standards (e.g., re homosexuality), is this not
a sign that God is 'giving over' his own professing people
to follow their own authority? If a church fails or refuses to
discipline ministers who deny Apostles' Creed-level doctrines
but allows them to serve in all their unbelief, is this not a signal
that God has already written 'Ichabod' (1 Sam. 4:21-22) over
that communion?

The Tragedy of the Original Sin (vv. 9, 18, 24, 28)
Because we meet with five Israelite kings within the confines
of one chapter we can't help but notice the repeated 'sins of
Jeroboam' formula. It appears four times, in the evaluations of
Zechariah (v. 9), Menahem (v. 18), Pekahiah (v. 24), and Pekah
(v. 28). The formula does not occur in reference to Shallum's

---

[13]Bruce Catton, *Glory Road* (Garden City, NY: Doubleday, 1952), 180-85.

one-month reign (cf. vv. 13-15). Each of the four kings 'did not turn away' from the sins of Jeroboam. The Jeroboam, of course, is not the recent 'son of J[eh]oash' (14:23) but the 'son of Nebat' who instituted the bull shrines (1 Kings 12:25-33). We read the tedious repetition of his name and hear the tragic dominance of his influence throughout 1–2 Kings. Two hundred years have passed since Jeroboam instigated his devious cult (931-732 BC) and its grip is undiminished, its poison still lethal. This was the 'original sin'—and is the tenacious sin—of the northern kingdom. Running into it four times in one chapter only increases one's sense of the tragedy and ruin such worship is bringing.

During World War II the Germans had French factories producing for the German war effort. To prevent sabotage the Germans had spread out production. One factory might make the chassis of a truck, another the engine—so it went. Now the laboratory of the French underground had developed an abrasive and, of course, placed it in the hands of underground workers in one of these truck factories. That worker might smear the abrasive on the bearings, or some other vital part; the truck would roll off the assembly line—in fact it might roll along fine for sixty miles before, mysteriously, breaking down. For a stretch of ten months 90 percent of the trucks put out by one assembly plant developed this strange problem.[14] Now, obviously, there is a quantitative difference between a truck's sixty miles and Israel's two hundred years—and yet an essential similarity. The trucks' problems did not develop from wear and tear over time; they stemmed *from the beginning*, from that 'factory installed' abrasive. And Israel's ruin was 'installed' from the very first, when her first king, Jeroboam son of Nebat, instigated that perverted bull worship that ate the fidelity out of Israel's vitals.[15] Here in 2 Kings 15 we come down within an inch of Israel's end and 'the sins of Jeroboam the son of Nebat' are still strangling the life out of her.

What an 'after-life' infidelity has, whether in doctrine, worship, or living. In 318 Arius touts that the Son of God

[14] *Secrets and Spies* (Pleasantville, NY: Reader's Digest, 1964), 131-32.

[15] On this point, cf. my *The Wisdom and the Folly: An Exposition of the Book of First Kings* (Ross-shire: Christian Focus, 2002), 164-66 (on 1 Kings 14:12-18).

is a created being and not equal with the Father, and today Jehovah's Witnesses propagate the same—a Son of God who is not God and a Savior who cannot save.[16] How crucial, then, not only for Christian leaders but for individual believers to 'watch your life and doctrine closely' (1 Tim. 4:16a, NIV). The destiny of those years later may depend on it.

---

[16]See Roger E. Olson, *The Story of Christian Theology* (Downers Grove: InterVarsity, 1999), 137-72.

21

Is the Grass Greener...?
(2 Kings 16)

Second Kings 15 has depicted the northern kingdom plummeting into political hades—and yet that account of Israel's tragedy was sandwiched by the entries of two Judean kings (Azariah/Uzziah and Jotham) that exude stability. So what if we emigrate to Judah? Maybe the grass is greener there? Maybe we could avoid this rapid rush to ruin as in Israel? Answer: Not likely; at least not now that Ahaz is on the throne. A whole chapter devoted to a southern king is unusual for 1–2 Kings so far. But the news is not good. I think the best way to get at the chapter's teaching is by a series of observations.

The gathering darkness in Yahweh's kingdom (vv. 1-4)
Chronology gets very sticky here. McFall places Ahaz between 735 and 715 BC and understands verses 1-2a as: In the seventeenth year of the break away kingdom of Pekah the son of Remaliah, Ahaz son of Jotham, king of Judah, became co-regent. Ahaz was twenty years old when he became co-regent, and he reigned sixteen years as king in Jerusalem.[1]

But chronology is the least of the problems, for the lights are going out in Judah. Our writer is blunt about Ahaz: 'he did not do what is right in the eyes of Yahweh' (v. 2b). Ahaz is the only king of Judah who receives this particular evaluation (we

---

[1]Leslie McFall, 'Has the chronology of the Hebrew kings finally been settled?,' *Themelios* 17/1 (Oct-Nov 1991): 9-10; see also John Bright, *A History of Israel*, 3rd ed. (Philadelphia: Westminster, 1981), 276.

are more accustomed to those who 'did right' but in a qualified way [15:3, 34], i.e., not like David).[2] Moreover, he aped the kings of Israel (v. 3a), shades of Jehoram and Ahaziah (8:18, 27)—and we know from chapter 15 where Israel is heading. But the writer says it gets much worse: 'and what's more [Heb., wĕgam], his son he caused to pass through the fire' (v. 3b). So the perversions of Israel do not satisfy Ahaz; he had to practice the horrors of paganism—child sacrifice, whether of a Molech or Baal variety.[3] And then he engaged in extra-temple worship 'in the high places and on the hills and under every green tree' (v. 4), probably involving the fertility rites cited back in 1 Kings 14:23. Normally the terminology of verse 4 describes what the people still did under a generally 'righteous' king (12:3; 14:4; 15:4, 35), but here the verbs are singular—Ahaz himself engages in this worship.

Remember the dark hint in verse 3b after the text tells us Ahaz made his son pass through the fire? The text continues: '...in line with the abominations of the nations Yahweh drove out before the sons of Israel.' This is a bit of innuendo. If Judah shares in the abominations of those nations, she will share their fate as well. Simply because this threat applies to the covenant nation of Judah does not mean that non-covenant nations (they prefer to call themselves 'secular states') are off the hook (see Amos 1–2). Of course, our abominations are often desacralized. In my own land our fertility rites are more often celebrated in university dormitories than at Asherah chapels and Molech receives his due in sterile clinics rather than at religious shrines. As of this writing, my own government cannot muster enough votes to stop the horror of 'partial-birth' abortion. The 'gathering darkness' is not confined to Judah, and organizing national prayer breakfasts or lobbying for evangelical chaplains in Congress will never disperse it.

---

[2]Some other kings of Judah—Jehoram (8:18), Ahaziah (8:27), and Manasseh (21:2)—'did evil in the eyes of Yahweh', which is the standard evaluation of the kings of Israel.

[3]Cf. Jer. 7:31; 19:5; Ezek. 16:21. On this whole matter, see John E. Hartley, Leviticus, Word Biblical Commentary (Dallas: Word, 1992), 334-37; R. D. Patterson and Hermann J. Austel, '1 and 2 Kings,' The Expositor's Bible Commentary, 12 vols. (Grand Rapids: Zondervan, 1988), 4:245-46; and John Bright, A History of Israel, 277.

The shameful recourse of Yahweh's vassal (vv. 5-9)
It was 734 BC and the sun was not shining outside the conference
room in Jerusalem where King Ahaz was conferring with his
foreign policy advisors. Rezin of Syria (Aram) and Pekah
of Israel were threatening to overrun Jerusalem—they were
besieging it but 'were not able to fight it out' with Ahaz (v. 5).
But it's worse than it looks. If we cheat and bring in the data
2 Chronicles 28 supplies, Judah is simply caving in: *Edomites* to
the southeast were invading; *Philistines* from the west had taken
territory and towns; *Syria* and *Israel* were inflicting staggering
losses in war and now these latter were investing Jerusalem
itself. So—you are in the conference room and you have few
options left, few buttons to push. But there was still the panic
button, and Ahaz's finger was on it.

It is usually thought that Syria and Israel (the 'Syro-
Ephraimite alliance') wanted Ahaz and Judah to join them in
an anti-Assyrian coalition. Ahaz refused and so they were on
the attack, wanting to overthrow Ahaz and install their own
toady in his place (Isa. 7:5-6).

And there was bad economic news: Rezin recovered the
port of Elath (restored to Judah by Azariah, 14:22), cleared
out the Judeans there, and, apparently left it for Edomites to
resettle (v. 6).[4] Elath (on the Gulf of Aqaba on the Red Sea) sat
at the terminus of two important land routes (one of which
was the King's Highway running through Transjordan all the
way north to Damascus) and as a port offered links to Arabia,
Africa, and even India.[5]

Ahaz is in deep trouble and appeals for help—to Assyria
(vv. 7-8). He acts not as a covenant believer but as a shrewd
politician. Ahaz sells his birthright at the very first: 'I am your
servant and your son' (v. 7a). I've a note here in my old study
Bible to 2 Samuel 7:14, which says that the Davidic king will
be Yahweh's 'son.' Ahaz repudiates the Davidic covenant as he
licks Tiglath-pileser's boots.[6] He wants to accept the Assyrians
as his personal savior—'Come up and save me from the grip

[4]Verse 6 is tricky. In the second half of the verse I follow the Masoretic marginal
reading, 'Edomites,' instead of 'Aramaeans.'
[5]Cf. 1 Kings 9:26-27; and Jeffrey R. Zorn, 'Elath,' ABD, 2:429.
[6]Cf. Walter Brueggemann, *1 & 2 Kings*, Smyth & Helwys Bible Commentary (Macon,
GA: Smyth & Helwys, 2000), 468.

of the king of Syria and from the grip of the king of Israel who are attacking me' (v. 7b). And, as usual in politics, a handsome bribe (v. 8) buys salvation (v. 9).[7] It may have been blatant unbelief but it was successful policy; he may repudiate the Davidic covenant but he saves his own skin. Ahaz could have put his attitude in verse (sung to the tune Gordon/Caritas = 'My Jesus, I Love Thee'):

> My Tig, I bribe thee, you know I'm your man;
> for thee Yahweh's promises I view as mere sand.
> You mighty oppressor, my savior art thou,
> if ever I needed you, dear Tiglath, 'tis now.

That is the 'faith' of the king of Judah.

Ahaz walks the way of human ingenuity. It may be *royal* human ingenuity, but it is still *human* ingenuity. This thinking says to itself, 'My troubles are too complex for me to lean upon Yahweh's assurances, but I see a clear and very obvious way to solve this problem.' Yahweh seems such a remote and ineffective help. I suppose Ahaz felt like H. G. Wells when he wrote Rebecca West:

> I can't—in my present state anyhow—bank on religion. God has no thighs and no life. When one calls to him in the silence of the night he doesn't turn over and say, 'What is the trouble, Dear?'[8]

Both Ahaz and H. G. longed respectively for help more 'tangible' than heaven's.

Shucked to the bone, the choice is between pragmatism or promise. (Ahaz had Yahweh's promise of deliverance through Isaiah [Isa. 7:3-9].) Do I go with what I am sure will work or wait for what God offers? Do I jump on an immediate solution

---

[7]On the plundering of temple treasures, whether by conqueror or resident monarch, see my discussion on 14:13-14 in chapter 19 above. On rendering *šōḥad* as 'bribe', see *The Wisdom and the Folly: An Exposition of the Book of First Kings* (Ross-shire: Christian Focus, 2002), 175-77. Richard Nelson insists the translation should be 'present' and that 'bribe' is 'indefensibly judgmental' (*First and Second Kings*, Interpretation [Louisville: John Knox, 1987], 225). He simply hasn't checked the consistent usage of *šōḥad* in the Old Testament; cf. Kohlenberger and Swanson, *The Hebrew English Concordance to the Old Testament* (Grand Rapids: Zondervan, 1998), 1556.

[8]Michael Coren, *The Invisible Man: The Life and Liberties of H. G. Wells* (New York: Atheneum, 1993), 116.

or submit to what God requires? Here is a man in a tense or disappointing marriage. Does he seek candidly and graciously to communicate his concerns to his wife, so that they can prayerfully, and perhaps with assistance (pastoral and/or professional), try to restore what has atrophied? Or does he insist on seeking his solace in an extra-marital relationship with a woman he has met at work because 'she understands me'? There are legions of ways we can become disciples of Ahaz. We simply say of any situation, 'My wisdom must handle this,' rather than 'My Father will give me what is good' (cf. Matt. 7:11).

The dubious innovation in Yahweh's worship (vv. 10-18)

This section is difficult—like the letters of Paul in which there are some things hard to understand (2 Pet. 3:16). Perhaps the best way to get a handle on it is to trace its content and go from there:

The new altar:	vv. 10-11
The new arrangements:	vv. 12-14
The new regulations:	vv. 15-16
The new rationale:	vv. 17-18

Choon-Leong Seow holds that 'Ahaz's innovations at the Temple are passed over without any theological judgments'.[9] Well, maybe, if one is only looking for explicit statements. But put your ear down on the text, and you'll hear some theological judgments. Let's walk our way through some of these details.

What are we to make of this new altar (vv. 10-11)? It was once held to be an *Assyrian* altar; it was held that, as the price of his subservience to Assyria, Ahaz had no choice but to introduce changes that reflected his homage to Assyria and its gods.[10] However, more recent opinion disputes this. For one thing, Assyria did not make religious impositions on its semi-independent vassal states (like Judah) as they might have

---

[9] In 'The First and Second Books of Kings,' *The New Interpreter's Bible*, 12 vols. (Nashville: Abingdon, 1999), 3:251.

[10] So the 2nd (1954) and 3rd (1970) editions of *The New Bible Commentary*, the former quoting A. T. Olmstead in support: 'As in all newly organized provinces, the cult of Ashur and the king had been established in Damascus, and the vassal rulers were ordered to follow this example' (p. 326).

done on provinces. Moreover, it seems that Assyrian altars were table altars (where food was placed for the 'divine meal') and not sacrificial altars.[11] Clearly, Ahaz's new altar was an altar for sacrifice. These considerations indicate that Ahaz was enamored with a *Syrian* altar.

The biblical text seems to support this latter contention. When Ahaz went to kowtow to Tiglath-pileser, verse 10 says 'he saw the altar which was in Damascus'. There is no indication of Assyrian pressure; on his own Ahaz seems to have taken a fancy to this Damascus altar. Surely we've read enough about Ahaz so far to know that he was very open to the 'contributions' of deviant religious practices (vv. 1-4). Moreover, 2 Chronicles 28:22-23 indicates that Ahaz had had a kind of love affair with Syrian worship before (cf. also Amaziah in 2 Chron. 25:14-16). So, for Ahaz, Assyria has become his salvation but Syria is his liturgist.[12]

There is also a dig at Ahaz in verses 12-14: he is a Jeroboam in Judah. Three times verse 12 explicitly mentions 'the king': 'So the king came from Damascus, and the king saw the altar, and the king came near to the altar and went up on it.' Long holds that Ahaz is acting 'as a royal priest, head of the state religion, like David and Solomon before him (cf. 2 Sam 6:17-18; 1 Kings 8:63), or given the [Deuteronomistic Historian's] negative attitude, like Jeroboam (1 Kings 12:32-33).'[13] But I think our writer casts Ahaz only in Jeroboam's image.[14] Ahaz 'drew near to the altar and went up upon it' (v. 12). That is the same language used of Jeroboam in 1 Kings 12:32-33 (three times!): 'he went up upon the altar.' So 'Jeroboam', pioneer of a deviant worship, is now in Judah. This is one way the writer can register his disgust over Ahaz. Jeroboam will spell ruin for Israel (2 Kings 17:21-23), and nothing better can be expected for Judah when Jeroboam's clone

---

[11]On this debate see M. Cogan, *Imperialism and Religion: Assyria, Judah and Israel in the Eighth and Seventh Centuries B.C.E.* (Missoula, MT: Scholars, 1974), 42-96, and John McKay, *Religion in Judah under the Assyrians* (London: SCM, 1973), 5-12.

[12]Ahaz had the former altar moved off to the north side (v. 14). Verse 15b may mean this old altar will be for Ahaz to use in seeking divine guidance (e.g., NIV) or that Ahaz will decide what is to be done with this altar (NJPS).

[13]Burke O. Long, *2 Kings*, The Forms of the Old Testament Literature (Grand Rapids: Eerdmans, 1991), 177.

[14]David and Solomon may have functioned in a quasi-priestly capacity, but when the text says they 'offered' sacrifices, it probably means they 'authorized' them but that priests actually offered them. We can be sure that Solomon did not himself offer the scads of sacrifices mentioned in 1 Kings 8:63!

rules there. Verse 13 probably intends us to understand that Ahaz himself performed priestly duties as he inaugurated the new altar into service. Once you see the Jeroboam connection, you can hardly hold that our writer views Ahaz's innovations in an objective and detached manner.

Verses 17-18 give more light on Ahaz's innovations but not without pain, since there are difficulties in the text and disagreement over how to take it. In order to get at this, let me set down the English Standard Version of these verses, particularly since it follows closely the given Hebrew text of verse 18:

> (17) And King Ahaz cut off the frames of the stands and removed the basin from them, and he took down the sea from off the bronze oxen that were under it and put it on a stone pedestal. (18) And the covered way for the Sabbath that had been built inside the house and the outer entrance for the king he caused to go around the house of the LORD, because of the king of Assyria.

Verse 17 evidently refers to the ten laver stands in 1 Kings 7:27ff.[15] Ahaz apparently cut down the stands and removed the lavers; he also relieved the twelve bronze bulls of the huge laver (1 Kings 7:23-26) that had to date rested on their haunches. Now NJPS puts 18b ('on account of the king of Assyria') immediately after verse 17. NJPS assumes that most of verse 18 is a parenthesis but that 18b qualifies verse 17, that is, Ahaz removes the bronze in order to have resources to pay tribute to Tiglath-pileser (cf. v. 8). But there is no bronze in the bribe of verses 7-8, only silver and gold.[16] If this is for tribute, it will be for later tribute. But I doubt that can be the case either, for the twelve bronze bulls seem to be present for Nebuchadnezzar to plunder much later (see Jer. 52:20).[17]

As a matter of fact, 'because of the king of Assyria' occurs at the end of verse 18, and it is more natural to take it as qualifying only the items mentioned there.[18] Exactly what verse 18 refers

---

[15]On which see my *Wisdom and Folly*, 76.

[16]Iain W. Provan, *1 and 2 Kings*, New International Biblical Commentary (Peabody, MA: Hendrickson, 1995), 246.

[17]Unless one deletes the bulls-clause from Jer. 52:20 (as does Holladay).

[18]In fact, the Hebrew construction changes at v. 18 with the direct objects placed first in the sentence. Because of this it would be better to translate the initial conjunction adversatively—'But...' This rather sets off v. 18 by itself and requires the 'because of the king of Assyria'-phrase to apply only to the items in this verse.

to is a puzzle for us at this point in time. What was the 'covered way for the Sabbath'? If it was built 'inside the house', is the 'house' the temple or the palace? The upshot is that Ahaz had to get construction crews working on architectural changes that apparently reflected his loss of royal prestige as a vassal of Assyria.[19]

All this means that the changes in verse 17 were not driven by a need for funds or because of Assyrian demands but simply because Ahaz decided to do so.

> It is simply that travel has broadened Ahaz's mind. He has gained some new ideas...Ahaz is presented as a king who is open to foreign *influence* in his religious policy (as in 16:2-4). He is not presented as one who is under foreign *control*. These are dark days, nonetheless. Never before has a Judean king taken it upon himself to redesign the Solomonic temple in such a way.[20]

What implications should we draw from this account of Ahaz's 'new measures'? First, *the king's innovations imply the deficiency of orthodox worship.* Ahaz apparently thought temple worship could be improved, that it lacked something, that an 'upgrade' was in order. Damascus novelty could enrich Jerusalem worship, and Ahaz himself would kick it all off in his priestly capacity.

But whenever we supplement or 'enrich' worship we are implying that our worship is somehow deficient. When my wife invites guests for dinner, I have noticed that women (single, married and/or mothers) will often ask if they can bring anything. The answer varies. Often it is, 'No, just come.' Other times, Barbara might accept an offer and ask for someone to bring a vegetable or salad. Now suppose some woman brings in her assigned vegetable dish but also carts in a full batch of pork loin and says, 'I know you're serving chicken enchiladas, but I thought some people might not care for them, so I brought this pork loin.' That means two things. One, she did not think my wife's planning and provision were sufficient, and two, she will never be invited back.

---

[19]Even the changes of v. 18 may not have been imposed by Assyria; Ahaz may have made them simply to remove a possible source of offense (Provan).

[20]Provan, *1 and 2 Kings*, 246.

I wonder if the church now runs the same danger? In principle, our worship is the same as Old Testament Judah's: prayer and praise based on atonement (sacrifice). That doesn't mean our worship can't have variety or that it must of necessity be tedious.[21] But why do we keep toying with worship, thinking that we have to soup it up with interviews or entertaining performances? Or clutter it up with scads of commercials, called announcements (or, in the supreme euphemism, 'opportunities for ministry')? Could it be that the church thinks the cross and the table are not enough? And so Ahaz is not the only one traveling to Damascus.

Second, *evil is helped by weakness as much as by wickedness* (vv. 10-11, 15-16). This implication depends on a particular view of Uriah (or Urijah) the priest as our writer portrays him. 'Uriah the priest' is mentioned five times (vv. 10, 11 [twice], 15, 16), and he does whatever King Ahaz tells him to do (vv. 11, 16). He raises no protests, he takes no stand. Whatever Ahaz commands, Uriah does. Now some simply can't see a negative tinge to Uriah here, because, citing Isaiah 8:1-2, they point out that he was a 'supporter of Isaiah'. But Isaiah 8 says nothing of Uriah as a supporter of Isaiah; it simply says that Uriah was to be used as a 'reliable witness' to authenticate Isaiah's billboard prophecy. One can accurately attest a document and still be a congenital yes-man.[22] Obviously, Uriah had a lot to lose should he refuse to go along with Ahaz's liturgical corruptions. Some of us know a little of that. Some of us know what it is to lose pensions or medical insurance because we could not continue association with a church denomination that refuses to be bound by the moorings of Scripture or credal orthodoxy. It can feel like your security has just been whumped in its solar plexus. But the way of peace Uriah-style never leads to righteousness but merely cooperates with wickedness. Often our call is to conflict rather than cooperation.

Benjamin Warfield once happened to meet Mrs. Stevenson, wife of the president of Princeton Seminary, on a Princeton

[21]At the church I serve our worship is carefully planned never to be exactly the same from Sunday to Sunday.
[22]Cf. Geoffrey Grogan, 'Isaiah,' *The Expositor's Bible Commentary*, 12 vols. (Grand Rapids: Zondervan, 1986), 6:67: 'Uriah the priest is probably the king's ally and instrument in apostasy who is named in 2 Kings 16:11. "Reliable witnesses" need not describe their character so much as their position as people of standing in the community.'

street. Mrs. Stevenson was worried about the fireworks that might erupt at the upcoming Presbyterian General Assembly. 'Dr. Warfield,' she pled, 'I hear there is going to be trouble at the General Assembly. Do let us pray for peace.' To which Warfield replied, 'I am praying that if they do not do what is right, there may be a mighty battle.'[23] That must be our attitude—not because we crave conflict but because we fear spinelessness that shares in other men's sins.

The slight hope for Yahweh's servants (vv. 19-20)

Sad to say that the best news about Ahaz is in verse 20a—'he was buried with his fathers.' And, although it may not yet be apparent there is a ray of hope in the last line of the chapter: 'And Hezekiah his son reigned in his place.'

We won't get to Hezekiah's reign until 2 Kings 18. And Hezekiah's rule won't lack its own problems. But, suffice to say, it *was* a time of religious reform and national deliverance. It will not be the final crescendo of the kingdom of God, but it will prove a period of refreshing, a time of some restoration, a breather from the intensity of wickedness under Ahaz.

I simply want to point out that God has a tendency to do this, to give these 'breathers' to his people. How merciful that he usually doesn't give us Ahaz-upon-Ahaz. How kind he is to respond to our need for relief. Such Hezekiah-times are not final solutions, but they are gracious provisions and should be received as such. William Cowper nicely captures this truth in his hymn (partly based on Habakkuk 3:16-19):

> Sometimes a light surprises the Christian while he sings;
> it is the Lord who rises with healing in his wings:
> when comforts are declining, he grants the soul again
> a season of clear shining, to cheer it after rain.

Who can say it better than that?

---

[23]Stanley W. Bamberg, 'Our Image of Warfield Must Go,' *Journal of the Evangelical Theological Society* 34 (1991): 235-36.

22

God of the Last Days
(2 Kings 17:1-23)

When we were living in Maryland I often had to drive the busy beltways of the Baltimore-Washington area. I believe it was on the beltway around D.C. that one reached a point, coming over a rise or rounding a curve, where a huge Mormon temple loomed ahead. It was so situated that it dominated the skyline and mesmerized one's attention until the motorway curved and traffic turned from it. Strategic visibility was written all over that monument. That temple almost mocked every motorist, as if to say, 'You simply cannot avoid me, can you?' It was a piece of visual domination.

Now 2 Kings 17:1-6 is a bit that way. Oh, it's loaded with problems and difficulties, but these do not detract from the dominating presence the writer wants us to feel. Six times in these verses he refers to the 'king of Assyria'. He fills the landscape and horizon. And because the king of Assyria so dominates the scene, Israel will cease to exist. Israel has lived in Assyria's shadow for some time but now she will be caught in Assyria's vise. The writer's preoccupation with the 'king of Assyria' is his way of getting you into the mood of this chapter.

Now there are problems. Verse 1 seems to say that Hoshea's reign starts from Ahaz of Judah's twelfth year. That could be if Ahaz became co-regent with his father Jotham in 743 BC and verse 1 was calculating from the start of Ahaz's co-regency.[1] In any case, the years 732/1-722 seem firm for Hoshea's reign.

During that reign, Shalmaneser V (727-722 BC) came up against Hoshea, who submitted to the Assyrian and began to pay tribute (v. 3). All was well until, for whatever insane reason, Hoshea conspired with Egypt and withheld tribute from Shalmaneser (v. 4).

Hoshea entered a conspiracy with So, king of Egypt (v. 4a). So what about So? We have to confess that our knowledge about So is not even so-so. Some propose that So is a place name, Sais, and that its ruler, Tefnakht, is Hoshea's recourse (e.g., Cogan and Tadmor). Others take So as an abbreviation for Osorkon IV (Kitchen). Or is So the Nubian Piankhy?[2] At present we cannot be definite about So's identity. Nor did it really matter for Hoshea since he was consigned to an Assyrian slammer (v. 4b),[3] Samaria besieged, taken after three years, and its people deported.[4]

One more historical conundrum. There has been much discussion over which Assyrian king did what in verses 5-6. Shalmaneser V besieged Samaria (v. 5) but he died about 722 BC when Samaria finally fell. Since Sargon II claims in his inscriptions that he conquered Samaria and captured and deported over 27,000 people,[5] some think that Sargon must have completed the conquest of Samaria upon Shalmaneser's demise and that verse 6 describes Sargon's work. However, it now appears that Shalmaneser V did capture Samaria (vv. 5-6a),

---

[1]See the discussion in J. N. Oswalt, 'Chronology of the OT,' ISBE, 1:683-84. For a recent re-evaluation of 2 Kings 17:1, see Rodger C. Young, 'When Was Samaria Captured? The Need for Precision in Biblical Chronologies,' *Journal of the Evangelical Theological Society* 47/4 (2004): 589-92.

[2]For a clear summary, see J. K. Hoffmeier, 'So,' ISBE, 4:558. Cf. also E. S. Meltzer, ABD, 6:76. On So = Piankhy, see the lucid argument by A. R. W. Green, 'The Identity of King So of Egypt—An Alternative Interpretation,' *Journal of Near Eastern Studies* 52/2 (1993): 99-108.

[3]Some read verse 4b and verses 5-6 chronologically, i.e., somehow Hoshea was captured and imprisoned and then Shalmaneser invested Samaria. Others read them as parallel, i.e., verse 4 reports Hoshea's fate, and verses 5-6 give greater detail about how that came about. For the latter, see C. F. Keil, *The Books of the Kings*, Biblical Commentary on the Old Testament (1876; reprint ed.,, Grand Rapids: Eerdmans, 1965), 411-12.

[4]They were deported hundreds of miles to the northeast. Halah was a little northeast of Nineveh. Gozan was located on the upper Habor River, a tributary of the Euphrates. These locations were within Assyria proper, while the 'towns of the Medes' were much further east—they were 'Frontiersville'. See *The Macmillan Bible Atlas*, 3rd ed. (New York: Macmillan, 1993), 115.

[5]See D. Winton Thomas, ed., *Documents from Old Testament Times* (New York: Harper Torchbooks, 1958), 58-63 (translated by D. J. Wiseman).

and that Sargon II retook the city in 720 BC. Sargon is likely the one responsible for deporting Israelites (v. 6b). The deportations must have occurred over a period of time, since Sargon had no control over 'towns of the Medes' (v. 6c) until about 716 BC.[6]

Since 2 Kings 17 is a long, intricate chapter, let me provide a reader's map before we go on to exposition.[7]

Flow of 2 Kings 17

(1) Event: the arrival of judgment, vv. 1-6
(2) Reflection: the abortion of salvation history, vv. 7-17
(3) Tragedy: apostasy is contagious, vv. 18-23
(4) Irony: the new syncretism, vv. 24-41

In this chapter, however, we will only cover verses 1-23.

I was recently reading a discussion by Walter Kaiser in which he stated, '[W]henever we are at a loss as to what we should preach on a passage, we will never go wrong if we focus on God, his actions and his requirements.'[8] I propose we approach verses 7-23 this way. This passage breaks down into three distinct parts, a reference to 'provoking' (or 'exasperating,' Heb. *kā'as*) Yahweh coming near the end of the one section (v. 11b) and at the end of another section (v. 17b). So our divisions are: verses 7-12, 13-17, and 18-23. Each of these begins with a distinct theological affirmation: Yahweh brought Israel up from Egypt (v. 7); Yahweh warned Israel by his prophets (v. 13); and Yahweh was very angry with Israel—enough to banish them from his presence (v. 18). On to the exposition.

The God who redeems (vv. 7-12)
Verse 7 explains why the Assyrian machine crushed and spit out Israel. It was because of ingratitude—they 'sinned against

---

[6]See the discussion by K. Lawson Younger, Jr., 'Recent Study on Sargon II, King of Assyria: Implications for Biblical Studies,' in *Mesopotamia and the Bible*, ed. Mark W. Chavalas and K. Lawson Younger, Jr. (Grand Rapids: Baker, 2002), 288-301. Cf. also M. Cogan and H. Tadmor, *II Kings*, Anchor Bible (Garden City, NY: Doubleday, 1988), 197.
[7]On the literary shape of 2 Kings 17, see also Richard D. Nelson, *First and Second Kings*, Interpretation (Louisville: John Knox, 1987), 229.
[8]Walter C. Kaiser, Jr., *Preaching and Teaching from the Old Testament* (Grand Rapids: Baker, 2003), 57.

Yahweh their God who brought them up from the land of Egypt, from under the grip of Pharaoh king of Egypt' (v. 7a). Yahweh their God is a liberating Lord, a God who redeems from bondage, but Israel seemed not to notice: 'they feared other gods' (v. 7b). Amazing grace is met with massive apostasy.

Verses 7-12 read like a digest of the Book of Judges and of Kings to this point. Two keynotes stand out—the passion they have and the standard they follow. They build high places 'in all their towns, from watchtower to fortified city' (v. 9b). The watchtower might serve for the protection of flocks in the wilderness (2 Chron. 26:10) or as a forward military outpost to detect or retard invasion.[9] Israel is so hot after perversion that she litters the land with high places from the most remote and sparse settlements to her major urban areas. They set up 'pillars and Asherah—posts on every high hill and under every green tree' (v. 10). 'They made offerings on all the high places' (v. 11a). The 'alls' and the 'everys' tell the story. Here was a people in heat for bastard worship.

But our summary also notes the standard they followed: 'they walked in the statutes of the nations whom Yahweh had driven out' (v. 8a), and 'they made offerings on all the high places like the nations Yahweh had exiled before them' (v. 11a). Not Yahweh's design, to be sure. Before Israel entered Canaan, Moses told them that they were to have absolutely no truck with the peoples in the land (i.e., à la Deut. 7:1-5, show no mercy to them, enter into no covenants with them, make no marriages with them, harbor no curiosity about their worship), 'for,' Moses continued, 'you are a people holy to Yahweh your God' (Deut. 7:6). So Israel is 'holy'—distinct, different, unique, unusual, unconventional. Israel's history did not follow Israel's call. Rather they were diligent to conform to the nations, to ape them and blend with them.

Diet Eman tells of life in Holland before the German occupation. Her family was quite close to another family in their church. Two girls in that family were her close friends. Diet's family often had Dutch soldiers for Sunday dinner before the war, since they lived next to an armory. But her friends' family avowed they could not do that because their family was so busy. Then came the Nazi occupation. One Sunday Diet was aghast

[9]Cf. Cogan and Tadmor, II Kings, 217.

when she entered her friends' house and saw a portrait of Hitler hanging above the piano. Moreover, German soldiers were entertained there that night.[10] Diet Eman (who would work for the Dutch resistance) would likely say this family had forgotten their 'Dutch-ness', so eager were they to fall in and coalesce with the occupying power. This was both Israel's standard and passion: to squeeze herself into the mold (cf. J. B. Phillips' rendering of Romans 12:2) of the nations (vv. 8, 11).

But we must never forget that, at its root, Israel's love affair with the nations is a *rejection of grace*. Verse 7 has a kind of textual dominance in this section, and it juxtaposes the anomaly of grace ('Yahweh their God who brought them up from the land of Egypt out from under Pharaoh's grip') and apostasy ('and they feared other gods'). Amazing grace should have been met with lasting gratitude.

Siegmund Weltlinger found out how fleeting gratitude is. He and his wife were taken in by the Möhring family in the Pankow district of Berlin, into their two room flat. The Weltlingers were Jews, hiding in Nazi-ville. In the spring of 1945 Russian troops entered Pankow. One Russian officer who entered the apartment assured the Weltlingers that the Russians would be good to them. Alas, however, when the whole apartment house was searched six revolvers were discovered along with some discarded uniforms. All in the housing complex were ordered outside, lined up against a wall. Things began to look deathly. Siegmund Weltlinger knew that many of these residents would have turned him in to the Nazis had they known he was hiding with the Möhrings. However, he stepped out and told the Russians that he was a Jew, and then: 'These are good people. All of them have sheltered us in this house. I ask you not to harm them. These weapons were thrown away by the Volkssturm.' His statement saved the lives of all the tenants. Weltlinger said that the people then became very kind to him and his wife—they were given an empty flat, and food and clothing. They could for the first time stand in the fresh air, walk in the street. But soon afterward the Russians were driven out of the area by an SS attack, and the residents Weltlinger had

---

[10]Diet Eman with J. Schaap, *Things We Couldn't Say* (Grand Rapids: Eerdmans, 1994), 41-42.

saved the day before suddenly became hostile again! Weltlinger said it was 'unbelievable'.[11]

That is the word one must write across Israel's history. Gratitude vanishes. Redemption finds only rebellion. Is this not one reason why the church celebrates the Lord's Supper so (hopefully) frequently? It fastens our eyes on our Redeemer and brings us to say:

> What language shall I borrow
> to thank thee, dearest Friend,
> for this thy dying sorrow,
> thy pity without end?

The 'nations' cannot lure us when grace clamps us in the bonds of gratitude.

The God who warns (vv. 13-17)

Before Yahweh brings his judgment he brings his truth. We might think otherwise after verses 7b-12—we expect a whiff of brimstone. Instead, 'Yahweh warned [or, testified against] Israel and Judah by the hand of all his prophets, every seer, saying, "Turn back from your evil ways..."' (v. 13a).[12] He sends prophets to call his people back to his law. Here is Yahweh's patience, Yahweh's restraint.

But the prophetic warnings receive the 'wilderness' response: 'But they did not listen, and they stiffened their neck like the neck of their fathers, who did not believe in Yahweh their God' (v. 14). The 'stiff neck' probably alludes to a farmer's difficulty with an obstinate draft animal that refuses to bend and accept the yoke. Israel was like this from Sinai to Canaan (see Exod. 32:9; 33:3, 5; 34:9; Deut. 9:6, 13; 10:16). And this resistance springs from unbelief (v. 14b). I call this the 'wilderness response' because verse 14 reflects Yahweh's exasperation with Israel during the wilderness wanderings at Kadesh-barnea: 'How long will this people despise me? And how long *will they not believe in me* in spite of all the signs I have done among them?' (Num. 14:11; see also Deut. 1:32; 9:23;

---

[11]Cornelius Ryan, *The Last Battle* (New York: Simon and Schuster, 1966), 462-63.
[12]Note the inclusion of 'Judah' here; the focus is on Israel, but Judah is no stranger to apostasy.

Ps. 78:32; 106:24). Where there is no faith there can be no fruit
of faith in obedience and submission. Where there is unbelief
what can we expect to see but a pile of deaf ears, stiff necks,
and rebellious hearts?

So we cannot be surprised at verses 15-17. They are sad but
not surprising. Read through verses 15-17 at a deliberate pace.
Feel the increasing weight each main clause adds to this mass
of apostasy. Three verses and ten main clauses summarize 200-
plus years of infidelity and crush the reader under its load:

> 'So they rejected his statutes and his covenant...and his
> testimonies'
> '(And) they went after worthlessness...and after the
> nations...'
> 'They forsook all the commandments of Yahweh...'
> 'They made for themselves molten (things)—two calves'
> 'They made an Asherah'
> 'They worshiped the host of heaven'
> 'They served Baal'
> 'They made their sons and their daughters pass through
> the fire'
> 'They practiced divination...'
> 'They sold themselves to do what was evil...'

We might comment on one or two items in this description.
Note the statement in verse 15b: 'They went after worthlessness
and became worthless' (see also Jer. 2:5). There is a word play
on the root *hbl*, the noun *hebel* referring to what is worthless,
useless, or futile. Here it refers to the nature of false gods—they
are nothing, zero, worthless. The 'worthlessness' of these
cipher-gods, however, does not simply lie in state. There is
a sad transformation that takes place in their worshipers—'they
went after worthlessness *and became worthless.*' We become
like what we worship. There was a clip in *Credenda Agenda*
several years ago about a four-year-old girl in North Wales
whose complexion had turned orangy. Her doctor discovered
she had been consuming 1.5 litres of Sunny Delight every day.
According to the report the manufacturers did admit that their
product would turn people yellow or orange but only when

slurped up in such nearly limitless amounts. This little girl had something of a *hebel*-experience: she became what she drank. This is why worship is different from getting a haircut or wearing green socks—it really changes *you*. You will become like what—or Whom—you worship.

Notice too the last clause of verse 17: 'And they sold themselves to do what was evil in Yahweh's eyes to exasperate him.' We may sometimes use this language of a politician who 'sells out' to certain interests. Actually, however, this language has already been used of King Ahab in 1 Kings 21:20, 25; the latter verse says: 'Only there was no one like Ahab, who sold himself to do what is evil in Yahweh's eyes—whom Jezebel his wife incited.' Now here in verse 17 this language is used of the nation—all Israel was 'Ahab-bing', giving themselves over to the power and control of evil, goading Yahweh to bring judgment.

The problem with this stretch of text is that the litany of apostasy (vv. 15-17) can eclipse the revelation of God (v. 13). Here is the God who warns, who in his grace sends his prophets to call his people away from their love affairs with their bastard deities.[13] And the New Testament refuses to allow us to treat Yahweh's warnings and Israel's failure as ancient history. 'See to it that you do not refuse him who speaks. If they did not escape when they refused him who warned them on earth, how much less will we, if we turn away from him who warns us from heaven?' (Hebrews 12:25, NIV). Hebrews assumes that Israel's apostasy is repeatable for professing Christians. In the context of that epistle to 'turn away from him' is to turn away from the Son of God who paved the way into the holy place with his own blood.

The God who judges (vv. 18-23)
The section begins with the anger of Yahweh (v. 18) and closes with the land of Assyria (v. 23)—where Israel was exiled as Yahweh's judgment. Let me allude to a couple of items before highlighting the dominant note of this section.

The writer hints at the *scope* of Yahweh's judgment. At the end of verse 18 he tells us that with Israel removed only the

---

[13]See discussion of Judges 6:7-10 in *Judges: Such a Great Salvation* (Ross-shire: Christian Focus, 2000), 91-93.

tribe of Judah remained—and the mention of Judah leads him into a short and sad parenthesis in verse 19: 'Even Judah did not keep the commandments of Yahweh their God, and they walked in the statutes of Israel which they practiced.' So even as he reports Yahweh's judgment on Israel he says in this 'pathetic' parenthesis that the same is coming to Judah as well.[14]

Verses 21-22 point to the *cause* of Yahweh's judgment. When Yahweh ripped the united kingdom apart (1 Kings 11), Israel made Jeroboam son of Nebat king (v. 21a). The form of the verb in verse 21b sums up the impact of Jeroboam's rule—he 'banished' or 'drove away' Israel from after Yahweh. The first verb of verse 22 can rightly be translated in a durative way—'the sons of Israel went on walking in all the sins of Jeroboam'—and so highlights the stranglehold and tragedy of Jeroboam's innovations. Israel was tenaciously faithful to Jeroboam. They stepped into their historical graves still worshiping his calves.

I recently saw a documentary on the Guyana suicides in 1978 under the aegis of Jim Jones. One marvels, I suppose, at the mesmerizing power a man can have over people to make them mentally and physically goosestep to his orders. The hold Jeroboam ben Nebat's cult had over Israel was something like that. Their very first king had driven the first nail into Israel's coffin and she never recovered.[15]

But the dominant note of this section is the *tragedy* of judgment. We hear it three times:

'So he removed them from his presence' (v. 18a)
'...until he threw them away from his presence' (v. 20b)
'...until Yahweh removed Israel from his presence' (v. 23a)

What did this being 'removed' or 'thrown away' from Yahweh's presence involve? At least, in part, exile from the land. This is clear from the sequence in verse 23: 'Yahweh removed Israel

---

[14]Cf. Pauline A. Viviano, '2 Kings 17: A Rhetorical and Form-Critical Analysis,' *The Catholic Biblical Quarterly* 49 (1987): 558-59. Some think that 'all the seed of Israel' in verse 20 includes Judah, but it is difficult to be sure. I take verse 19 as parenthetical (about Judah) and verse 20 as picking up with the northern kingdom again.

[15]See my discussion on 2 Kings 15, 'the tragedy of the original sin,' for a similar emphasis. Jeroboam's dominant influence, however, does not negate Israel's responsibility.

from his presence…and so Israel was exiled from its (or, his) land.' John Bimson sums it up nicely:

> When God is spoken of as removing his people from his presence… the reference is to their being driven from the land. This is not because the writer thought of Yahweh as somehow restricted to the land of Israel, but because he regarded the land as the primary arena in which Yahweh's purposes for his people were fulfilled.[16]

But I wonder if that catches quite all of it. I think we must understand that being removed/thrown away from Yahweh's presence is not only a matter of geography but of fellowship; it is not simply location but rejection. And nothing is sadder.[17]

Donald Cargill's act at Torwood in Stirlingshire in September 1680 was controversial even at the time. He preached from Ezekiel 21:25-27 and then solemnly proceeded to declare excommunication upon Charles Stuart, king of England, upon the Dukes of York, Monmouth, Lauderdale, Rothes, and upon General Dalziel and Sir George Mackenzie, for their sins and their cruelties upon the Lord's people. The following year the Duke of Rothes became dangerously ill. Inconsistently enough, he wanted some of his wife's persecuted Presbyterian ministers to counsel and pray with him in his last hours. Referring to Cargill's action at Torwood, Rothes told one of the ministers: 'We all thought little of what that man did in excommunicating us; but I find that sentence binding upon me now, and will, I fear, bind to eternity.' To this Alexander Smellie added, 'Thus Lord Rothes went out into the night.'[18]

Some will fault me for, among other things, individualizing what is corporate (Israel) in the text. But we can use the corporate to keep us from feeling the sting we should feel. And we must understand that being removed from the Lord's presence may involve more than ending up in Assyria.

---

[16]John J. Bimson, '1 and 2 Kings,' *New Bible Commentary*, 4th ed. (Leicester: Inter-Varsity, 1994), 377.

[17]One finds the same language used of Judah in 23:27 and 24:3.

[18]Alexander Smellie, *Men of the Covenant* (New York: Fleming H. Revell, n.d.), 284-85; and W. M. Hetherington, *History of the Church of Scotland* (Edinburgh: John Johnstone, 1841), 471-72.

23

A Religion Fair?
(2 Kings 17:24-41)

Occasionally one hears of a 'job fair' perhaps held in a shopping mall or a university facility. It may be geared for upcoming graduates from colleges or trade schools. Representatives of different companies are on hand to speak with prospects about opportunities available with their respective firms. The options are legion, limited only, I suppose, by applicants' interests and aptitudes—and available positions.

That is something like the state of affairs in Samaria after the Israelites had been carried off. The influx of transplants under the Assyrian relocation program brought their own religious traditions and preferences to their new home. It was a religion fair—a cafeteria of devotional possibilities. One could worship Nergal with the folks from Cuth (v. 30) or practice up on child sacrifice to Adrammelech (v. 31)—or whatever. Samaria was a hodge-podge of religious diversity. I've no intention of discussing the various 'cults' extant in Samaria at this time; we haven't enough data for that anyway. But we can discern certain *types* of religion in this section and it would be profitable to work our way through them.

Coping Religion (vv. 24-28)
New residents come to Samaria 'from Babylon, Cuthah, Avva, Hamath, and Sepharvaim' (v. 24). Cuthah may well be Tel

Ibrahim, twenty miles northeast of Babylon. Avva's location is uncertain. If Hamath is Hamath on the Orontes, it would be about 120 miles north/northeast of Damascus. Some suggest that Sepharvaim may be Sibraim near Damascus.[1] Since these new residents came from various locations, one may suppose 'that the deportations listed in 2 Kings 17:24 resulted from several Assyrian campaigns during the reign of more than one monarch'.[2] Verse 24 then summarizes several waves of Assyrian resettlements. Now Israel is largely peopled with pagans.[3] They don't bother themselves about Yahweh and that becomes a problem.

At first these imports 'did not fear Yahweh' (v. 25a), and so 'Yahweh sent lions among them, which were killing some of them' (v. 25b).[4] The official dispatch to Assyria reports the lion scourge and proposes the reason is that the settlers 'do not know the *mišpaṭ* of the god of the land' (v. 26). *mišpaṭ* can be 'requirement' or 'ordinance', but here it may well refer to the 'rites', the ritual practices, by which Yahweh was to be worshiped.[5] The king of Assyria directs them to require one of the exiled priests to go back and teach the people these rites (v. 27).

Lion attacks, of course, are not amusing, but one senses a hint of irony here. For one thing, the 'newly settled nations behave more correctly than did their predecessors in the land'.[6] At least these pagans are concerned to pacify Yahweh, which is more than can be said for Israel (see vv. 7-17). Then too the priest who comes to enlighten these pagans settles in Bethel,

[1]See T. R. Hobbs, *2 Kings*, Word Biblical Commentary (Waco: Word, 1985), 237, and D. J. Wiseman, *1 & 2 Kings*, Tyndale Old Testament Commentaries (Leicester: Inter-Varsity, 1993), 268-69.

[2]M. Cogan, *Imperialism and Religion: Assyria, Judah and Israel in the Eighth and Seventh Centuries B.C.E.* (Missoula, MT: Scholars, 1974), 101 (fn 23).

[3]Cf. Cogan, *Imperialism and Religion*, 101: 'The upshot of these incessant transfers [Israelites out, pagans in] was a shift in the ethnic make-up of north Israel in favor of the foreign settlers. While our sources do not tell of a systematic Assyrian depopulation of the Ephraimite hill country, it seems clear that the native Israelites left on the land were not, as Noth contended, "numerically much greater" than the "foreign upper class" settlers. The opposite was the case. Sargon's exile of 27,290 Israelites from Samaria was but the final stage in a bitter four-year struggle to subdue the rebellious city.'

[4]On lion plagues, see the annals of Assurbanipal (669-633 BC) in D. D. Luckenbill, *Ancient Records of Assyria and Babylonia*, 2 vols. (London: Histories & Mysteries of Man, 1989 [reprint]), 2:363 (sect. 935).

[5]M. Cogan and H. Tadmor, *II Kings*, Anchor Bible (Garden City, NY: Doubleday, 1988), 210.

[6]Hobbs, *2 Kings*, 237.

one of the original sites for calf worship (1 Kings 12:25-33). Does that indicate his preference for Jeroboam theology? In any case, any priest from the former northern kingdom would likely propagate more syncretism than orthodoxy.

Conceivably the lion scourge could have proven an initial opportunity for these people to turn to Yahweh. Not much chance of that happening, however, when their evangelist is a northern priest. At any rate, getting rid of the lions is the important thing and if some recognition of Yahweh secures that end that is all that matters. That's what religion ought to do—help one cope with the troubles and tensions of life. This sort of religion is primarily pragmatic and can therefore be crassly manipulative.

Quite a furor arose over the 1936 Olympics. They were to be held in Berlin in Nazified Germany. Because of that regime's anti-Semitic policies some in Great Britain, France, and the United States wanted to boycott the games. But they went on. And there were several Jews among Germany's athletes. Captain Wolfgang Fürstner, a Jew, was in charge of erecting and managing the Olympic village. Anti-Semitic posters along the highways were taken down. No one saw any notices barring Jews from resorts. An anti-Jewish newspaper disappeared from the newsstands in Berlin. Visitors flocked to Berlin and were welcomed enthusiastically. Many left with wonderfully favorable impressions of Hitler's reich.[7] But it was all window dressing. Adolf was simply playing his cards to obtain favorable world opinion.

And some religion can be that pragmatic. We must do something to get rid of these lions. So some crave a 'protective' faith that charms away troubles, that deals with threats to one's security. The big question is not: Is it true?, but: Will it work to avoid discomfort? To ward off disaster? In the wake of catastrophes, like 9-11, comes the question, 'Where is/was God?' Nothing wrong with asking that question but sometimes there's a fallacious assumption behind it, namely, that God is supposed always to make life safe; that God is my existential pacifier and if he does not guarantee my security, of what use is he? Religion, you know, should get rid of the lions for you.

---

[7]John Toland, *Adolf Hitler* (New York: Ballantine, 1976), 392-93.

Creative Religion (vv. 29-33)

The new residents were very religious; they wasted no time in installing their gods and worship centers (vv. 29-31).[8]

> (29) However, each nation continued to make its own gods and to set them up in the cult places which had been made by the people of Samaria; each nation [set them up] in the towns in which it lived. (30) The Babylonians made Succoth-benoth, and the men of Cuth made Nergal, and the men of Hamath made Ashima, (31) and the Avvites made Nibhaz and Tartak; and the Sepharvites burned their children [as offerings] to Adrammelech and Anamelech, the gods of Sepharvaim. (NJPS)

The operative word in these verses is the damning little verb 'make' (or 'made'). Our writer uses it six times in verses 29-31 to describe the 'making' of gods. It is the very common verb '$\bar{a}\acute{s}\bar{a}h$ (to do, make), used over 2600 times in the Old Testament. One wouldn't think much of it except that when the writer piles it up, as he does here, one suspects that he is being sarcastic. They made...they made...they made—that is pagan religion, do-it-yourself devotion. This is the very same biblical sarcasm one finds in 1 Kings 12:31-33 where the writer describes the inauguration of Jeroboam's bull worship, using '$\bar{a}\acute{s}\bar{a}h$ eight times in three verses, in order to mark the stupidity of such 'spirituality'.[9]

The Israelites, called the 'Samarians' (v. 29), had even helped in this venture because they had 'made' the high places which the new residents now used. So here is creative religion. Religion is what you like to make ('$\bar{a}\acute{s}\bar{a}h$) of it. And it can be so comprehensive and ecumenical—you can both worship Yahweh and serve your own favorite gods (v. 33). You can make it as you like it.

Charles Colson tells of a conversation he had with a neighbor. She was so excited about her church. Colson tried to point out graciously that the group was a cult that believed neither in the resurrection nor the deity of Christ. The woman was unmoved. She simply exclaimed, 'Oh, but the services are so wonderful.

---

[8]Nergal, worshiped by the people from Cuth, was god of the plague and underworld, but the precise identifications of the other deities are elusive.

[9]See *The Wisdom and the Folly: An Exposition of the Book of First Kings* (Ross-shire: Christian Focus, 2002), 143-45.

I always feel so good after I've been there!'[10] What is true takes second place to what I enjoy. What I like rules.

But the 'creativity' of paganism creeps into the church as well. Jim Nelson Black tells of the first official event at the meeting of the World Council of Churches General Assembly in Canberra, Australia. It was a pagan purification ritual—delegates walked through the smoke of burning leaves while insect noises were played on loudspeakers. Aborigines clad in loincloths danced in circles around the group. South Korean minister Reverend Chung Hyun Kyung called on the spirits of the dead. She called for delegates to read the Bible from the perspective of 'birds, water, air, trees.' She told them to think 'like a mountain'. Afterward an Anglican minister of Indian origin said, 'I left that behind to become a Christian.'[11]

So pagan religion creates what it likes; biblical faith receives what is revealed. Pagans worship based on what they prefer; biblicists must worship based on what God declares. The biblical worshiper must submit; the pagan worshiper may concoct. And when pagan worship mixes with true worship (v. 33) we have more Canberras.

Covenant Religion (vv. 34-40)
Verse 34 stands in formal contradiction to verse 33. In verse 33 the imported residents are 'fearing Yahweh and serving their own gods', while verse 34 denies this: 'They are not fearing Yahweh'—nor, for that matter, are they living in line with the statutes, ordinances, instruction, and commandments Yahweh had directed Israel to keep.[12] We'll likely miss our cue unless we realize, as Iain Provan holds, that verses 25-33 drip with irony.

Some years back when our sons were young I somehow obtained (he may have given it to me) a sheet of paper with our middle son's writing. In this brief message he told how he despised the seminary where I taught, railed, I believe, at its president, and entered several other 'exhibits' of evidence (perhaps how he detested our church, and so on). I was shocked.

---

[10]Charles Colson, *Against the Night* (Ann Arbor: Servant, 1989), 98.

[11]Jim Nelson Black, *When Nations Die* (Wheaton: Tyndale House, 1994), 202.

[12]The 'statutes' and 'ordinances' are obviously Yahweh's, even though the text literally reads 'their statutes' and 'their ordinances'.

I showed it to our department secretary at the seminary and she was non-plussed. What had I done? I was utterly unaware of inflicting such severe psychological damage on him. Visions of therapy danced in my head. When I was able to ask him about it, Seth simply said, 'Oh, Thursday [or whatever day it had been] is "Opposite Day".' Which means a kid writes the very reverse of what he really feels. In short, his note was full of irony, and, because I didn't detect that, I misinterpreted it.

Now biblical writers are not likely to set down a blatant contradiction (though there are plenty of biblical critics who assume they were such nincompoops). Nor need we think that happened here—not if we see the irony.

> We must reckon, then, with the presence of irony in 2 Kings 17:25-33. It is not a passage meant to be taken at face value. The authors are simply setting up a particular point of view in order to demolish it—rather in the manner of a participant in a debating competition. The tone of the passage is best caught, in fact, if the reader mentally supplies quotation marks to the words "worship" and "worshiped" [lit., "fear," "feared"] in the NIV translation of verses 28 and 32-33. For we are certainly not to regard the "worship" described in these verses as true worship—as verses 34-39 make clear.[13]

Even in verse 33 we sense our writer has tongue in cheek when he says, 'they were fearing Yahweh *and* they were serving their own gods' (emphasis mine). Verse 34 then says it in bald prose: 'they were not fearing Yahweh.'

At the end of verse 34 the writer refers to what Yahweh had commanded the sons of Jacob or Israel. And in verses 35-39 he inserts a flashback, rehearsing, in second-person address, the terms of Yahweh's covenant. The first verb of verse 35 should be construed as a pluperfect—'Now Yahweh had cut a covenant with them and commanded them...'[14] He is taking us back into exodus-time.

Note how stringently the covenant insists on exclusive devotion to Yahweh. One runs into three negativized verbs in

---

[13]Iain W. Provan, *1 and 2 Kings*, New International Biblical Commentary (Peabody, MA: Hendrickson, 1995), 250-51.

[14]One meets instances of *waw* consecutive + imperfect = pluperfect a number of times in narrative. For some examples and explanation, see Bruce K. Waltke and M. O'Connor, *An Introduction to Biblical Hebrew Syntax* (Winona Lake, IN: Eisenbrauns, 1990), 552-53. Among English versions NRSV, JB, NJB, NLT, and TEV translate as a pluperfect; NIV and REB render 35a a bit differently but in any case recognize the flashback.

verse 35: Israel must not bow down, serve, or sacrifice to other gods. Verses 36-37 invert normal grammar and put the direct or indirect objects first in the clauses for emphasis:

> But *Yahweh* who brought you up from the land of Egypt with great might and with an arm stretched out—*him* you must fear, and *to him* you must bow down, and *to him* you must sacrifice, and *the statutes and ordinances and instruction and commandment which he wrote for you,* you must be careful to do…

He does the same in verse 38 ('the covenant') and verse 39 ('but Yahweh your God you must fear'). And lest we miss the point, he hammers it into us three times: 'You shall not fear other gods' (vv. 35, 37, 38). Covenant religion is exclusive religion, the faith that bashes our both-ands to bits with its either-or.

Verse 40, I think, gives Israel's response to the (ongoing) covenant proclamation of verses 35-39: 'But they did not listen; instead they went on acting in line with their former custom.'[15] Israel had no stomach for covenant religion.

Covenant religion tolerates no 'Yahweh-plus' sentiments. You must fear Yahweh and no other. When I was very small my father used to fix my bread for me at meals. World War II had been over for four or five years, but my father was still living with a ration mentality. So, before he prepared my slice of bread he would ask, 'You want butter or jelly?' (It wasn't actually butter but margarine.) It was one or the other. One might wonder why there was no other possibility; one might lust for a butter-plus option. But the universe of our household was an exclusive universe: it was always either-or. Covenant

---

[15]Some disagree and take verse 40 with verse 41 as the response of the imported nations. This seems appropriate since 'acting in line with their former custom' in 40b seems to pick up 'acting in line with (their) former customs' in 34a, where it refers to the imported peoples. However: (1) 'But they did not listen,' 40a, immediately after verses 35-39, more naturally points to Israel; (2) since irony pervades the passage we might assume it in 40b—as the imports kept acting in line with their former customs (34), so Israel, not to be out-paganed by pagans, did the same; and (3) Israel *did* have a 'former custom' of worshiping idols while in Egypt (Ezek. 20:7-8; Josh. 24:14). Richard Nelson nicely captures the thrust: 'These foreigners parody Israel. Trying to fear the Lord in their syncretistic way (vv. 32, 33, 41), they really do not fear God at all (v. 34), for they do not follow the law of Deuteronomy. If you want to see what Israel was like, the narrator suggests to exilic readers, go look at these contemporary foreigners who are "doing according to their former manner" even "to this day" (v. 34a) just as Israel used to do (v. 40)' (*First and Second Kings*, Interpretation [Louisville: John Knox, 1987], 232).

religion is that way. It carries a fundamental intolerance at its center: Yahweh or other gods. If Jesus is Lord, all competitors must be excluded. As I have noted before, pagan religions were not like this. No pagan deity worth his/her salt ever got its divine bowels in an uproar if one of its devotees worshiped or prayed or sacrificed to another god or goddess. Only biblical, covenant religion carries this virulent animosity toward all would-be competitors. One suspects this unique religion is also the true religion.

Condemning Religion (v. 41)

Verse 41 comes back to the 'new' nations who had been resettled in Samaria: 'So these nations went on "fearing" Yahweh and they kept serving their idols; moreover, to this day their children and children's children go on doing as their fathers had done.' We've seen it before; the boring binge of bondage—they serve their idols and their descendants follow along in lockstep down through the years. One generation embraces falsehood and virtually dooms their descendants unless God in his grace interrupts this nexus of damnation.

Joseph P. Kennedy was father of a U. S. president, an attorney general, and a senator. The last, Edward (Ted), is still extant. One of Joseph's daughters had a drinking problem, a reaction, perhaps, to a cheating husband. One grandchild became a drug addict and four grandchildren abused drugs, one dying as a result. Two grandchildren declared themselves alcoholics and another went to AA meetings. One was accused of raping a woman. He was found not guilty but then got into a fight in a Virginia bar and pleaded no contest to a charge of assault and battery.[16] One cannot negate personal responsibility, but at the same time one cannot help but wonder if much of this is not the fruit of the hard, driving, and immoral Joe Kennedy. A legacy is a frightening thing.

Verse 41 breathes such an air of hopelessness, succeeding generations aping the commitments of the former ones. Religion is not necessarily a good thing. There's such a thing as condemning religion; there's such a thing as a religion that damns.

---

[16]Ronald Kessler, *The Sins of the Father* (New York: Warner, 1996), 402-3.

Bleak is the word for 2 Kings 17. Yet there is a minuscule ray of light for Israel. Naturally, it's in the covenant promise in verse 39b: 'And *he* will deliver you from the hand of all your enemies.'[17] But that hope depends on whether they fear Yahweh (v. 39a).

---

[17]Cf. Paul R. House, *1, 2 Kings*, New American Commentary (Nashville: Broadman & Holman, 1995), 345.

The Last Days

2 Kings 18–25

24

Fresh Air, Dark Day
(2 Kings 18)

Second Kings 18 is a bit like May 2, 1863. Then, near Chancellorsville, Virginia, 45,000 Confederate troops under General Robert E. Lee faced a northern army twice their number. Lee and his lieutenant general, 'Stonewall' Jackson, held conference, after which General Jackson took 25,000 southern troops, marched the length of the northern army's front, and came late in the afternoon to a position due west of the northerners. Jackson's troops seemed to rise out of nowhere as they smashed into the exposed right flank of the northern line. One federal corps was routed; the whole right half of its battle line was disrupted.[1] Darkness and the tangled woods kept the Confederates from capitalizing on their triumph. However, it was a plan that went right, with all the advantage of a luscious surprise. And yet that night General Jackson was shot down by his own troops. He and a small group of riders were scouting the lines. They were riding back into the southern lines but southern troops had not been told that such a party was out. Hence in the dark Jackson & Co. were taken for northern troops and fired upon. In little more than a week Jackson would die from complications from his wounds. Chancellorsville—a brilliant victory in the afternoon and a tragic loss at night.

---

[1] Cf. Bruce Catton, *This Hallowed Ground* (Garden City, NY: Doubleday, 1956), 238-44.

Now that is the way 2 Kings 18 strikes one if taken by itself.[2] Here is such a breath of fresh air at the first (vv. 1-8)—it's as if David were reigning again. And yet it's such a dark day at the close, for Hezekiah is besieged in Jerusalem, shut up 'like a caged bird' (according to Sennacherib), and—as far as the media could see—without any hope at all. Things have gone from bright to bleak.

Before wading into the exposition of the chapter, I want to provide an overall sketch of its development; sometimes it is useful to see the 'bones' of a long piece of text.

2 Kings 18

A breath of fresh air (Hezekiah), vv. 1-8

A blast of stale air (Assyria), vv. 9-16

      Shalmaneser 'came up' (*'ālāh*), vv. 9-12
      Sennacherib 'came up' (*'ālāh*), vv. 13-16

First speech: trust (*bāṭaḥ*), vv. 17-25

      Exposure (Egypt), vv. 21, 24b
      Politics, v. 22
      Mockery, vv. 23-24a
      'Revelation,' v. 25

Second speech: deliverance (*nāṣal*), vv. 26-35

      The power of intimidation, vv. 26-27
      The attempt at division, vv. 28-32
      The logic of history, vv. 33-35

The end to a dark day, vv. 36-37

With this summary as our reference point, let's move on to exposition.

---

[2]And I almost have to do that—unless you want a chapter of fifty pages covering chapters 18–19. 2 Kings 18 is not the whole story, but it is legitimate to take it, for the present, by itself.

Relief may surprise us (vv. 1-8)
Major change came to Judah about 715 BC.[3] A new David
appeared. Hezekiah 'did what was right in Yahweh's eyes in line
with all that David his father had done' (v. 3). No qualifications.
In 14:3 Amaziah did right 'yet not like David his father', and in
1 Kings 15:11 Asa did what was right as David had, but he didn't
put the 'high places' out of business (v. 14a). But this new David
removes the high places, shattering the symbols of male deity
(pillars) and hacking down those of female deity (Asherah)—he
even pounds to bits the bronze serpent from Moses' time
(Num. 21:4-9) since the people were venerating it (v. 4).

However, the writer says that Hezekiah's premier virtue was
that 'he trusted in Yahweh, the God of Israel' (v. 5a).[4] He goes
on to flesh out what this trust involved: 'he clung [*dābaq*, cf.
Gen. 2:24, 'and he shall cling to his wife'] to Yahweh,' he 'did
not turn back from him', and he 'kept his commandments which
Yahweh had commanded Moses' (v. 6). So 'Yahweh was with
him' and 'wherever he went out he was successful' (v. 7a)—so
successful that he rebelled against the king of Assyria (v. 7b)
and swept through Philistia all the way to Gaza, the Philistines'
southernmost major city (v. 8).[5] In view of all this, Iain Provan
draws attention to some interesting parallels:

> The consequence of this religious faithfulness was that Hezekiah's
> military exploits paralleled David's in a way that was not true of

---

[3]The chronology is tough here. Leslie McFall, assuming a co-regency, construes
verses 1-2 to mean: In the third year of Hoshea son of Elah, king of Israel, Hezekiah
the son of Ahaz, king of Judah, *became co-regent*. He was twenty-five years old when
he *became king*, and he reigned twenty-nine years *as king* in Jerusalem. See again
McFall's article in *Themelios* 17/1 (Oct-Nov 1991): 9. In this case Hezekiah becomes co-
regent about 729 BC, becomes sole ruler in 715 BC and reigns until 686 BC. We do know
that Hezekiah's fourteenth year (v. 13), when Sennacherib invaded, was 701 BC.

[4]The Hebrew places 'in Yahweh, the God of Israel' first in the sentence for emphasis;
the stress is on the object of Hezekiah's trust. Hezekiah was unique among the kings
of Judah in this regard—'after him there was no one like him among all the kings
of Judah, nor was there any (like him) before him.' Some may think this contradicts 23:25
(of Josiah), but long ago Thenius explained that 18:5 'is not in contradiction with chap.
xxiii.25, for its application must be restricted to the single characteristic of trust in God.
In this particular Hezekiah showed himself the strongest, whereas, in xxiii.25, strict
fidelity to the (Mosaic) Law is applauded in Josiah' (cited in K. C. W. F. Bähr, *The Books
of the Kings*, Lange's Commentary on the Holy Scriptures, in vol. 3, *Samuel-Kings*
[1868; reprint ed.,, Grand Rapids: Zondervan, 1960), 204).

[5]Second Chronicles 29-31 contains much more about Hezekiah's religious reforms,
with only chapter 32 covering the Assyrian invasion.

any of the rest of his descendants. Only of David and Hezekiah among the Davidic kings is it said that *the LORD was with him* (v. 7; cf. 1 Sam. 16:18; 18:12, 14; 2 Sam. 5:10) and that the king *was successful* in war (Hb. *śkl*, v. 7; cf. 1 Sam. 18:5, 14, 15). Only David and Hezekiah, furthermore, are said to have *defeated* the Philistines (Hb. *nkh*, v. 8; cf. 1 Sam. 18:27; 19:8; etc.). As similar to David as he was, he was by the same token utterly dissimilar to Ahaz, for he would not continue to *serve* the king of Assyria (Hb. *'bd*; contrast Ahaz's description of himself as "servant" in 2 Kings 16:7) but *rebelled* against him.[6]

So David reigns again! It was almost too much to hope for.

Think of Hezekiah's reign in light of Judah's previous 150 years. Godly Jehoshaphat's stupid marriage alliances with Ahab's family not only guaranteed wicked kings (Jehoram, Ahaziah) to Judah but nearly wiped out the Davidic dynasty (Athaliah). Kings followed who were doing 'what was right' but never getting extreme about it (Joash, Amaziah, Uzziah, and Jotham). Then with Ahaz (ch. 16) it looks like Judah is plunging into the pit. How amazing that after Ahaz we have David *redivivus*.

Is this not typical of God's way with his kingdom and people? Either from enemies without or from danger within, the church sometimes looks like there is nothing that can stop her extinction. And then God sends a 'recovery' time, one of those 'Hezekiah interludes'. Idi Amin, for example, did not remain in power forever, and today the church in Uganda knows life without that butcher. Many of us have seen church denominations slide from vital evangelical faith to bland religious pluralism, usually when they abandon confidence in the authority of the Bible. We watch them go from virility in faith to impotence in witness. But I can think of one or two denominations that have gone from doctrinal drifting back to biblical authority. It surprises us. That's not what usually happens. But sometimes God's relief surprises us, and we can only be grateful. So—we must have done with a faithless pessimism that imagines God abandons his work. At the same time we must not make an idol out of Yahweh's times of relief.

---

[6]Iain W. Provan, *1 and 2 Kings,* New International Biblical Commentary (Peabody, MA: Hendrickson, 1995), 253.

We must not identify his kind interludes with the final kingdom of God. Hezekiah reigns now, but Manasseh (ch. 21) is coming and the darkness will get darker. We are to be grateful for goodness and mercy given us in the present moment.

Faith still has its problems (vv. 9-16)
We wonder why we have a rehash of the fall of the northern kingdom in verses 9-12 (see 17:1-6). Why do we need to hear again about all that happened ca. 724-722 BC during Shalmaneser V's investment of Samaria (vv. 9-10), about the destinations of departed Israelites (v. 11),[7] and the reason for the whole disaster (v. 12)? A long chapter (2 Kings 17) seemed to cover that. But it's likely the writer wanted to remind us 'of the kind of environment in which Hezekiah pursued this bold policy'[8] of rebelling against Assyria (vv. 7-8). There's an old gospel chorus that goes: 'It is no secret what God can do— what he's done for others, he'll do for you.' I'm not sure that's an accurate assumption about the Lord's ways but it's a fine analogy for the king of Assyria: what he'd done to others, he'll do to you! Hence we understand the gutsiness of Hezekiah's revolt—that's why verses 9-12 appear here.

True to predictable Assyrian form 'Sennacherib king of Assyria came up against all the fortified cities of Judah and seized them' (v. 13), and it looks terribly dark in Judah in 701 BC. But this should not have been! If Hezekiah is everything that verses 1-8 say he is, surely such devotion to Yahweh would be sufficient to bring God's blessing rather than Assyria's presence. Now Judah's principal towns are in Assyrian hands and Jerusalem will be next. None of this should be happening, for Hezekiah's been so, well…good. 'How could Jerusalem be in such dire straits when Hezekiah was so righteous?'[9]

But we're not surprised. We've run into this before. The text is simply teaching that faith is not a prophylactic that shields one from all disasters. You can cling to the Lord and the Assyrians will

[7]For these locations see our discussion in the first part of chapter 22 above.
[8]Provan, *1 and 2 Kings,* 253.
[9]Richard D. Nelson, *First and Second Kings,* Interpretation (Louisville: John Knox, 1987), 236. This situation (distress coming to a righteous king) would give dyspepsia to those poster boys of Old Testament criticism, the Deuteronomistic editors. For them, such things are not supposed to be. Apparently the story was so rooted in history that they couldn't doctor it up.

come. This does not overthrow the overall promise of blessing and help given to faith and obedience (e.g., Deut. 28:1-14; Ps. 37:3-9) but recognizes that such blessing often can be diluted with trouble and grief. If it were not so, our faith would likely become magic. Many folks who get 'disappointed with God' have walked by this prophylactic faith. One gives himself to earnest prayer but his wife still dies of cancer, and he never prays again. A woman who is a diligent children's worker in the church is abandoned by her husband, and she abandons the church. A lady in the early stages of Alzheimer's tells her pastor that she says her prayers every night and it sounds as if this practice is a kind of religious rabbit's foot. So 2 Kings 18 can prove a helpful corrective. It tells you that you can be a king who trusts and obeys Yahweh and who reforms the nation's worship and yet your enemy may come and crush your land, deport its population, and await the moment when he can impale the king's carcass on a stake outside the city wall. It's helpful to faith to know that.

Verses 14-16 present another problem faith has: it can cave in. In face of Assyria's onslaught 'Hezekiah king of Judah sent to the king of Assyria at Lachish, saying, "I have done wrong; turn away from me; what you lay upon me I will bear"' (v. 14a). Sennacherib was typically exorbitant: 300 talents of silver, 30 talents of gold (v. 14b).[10] Hezekiah drained the temple and royal treasuries, even stripping gold from overlaid temple doors (vv. 15-16). First and Second Kings always views draining the treasuries in a negative way. A foreign king may pilfer them as Shishak did in Rehoboam's reign (1 Kings 14:25-26), or the funds may be used to bribe foreign kings to intervene on Judah's behalf, as per Asa and Ahaz (1 Kings 15:18-19; 2 Kings 16:8-9), or they may be used to buy off an aggressor, either successfully (as Joash, 2 Kings 12:17-18) or unsuccessfully (as Hezekiah, vv. 14-16). But the writer always takes a dim view of it. So here Hezekiah fails in faith—and in wisdom, for Sennacherib

---

[10]Sennacherib's annals claim 800 rather than 300 talents of silver; see D. D. Luckenbill, *Ancient Records of Assyria and Babylonia,* 2 vols. (reprint ed.,, London: Histories & Mysteries of Man, 1989), 2:120-21, 143. There are various explanations for this silver discrepancy. It may be Sennacherib simply lied, or rather, exaggerated (cf. G. H. Jones, *1 and 2 Kings,* New Century Bible Commentary, 2 vols. [Grand Rapids: Eerdmans, 1984], 2:565).

still sends his lackeys to demand the surrender of Jerusalem.[11] Assyria is always a poor investment.

Someone may object: But this contradicts verses 1-8. I thought Hezekiah was the premier believer among all the kings of Judah. How can this God-truster, Yahweh-clinger, commandment-keeper of verses 5-6 become such a glob of Jello here?

Bähr long ago gave us the answer: we must recognize that 18:1-8 is a *summary* of Hezekiah's whole reign, just as 16:1-4 is a summary of Ahaz's entire reign.[12] So the trust and obedience verses 1-8 speak of are what Hezekiah came to have as a result of the whole Assyrian threat. True, verses 1-8 specify some of Hezekiah's initial reforms; but primarily they are giving an evaluation of Hezekiah's total reign not of a particular failure. There is no conflict between an overall trend of faith that nevertheless experiences lapses of faith. Sometimes faith has its 'wobblies'—and they can be severe.

Faith Cook tells the story of Chinese pastor Wang Ming-Dao. He was the highly respected pastor of the Christians' Tabernacle in Peking. Soon after coming to power in 1949, the Communists carted Wang and his wife Jing Wun off to prison, he being sentenced to fifteen years. His last message to his congregation had declared, 'We shall make whatever sacrifice is required of us in being faithful to God. Regardless of how others may twist the truth and slander us, *we because of our faith shall remain steadfast.*'

Wang was fifty-five and his imprisonment was brutal. His captors knew what a 'catch' it would be if they could get Wang to renounce his faith. Constantly they barraged him with bribes, threats, and insinuations. And his Lowest Majesty himself joined in—pressing doubts upon him even about the existence of God. Finally, he appealed for clemency on the basis of his willingness to cooperate, and then, after hearing of his wife's plummeting health, he wrote all that was asked of him, even agreeing to join the government-infested Three-Self Patriotic Movement. So, in 1956 he was released. And yet he was not

---

[11]Cf. K. D. Fricke, *Das zweite Buch von den Königen*, Die Botschaft des alten Testaments (Stuttgart: Calwer, 1972), 259.

[12]K. C. W. F. Bähr, *The Books of the Kings*, 202.

free, for his conscience held him captive. He had never lacked integrity before, but now he had given in. He wandered streets near his home muttering, 'I am Peter'—or, 'I am Judas.' Since Wang was not fully cooperating, he knew he would soon be rearrested. So Wang and his wife reported to the authorities; he told them his statements had been false. He was—of course—promptly thrown back into prison and sentenced for life. Back in his prison cell, however, the Lord used Micah 7:9 (Well, look it up!) to restore Wang to himself.[13] None of us can throw stones in light of what Wang endured. And yet it is true that people of great courage and strong faith can crumble. And the best antidote any believer has is realizing that faith-eclipse can happen to him/her and praying that it won't.

Folly can be exposed (vv. 17-25)

'Then the king of Assyria sent the Tartan, the Rabsaris, and the Rabshakeh from Lachish to King Hezekiah at Jerusalem with a sizable army' (v. 17a).[14] But what on earth are these Assyrians doing outside Hezekiah's capital? Didn't Hezekiah just agree to Sennacherib's exorbitant tribute? Wasn't that the rationale for paying tribute—Sennacherib was to buzz off (v. 14a)? Why is Sennacherib not content with that? Why does he now also demand the surrender of Jerusalem?

So Sennacherib seems to be a rascal and is certainly a conundrum. In fact, the ins and outs of this whole episode pose one of the major problems in Old Testament history. I'm not about to explain six views of the problem in twenty pages because I want you to read the rest of this book. So I'm simply going to give my own reconstruction of the affair.

An interesting pattern appears in Sennacherib's annals of his third campaign (701 BC). Lule, king of Sidon, runs off in

[13]Faith Cook, *Singing in the Fire* (Edinburgh: Banner of Truth, 1995), 21-32.

[14]It is a bit slippery to specify the exact responsibilities of these Assyrian functionaries. The Tartan was a field marshal, next in rank to the king, who led military campaigns if the king himself did not go; the Rabsaris, 'chief of the royal attendants,' was a senior administrative official close to the king; and the Rabshakeh, lit., 'chief cupbearer,' was a high official whose duties were restricted to court and the king's person. See D. J. Wiseman, 'Rabsaris,' 'Rabshakeh,' ISBE, 4:30-31, and M. Cogan and H. Tadmor, *II Kings*, Anchor Bible (Garden City, NY: Doubleday, 1988), 229-30. The location of the 'upper pool' in v. 17b is uncertain—some argue for a location on the north outside the city walls at the upper end of the Central Valley (see Cogan and Tadmor, *II Kings*, 230, and V. Fritz, *1 & 2 Kings*, A Continental Commentary [Minneapolis: Fortress, 2003], 370).

fright when the Assyrians come; Sennacherib places Ethbaal on the throne and imposes tribute upon him. Rebellious Sidka, king of Ashkelon, Sennacherib carts off to Assyria and reinstalls the former king Sharru-lu-dari and imposes tribute on him. And Sennacherib wiped out the rebellious governors of Ekron and impaled their bodies on stakes around the city, then reinstalled Padi, the previous king—and imposed tribute on him.[15] Sennacherib also claims he imposed additional tribute on Hezekiah, although he does not mention removing Hezekiah from kingship. In the first three cases he imposes the tribute upon the one he has decided will reign. Could this be at least the initial impression he wanted to make in Hezekiah's case? Tribute gets imposed on kings Sennacherib authorizes to reign; the fact he lays tribute on Hezekiah indicates that he has—despite Hezekiah's rebellion—agreed to accept his subservience and allow him to continue as king. It could be that Sennacherib was occupied with fighting off the Egyptians at the time (19:9) and didn't want to clutter up his 'to do' list before he could give full attention to Hezekiah.

Apparently Hezekiah was under no loyalty oath to the king of Assyria—he was simply required to pay annual tribute.[16] But when he rebelled he withheld that tribute. Sennacherib, however, was not about to let Hezekiah off scot-free.[17] So, though he had agreed about the tribute and apparently withdrawing from Hezekiah, he then reneged and sent his agents and an army to demand Jerusalem's surrender (vv. 17ff.). Am I supposing Sennacherib went back on his word? Let me ask you a question: When did you last trust an Assyrian? Thought so.[18]

---

[15]Luckenbill, 2:119-21, 142-43.

[16]See the study by H. Tadmor, 'Treaty and Oath in the Ancient Near East: A Historian's Approach,' in *Humanizing America's Iconic Book* (Chico, CA: Scholars, 1982), 127-52.

[17]On Assyrian methodology in dealing with rebel territories, see the helpful study by Robert D. Bates, 'Assyria and Rebellion in the Annals of Sennacherib: An Analysis of Sennacherib's Treatment of Hezekiah,' *Near Eastern Archaeological Society Bulletin* ns 44 (1999): 39-61; also A. Kirk Grayson, 'Assyrian Rule of Conquered Territory in Ancient Western Asia,' *Civilizations of the Ancient Near East*, 4 vols. (New York: Charles Scribner's Sons, 1995), 2:959-68.

[18]Isaiah 33:8 may reflect Sennacherib's perfidy: 'He has broken the covenant; he has despised cities [or, witnesses]; he does not regard man.' Most English translations render the verbs in the passive voice but they are properly active. The New Berkeley Version gets it right. For the possible Sennacherib background to Isaiah 33, see John N. Oswalt, *The Book of Isaiah: Chapters 1-39*, New International Commentary on the Old Testament (Grand Rapids: Eerdmans, 1986), 590.

Now you must realize there are some 'supposings' in any historical reconstructions, so we must not be cocksure about this one. But my hunch is that in his heart of hearts Sennacherib really preferred to see Hezekiah's corpse impaled on a stake outside the walls of Jerusalem.

So here is the Rabshakeh demanding that King Hezekiah come out (v. 18a), but, perhaps to retain a tad of royal dignity, three of Hezekiah's cabinet ministers come out instead (v. 18b).[19] The Rabshakeh then harangues Eliakim, Shebna, and Joah.

A general outline of the Rabshakeh's first speech appears in the structured outline at the beginning of this chapter. I will, however, take up the exposure-theme last.

The Rabshakeh may have had speech classes, for he organizes his pitch around the theme of 'trust'. The root (*bāṭaḥ*, to trust, rely) appears seven times in verses 19-24. Part of his argument consists of a political ploy (v. 22):

> And if you should say, 'It's in Yahweh our God that we trust'—Is not he the one whose high places and altars Hezekiah has taken away, so that he said to Judah and Jerusalem, 'It is before this altar you are to worship in Jerusalem'?

This tells us Assyria had a fine intelligence network. We might think that the Assyrian is bungling the case here—he doesn't know, pagan that he is, that Hezekiah's reforms would have been *pleasing* to Yahweh. But that is beside the point. He doesn't care about religion but politics. The Rabshakeh likely knows that not everybody in Judah was smack-happy over the king's reforms. If his rhetoric can stir up some high-place-loving sourpusses it can only help Assyria's case.[20] He wants to stoke the embers of Judean rancor and bitterness over the king's reforms.

He also engages in sheer mockery. He offers Jerusalem a deal: Assyria will give them 2,000 horses. Of course, he suggests, you won't be able to furnish decently trained riders for them. 'You are no match for even the lowest ranking Assyrian official' (v. 24a, TEV). One of my brothers used to show his

[19]R. de Vaux identifies their respective offices as vizier, secretary, and herald (*Ancient Israel*, 2 vols. [New York: McGraw-Hill, 1965], 1:129-32).

[20]See Paul R. House, *1, 2 Kings*, New American Commentary (Nashville: Broadman & Holman, 1995), 359. It is conceivable that the Rabshakeh's 'misunderstanding' could be intentional, much like the Serpent's in Genesis 3:1.

contempt for another basketball player by saying he 'couldn't fight his way out of a wet paper bag'. That is the Rabshakeh's tone here: pure scorn.

And then he waxes religious and makes a claim to special revelation. The very One in whom Judah trusts is, in fact, against them. It was Yahweh himself, he declares, who told Sennacherib to assault Jerusalem and lay it waste (v. 25). Assyria is only obeying the will of Judah's god. We might say, to pervert the hymn title, that the Assyrians claim to be 'channels only'.

The saddest point in the Rabshakeh's argument comes in his exposé of Judah's trust in Egypt:

> You rely, of all things, on Egypt, that splintered reed of a staff, which enters and punctures the palm of any one who leans on it! That's what Pharaoh king of Egypt is like to all who rely on him (v. 21, NJPS).[21]

The Egyptian war machine was Judah's hope (v. 24b).

One cheer for Egypt—at least they showed up. Egypt and allies met Sennacherib at Eltekeh (eleven miles south/southwest of Joppa). It was an Assyrian success and Egypt & Co. withdrew south to Gaza. However, while Sennacherib had his forces split between Libnah and Jerusalem, Egyptian forces came back quietly, led by Tirhakah, brother of the new Ethiopian Pharaoh Shebitku. Sennacherib learned of the potential attack, brought his forces together to strike back, and the Egyptians decided there was no place like home.[22]

We don't know if Hezekiah himself was an ardent supporter of the alliance with Egypt, but at least there was a strong pro-Egyptian party at court. But Isaiah the prophet made no bones about his politics: he blasted the Egyptian alliance as useless, stupid, and idolatrous (see Isaiah 30, 31).[23]

---

[21]Egypt's unreliability was proverbial; see Isaiah 30:7 and Ezekiel 29:6b-7.

[22]See K. A. Kitchen, *On the Reliability of the Old Testament* (Grand Rapids: Eerdmans, 2003), 16, 40-41, 611. See also his article 'Egypt', NBD, 298. The claim that Tirhakah was too young to lead an army in 701 BC is baseless; see A. R. Millard, 'Sennacherib's Attack on Hezekiah,' *Tyndale Bulletin* 36 (1985): 63-64, and the studies by Kitchen cited in his notes.

[23]Cf. Derek Thomas, *God Delivers: Isaiah Simply Explained* (Darlington: Evangelical Press, 1991), 198-99; and Robert B. Chisholm, Jr., *Handbook on the Prophets* (Grand Rapids: Baker, 2002), 75-78.

And the Rabshakeh seemed to know it was useless and stupid. But it is sad when an Assyrian has to teach you how flimsy and foolish and fragile is the object of your trust. It's sad when an Assyrian can divine that you trust Egypt more than Yahweh. It's sad when an Assyrian can expose your folly rather than your faith.

I heard a fascinating story on a recent radio program. A man in Florida was abusive to his wife and children so they left him to live elsewhere. They kept a low profile because they did not want husband and father to be able to locate them. Then came 9-11. He then claimed his wife died in the World Trade Towers, on floor number whatever. He then gets a million dollars from the government. He phones an older son and tells him the family has come into some money and mentions the name of his previous insurance agent who 'was working on it'. The son calls his mother, the mother calls the insurance agent, whose wife is shocked because her husband's client's wife is still alive! Donna is alive! Some Channel 9 in Florida then did an interview with the husband in his Pennsylvania home where he now lived. He went on about his wife's death, about how tragic it was. Then the interviewer told him she had just interviewed Donna. Was it the right Donna Lee? Yes—and he was exposed on camera.

It's frightening when things appear as they really are, when even Assyrians know we have more faith in Egyptians than in Yahweh. And it was not only Egypt. Isaiah scored Judah for trusting in all her military preparedness (Isa. 22:8-11). Nothing wrong with such preparations if they are done under faith and not instead of faith, but, Isaiah accuses, 'you paid no attention to God, who planned all this long ago and who caused it to happen' (Isa. 22:11b, TEV). 'Why bother with faith when you have walls, water, and weapons?'[24] Making alliances and building walls, i.e., our activity, too often becomes a substitute for faith instead of an expression of faith. The church is not immune to this trap. How easy it is to think that we can minister because we have resources, we have programs, we have (perhaps) political clout, we have conferences—and software and fax numbers. At such times an Assyrian can do us a real service.

---

[24]J. A. Motyer, *The Prophecy of Isaiah* (Downers Grove: InterVarsity, 1993), 185.

Logic turns into stupidity (vv. 26-35)

There's a brief interruption—Hezekiah's henchmen plead with the Rabshakeh to be professional, follow protocol, and speak in Aramaic, the current lingua franca of diplomacy. Besides, they so much as say, we don't want these poor wretches standing guard on the wall to understand what you're saying (v. 26). This appeal only goaded the Rabshakeh to go on using the Judean dialect. He may have been chosen for this task precisely because he possessed such facility with the local language. He disdained their request—his primary audience, he said, was precisely those fellows 'sitting on the wall, who are doomed to eat their own dung and to drink their own urine along with you' (v. 27b; the last three words are telling—not even the 'uppercrusts' will escape the ravages of the siege). So much for the Assyrian's intimidation. He then moves on to show these Judeans a more excellent way: they should surrender and then each one can 'eat from his own vine, each from his own fig tree, and each can drink from the waters of his own cistern' (v. 31). A much healthier diet! Surely, he implies, you prefer water to urine, grapes and figs to dung. Why back yourselves into a meatgrinder when you can come out and enjoy the tender mercies of Assyria? Of course, we'll have to 'relocate' you, but that won't be so bad (v. 32).

But the Rabshakeh wants to divide as well as intimidate. If he can get Jerusalem to capitulate he will save much Assyrian sweat and time. So he wants to drive a wedge between the people and Hezekiah.[25] Four times then he seeks to undermine the people's confidence in Hezekiah's leadership:[26]

'Don't let Hezekiah deceive you' (v. 29)
'Don't let Hezekiah make you trust in Yahweh' (v. 30)
'Don't listen to Hezekiah' (v. 31)
'Don't listen to Hezekiah, for he misleads you' (v. 32)

If he can get popular sentiment to clash with royal policy, he will get both a city and a promotion.

---

[25] Note that throughout the chapter the Rabshakeh only calls Judah's king 'Hezekiah'; he never alludes to him as 'King Hezekiah'. In contrast, he can spiel off the Assyrian king's nomenclature (vv. 19, 29). This is an intentional 'put down' of Hezekiah. See Fricke, *Das zweite Buch von den Königen*, 261.

[26] Roger Ellsworth, *Apostasy, Destruction and Hope: 2 Kings Simply Explained* (Darlington: Evangelical Press, 2002), 209; and Fricke, p. 265.

In this second speech the Rabshakeh has used intimidation and tried to foment division. He now moves on to the clencher of his argument—logic. The key verb of this speech is 'deliver' (Heb., *nāṣal*). Forms of the verb appear nine times in the Hebrew text (in vv. 29, 30, 32, 33, 34, 35), and it is the key word in the Rabshakeh's logical finale (= vv. 33-35):

> (33) Has any of the gods of the nations ever delivered his land from the hand of the king of Assyria? (34) Where are the gods of Hamath and Arpad? Where are the gods of Sepharvaim, Hena, and Ivvah? Sure—they delivered Samaria from my hand! (35) Who is there among all the gods of the lands who has delivered their land from my hand, that Yahweh should deliver Jerusalem from my hand?[27]

And it is a telling argument; it can claim history as its witness. Off the top of his head the Rabshakeh names half a dozen hopeless cases. The Assyrian steamroller flattens every land in its path. No divinity has been able to protect its people from the invincible hosts of the god Assur (cf. v. 35a). And then the Rabshakeh said something asinine (v. 35b). By a leap of faith and defect of logic he assumes that Yahweh is simply another generic deity of a minuscule kingdom who is no match for a world-class empire. Something snapped somewhere when he said that. He had stepped over a line. He had gone too far. It was the beginning of the end.

Words can have consequences. At one of the Saturday evening discussions at Sandfields a man rose and complained, 'I cannot believe in the deity of Christ.' The moderator and pastor, Martyn Lloyd-Jones, sized the fellow up and countered, 'You have said that more than once. Very well, you will say it no more here, you must go!'[28] Words can get one kicked out of a Christian meeting, and rightly so. And the Rabshakeh's words will bring dire consequences as well, for his words mock Yahweh as a no-count deity from Nowheresville (cf. 19:22).

---

[27]For some of the locations in verse 34, see comments on 17:24. If Hamath is 120 miles NNE of Damascus, Arpad is that far again north of Hamath; it is identified with Tell Erfad, 25 miles north of Aleppo. The site of Hena is unknown. I have followed B. O. Long in translating the last clause of verse 34; it is a piece of sarcasm (*2 Kings*, The Forms of the Old Testament Literature [Grand Rapids: Eerdmans, 1991], 216).

[28]Iain H. Murray, *David Martyn Lloyd-Jones: The First Forty Years 1899-1939* (Edinburgh: Banner of Truth, 1982), 233.

And Yahweh, who will not give his glory to another (Isa. 42:8; 48:11), will see that the Assyrians pay dearly for the Rabshakeh's logical fallacy.

After the Rabshakeh ceased his bluster all was quiet. The king's orders were to give no response. The Rabshakeh stands there expectantly, but Eliakim, Shebna, and Joah turn and walk off. With robes ripped in anguish they come and report all to Hezekiah. The fortunes of Judah will change soon but don't rush from chapter 18 too quickly. Let the scene of verses 36-37 sink into your soul. It's quite authentic. Do not the affairs of Yahweh's people in this world often look just that bleak?

25

The Terror of the Night
(2 Kings 19)

The chapter division in our Bibles is not all that bad; chapter 18 closes at the end of a scene. Moreover, chapter 19 develops in a symmetrical pattern, and since it also is a long chapter it will be useful to have that pattern in front of us:

Development of 2 Kings 19

King's plea, vv. 1-4
Prophet's assurance, vv. 5-7
Assyria's propaganda, vv. 8-13

King's prayer, vv. 14-19
Prophet's assurance, vv. 20-34
Assyria's termination, vv. 35-37

I will follow this literary break-down in the exposition, though I will combine the first three sections under one head.

Before Dawn: Has Anything Changed? *(vv. 1-13)*
All is distress and anguish in Jerusalem. And probably repentance too. Ripping clothes and donning sackcloth (vv. 1, 2) signals agony and grief and sometimes the sackcloth was a token of repentance (see Jonah 3:5, 8; Dan. 9:3; Neh. 9:1).[1] In any case, Hezekiah's words more than his wardrobe express repentance. He sends Eliakim and Company to Isaiah, lamenting that 'this day is a day of distress and

---

[1] See L. G. Herr, ISBE, 4:256.

punishment and contempt' (v. 3). 'Punishment' (*tôkēḥā*) can mean 'rebuke' but passes over into 'chastisement' and 'punishment' (Ps. 149:7; Hos. 5:9).[2] 'Contempt' may have a similar nuance if it means the contempt which God holds toward his unfaithful people.[3] 'The crisis is so dire,' Hezekiah says, 'and yet we have no strength or resources to face it.'[4]

Yet for all his agony Hezekiah put his finger on the major matter: the king of Assyria had sent the Rabshakeh 'to ridicule (*ḥārap*) the living God' (v. 4a). That puts Sennacherib in a Goliath role, for that brute had ridiculed both Israel's army and Israel's God (1 Sam. 17:10, 25, 26, 36, 45)—and ended up with a rock in his head.[5] Hezekiah feels no such certainty about Sennacherib but musters a 'perhaps': 'Perhaps Yahweh your God will hear all the words…and will punish (him) for the words which Yahweh your God has heard' (v. 4a).

Isaiah, however, is not into 'perhapses'. He is all brevity and dogmatism:

> Here's what Yahweh says: 'Don't be afraid of the words which you have heard, words with which the servants of the king of Assyria have blasphemed me. Look, I am going to put a spirit in him, he shall hear news, and shall return to his own land, and I shall make him fall by the sword in his own land.' (vv. 6b-7)[6]

'Isaiah offers very specific promises, ones that will prove he is either a true prophet or a liar.'[7] But as usual the Assyrians

---

[2]NIDOTTE, 2:444, and Bähr and Patterson & Austel among commentators.

[3]Per E. J. Young, *The Book of Isaiah*, New International Commentary on the Old Testament, 3 vols. (Grand Rapids: Eerdmans, 1969), 2:473.

[4]This seems to be the sense behind 3b: 'For children have come to the point of birth, and there is no strength to give birth.'

[5]The root *ḥrp* (defy, mock, ridicule) occurs six times (five as a verb, once as a noun) in 1 Samuel 17 and is the interpretive key to the David-Goliath story; see my *1 Samuel: Looking on the Heart* (Ross-shire: Christian Focus, 2000), 144-54. Here in 2 Kings 19 the verb appears four times (vv. 4, 16, 22, 23).

[6]Some think Isaiah is cutting down Sennacherib's servants (my translation) by calling them 'lads' (plural of *na'ar*), but this is unlikely; see T. R. Hobbs, *2 Kings*, Word Biblical Commentary (Waco: Word, 1985), 275.

[7]Paul R. House, *1, 2 Kings*, New American Commentary (Nashville: Broadman & Holman, 1995), 366. Alec Motyer points out that Isaiah makes no reference here to the devastation of the Assyrian army by the angel of the LORD (see v. 35); however, he had already predicted that in Isaiah 14:24-27. 'If only Hezekiah had believed [that] word when it was first spoken!' See Motyer, *The Prophecy of Isaiah* (Downers Grove: InterVarsity, 1993), 279.

get more media hype and so Sennacherib's message naturally eclipses both Isaiah's and Hezekiah's in length.

Verses 8-9 give us a geographical update. Sennacherib had finished off Lachish and was now reducing Libnah (v. 8), probably to the north/northeast of Lachish.[8] Hearing of Tirhakah's foray (v. 9) probably didn't alarm Sennacherib; he simply renewed his efforts to reduce Jerusalem by psychology rather than arms, the latter being such a cursed inconvenience.[9] In his message Sennacherib admonishes Hezekiah against religious naïveté—'Don't let your god in whom you trust deceive you' (v. 10). In 18:29 Jerusalem's residents were warned not to let Hezekiah deceive them. Now Yahweh has become the deceiver! Sennacherib presses all the force of his 'historical argument' on Hezekiah. He begins with, 'Look, *you* [emphatic] have heard…,' as if to suggest: 'It's all well and good, Hezekiah, to prop up the national religious faith, but *you* know better— you know the facts of history. You've surely read the proud reports of Assyria's conquests [v. 11a]. So what makes you think that you, Hezekiah, are special? [v. 11b].' Sennacherib's predecessors brought nations to ruin; did any of their deities deliver them (v. 12)?[10] 'Can you name one, Hezekiah?' Off the top of his head Sennacherib can add half a dozen kings who are now in Losers' Land (v. 13).[11]

Now the interesting thing about the first chunk of chapter 19 is that nothing has changed. To be sure, Isaiah has proclaimed Yahweh's assurance that Sennacherib will vamoose (vv. 5-7).

[8]The site of Libnah is uncertain. Some favor Tell Bornat, five miles south of Gath (if Gath = Tell es-Safi). Carl Rasmussen prefers Khirbet Tell el-Beida, twenty miles SW of Jerusalem, eight miles NE of Lachish (*Zondervan NIV Atlas of the Bible,* 243). For discussion see John L. Peterson, 'Libnah,' ABD, 4:322-23.

[9]See my discussion in the previous chapter about the Egyptian-Ethiopian threat, where I drew upon K. A. Kitchen's reconstruction (see fn 22 there).

[10]Of the places mentioned in v. 12: Gozan is on the upper Habor River, a tributary of the Euphrates, about 220 miles (for a crow) east of the NE corner of the Mediterranean Sea. Haran is west of Gozan on the Balik River. Rezeph was an important caravan center on the route from the Euphrates to Hamath, located about 125 miles ENE of Hamath (Wiseman, 'Rezeph,' NBD, 1019). The 'sons of Eden' were the people of Bit Adini (an area in N. Syria between the Balik and the Euphrates), who were resettled in Telassar (location unknown).

[11]On the place names in v. 13, see footnote 27 in the previous chapter. Some translations refer to 'the king of the city of the Sepharvaim.' However, the Hebrew behind 'of the city of' may be a place name, Lair, which Cogan and Tadmor identify as the city Lahiru in northeastern Babylonia (*II Kings,* Anchor Bible [Garden City, NY: Doubleday, 1988], 235).

But he still seems very much there. The pressure is still on Jerusalem. Nothing has changed since chapter 18. Assyria's arguments are the same; Assyrian arrogance is the same. Judah has Yahweh's word promising relief, but it's still night in Jerusalem. Nothing has changed.

On June 28, 1865, the Confederate raider *Shenandoah* seized and destroyed eleven northern whaling ships in the Bering Sea. General Lee had surrendered his troops on April 9, and others followed not long after that. But the captain of the *Shenandoah* would not hear that the American Civil War was over until August 2. That's why on June 28 the crew was still fighting the war even though the war was over.[12] Nothing had changed.

Is that not exactly what many of Yahweh's people face repeatedly? Some trouble besets them, some distress pulls them down, and, though they know the biblical assurances of God's faithfulness (they can quote them), still nothing changes and they go on and on in their trouble. Which is why we use 'how-long?' prayers (Ps. 13:1-2). We are assured of the 'glory about to be revealed in our case' and yet find ourselves wading through 'the sufferings of the present time' (Rom. 8:18). And who can deny that it frightens us a bit when we find the believer in Psalm 88 still walking in darkness at the end of his prayer? If Sennacherib can awaken us to a reality of Christian experience, his life will not have been in vain.

Prayer: Getting Our Bearings (vv. 14-19)

Hezekiah drops anchor in the storm: he goes again to the house of Yahweh (v. 14; see also v. 1) and prays. T. R. Hobbs breaks down the prayer as invocation (v. 15), complaint (vv. 16-18), and supplication (v. 19).[13] I will follow his outline, except that I want to back up and take in verse 14.

Disclosure (v. 14). The latest message from Sennacherib may have been delivered both orally (cf. vv. 9b-13) and in written form. In any case, Hezekiah reads the documents, goes to Yahweh's house, and spreads Sennacherib's message out before Yahweh (v. 14). 'Hezekiah solemnly hands over

---

[12]This clip was in an old issue of *Civil War Times Illustrated*.

[13]T. R. Hobbs, *2 Kings*, Word Biblical Commentary (Waco: Word, 1985), 270.

the letter, the documentary blasphemy, to Jehovah.'[14] For this reason desperation is laden with hope, for Yahweh does not stand passively on the side when someone mocks his name and character. But, for Hezekiah, this is an Old Testament instance of letting your 'requests be made known to God' (Phil. 4:6), of simply casting his burden on the Lord (Ps. 55:22)—and that perhaps because there is nothing else he can do. Hezekiah's prayer begins with a disclosure of his helplessness. That's where, if we knew the truth, prayer always begins. 'Helplessness becomes prayer the moment that you go to Jesus and speak candidly and confidently with him about your needs.'[15]

Invocation (v. 15). We may not give much thought (and wrongly so) to how we address God, but Hezekiah does stellar work here:

Yahweh, God of Israel,
enthroned above the cherubim,[16]
you are God, you alone,
of all the kingdoms of the earth;
you have made heaven and earth.

Hezekiah comes to a God of intense presence ('enthroned above the cherubim'), sovereign sway ('God...of all the kingdoms...'), and massive power ('you have made heaven and earth'). Yahweh is specially present to Israel in his temple ('enthroned above the cherubim') but that does not mean he has gone AWOL among the nations or throughout the world.[17] In one sentence Hezekiah confesses that he approaches a God who is near, vast, and mighty. One who is accessible, sovereign, and

---

[14]K. C. W. F. Bähr, *The Books of the Kings*, Lange's Commentary on the Holy Scriptures, in vol. 3, *Samuel–Kings* (1868; reprint ed.,, Grand Rapids: Zondervan, 1960), 210. R. S. Wallace nicely captures a bit of irony: 'Sennacherib in dictating his letter has indeed provided Hezekiah with most eloquent means of fellowship with God' (*Readings in 2 Kings* [Eugene, OR: Wipf and Stock, 1997], 168).

[15]O. Hallesby, *Prayer* (London: Inter-Varsity, 1948), 23.

[16]The phrase is a bit difficult, partly because there is no preposition in the Hebrew—it could be 'over'/'above' or 'between' if the reference is to the cherubim on the ark of the covenant (Exod. 25:10-22), or 'among' if one thinks of the carved cherubim in the temple as well (cf. 1 Kings 6:29).

[17]Cf. John Bimson, '1 and 2 Kings,' *New Bible Commentary*, 4th ed. (Leicester: Inter-Varsity, 1994), 380. By the way, note Calvin's rich exposition of Hezekiah's prayer in the Isaiah parallel (Isa. 37:14-20): *Commentary on the Book of the Prophet Isaiah*, in vol. 8 of *Calvin's Commentaries*, 22 vols. (reprint ed.,, Grand Rapids: Baker, 1999), 118-26.

able. He packs a three-point sermon into the opening lines of his prayer! And the twist is that it's not only true but helpful. Is this not precisely what Hezekiah needs to remember in the present distress? What better way for Hezekiah to encourage Hezekiah than to rehearse God's majesty as he requests God's help? Speaking truth about God to God may stir up assurance in God. Is this a cue for us to take more care about our address to God, about the way we begin our prayers?

Complaint (vv. 16-18). Now Hezekiah appeals to Yahweh's senses: 'Turn your ear and hear; open, Yahweh, your eyes and see; and hear the words of Sennacherib which he has sent to ridicule the living God' (v. 16). And then Hezekiah confesses two truths. Truth one: The kings of Assyria really have wasted nations and their lands and have pitched their gods into the fire (vv. 17-18a). Truth two: Those were not real gods but the work of men's hands, 'and so they destroyed them' (v. 18b).[18] Truth one is neutered by truth two. In all her conquests Assyria had never run up against a real deity. In his plea to Yahweh Hezekiah confesses the big fact ('for they are not gods') that makes all the difference in the world.

When the Allies arrived and liberated Paris in 1944 church bells, silent during German occupation, now erupted in a cacophony of joy. But the bells of Saint-Philippe du Roule did not ring. Apparently many parishioners called Canon Jean Muller that Thursday evening to urge that the church's bells join the chorus. On the following Sunday Muller thanked all who had called him to ask him to ring the church's bells. Then he said: 'I should also like to remind you of something you all forgot in your excitement that day. There are no bells in the belfry of Saint-Philippe.'[19] It seems to me that was a significant piece of information. The bells of Saint-Philippe did not ring

---

[18]Normally Assyrians seem to have treated captured images with respect, sometimes returning them to their bereft devotees after holding them in Assyria for a while; see M. Cogan and H. Tadmor, *II Kings*, Anchor Bible (Garden City, NY: Doubleday, 1988), 236. See also Cogan's discussion of 'Assyrian Spoliation of Divine Images' in *Imperialism and Religion: Assyria, Judah and Israel in the Eighth and Seventh Centuries B. C. E.* (Missoula, MT: Scholars, 1974), 22-41. Assyrians did, however, also destroy images (see *Imperialism*, 24, and, e.g., D. D. Luckenbill, *Ancient Records of Assyria and Babylonia*, 2 vols. [London: Histories & Mysteries of Man, 1989 reprint], 2:308, 310 [of Assurbanipal]).

[19]Larry Collins and Dominique Lapierre, *Is Paris Burning?* (New York: Simon and Schuster, 1965), 258.

because it had no bells; the nations' gods did not rescue them from Assyria because they were not gods. So what will happen to Assyria when Assyria picks a fracas with 'something' she has never met before—Yahweh? In his prayer Hezekiah confessed truth (v. 18b) and so edged close to hope. Prayer often does that. In prayer we get a fresh glimpse of the Hearer of prayer and so get our bearings again.

Supplication (v. 19). Hezekiah's petition is two-pronged—emergency and testimony. 'And now, Yahweh our God, save us from his hand' (v. 19a). Requests are fairly simple and direct when the terror of the world is outside your walls. But there is an additional petition (which actually indicates the result should Yahweh save Jerusalem): 'And let all the kingdoms of the earth know that you, Yahweh, are God all by yourself' (v. 19b). Yahweh's deliverance at Jerusalem will magnify Yahweh's reputation throughout the world. Dozens of deities had proven helpless against the mighty Sennacherib and Sennacherib's lord, Assur; but when Assur meets Yahweh and gets creamed he will go (as it were) and join the other loser gods. Hezekiah's plea has its eye on his trouble and on Yahweh's glory—and when we are concerned with God's glory we are likely to be heard.[20]

Luther seemed to think so. In 1540 his friend Frederick Myconius became terribly ill. He and his friends thought he would shortly die. One night with his trembling hand he wrote a farewell note to Luther, whom he deeply loved. Upon receipt Luther shot back his reply: 'I command thee in the name of God to live because I still have need of thee in the work of reforming the Church...The Lord will not let me hear while I live that thou art dead, but will permit thee to survive me. For this I am praying, this is my will, and may my will be done, because I seek only to glorify the name of God.' Myconius had already lost his faculty of speech when Luther's letter came. But in a brief time he was well again and survived Luther by two months![21] 'May my will be done, because I seek only to glorify the name of God.' When the driving passion of our prayers is Yahweh's honor a strange confidence begins to seep into them.

---

[20] This is not invariably the case, however. Sometimes Yahweh may choose to suffer shame and apparent defeat in order to awaken Israel (for example) to her need; 1 Samuel 4 is a case in point.
[21] Cited in Hallesby, *Prayer*, 103.

Prayer is frequently unnerving because it is the activity we engage in between catastrophe and deliverance. But if we pray truth, as Hezekiah did, we will find it not only reaches God but anchors us.

Prophecy: A Love Affair with Predestination (vv. 20-34)

Prayer does not change things but prayer lays hold of God who changes things. Isaiah assures Hezekiah that Yahweh has heard his prayer (v. 20). And the fact that Isaiah's prophecy rather than Sennacherib's threat dominates the chapter is a sign that augurs well for Jerusalem. Isaiah's prophetic word breaks down into three sections, dealing with arrogance (vv. 20-28), discouragement (vv. 29-31), and fear (vv. 32-34). The arrogance is Assyria's, the discouragement and fear Jerusalem's. I want to treat the 'discouragement' and 'fear' sections first and take up the put-down of Assyria last.

In verses 29-32 Isaiah proclaims a sign to Jerusalem—one for the near future not for the immediate present. Isaiah's assurance here assumes that the land has been devastated and untended because of the Assyrian invader. When Yahweh delivers Jerusalem, how will they eat? The 'sign' answers that: 'This year you eat what grows of itself, and the next what springs from that; and in the third year, sow and reap, and plant vineyards and eat their fruit' (v. 29, NJPS). Oswalt (drawing upon Delitzsch) has, I think, the simplest and most likely explanation of this:

> ...while three actual calendar years are intended, only about fourteen to fifteen months would be covered. This view involves the suggestion that the prediction was made in the fall, as 'this year' in which the accidental growth was being eaten was drawing to a close...The deliverance would not come in time for the fall planting to be done, meaning that only what came up from the roots of previous plants would be available during the next year. But by the following fall, when the third calendar year was beginning, normal life could resume, for the Assyrians would be gone.[22]

By the time the 'third year' came and Judean farmers were planting their crops they might realize that Yahweh's word was

[22]John N. Oswalt, *The Book of Isaiah: Chapters 1-39* (Grand Rapids: Eerdmans, 1986), 665.

coming true. 'We're planting—there will be a harvest this year.'
Then they would know that Yahweh had been at work in all
this, not least in basic provision and mere survival.

But that survival looked highly unlikely just now. That
these leftovers of Judah could prosper again (the root and fruit
imagery, v. 30) seemed like a pipe dream. One can imagine
Assyrians in their camp around Jerusalem playing Frisbee
or poker, waiting for Sennacherib's forces to come up from
the west to put the finishing touch on Jerusalem. But Yahweh
said, 'From Jerusalem will go forth a remnant, and survivors
from Mt. Zion' (v. 31). And Yahweh knows his promise sounds
laughable to those impressed by appearances; that's why he
adds, 'the zeal of Yahweh of hosts will do this.' As if to say,
'Impossible as it looks, you must understand that Yahweh
is in a passion about this and he will see it's done no matter
what' (cf. Isa. 9:7 in context). So Yahweh's encouragement to
his hopeless people is: you will survive and be provided for
and begin to prosper again.

The prophet then adds another assurance (vv. 32-34) meant
to quiet Jerusalem's fears. Yahweh explains that Sennacherib's
return to his own land (cf. v. 28b) will be before he can even
lay a finger on Jerusalem. He will not enter the city, shoot an
arrow against it, bring on his infantry with their shields, or start
moving dirt for a siege ramp (v. 32). Sennacherib will simply
go home (v. 33), Isaiah says, because Yahweh is our Shield and
Defender (v. 34). He, not Sennacherib, will surround the city
to save it for his own praise ('for my own sake,' here likely
means to show his supremacy in face of Assyrian blasphemy)
and for his own promises ('for the sake of David my servant,'
i.e., because of his covenant to maintain David's royal line until
the new David appears).

Yahweh, then, not only blasts Assyria's pride (vv. 20-28) but
is careful to quiet his people's fears (vv. 29-31, 32-34). The latter
is as essential as the former and Yahweh does not forget to do
so. I occasionally have heard from friends who attend staunchly
'evangelistic' churches. Every service, apparently for worship,
is pitched to call the lost to repentance. Most every sermon
targets the unsaved (at least at the end). The never-missed
'invitation' calls unbelievers to faith. No need to debate the

merits or otherwise of this—except to say that such ministries are neglecting a whole 'audience'. They seek the lost but fail to feed the sheep. They want to bring conviction to sinners but never bring encouragement to believers. They try to disturb the unrepentant but seldom comfort the saints. Yahweh is not like that. He deals with Sennacherib but never forgets the fears and tremblings of his people. He has a word for the reprobate but is always eager to console his church.

Now let us step back to verses 20-28 where Isaiah turns the guns of Yahweh's word upon Sennacherib. The prophet begins with a startling picture of Zion/Jerusalem scorning the Assyrian:

> Virgin Daughter Zion despises you, she mocks you;
> Daughter Jerusalem shakes her head behind you (v. 21b).

Zion/Jerusalem has nothing but contempt for Assyria as its decimated army plods back home.[23] That is the introductory picture.

Yahweh's word is spoken against Sennacherib (v. 21a) and he begins by *specifying his sin:*

> Whom have you ridiculed and blasphemed?
> And against whom have you made such loud talk and lifted high your eyes?
> Against the Holy One of Israel! (vv. 22-23a)

The ridicule is that of 18:30, 32b-35 and of 19:10-13. It is the ridicule that says that Yahweh will not and cannot save, that says nothing and no one can stop Assyria.

Then Yahweh says that he has obviously been *hearing his words,* for he 'quotes' Sennacherib's boasts ('you have said,' v. 23). Technically, of course, Sennacherib might give credit to Assur for his success but in actual fact he loves to exercise his egomania, to indulge his own deity complex:

---

[23]Cogan and Tadmor, *II Kings,* 237, think shaking the head is a figure not merely of scorn but of sorrow and commiseration, as if Jerusalem says (tongue-in-cheek, of course), 'Poor Assyria, how you do suffer!' However, the verb used here (*nûaʿ* + 'head') connotes derision and hostility (see Lam. 2:15; Ps. 22:7; 109:25; cf. Iain Provan, *Lamentations,* New Century Bible Commentary [London: Marshall Pickering, 1991], 74).

With my many chariots
I have gone up the heights of the mountains,
    to the far recesses of Lebanon;
I felled its tallest cedars,
    its choicest cypresses;
I entered its farthest retreat,
    its densest forest.
I dug wells
    and drank foreign waters,
I dried up with the sole of my foot
    all the steams of Egypt (vv. 23-24, NRSV).[24]

Sennacherib was simply following good Assyrian tradition. Assur-nasir-pal (884-858 BC) claimed he climbed up into Mount Amanus (the range off the NE 'corner' of the Mediterranean Sea) and cut down beams of cedar, cypress, juniper, and pine.[25] Assyrian kings often boasted of overcoming massive difficulties, as witness Sennacherib himself:

> I had my camp pitched at the foot of Mount Nipur and with my picked bodyguard and my relentless warriors, I, like a strong wild-ox, went before them (led the way). Gullies, mountain torrents and waterfalls, dangerous cliffs, I surmounted in my sedan chair. Where it was too steep for my chair, I advanced on foot. Like a young gazelle I mounted the high(est) peaks in pursuit of them. Wherever my knees gave out, I sat down on (some) mountain bowlder [sic] and drank the cold water from the water skin (to quench) my thirst. To the summits of the mountains I pursued them and brought about their overthrow. Their cities I captured and I carried off their spoil; I destroyed, I devastated, I burned (them) with fire.[26]

One or two minor problems of interpretation do not fuzzy Sennacherib's meaning in our text. He is saying that he is unstoppable—nothing has been or will be able to stand in his way.[27]

---

[24]The first 'I' and the fourth 'I' (in the NRSV quote) are emphatic. Sennacherib is pounding his hairy chest a bit here.

[25]Luckenbill, *Ancient Records of Assyrian and Babylonia*, 1:167; so Shalmaneser III as well, 1:205, 216.

[26]Luckenbill, 2:122. See also 1:142, 149-50, 152-53, 155 (Assur-nasir-pal), 1:213, 218f. (Shalmaneser III), and 1:256 (Shamshi-Adad V).

[27]Oswalt, *Isaiah*, 661.

Which is always a stupid thing to say. They said the British liner *Titanic* (largest movable man-made object to date) was so well built that 'God himself couldn't sink this ship'.[28] But, apparently, he did. On its maiden voyage no less (April 14, 1912), with the loss of 1,500 lives.

So Yahweh replies to Sennacherib's arrogance by *exposing his ignorance* (vv. 25-26).

> Have you not heard?
> It was long ago I did it,
> from ancient days that I planned it;
> now I have brought it about
> —that you should make fortified cities crash into piles of ruins,
> and their residents,
> stripped of strength,
> are terrified and ashamed;
> they are plants of the field
> and shoots of grass,
> grass on the rooftops,
> a blighted thing before it can come up.

'Have you not heard?' Well, no, for Sennacherib is dense as a post when it comes to recognizing Yahweh. Isaiah later voices the same predestinarian argument in Yahweh's name about the rampaging victories of the Persian Cyrus, who conquers nations and tramples kings. 'Who has worked and done this, calling the generations from the beginning? I, Yahweh, the first—and with the last things I am he' (Isa. 41:4). Strangely enough, world conquerors are an abysmally ignorant species—they have no clue why they have been so victorious.

Yahweh, however, has had enough of Sennacherib's rage and arrogance (vv. 27-28a) and so tells him that he is *preparing his exile*—from Judah: 'I shall place my hook in your nose and my bridle (muzzle?) on your lips, and I shall bring you back by the way you came' (v. 28b). Here's a touch of irony, for Assyrians knew a bit about putting hooks in noses and similar 'treatments'. Tiglath-pileser I (1115-1076 BC) boasted, 'I attached to their noses ropes (and) took them to my city,'[29] Assurbanipal

---

[28]John Blanchard, *Is God Past His Sell-by Date?* (Darlington: Evangelical Press, 2002), 160-61.

[29]As cited from A. K. Grayson in B. O. Long, *2 Kings*, The Forms of the Old Testament Literature (Grand Rapids: Eerdmans, 1991), 231.

(669-633 BC) 'pierced the lips' of Elamite captives and hauled them off to Assyria. Of a certain Uaite' he says:

> ...I pierced his chin with my keen hand dagger. Through his jaw... I passed a rope, put a dog chain upon him and made him occupy... a kennel of the east gate of the inner (wall) of Nineveh...[30]

But the imagery in 28b may also imply that Sennacherib is a 'bulky beast' who must be forced to do his owner's bidding by bit and bridle. 'It is a vast come-down to go from self-made ruler of the world to stubborn mule,'[31] or, perhaps more accurately, to Yahweh's ass.

But the keynote of this section is verses 25-26 in which Yahweh smacks Sennacherib's arrogance right between the eyes. After citing a few lines of Sennacherib's boasting (vv. 23-24) Yahweh retorts: 'Have you not heard? Long ago I did it; it was from ancient days that I planned it' (v. 25). In other words, long before Sennacherib was ever a blip on the screen of history Yahweh had ordained his victories and conquests. Knowing the true explanation sucks the pride out of one's balloon.

During the U. S. Senate hearings on the Watergate scandal in 1973-74, committee chairman Sam J. Ervin, Jr., had to go to Cincinnati to deliver a commencement address at the University of Cincinnati. When Ervin returned to his motel suite afterward, he found two Cincinnati police officers awaiting him. Their chief indicated he had received a call threatening to kill Ervin and so these two officers were to spend the night in his suite and look after him while he was in Cincinnati. Then came the 'downer'. 'I don't know how much the chief is concerned with your assassination,' one of the policemen mused, 'but I am absolutely convinced he doesn't want it to happen in Cincinnati!'[32] If the special protection had given Ervin any delusions of personal importance that quip should have disabused him of such ideas.

So with Sennacherib. The Assyrian can brag all he wants (vv. 23-24), but the fact is he is only carrying out what Yahweh had long ago decided he should do. In short, a little

---

[30]Luckenbill, 2:306, 319.

[31]Oswalt, *Isaiah*, 663.

[32]Paul F. Boller, Jr., *Congressional Anecdotes* (New York: Oxford, 1991), 175.

predestination cuts arrogance down to size. Predestination, of course, makes some Christians nervous; they shudder at the mention of the 'P-word'. All I can say is: If you don't want predestination, well then, go ahead and live a comfortless life, bite your nails and swallow your tranquilizers and eat your guts out as you watch the evening news. Some of us prefer, however, the pillow of predestination, that is, of having a God big enough that he is never surprised by the blathering Sennacheribs of this age.

After Dark: The Terror of the Lord (vv. 35-37)

'On that night the Angel of Yahweh went forth and struck down 185,000 in the camp of Assyria; and when they rose early in the morning, why, they were all corpses!' (v. 35).[33] (Yahweh had never promised to preserve the Assyrians from the 'terror of the night' [cf. Ps. 91:5].) Sennacherib simply pulled up stakes and returned to Nineveh (v. 36; cf. v. 33). Some twenty years later while Sennacherib was worshiping 'in the house of Nisroch his god', two of his sons assassinated him (v. 37).[34]

Verses 35-37 constitute the literary step-child in scholarly study of 2 Kings 18–19. This is primarily because of verse 35, which speaks of divine intervention; even the concept gives some biblical scholars an allergic reaction. Anything theological seems immediately suspect to them. We are assured, therefore, that this verse is a 'later addition'[35] and thus are saved from a brush with the Angel of Yahweh. But let us evaluate these verses a bit more.

First, there are literary considerations. Verses 35-37 are the climax of the whole chapter, especially after the three segments of Isaiah's prophecy have somewhat delayed that climax. And

---

[33]I have translated literally. The writer is not being ridiculous. When the writer says, 'they rose,' he doesn't mean those who have been wiped out. He refers probably to the Assyrians who survived; NASB takes it generally, 'when men rose early'; others, apparently assuming the whole Assyrian army is now outside Jerusalem, take 'they' as the citizens of Jerusalem (so Robert Cohn). On the Angel of Yahweh, see Alec Motyer, *Isaiah*, Tyndale Old Testament Commentaries (Leicester: Inter-Varsity, 1999), 231.

[34]No one can identify a deity named Nisroch. Perhaps it was Nusku, or possibly Assur (Wiseman), but at present we do not know. The Babylonian Chronicle and Assyrian sources confirm Sennacherib's murder by his son or sons; see Kenneth A. Kitchen, *On the Reliability of the Old Testament* (Grand Rapids: Eerdmans, 2003), 42.

[35]See, e.g., G. H. Jones, *1 and 2 Kings*, New Century Bible Commentary, 2 vols. (Grand Rapids: Eerdmans, 1984), 2:569, 582.

verse 36 is necessary in order to fulfill verses 28 and 33. And verse 37 is no mere footnote; it is necessary in order to fulfill verse 7 ('and he shall return to his own land, and I shall make him fall by the sword in his land'). Verse 37 avers that it was indeed the sword that dispatched Sennacherib. The fact that his death in verse 37 occurs twenty years after his assault on Jerusalem is no skin off the Bible's nose. The biblical writer only intends to show the certainty of Yahweh's word (v. 37 fulfilling v. 7) not to give a summary of Sennacherib's last twenty years. But it is important to show that verse 7 is fulfilled — Yahweh's judgment doesn't merely fall on Assyria's army but follows the blasphemer himself until it liquidates him. Verses 35-37 function as a proper and needed climactic summary to chapters 18-19.

But, second, what about the suspect 'theological interpretation' of verse 35? Is this simply a piece whose 'God talk' gives it away as later legend? Hardly. Millard and Kitchen have demonstrated that other ancient Near Eastern accounts regularly speak of divine intervention and historical events together. Pagans combined religious ideology and historical data in the same materials without blushing. Sometimes it can be shown that such 'theological-historical' accounts were written down soon after the occurrences they described. There were no editors coming along in the next two centuries to doctor them up with sundry theological/legendary notes. Even Sennacherib's own annals combine reports of military victories and 'divine intervention' in records written down within a year after the events related. As Kitchen says, 'If Assyrian theological interpretation can be part of their *original* account, then *exactly the same* should apply to the Hebrew text.'[36]

Thirdly, there are historical data that need explaining. Sennacherib returned to Assyria (v. 36). Verse 35 supplies the reason. Assyrian kings do not report their failures and disasters in their annals. They don't mind rehearsing difficulties and obstacles which they surmount. But Sennacherib is not going to tell you that he walked away from Jerusalem like a whipped puppy because his army was riddled with death. So Sennacherib's silence is rather eloquent. Had he reduced

---

[36]See K. A. Kitchen, *Reliability,* 47-51 (quote from p. 50, emphasis his); and A. R. Millard, 'Sennacherib's Attack on Hezekiah,' *Tyndale Bulletin* 36 (1985): 72-77. On the possible numbers in the Assyrian army, see Oswalt, *Isaiah,* 669-70.

Jerusalem he would have boasted about it. But he never claims to have taken Jerusalem. There is, however, a superb series of reliefs, excavated at Nineveh, depicting Sennacherib's conquest of Lachish. The reliefs in the palace covered the walls of a chamber 38 feet long and 18 feet wide. Why all the splash about Lachish? If Sennacherib had a Lachish Room, why didn't he have a Jerusalem Room? Was the focus on Lachish a sort of sop for not reducing Jerusalem? In any case, that Sennacherib did not take Jerusalem is a historical fact—and I would say verse 35 is the historical explanation.

'Walk about Zion and go around her; count her towers' (Ps. 48:12, NASB). Yes, now that the Assyrians are gone one can do that. Count her towers. They are all there, aren't they? The people of God are, admittedly, pretty pathetic, but if you assault them you will find their God is able to deliver them—and, if you mock their God, watch out for the terror of the night.

26

Yahweh Is All You Need! Or Is He?
(2 Kings 20)

Someone asked Senator Zebulon Vance, campaigning in North Carolina, where he stood on the subject of Prohibition. Vance answered: 'I will respond to the gentleman's question by saying that my head is strongly inclined to the great policy of prohibition, but my stomach yearns the other way. I may say therefore I truthfully declare myself as being divided on the issue.'[1] So Vance was both for and against Prohibition. Here was Vance dry and Vance wet. Even in politics most think that is inconsistent.

That is a bit like Hezekiah in 2 Kings 20. The chapter provides two pictures of Hezekiah. In one he walks by faith (vv. 1-11); in the other he walks by sight (vv. 12-19). In the first section he seems to believe 'Yahweh is all you need', while in the second he seems to say, 'I'm not so sure about that.'

The chapter follows a generally regular development and it might be helpful to map out its structure prior to exposition (see next page).

And one chronological clarification as well. It may be helpful to know that chapter 20 happened *before* 18:13–19:36 even though it is related *after* it. Verse 6 shows that Jerusalem's deliverance from the Assyrians is yet to come and the fact that Hezekiah's coffers are full (v. 13) makes sense before he had to fork over tribute to Sennacherib (18:13-16). This is not so

---

[1]Paul F. Boller, Jr., *Congressional Anecdotes* (New York: Oxford, 1991), 115.

Plan of 2 Kings 20

Time and circumstance, v. 1a
  Coming of prophet, v. 1b
    Message (death), v. 1c
      Hezekiah's response, vv. 2-3 (prayer)
    Message (deliverance), vv. 4-6
    (Fulfillment, v. 7)
      Hezekiah's response, vv. 8-11 (sign)

Time and circumstance, vv. 12-13
  Coming of prophet, v. 14a
  + questions and answers, vv. 14b-15
    Message (exile), vv. 16-18
      Hezekiah's response, v. 19

unusual; chronology does not hold biblical writers hostage. The story in Judges 19–21 stands at the end of that book and yet actually occurred early in the judges' period.[2] Or why did Isaiah give us five chapters of his preaching before telling us of his call to prophesy in Isaiah 6?[3]

Merodach-baladin (v. 12) was nearly a perennial pain for Assyria. He stirred up the international pot after Sargon II's death (705 BC). Sennacherib claims to have defeated him in his first campaign (in 702). It was likely at about that time that Merodach-baladin's envoys visited Hezekiah under the guise of congratulating him on his recovery. If Hezekiah's illness/recovery occurred in 702/701, his fifteen additional years would take him to his death in 686.[4] God then grants Hezekiah a gracious recovery, the Babylonian schemers arrive to beef up

---

[2] See my *Judges: Such a Great Salvation* (Ross-shire: Christian Focus, 2000), 211fn. See also my discussion of 1 Samuel 28:3-25 (which is out of chronological order—and significantly so) in *1 Samuel: Looking on the Heart* (Ross-shire: Christian Focus, 2000), 236-38.

[3] Cf. B. S. Childs, *Introduction to the Old Testament as Scripture* (Philadelphia: Fortress, 1979), 331; and J. N. Oswalt, *The Book of Isaiah: Chapters 1-39*, New International Commentary on the Old Testament (Grand Rapids: Eerdmans, 1986), 173-75. Both 2 Chronicles 32 and Isaiah 36–39 report Hezekiah's illness and the Babylonians' visit after the deliverance of Jerusalem. In Isaiah, therefore, as in 2 Kings, chs. 38–39 occur before chs. 36–37. Is Isaiah or Kings original? I don't know—and don't care. On the place of Isaiah 38–39 in that book, see Oswalt, 672-73.

[4] See W. S. LaSor, 'Merodach-baladin,' ISBE, 3:325-26; and Eugene H. Merrill, *Kingdom of Priests* (Grand Rapids: Baker, 1987), 417-18.

the coalition, the Assyrians shove Merodach-baladin off the stage of history, defeat Egyptian forces coming to Judah's aid (cf. 18:21; 19:9), and ravage Judah within an inch of its life. Now, bereft of both his Babylonian and Egyptian crutches, Hezekiah throws himself upon Yahweh for deliverance (ch. 19). But our writer is not interested in a flowing chronological package. He tells us first of Yahweh's deliverance of Jerusalem (chs. 18–19) and then gives us a flashback into the middle of that drama, one that focuses on Hezekiah's illness and recovery (ch. 20), where he can set before us the stark contrast between walking by faith and walking by sight.

God's servant walks in faith and enjoys his compassionate word (vv. 1-11)

Hezekiah is seemingly in his last illness (v. 1a). The grim reaper will get to him before Sennacherib does. And this was Yahweh's initial word to him: 'Give commands to your household, for you are going to die and not get well' (v. 1b). That's pretty direct and clear. And kind. Would that some families and medics were that straight–forward so that a loved one could have a distinct opportunity to prepare for death.

But Isaiah's news goads Hezekiah to prayer. He turns his face to the wall and moans: 'Please, Yahweh, remember how I have walked before you in fidelity and with a whole heart, and how I have done what is good in your eyes' (v. 3a). Then uncontrollable weeping (v. 3b). I don't think Hezekiah's prayer is mere selfishness nor that he is simply tooting his own horn. We have already read of his 'Davidic' ways (18:-1-8). His prayer follows the Psalm-pattern of appealing to one's faithfulness as a reason to be heard or delivered (see Pss. 7:3-5; 17:1-5; 18:20-26; 26:1-7; 44:17-22). There is no thought of sinless perfection in this but only of covenantal obedience. It may seem surprising that Hezekiah had the gall to so much as ask Yahweh to reverse his clear word. I am not smart enough to know if Hezekiah acted solely on instinct here or partly on reason. But there have been others who apparently thought that Yahweh's hard word may not be his last word but rather a call to prayer for new mercies (Exod. 32:7-14; 2 Sam. 12:13-22). Sometimes what sounds like a final decree is a subtle invitation.

Isaiah has not gotten out of the middle court when Yahweh sends him back to the king with his revised word:

> Here's what Yahweh, the God of David your father, says: 'I have heard your prayer, I have seen your tears. Look, I'm going to heal you—on the third day you will go up to the house of Yahweh. And I shall add fifteen years to your days, and from the grip of the king of Assyria I will deliver you and this city, and I shall defend this city for my sake and for the sake of my servant David' (vv. 5b-6).

Instead of death there will be recovery; instead of a funeral, worship; instead of defeat, deliverance. What an answer Hezekiah received to his prayer! Yahweh is hearing, healing, adding, defending. What a kind God he has: 'I have heard your prayer; I have seen your tears' (v. 5). Not to mention that Yahweh assures him that he will handle all this Assyrian mess.

Divine healing does not exclude human means. Hence Isaiah instructs them to use a poultice of figs on Hezekiah's boil (or rash [NJPS] or skin disorder) and he recovered (v. 7).[5]

Yahweh's promise was a bit staggering—he would not only heal Hezekiah but heal him quickly and completely, for the king would go to the temple to worship on 'the third day' (v. 5). Hezekiah had asked for an immediate sign to assure him of that promise.[6] We cannot be sure of what the sign involved. Isaiah said, 'The shadow has moved ten steps, or should it return ten steps?' (v. 9b, lit.). The steps were apparently something King Ahaz had constructed (v. 11). Some guess that the text refers to some type of sundial, but it could be only a set of stairs on which shadows were cast indicating a particular time of the day.[7] In

---

[5]See John H. Walton, Victor H. Matthews, and Mark Chavalas, *The IVP Bible Background Commentary: The Old Testament* (Downers Grover: InterVarsity, 2000), 407.

[6]Some wonder why Hezekiah asks for a sign in verse 8 after he had already recovered in verse 7. Only a tad of sense tells one that he asked for the sign pre-recovery. The more natural way to take verse 8a is to translate the initial verb as a pluperfect, 'Now Hezekiah *had* asked Isaiah' (as do NIV, NBV, and NLT), so placing his request back in the verses 4-6 situation. A *waw* + imperfect verb form can sometimes be a pluperfect; I have already cited Waltke and O'Connor in this regard (*An Introduction to Biblical Hebrew Syntax* [Winona Lake, IN: Eisenbrauns, 1990], 552-53); see also A. B. Davidson, *Hebrew Syntax*, 3rd ed. (Edinburgh: T. & T. Clark, 1896), 72-73; Davidson tries so hard (and unsuccessfully) to slither out of the examples he cites! One could also look on verse 7 as a parenthesis and connect verse 8 directly to verse 6.

[7]See *Bible Background Commentary,* 407; and Richard D. Patterson and Hermann J. Austel, '1, 2 Kings,' *The Expositor's Bible Commentary*, 12 vols. (Grand Rapids: Zondervan, 1988), 4:274 (drawing on E. J. Young).

any case, Hezekiah asked for the 'hard' option, for the shadow to turn back. This was no natural affair—Isaiah cried to Yahweh to make it happen (v. 11a). It need not have involved any cosmic glitches—the Lord may have refracted the sun's rays. Perhaps it suggested that as time 'went backwards' on the steps, so Yahweh was 'backing up' time in giving the king fifteen more years.

What are we to take away from this segment of text? Are we not to see Yahweh's compassion in delivering his royal servant from death and distress? Someone, however, may wonder why Yahweh shows his compassion in such a distressful manner. Why did he torture Hezekiah with a sentence of death before 'reversing' his word and giving him fifteen additional years? I don't think I know the answer to that, and, even if I did, it wouldn't be profitable. But Yahweh indicates that Hezekiah's prayer was at least one decisive matter behind his 'revised' word: 'I have heard your prayer; I have seen your tears' (v. 5). Yahweh does not ignore us but delights to grant our pleas. Apparently he loves to lift our anguish. Our prayers matter to him. We forget that. We can drop into paganism as soon as we're on our knees. We easily think we must pry benefits out of a reluctant God. How often we need John Newton to the rescue to jump-start the proper attitude in us:

Come, my soul, thy suit prepare:
    Jesus loves to answer prayer;
he himself has bid thee pray,
    therefore will not say thee nay…

Thou art coming to a King,
    large petitions with thee bring;
for his grace and power are such,
    none can ever ask too much…

Then too we see that Yahweh's compassions may come to us packaged in hard providences. We never expected to see the glad word of verses 5-6 come out of the sad wrapping of verse 1. Only the chemistry of Yahweh's kindness could produce that.

A musician and composer was in deep trouble. He was heading for financial disaster. He drove himself pitilessly to recover from one failure after another and so his health began to fail. By 1741 he was swimming in debt and would surely land in debtor's prison. But he received a commission from a Dublin charity to compose a work for a benefit performance. He went to work, rarely leaving his room, hardly stopping for food, never out of his house for three weeks. Three parts and the orchestration—260 pages of manuscript—were finished in 24 days. So Georg Frideric Handel produced *Messiah*. At its premiere *Messiah* raised 400 pounds and freed 142 men from debtor's prison. One of his biographers claimed that '*Messiah* has fed the hungry, clothed the naked, fostered the orphan...more than any other single musical production in this or any country.' And Handel's fortunes turned for the better.[8] But it hadn't looked like that in April, 1741, when he gave his 'farewell' concert.

The point is not that God will always turn trouble to success but that, as with Hezekiah, God's compassions lie hidden in a bundle of trouble. This will not save us distress but may save us from despair. Perhaps we need the help of Newton's friend, William Cowper, here:

Ye fearful saints, fresh courage take;
    the clouds ye so much dread
    are big with mercy,
    and shall break in blessings on your head.

Judge not the Lord by feeble sense,
    but trust him for his grace;
    behind a frowning providence
    he hides a smiling face.[9]

God's servant walks in folly and receives his severe word (vv. 12-19)

Ah, visitors! From Babylon no less! Merodach-baladin sent an embassy to Hezekiah with congratulations on his recovery (v. 12).[10] One needn't marvel that Hezekiah is impressed. There's something gratifying, is there not, to discover that people far

---

[8]Patrick Kavanaugh, *The Spiritual Lives of the Great Composers* (Nashville: Sparrow, 1992), 5-6.

[9]From his hymn, 'God Moves in a Mysterious Way.'

[10]Biblical Merodach-baladin is Marduk-apla-idinna II of Assyrian and Babylonian sources.

away have an interest in you? It is heart-warming to see that you matter to important people. 'So Hezekiah paid attention to them[11] and showed them all his treasure house—the silver and the gold and the spices and the fine oil, as well as his armory and all to be found in his treasuries; there wasn't a thing Hezekiah did not show them in his house and all his realm' (v. 13). It all went beyond condolences and congratulations. The 'letters' (v. 12) the Babylonians brought were not get-well cards. They likely spelled out the 'hidden agenda' (Motyer). So Hezekiah wasn't simply taking them on a tour but showing them his resources—the sort of punch he could bring to the table in an alliance against Assyria.[12]

Isaiah must've smelled what was going on. The prophet does not suffer from reticence and so goes to the king and 'one-ups' him: What did these men say? Where do they come from? (v. 14). When the king answers, the prophet presses him: 'What have they seen in your house?' (v. 15a). Hezekiah is quite open and emphatic: 'Everything that's in my house they have seen; there's not a thing I did not show them in my treasuries' (v. 15b).[13] That brings on the key moment, as if Isaiah says, 'Okay then, you need to hear the word of Yahweh about this situation' (v. 16):

'The days are coming when everything in your palace, everything that your ancestors have amassed till now, will be carried off to Babylon. Not a thing will be left,' Yahweh says. 'Sons sprung from you, sons fathered by you, will be abducted to be eunuchs in the palace of the king of Babylon' (vv. 17-18, NJB).[14]

So flattery can be fulfilling and plots are thrilling—and all of it idolatrous. You cannot, Isaiah would say, lean on Yahweh's arm (cf. Isa. 33:2) and on Babylon's arm (here) or on Egypt's arm

---

[11]BDB, 1034, would take the verb (lit., to hear) here as 'listen to, yield to'. A few Hebrew manuscripts have the same reading as the parallel in Isaiah 39:2, 'rejoiced over.'

[12]Alec Motyer nicely captures Hezekiah's likely thrill: 'Imagine them coming all that way to see me! Imagine Merodach-Baladin wanting me as an ally!' (*Isaiah*, Tyndale Old Testament Commentaries [Leicester: Inter-Varsity, 1999], 240).

[13]My translation picks up the emphasis of the Hebrew which places the object-clauses before the verbs for emphasis. The verb 'to see/show' (*rā'āh*) occurs five times in verses 13-15.

[14]It is difficult to decide whether *sārîsîm* in verse 18 is 'eunuch' or 'official' in this context. See Gordon H. Johnston, NIDOTTE, 3:288-95.

(Isa. 30:1-5; 31:1-3). Hence both the stockpiles Hezekiah boasts of and the sons he fathers will be carted off; both possessions and people are destined for Babylon.

So verses 16-18 control (we might say) the rest of 2 Kings. Come 2 Kings 21 we will discover that Manasseh puts Judah beyond the point of recovery, but chapter 20 shows us that the road to Babylon began with the folly of godly king Hezekiah.

We should note Hezekiah's response in verse 19 to Yahweh's word: 'Hezekiah said to Isaiah, "The word of Yahweh which you have spoken is good." Now he said [= thought], "Is this not the case, if there will be peace and security in my days?"' But what sort of response is this? Certainly a submissive one (v. 19a). But what are we to make of his rationale in 19b? Probably a majority of commentators assume it reflects Hezekiah's self-centeredness. 'At least this disaster won't hit under my watch!'[15] Verse 19 then works on a contrast that boils down to submission-yet-selfishness.

This, however, is not the only way to read 19b. The halves of the verse may stand in parallel rather than contrast. That is, 19b may spell out why Yahweh's word is 'good', in that the king recognizes the mercy and restraint in Yahweh's word. After all, it could have been much worse—the judgment could have been immediate, perhaps Yahweh giving Hezekiah over to the Assyrians after all. On this view, Hezekiah is saying Yahweh's word is 'good', that is, kind, in that the judgment has been postponed. So 19b would not reflect Hezekiah's self-centredness but his gratitude.[16] I refuse to die for this matter, but if forced to vote I would take this second view.

What then do we see here in verses 12-19? We see a king who finds it hard to be steadfast. We see a king who seems to

---

[15]See, e.g., the commentaries by Provan and Cogan & Tadmor.

[16]One can find this view in C. F. Keil, J. R. Lumby (in the old Cambridge Bible for Schools and Colleges), H. L. Ellison (in 2nd ed. of *New Bible Commentary*), and in Calvin. Calvin wrote that Hezekiah 'gives thanks to God for mitigating the punishment which he had deserved; as if he had said, "The Lord might have suddenly raised up enemies, to drive me out of my kingdom; but he now spares me, and, by delaying, moderates the punishment which might justly have been inflicted on me."' He continues: '[W]hile he wished well to those who should live after him, yet it would have been undutiful to disregard that token of forbearance which God gave by delaying his vengeance; for he might have been led by it to hope that his mercy would, in some degree, be extended to posterity' (*Commentary on the Book of the Prophet Isaiah*, in vol. 8 of *Calvin's Commentaries*, 22 vols. [reprint ed.,.; Grand Rapids: Baker, 1999], 192-93).

do better in sickness (vv. 1-11) than in health (vv. 12-19), who perhaps handles blight better than blessing. This is the king of 18:1-8, who trusted Yahweh (18:5), and yet seems to think Yahweh needed a little help from Babylon. How fragile our faithfulness; how changing our consistency; how easily our faith can fade.

Baseball lore tells of 'Happy Jack' Chesbro, who pitched for the New York Highlanders (later Yankees) in 1904. A pitcher today who chalks up twenty wins has had a superb season. But that was nothing for Chesbro. He long passed that. Near season's end he had given New York forty-one wins. Then, on the final day of the season, with the league pennant hanging in the balance, Happy Jack went to the mound looking for win number forty-two. But in the final play in the last inning of the game, Chesbro let go with a wild pitch that allowed a runner to score and lost the ball game and the pennant. After all he'd done. Winning an amazing forty-one games. Perhaps being the major reason New York was even vying for the pennant. And then a wild pitch that ended it all.[17] It's hard to be consistent about consistency.

This closing scene of Hezekiah's reign means to impress us with that. It's not a failure unique to royalty but dogs all God's people. And if we see how quickly we can contradict our commitments and how easily we fall, perhaps the Spirit will work in us a holy fear and a sacred caution that will make us cry out for God to keep us. That is apparently what happened in Simon Peter's case. There he was at 'the Lord's Breakfast,' answering essentially the same question for the revealing third time. And he simply had to blurt out, 'Lord, you know everything; you know that I love you' (John 21:17). But there were no superlatives about how much he loved Jesus. There were no pledges that even if all others forsook Jesus, Peter would stand as the lone faithful one (Mark 14:29). That seems to have gotten knocked out of him. Fear made Peter cautious. So should this text do for us. It is when Scripture makes us tremble that we are actually the safest.

So Hezekiah's reign comes to an end. Fifteen more years don't last forever. But even the customary formula is spiced up a bit

---

[17]*Bill Stern's Favorite Baseball Stories* (Garden City, NY: Blue Ribbon, 1949), 126-27.

for Hezekiah with the memory of his famous water delivery system (v. 20).[18] He did what was right like David (18:3) but 20:12-19 shows he is not the 'David' to come.

[18]See the fine summary in Alfred J. Hoerth, *Archaeology and the Old Testament* (Grand Rapids: Baker, 1998), 344-46.

27

The Point of No Return
(2 Kings 21)

A few weeks ago during a scrumptious spaghetti supper, Andrew, one of my friends, told us that we were overdue for a hurricane. We live some seventy miles from the Mississippi gulf coast and periodically such storms can batter the daylights out of the area. Coastal residents hurriedly prepare for such a storm's landfall: storm shutters are closed or sheets of plywood nailed up over windows, and so on. Authorities may urge evacuation along designated routes. There are always some who choose to stay and 'ride out' the storm. It was something like that in Judah during the reign of Manasseh. Without the evacuation option. Manasseh was 'the worst king ever'.[1] Remnant believers simply had to batten down the hatches and hope to ride out the storm. And it was a long storm. Evil reigned. Manasseh would make Athaliah and Ahaz look like Kiddie Skool.

The breakdown of the chapter is simple:

> A dark regime, vv. 1-9
> A hard word, vv. 10-15
> A bloody time, v. 16

---

[1] Richard D. Nelson, *First and Second Kings*, Interpretation (Louisville: John Knox, 1987), 247. Roger Ellsworth tells of a student who complained to his professor that he did not deserve the low grade on his paper. 'I know,' the prof shot back, 'but this school does not have a lower grade than the one on your paper!' So one can't find a grade low enough for Manasseh. 'Manasseh plumbed the depths of evil in an unprecedented and particularly grievous way, and did so for a prolonged period of time' (*Apostasy, Destruction and Hope* [Darlington: Evangelical Press, 2002], 233-34).

A shameful record, vv. 17-18
A fearful hold, vv. 19-26

Now let us move on to the testimony of this chapter. I'll try to present that testimony under the rubric of certain 'pairs' the text suggests.

Chronology and Mystery (v. 1)

Manasseh's fifty-five years give chronologists fits. If one counts them from the end of Hezekiah's reign (687/686 BC) one ends up well into Josiah's reign, which began about 640 BC (cf. 22:1). Hence some would posit that Manasseh was co-regent with Hezekiah for ten-plus years (ca. 697-686) and then ruled by himself until about 642. If that were so, verse 1 means that Manasseh was twelve years old when he became co-regent and he reigned fifty-five years as co-regent and sole king in Jerusalem.[2]

But Manasseh's fifty-five years are more of a theological than a chronological problem. Manasseh's fifty-five years constitute the longest reign of any king of Judah or Israel. Yet in them he wiped out Hezekiah's reforms, exponentially increased wickedness, and exhausted the patience of God (cf. 23:26-27).[3] Why so long to do so much damage? If 'the years of the wicked will be short' (Prov. 10:27), why weren't they? Why make Manasseh an exception? Cohn is right: In spite of his gross godlessness, at least as far as 2 Kings 21 goes 'Manasseh meets with no reported personal or professional adversity. The narrator tells of his long reign and peaceful burial in a garden.'[4] And we wonder why God does that. Why does God allow this godless geek 55 years to wreak ruin?[5]

---

[2] Cf. the discussion in T. R. Hobbs, *2 Kings*, Word Biblical Commentary (Waco: Word, 1985), 304, and, again, Leslie McFall, 'Has the chronology of the Hebrew kings been finally settled?,' *Themelios* 17/1 (Oct-Nov 1991): 9-10. For references to Manasseh in extra-biblical materials, see the summary in Iain Provan, V. Philips Long, and Tremper Longman III, *A Biblical History of Israel* (Louisville: Westminster/John Knox, 2003), 274-75.

[3] K. D. Fricke, *Das zweite Buch von den Königen*, Die Botschaft des alten Testaments (Stuttgart: Calwer, 1972), 299.

[4] Robert L. Cohn, *2 Kings*, Berit Olam (Collegeville, MN: Liturgical, 2000), 149.

[5] I can't pretend to know. One possibility is that Manasseh's reign in itself was part of God's judgment on Judah. Isaiah 3, for example, gives two answers to the question, How does a nation know it is under divine judgment? Answer: (1) by the wicked quality of its leaders (3:1-15), and (2) by the trivial preoccupations of its women (3:16–4:1).

It's only a numeral and yet it is a mystery. But we are awash in mysteries. Joseph Smith, Jr.'s polygamy was conveniently authorized by subsequent 'divine revelation'; over sixty residents of Palmyra, New York, certified Smith and his father to be 'destitute of moral character'; no evidence supports (and much doesn't) the existence of civilizations, flora, fauna, topography, and geography described in *The Book of Mormon*; and specific prophecies of Joseph Smith himself have proved false.[6] Yet more than ten million people are Latter Day Saints.

There are some 100,000 billion complex cells in the human body; the human hand has over 652,000 nerve endings; the retina of the human eye contains some 124 million rod-shaped cells to distinguish light from darkness and about six million cone-shaped cells responding to millions of variations of colour; the human heart beats some 100,000 times per day, pumping blood through 80,000 miles of blood vessels—on and on it could go. And yet Stephen Jay Gould claims 'Human beings arose as…a kind of glorious cosmic accident resulting from the catenation of thousands of improbable events'.[7] Is such 'faith' a mystery or what?

In June 1661 James Guthrie sealed his faith with his neck; afterwards his head was struck off and placed on display high above the Netherbow Port of Edinburgh, where it remained, bleached and bony, for twenty-seven years. Yet little Willie Guthrie would repeatedly traverse the cobblestones to a place where he could gaze on that gruesome token. He would then hide himself away for hours at home, and, when found, would cry, 'I've seen my father's heid! I've seen my father's heid!'[8] Wasn't government butchery enough? Why did little Willie have to be traumatized by their ghoulish display?

Lots of mysteries. Why does a character like Joseph Smith spawn such a 'successful' movement? Why doesn't Gould have ability to assess evidence? Why did wee Willie Guthrie have to

---

Sometimes (for we cannot make this universal) inept and wicked rulers are not the reason for judgment to come but are part of a judgment that has already arrived.

[6]Walter Martin, *The Kingdom of the Cults*, rev. ed. (Minneapolis: Bethany House, 2003), 203-23.

[7]John Blanchard, *Is God Past His Sell-by Date?* (Darlington: Evangelical Press, 2002), 116-18.

[8]Jock Purves, *Fair Sunshine*, rev. ed. (Edinburgh: Banner of Truth, 2003), 7-10.

be devastated? And why fifty-five years for wicked Manasseh to operate his playground of iniquity? Such mysteries should humble us. Believers who hold a high (proper) view of the Bible's authority, who think (rightly) that the Bible teaches coherent doctrine and clear morality, may especially need this counsel. Sometimes some of these folks can give the impression that with their biblical and doctrinal knowledge they have pretty well sewed up the rough edges of life as well. But sane Christians know that biblical clarity does not eliminate life's puzzles. Having some knowledge of God's truth does not mean we comprehend God's ways. And so we often find ourselves asking 'But why is God doing it this way?' That may have been precisely the question of some believers in Judah who lived their entire lives under the reign of Manasseh.

Perversion and Privilege (vv. 2-9)

Verses 2-9 are a summary section, reporting a new paganism (vv. 3-6), a scorned privilege (vv. 7-8), and a certain doom (vv. 2, 9) of Judah under Manasseh.[9] Readers must make careful note of verse 2-7, the list of Manasseh's perversions, because they form a direct contrast to 18:3-8, where the writer tabulated the reforms of Hezekiah's reign. Hence, 21:2-7 reverses all of 18:3-8.

The writer itemizes Manasseh's apostasy so that we readers will feel its cumulative weight. Manasseh re-instituted *fertility* worship: 'he erected altars for Baal and he made an Asherah' (v. 3b). This was in the tradition of Ahab, the infamous 'antichrist' of the northern kingdom ('as Ahab king of Israel had done,' v. 3c). Manasseh even installed an Asherah image in the temple itself (v. 7a). And Manasseh gave himself to *astral* worship—'he bowed down to all the host of heaven and served them' (v. 3d). Again, altars to sun, moon, and stars had squatters' rights in both courts of the temple (v. 5).[10] Borrowing a page from Ahaz's scrapbook (16:3), Manasseh stooped to the horror of *child sacrifice* (v. 6a) and also gave himself over to all kinds of

---

[9]Note the 'nations' at the beginning and end of this section (vv. 2 and 9). That Yahweh both 'dispossessed' (v. 2) and 'exterminated' (v. 9) these nations shows such a dark end awaits Judah since Manasseh has practiced the 'abominations' of the nations (v. 2) and led Judah to do more evil than the nations (v. 9).

[10]On the 'problem' of the two courts, see Hobbs, *2 Kings*, 305-06.

divination, or, as we might say, trafficking in the dark powers ('practiced sorcery and divination, and consulted mediums and spiritists,' v. 6b, NIV). Manasseh 'multiplied doing evil' (v. 6c) and brought it as a perverse art to ever grosser depths.

Now step back from this pile of paganism and note the common virus that infects it all. It's all about *control*.[11] In fertility worship I use my practice of sex to manipulate or encourage the heavenly powers to act in the same way and grant fertility. In astral worship I seek out omens that are indicators of future events; likewise in spiritism I want the secret knowledge that will enlighten me on how to act or react in view of what is coming. By sacrificing my child I show how dead earnest I am, what an extreme price I am willing to pay, and so should be able to 'purchase' the favor I desire. Paganism is the way I *manage* my life over against the various 'powers' that may determine it. Paganism is light years away from biblical religion with its sovereign God who walks before and beside me in both green pastures and dark valleys all the way to my final residence.

The real tragedy appears, however, not in what Manasseh embraced but in what he abandoned. There's a hint of this in verse 4 in its reference to 'the house of Yahweh of which Yahweh had said, "In Jerusalem I will put my name."' But verses 7-8 flesh out the matter, when they speak of the Asherah-image Manasseh placed in the house

> (7) of which Yahweh had said to David and to Solomon his son, 'In this house and in Jerusalem which I have chosen out of all the tribes of Israel I will put my name for all time; (8) and I will not make Israel's feet wander anymore from the land that I gave their fathers; only they must take care to do in line with all I have commanded them—all the instruction that Moses my servant commanded them.'

Here was reality given (v. 7)—Yahweh 'put his name' in the temple and in Jerusalem. Yahweh's 'name' is another way of saying Yahweh himself and all that he has revealed himself to

---

[11]Cf. Walter Brueggemann, *2 Kings*, Knox Preaching Guides (Atlanta: John Knox, 1982), 89:Manasseh 'prefers to trust in the religious manipulations which keeps [sic] security for his realm in his own hands. Thus the worship of these other gods is finally technique, a way to manage political reality for our own interests...'

be.[12] Here was security assured (v. 8a)—rest and stability in the land. Here was fidelity demanded (v. 8b)—the obedient response for Yahweh's gifts of his presence and preservation. But they didn't listen (v. 9a) and Manasseh duped them into his super-paganism anyway (v. 9b). Think of the treasure Manasseh despised—for Yahweh who put his name in the temple is the atonement-providing (altar of sacrifice; cf. Lev. 16:1-16), people-sustaining (showbread, cf. Exod. 25:23-30), prayer-hearing (altar of incense, cf. Exod. 30:1-10; Rev. 8:3) God. And Manasseh would have none of him.

Fred Astaire and Ginger Rogers were about to star in *Shall We Dance* (1937). George Gershwin had written the musical score. Choreographer Hermes Pan was about to start rehearsals; he walked on to an assigned stage on the set and ask a pianist who was already there to play part of the score. Pan told him he was to begin rehearsals the next day and had not heard the musical score yet. The pianist played the title song. Pan asked him if he couldn't play it a little faster. He did. Pan complained that it had such a strange tempo and that it was almost like a march. The pianist played it for him a number of different ways but couldn't satisfy the choreographer. Finally, Pan announced, 'Gershwin or no Gershwin, this isn't for me. This is not my type of dance feeling. I don't know what to do with it.' Pan went off to a meeting with Astaire, the producer, and someone else to discuss the problem with the music. A few minutes later the 'pianist' walked into the meeting. It happened that he was the great Gershwin himself. Pan wanted to become suddenly invisible. 'I'm sorry,' he cried, 'I didn't realize who you were.'[13]

Maybe that was Manasseh's problem—he didn't know who Yahweh was. Or perhaps it was worse—he didn't care who Yahweh was. The presence (v. 7) and promise (v. 8) of Yahweh are his people's infinite treasure and highest privilege. And Manasseh despised them.

---

[12]See J. A. Motyer, 'Name,' NBD, 3rd ed., 801-02; Walter C. Kaiser, Jr., *Toward an Old Testament Theology* (Grand Rapids: Zondervan, 1978), 106-07, 120-21. 'Putting' the name in a place likely carries overtones of ownership and conquest; cf. G. J. Wenham, 'Deuteronomy and the Central Sanctuary,' *Tyndale Bulletin* 22 (1971): 112-14.

[13]Paul F. Boller, Jr., and Ronald L. Davis, *Hollywood Anecdotes* (New York: William Morrow, 1987), 272.

Depravity and Disaster (vv. 10-16)

Now we hear the prophetic announcement of judgment in its usual 'because' (v. 11a)-'therefore' (v. 12a) form. Verses 10-11 briefly recapitulate the crimes of verses 2-7 as the rationale for the following judgment (vv. 12-15). The writer does not say Manasseh's evil eclipsed that of any king of Judah to date; he says that Manasseh's wickedness outstripped that of the Amorites, the pagan, pre-Israelite residents of Canaan (v. 11)! After the actual announcement of judgment in verses 12-15, the writer adds an 'and-this-too' note in verse 16: 'And what's more Manasseh poured out very much innocent blood, to the point that he filled Jerusalem from end to end—beside his sin which he made Judah sin, by doing what is evil in Yahweh's eyes.'[14] Manasseh smashed and crushed as he liked and woe betide the protester.

The judgment, then, is unsurprising but very graphic. Yahweh depicts the coming disaster via four images. First, both ears of anyone hearing of Jerusalem's ruin will 'tingle' (v. 12; see 1 Sam. 3:11; Jer. 19:3). The idea is that the horror of a message that is heard produces an adverse physical reaction. Habakkuk uses the same verb to describe how his lips 'quiver' in fright over Babylon's coming invasion of Judah (Hab. 3:16). So the ears 'tingling' speak of the *terror* of judgment. Next, Yahweh uses building imagery, but of deconstruction rather than construction: 'And I shall stretch out over Jerusalem the measuring line of Samaria and the level of the house of Ahab' (v. 13a). Yahweh had already made history of both Samaria (cf. 17:6) and of Ahab's dynasty (cf. 10:17) and Jerusalem was next in his demolition program. So verse 13a implies the *inevitability* of judgment. Third, Yahweh uses kitchen language: 'I shall wipe away Jerusalem as one wipes a dish, wiping it and turning it upside down' (v. 13b). The dish or bowl is wiped clean and then flipped over to show there is not a drop or lick of anything in it—a graphic picture of the *totality* of judgment. Finally, Yahweh vows to abandon his people, give them up to their enemies' will, so that they will be 'spoil and plunder' for

---

[14]Note how 16b casts Manasseh as the 'Jeroboam' of the southern kingdom—'his sin which he made Judah sin.' It's a take-off on the refrain of the northern kings—so-and-so 'walked in the way of Jeroboam and in his sin which he made Israel to sin' (e.g., 1 Kings 15:26, 34). See comments on 2 Kings 17:21-23 above.

all their enemies (v. 14). The people will be 'easy pickings' for the invaders; they will be able to do nothing to prevent this. So the spoil and plunder imagery points to their *helplessness* in judgment.

Now our writer and the prophet he quotes are not teaching a doctrine of 'condemnation by Manasseh alone' (cf. v. 11). Rather, there's been an ongoing tradition of evil in Israel ever since Yahweh redeemed them from slavery (v. 15).[15] Their whole 'national' history has been one long exercise in 'aggravating' Yahweh. Manasseh's depravity simply put them 'over the top', as we say. Manasseh's massive wickedness added to the nation's cumulative apostasy puts Judah beyond hope of recovery. Because of Manasseh Judah had reached the point of no return. This is clearly the writer's point in 23:26.

This is a solemn matter: that iniquity can pass a point that places a nation, or an individual, beyond hope of recovery and makes judgment irreversible. The fact that *we* don't know where that point is should sober us. Several years ago our local newspaper reported a birthday celebration. Byung Soo Kim was an engineering student at the University of Michigan. Eleven of his friends had gathered in an apartment one Friday evening to celebrate Kim's twenty first birthday. Kim had determined how he wanted to celebrate—he would down a shot of scotch for every year of his life. He downed twenty shots in ten minutes and passed out before the climactic one. He was found blue and unconscious early the next day; he died at a hospital where he had been admitted with a blood alcohol level of 0.39 percent. He had a limit. He didn't know what it was. He went beyond it, and it destroyed him. That's how it is with idolatry and depravity. There's a line we can cross and we don't know where it is. This ought to scare us into repenting. A broken and crushed heart (Ps. 51:17) doesn't look all that bad when one considers the alternative.

Memory and Legacy (vv. 17-22)
There it was in bold print from the Associated Press: 'State most corrupt in the nation.' The clip referred to a study of

---

[15]Victor P. Hamilton, *Handbook on the Historical Books* (Grand Rapids: Baker, 2001), 462.

corruption among public officials, and, according to said study, my current state of residence, Mississippi, has taken the laurels for most corrupt. Louisiana is apparently losing its reputation to Mississippi. Now the article does suggest some qualifiers. For example, the ranking may only indicate which state has the highest rate of crooked officials who get caught. That may imply that we have the most stupid crooked officials but that we may not be the absolutely most corrupt state. I trust you can discern the fine distinction. But the fact is my state is unique and one should not be ecstatic over that uniqueness.

And Manasseh was unique. The writer even felt compelled to change up the standard summary formula for Manasseh. That formula always begins, 'Now the rest of the acts of so-and-so and all that he did...' That summary formula (for kings of Judah) occurs fifteen times in 1–2 Kings.[16] Usually it simply has that standard footnote form—you can find the record of this king's acts in the chronicles. Occasionally, the writer will add a mention of the king's might or cities built or war record or, in Hezekiah's case, his water system (cf. 1 Kings 15:23; 22:45; 2 Kings 20:20). Only Manasseh garners a special notation for his sin: 'Now the rest of the acts of Manasseh and all that he did—including his sin which he sinned, are they not written...?' (v. 17). That does not mean the rest of Judah's kings were stalwarts of righteousness but only that Manasseh was so much the epitome of wickedness that one could not tell his story without wallowing in the details of his wickedness. 'The sin which he sinned' was 'written', recorded in clear and fluent Hebrew in all its shame and scandal. What a memory to leave. Manasseh, the only king specially noted for his sin.

But verses 19-22 suggest that Manasseh not only left a memory but passed on a legacy. The writer's triple emphasis depicts Manasseh's son Amon as a Manasseh-clone:

> And he did evil in Yahweh's eyes *as Manasseh his father had done*; and he walked in all the way *which his father had walked*, and he served the idols *that his father had served...* (vv. 20-21).

[16]To wit: 1 Kings 14:29; 15:7, 23; 22:45; 2 Kings 8:23; 12:19; 14:18; 15:6, 36; 16:19; 20:20; 21:17, 25; 23:28; 24:5.

Amon simply goose-stepped to Manasseh's standards.

But wait a minute. Doesn't 2 Chronicles 33:1-20 tell us that when the Assyrians carted Manasseh off to Babylon, he humbled himself before God, that he repented, and that his repentance must have been genuine since, upon restoration to his throne, he tried to eradicate his previous corruptions? Are we dismissing 2 Chronicles 33 as irrelevant or misleading? Certainly not. In fact, we've every reason to take 2 Chronicles 33 as historically reliable.[17] But perhaps 2 Kings 21 doesn't mention the matters noted in 2 Chronicles 33 because they didn't make much difference. Don't misunderstand. Better Manasseh repent than not repent. Better that he seek to undo damage he had done than ignore such. Wonderful to hear of Manasseh's wonderful conversion. But his new, personal relationship with Yahweh didn't affect all that much. The disaster had been inflicted, the poison administered. Whatever change had come to Manasseh had no impact on Amon (vv. 20-21). Manasseh had already made his impression there.

There may be a warning for us here. A healthy spiritual legacy seldom flows from a late and sudden conversion but from the practice of lifelong and attractive godliness.

Murder and Promise (vv. 23-26)

> The servants of Amon conspired against him and put the king to death in his palace. Then the people of the land struck down all those conspiring against king Amon; and the people of the land made Josiah his son king in his place (vv. 23-24).

We don't know why Amon's servants assassinated him. Was it political? Was Amon still trenchantly pro-Assyrian while a palace clique favored alignment with Egypt?[18] We can't be sure. Sometimes we just can't get *behind* the text. Nor do we have much certainty over 'the people of the land' in verse 24. Does this term refer to the people of Judah in general or outside Jerusalem — or to a sort of elite group among them — who may have had particular loyalty to the Davidic monarchy? Why bore

---

[17]See the study by Brian Kelly, 'Manasseh in the Books of Kings and Chronicles (2 Kings 21:1-18; 2 Chron 33:1-20),' in *Windows into Old Testament History* (Grand Rapids: Eerdmans, 2002), 131-46.

[18]Cf. Eugene H. Merrill, *Kingdom of Priests* (Grand Rapids: Baker, 1987), 442.

you with all seven views of such a matter?[19] We do know Amon
was murdered, that his assailants were brought to justice, and
that 'the people of the land' apparently thought of no one else
but Amon's son to succeed him. Hence young Josiah reigns.

I don't know much about 'the people of the land'—that is,
I don't know how deep their faith or how earnest their piety
was. But it is fascinating that after fifty-five years of Manasseh
and two years of Manasseh, Jr., they do not cast aside the
Davidic succession of kings and deem it an outmoded tradition
fit only for the political landfill. After over a half-century of
disenchantment who could blame them had they said they
were finished with David's line of kings since it gave them
only rogues and bums? Yahweh's promise to David in the
'Davidic covenant' must have had a tenacious hold on their
consciousness. According to that promise, David's kingdom was
to be a 'forever' kingdom (2 Sam. 7:12-16) for the lasting security
of Israel (2 Sam. 7:10-11a) and the ultimate benefit of humanity
(2 Sam. 7:19), a kingdom whose eventual coming is utterly
certain (2 Sam. 23:1-3a, 5) and whose Final Representative is
refreshingly attractive (2 Sam. 23:3b-4).[20] They hadn't seen any
royal 'attractiveness' for decades, and yet, in line with Yahweh's
promise, they install an eight-year-old descendant of David as
king. And how could they know he wouldn't prove Manasseh
III? Or how could they be sure he could bring any ultimate
good since Manasseh had made judgment certain for Judah?
But, like dropping anchor to ride out a furious storm, they hold
to Yahweh's kingdom promise in spite of the disappointments
and wickedness that have closed in on them.

During the 'Market Garden' offensive in Holland during
World War II, British wounded lay in the Schoonoord Hotel in
Oosterbeek under the watchful eyes of German guards. Dutch
volunteers and British medics cared for these casualties as best
they could during the fury of battle. Hendrika van der Vlist,
the daughter of the hotel's owner, was nursing the wounded
and also keeping a diary. One entry read:

[19]Especially when, if interested, you can read for yourself. G. H. Jones (*1 and 2 Kings*,
New Century Bible Commentary, 2 vols. [Grand Rapids: Eerdmans, 1984], 2:483-84)
has a lucid survey of various views; one could add Cogan and Tadmor, *II Kings*, Anchor
Bible (Garden City, NY: Doubleday, 1988), 129-30, and Hobbs, *2 Kings*, 310-11.
[20]These points are fleshed out in my *2 Samuel: Out of Every Adversity* (Ross-shire:
Christian Focus, 1999), 72-85, 245-47.

Sunday, September 24. This is the day of the Lord. War rages outside. The building is shaking. That is why the doctors cannot operate or fix casts. We cannot wash the wounded because nobody can venture out to find water...[21]

Maybe Miss van der Vlist was simply being emphatic about the fact that it was Sunday that day in 1944. But I find the juxtaposition of her sentences interesting: This is the day of the Lord. War rages...the building is shaking...we can't wash the wounded. And yet in the middle of all the fury of destruction one fact remains non-negotiable: This is the day of the Lord. As if to say, He *is* in control in spite of the chaos all round. There *is* a bastion of sanity in this trouble, a sovereignty that somehow rules this mess.

That, I propose, is the way Yahweh's promise to David of an everlasting kingdom must function for us in the upheaval and bedlam of our history. The people of the land didn't have all the answers to their nation's troubles. But they seemed to know the next step—place another descendant of David on the throne. That may not solve today's troubles. But it's the promise, and the promise is the anchor until fulfillment comes.

---

[21]Cornelius Ryan, *A Bridge Too Far* (New York: Simon and Schuster, 1974), 547-48.

28

Can a Reformation Save Us?
(2 Kings 22:1–23:30)

I find the first two chapters of J. C. Ryle's *Christian Leaders of the 18th Century* very stirring. (That's a bit misleading. I find almost everything J. C. Ryle wrote very stirring.)[1] In those chapters he traces the abysmal condition of both state and church in England in the mid-1700s. Left to herself, he says, the Church of England 'would probably have died of dignity'—and to some degree it didn't even have that. Into these bleak days, however, God sent the Christ-conquered, cross-proclaiming preachers of the Evangelical Revival, whose work and message had a salvaging effect on church and country. Dead churches weren't the only 'victims' of gospel resurgence—so were filthy prisons and slave trafficking.[2]

The needs of our own times and such memories of previous days often stir pleas for revival or calls for reformation. We are aware, after all, of the church's deficiencies (at least in the West): she needs to recover doctrinal purity, vital worship, bold witness, personal godliness, and social impact. We sense instinctively that the church's problems do not stem from a lack of a leadership development program, the absence of

---

[1] One of the kindest things my father did was to commend (and eventually give me his set of) Ryle's *Expository Thoughts on the Gospels*. He was fond of saying, 'Anything Ryle writes is good,' and I think he was right!

[2] Cf., in brief compass, Williston Walker, *A History of the Christian Church*, rev. ed. (New York: Charles Scribner's Sons, 1959), 469-72; see also Earle E. Cairns, *An Endless Line of Splendor* (Wheaton, IL: Tyndale House, 1986), chap. 10.

a bus ministry, the want of a music program for eight-to-ten year-olds, or the failure to install a new state-of-the-art sound system—though a legion of brochures and catalogs come to us offering to redress these horrendous shortcomings. No, but if the church could experience a reformation in the really essential areas, well then, it would have a most salutary effect not only on the church but on the nation. Shades of eighteenth-century England perhaps. In any case, we tend to surmise that if there were a reformation in the church it would prove to be some kind of solution at least. But that is not always so. There was a sweeping reformation in Judah under King Josiah. There was a desperate need for it after nearly a half-century of Manasseh–Amon style of paganism. But it was an exercise in futility. The reformation could not save the nation. It was too late for that.

Before getting into the exposition, let me indicate how these chapters seem to be packaged. G. H. Jones is helpful here: he draws on N. Lohfink's observation that major sections begin with 'the king sent' or 'the king commanded'.[3] If we pull 23:4-20 into this scheme our major sections would be:

The king sent:	22:3-11
The king commanded:	22:12-20
The king sent:	23:1-3
The king commanded:	23:4-20
The king commanded:	23:21-23

This leaves 23:24-30 to clean up and summarize. The record of Josiah's reign seems to have been carefully put together. Our exposition, however, will touch on thematic highlights rather than slavishly following these literary divisions.[4]

The Flexible Forbearance of Yahweh (22:1-20)

Fresh air begins to blow into Judah with the accession of eight-year-old Josiah (v. 1).[5] He receives kudos from our writer (v. 2):

---

[3]G. H. Jones, *1 and 2 Kings*, New Century Bible Commentary, 2 vols. (Grand Rapids: Eerdmans, 1984), 2:608; see also B. O. Long, *2 Kings*, The Forms of the Old Testament Literature (Grand Rapids: Eerdmans, 1991), 256.

[4]2 Kings 22–23 is at the center of a vigorous critical debate. I will deal with some of these matters later in the chapter—though not in detail because I'm trying to keep this relatively interesting.

[5]Josiah reigns ca. 640-609 BC. His mother Jedidah was from Bozkath, a town in the lowland hills of Judah (Josh. 15:39); its precise location is unknown.

he joins seven other kings of Judah who do 'what is right' in
Yahweh's eyes,[6] but only two others share with him a favorable
comparison with David.[7] Josiah's steadfastness ('he did not
turn to right or left,' v. 2b) places him in a league with Hezekiah
(18:6). How good Yahweh is to send a Josiah after the Manasseh-
Amon debacle.

Our writer zeroes in on the eighteenth year of Josiah (v. 3a;
ca. 622 BC, when Josiah was twenty-six years of age) and the
premier event that made that year so notable. The story breaks
down into three distinct sections:

> Priestly discovery, vv. 3-10
> Royal distress, vv. 11-14
> Prophetic clarity, vv. 15-20

Let's briefly recapitulate the story.

King Josiah sends Shaphan the scribe to the temple to see that
arrangements are carried out for paying workers and purchasing
materials for the current temple repair project. Verses 4-7 consist
entirely of Josiah's instructions. Note that nothing is said about
the king's orders being carried out. Rather the next thing we hear
is Hilkiah the high priest saying to Shaphan, 'The book of the
law I have found in the temple of Yahweh' (v. 8a).[8] Hilkiah gives
the book to Shaphan who reads it (whether all or part we do not
know; v. 8b). Shaphan's report to Josiah (v. 9) informs us that
the king's orders have been executed, but the focus remains on
the 'book': 'A book [emphatic] Hilkiah the priest has given me'
(v. 10a). Shaphan reads the book in the king's presence (v. 10b),
Josiah rips his clothes in anguish (v. 11) and orders a five-man
commission to go obtain prophetic direction and light on the

---

[6]Asa, 1 Kings 15:11; Jehoshaphat, 22:43; Joash, 2 Kings 12:2; Amaziah, 14:3;
Azariah (Uzziah), 15:3; Jotham, 15:34; and Hezekiah, 18:3.

[7]Asa, 1 Kings 15:11, and Hezekiah, 2 Kings 18:3. On Josiah's stature in 1–2 Kings,
see Gerald Eddie Gerbrandt, *Kingship according to the Deuteronomistic History*, SBL
Dissertation Series (Atlanta: Scholars, 1986), 48-50.

[8]The wooden translation reflects the Hebrew's placing 'the book of the law' in
emphatic position. It was no strange, unknown document but one that, though obscured
for some time, was nevertheless perfectly identifiable to Hilkiah. See Iain Provan, *1 and
2 Kings*, New International Biblical Commentary (Peabody, MA: Hendrickson, 1995),
271, who argues that there is 'no reason to think, then, that the loss or concealment
of the book is being presented as anything other than a recent event, occurring during
the long reign of the apostate Manasseh'.

matter (vv. 12-13). Huldah's door (v. 14) is like the entrance to the emergency room, for Yahweh's furious rage has been ignited against Josiah's realm 'because our fathers have not obeyed the words of this book' (v. 13).

We wonder, however, what exactly was 'this book'? Most seem to think that Hilkiah's 'book of the law' was Deuteronomy or a substantial chunk of it (cf., for the terminology, Deut. 28:61; 29:21; 30:10; 31:26). I have no problem with this identification so long as 'Deuteronomy' is understood as the document from the time—and from, substantially, the mouth—of Moses.

Why do I say that? Narrow your eyes and try to concentrate really hard on the rest of this paragraph. Nineteenth-century Old Testament criticism held that Deuteronomy (most of it) was produced in King Josiah's own time by a reform-minded group, stashed in the temple, 'discovered' by Hilkiah (who may have been in on the ruse), accepted by Josiah, and the reformation was on. On this view, Deuteronomy didn't originate with Moses, but the seventh-century BC writers cast Deuteronomy in the form of speeches by Moses so that it would pack greater 'authority' in Josiah's time. (Folks would more likely listen to 'Moses' than to a bunch of reforming agitators.) So the book was a fraud, but a pious fraud, since the goal was reform, particularly the centralization of worship in Jerusalem. Let a hundred years or so go by and this original critical position becomes so nuanced, modified, adjusted, and disputed that hardly anyone holds it any more (except perhaps in undergraduate religion courses whose teachers sometimes keep regurgitating views from 150 years ago). Scholars have then proposed a welter of dates and origins for the book.[9] And yet, like granny's girdle being found in the attic long after she's gone, the impress of nineteenth century criticism remains—many still insist that Deuteronomy was first published (even if containing older materials) in Josiah's time.[10] However, when there is such a plethora of views on the

[9]For brief reviews, cf. Christopher Wright, *Deuteronomy*, New International Biblical Commentary (Peabody, MA: Hendrickson, 1996), 6-8, and W. S. LaSor, D. A. Hubbard, and F. W. Bush, *Old Testament Survey*, 2nd ed. (Grand Rapids: Eerdmans, 1996), 114-17. For more detail, see J. G. McConville, *Deuteronomy*, Apollos Old Testament Commentary (Leicester: Apollos, 2002), 21-33.
[10]See M. Weinfeld, ABD, 2:174 (seventh century BC.), and, in popular form, B. W. Anderson, *Understanding the Old Testament*, 4th ed. (Englewood Cliffs, NJ: Prentice-Hall, 1986), 376-79.

matter, one divines that a good bit of guesswork is going on. I then remain unrepentant over taking the claims of Deuteronomy itself at face value and attributing it to Moses.[11]

But Josiah was not unrepentant toward the threats in the book of the law. He has a law word and now seeks a prophet word (v. 13), perhaps to discover how soon judgment will strike and if there is any hope of averting it. Huldah's prophecy (vv. 15-20) makes two points. First, there is no hope: Yahweh is 'bringing disaster against this place and its residents' because they have forsaken him, and the inferno of his rage will not be put out (vv. 16-17). Second, there is some mercy: Since King Josiah's heart was 'soft' when he heard the threats of the law and since he humbled himself, tore his clothes and wept in Yahweh's presence, Yahweh will bring Josiah to his grave in peace and not allow him to see the disaster that will wash over Judah (vv. 18-20). So judgment is certain, but judgment is delayed; disaster is on the way, but disaster is not yet—thanks to the repentance of one man.

The text places major attention on Josiah's trembling response. And perhaps we find such acceptance and anguish over Yahweh's word so impressive because it seems so rare. I have always been astounded over Abraham Lincoln's attitude in a dispute during the War between the States. (Some readers may choose to be offended by this; please remember—I'm quoting.) A committee headed by Owen Lovejoy had urged Lincoln to consider a plan for mingling eastern and western troops and Lincoln, assenting, wrote a note to Secretary of War Edwin Stanton suggesting the same. Lovejoy took the note to Stanton, who asked if Lincoln had given the order. When he was assured of that, Stanton exclaimed, 'Then he is a damned fool!' Lovejoy brought news of Stanton's reaction back to the White House. 'Did Stanton say I was a damned fool?,' Lincoln asked. 'He did, sir, and repeated it' was the reply. The President mused a bit and then said: 'If Stanton said I was a damned fool then I must be one. For he is nearly always right, and generally says what he means. I will stop over and see him.'[12] I cannot

---

[11]R. K. Harrison's discussion is still worth reading; see his *Introduction to the Old Testament* (Grand Rapids: Eerdmans, 1969), 637-53.
[12]Carl Sandberg, *Abraham Lincoln*, One Volume Ed. (New York: Harcourt, Brace, Jovanovich, 1974), 354.

comprehend it. I would have fired Stanton with no severance package. But Lincoln didn't; he received a critical word with genuine meekness.

That's what is so apparent in Josiah. He does not throw Hilkiah into the slammer for passing on such a disturbing book nor bawl Shaphan out for reading him such horrific threats. No, his heart is 'soft' (v. 19a), he tears his clothes and weeps. And Yahweh does not ignore this, rather he 'hears' (v. 19b), for here is a man doing exactly what Yahweh wants—trembling over his word (Isa. 66:2). Yahweh's word can make a tremendous impression on a soft heart.

So Yahweh's forbearance gives what appears to be a flexibility to his ways (actually it's all a part of his 'standard' character): he will not alter the fact of judgment but will put off the time of judgment. At this some wag might interject his curious 'what if': Instead of the wicked and weak kings after Josiah, what if Josiah had been followed by a string of 'Josiahs'—would God go on forbearing and putting off judgment? What would Yahweh have done then? The answer, of course, is: Wouldn't Yahweh think that a delightful dilemma? How could that ever be a difficulty for him who delights in mercy?

The Unquenchable Wrath of Yahweh (23:1-27)
Here is another lengthy chunk of text and it will help to have a general map of it:

>Covenant renewal, vv. 1-3
>Intensive reform, vv. 4-20
>Scriptural Passover, vv. 21-23
>Unique king, vv. 24-25
>Unchanged destiny, vv. 26-27

That will give us the run of the text. All Judah enters into a commitment 'to follow Yahweh and to keep his commandments, his testimonies, and his decrees with all the heart and all the soul' (v. 3). This then leads, it seems, to Josiah's thorough-going reform program (vv. 4-20), but that may not be exactly the case. We need to take time out to deal with the 'problem' of 23:4-20.

The writer of Kings focuses on Josiah's eighteenth year (22:3; 23:23); apparently he highlights one year of Josiah's reign to give a flavor of the whole. And in his narrative it looks like Josiah's reforms (23:4-20) are the consequence of the discovery of the Book of the Law and the covenant renewal. Note, however, the broad order of 2 Kings compared with that of 2 Chronicles:

2 Kings		2 Chronicles
Law discovery, 22:3-20		Worship reform, 34:3-7
Covenant renewal, 23:1-3		Law discovery, 34:8-28
Worship reform, 23:4-20		Covenant renewal, 34:29-33
Passover celebration, 23:21-23		Passover celebration, 35:1-19

Here are clues to the interests of the respective writers: Chronicles spends far more time on the Passover than Kings, while Kings gives far more space to the purification of worship, something Chronicles briefly summarizes. However, though not fixated on chronology, the Chronicler does give us more chronological precision on the worship reforms (= 34:3-7): (1) In Josiah's eighth year (632 BC, when he was sixteen years old) he 'began to seek the God of David his father' (v. 3a); (2) in his twelfth year (628 BC, at twenty years old) he 'began to purge' Judah and then extended his image/altar-bashing to the former northern kingdom (vv. 3b-7); and (3) in his eighteenth year (622 BC, at twenty-six years of age) came the discovery of the Book of the Law and renewal of the covenant (vv. 8ff.).

Chronicles is clear: Josiah's reforms were both begun and to a large extent complete *before* Hilkiah's discovery of the Book of the Law. Why does Kings relate them *after* that discovery, giving the impression that the Book of the Law drove those reforms? Is that not deceptive or misleading?

So we need to look at 2 Kings again. First, note that Kings *implies* that Josiah's reforms were underway before Hilkiah's discovery of the Law (22:3-7), for it would seem likely that repairing the temple also involved at least some purging of the temple. Secondly, note that the covenant renewal (23:1-3) and the Passover celebration (23:21-23) are specifically tied to the book that was found (23:2, 3, 21), as are the reforms of verse 24, but that nothing in the reforms of 23:4-20 is related to that book. Thirdly, anyone in a reflective mood might wonder whether all the reforms (and travel required) in 23:4-20 could have been carried out within the confines of one year (the eighteenth year of Josiah's reign). Hence, I think the writer of Kings has left us clues about what he is doing in 23:4-20: he is giving us a *topical survey* of Josiah's reforms out of strict chronological order (a perfectly legitimate practice, by the way).[13]

Now why would he want to do that? Why would he insert 17 verses itemizing Josiah's reforms along with the covenant renewal and Passover celebration? Because he is building up to the climax of his chapter in verses 26-27. He wants to beef up (and that truly) the record of Josiah's reforms, to depict how very intense and massive and detailed those reforms were, so that verses 26-27 will slap his reader in the face with the greatest force. He wants to send us reeling and the way he does so is to pack the chapter full of all Josiah's reforms so that verses 26-27 will deliver their maximum jolt to us.

We'll come back to this, but let's get a feel for the thoroughness of Josiah's reform by taking a brief walk through verses 4-20. We cannot be sure of all the details but one might suggest this is Josiah's twelve-step 'de-Manassehfication' program.

1. Removing pagan vessels from temple (v. 4)
2. Deposing pagan clergy (v. 5)
3. Pulverizing the Asherah image (v. 6)
4. Wrecking the male prostitutes' temple apartments (v. 7)
5. Defiling Judah's high places, deposing their priests (vv. 8-9)
6. Desecrating Tophet, the place of child sacrifice (v. 10)
7. Removing and destroying sun worship paraphernalia (v. 11)[14]
8. Smashing royal idolatrous altars (v. 12)
9. Eliminating Solomon's folly (v. 13)
10. Destroying the props for fertility worship (v. 14)
11. Pulling down/defiling Jeroboam's Bethel worship center (vv. 15-16)
12. Purge throughout northern cities (vv. 19-20)

---

[13]I have cribbed everything in this discussion from D. W. B. Robinson, *Josiah's Reform and the Book of the Law* (Tyndale Press, 1951), 3-25; David L. Washburn, 'Perspective and Purpose: Understanding the Josiah Story,' *Trinity Journal* 12NS/1 (Spring 1991): 59-78; and Richard L. Pratt, Jr., *1 and 2 Chronicles*, Mentor (Ross-shire: Christian Focus, 1998), 472-76.

[14]On verse 11, see Washburn, 'Perspective and Purpose,' 71-73.

That's quite impressive and seems very thorough. And the practice of 'defiling' (the verb *ṭm'* is used four times, vv. 8, 10, 13, and 16) underscores the thoroughness of Josiah's activity. H. L. Ellison puts it well:

> The frequent mention of defiling in this section (8, 10, 13, 16) and the defiling by certain acts (4, 6, 14, 16, 20) is explained by the fact that a sanctuary or high place did not lose its sanctity by the cult objects and buildings being destroyed. It needed more drastic action to make the spot 'profane' or ordinary. Unless this action was taken the sanctuaries would be restored at the next relapse.[15]

Solzhenitsyn describes a 'political' example of this sort of thing. Zoya Leshcheva's whole family had been submerged in the Soviet prison 'sewer system' because of their faith. Zoya herself had been apprehended when ten years old, later sent (for her religious stubbornness) to an orphanage for retarded children. She refused to stoop to the thieving and cursing of most of the kids but instead came to win them over to her own point of view. Which was, not remarkably, anti-Stalinist. There was in the orphanage courtyard one of those mass-produced plaster statues of Stalin. Mocking graffiti began to appear on it. The administration kept repainting the statue to keep Stalin pure. In spite of the authorities' watchful effort the graffiti kept appearing and the kids kept laughing. One morning 'Dagon' fell—they found the statue's head knocked off and turned upside down with feces in the not so oddly empty head. Of course, it was declared a terrorist act and all 150 children were threatened with execution if no one owned up. So Zoya claimed responsibility: 'I did it all myself! What else is the head of that papa good for?'[16] One assumes that statue was taken out of circulation. That is what 'defiling' does—hence Josiah's practice as Ellison explains it.

Now let's come back to the way the whole chapter leads up to verses 26-27. We read of a royal and national recommitment to Yahweh's covenant law (vv. 1-3), of extensive and thorough

---

[15]H. L. Ellison, 'I and II Kings,' *The New Bible Commentary*, 2nd ed. (Grand Rapids: Eerdmans, 1954), 331.

[16]Aleksandr I. Solzhenitsyn, *The Gulag Archipelago: 1918-1956*, abridged by Edward E. Ericson, Jr. (New York: Harper & Row, 1985), 276-77.

royal reforms (vv. 4-20), of a keeping of the Passover that
eclipsed all others for centuries (vv. 21-23), of still more royal
anti-paganism (v. 24), and—a superlative at the last—of a king
without parallel: there was no one like Josiah for wholeheartedly shaping his life after God's law (v. 25). And none of
it seemed to do any good:

> Yet Yahweh did not renounce the heat of his great anger which
> blazed out against Judah because of all the provocation Manasseh
> had offered him. Yahweh decreed, 'I will thrust Judah away from
> me too, as I have already thrust Israel; I will cast away Jerusalem,
> this city I had chosen, and the Temple of which I had said: There
> my name shall be' (vv. 26-27, JB).

As we have seen already, Manasseh (ch. 21) had put Judah
beyond the line of hope. It is very sobering: there *is* such a thing
as the hot heat of Yahweh's anger that no amount of repentance
or reform can dampen or douse. We've already known this but
somehow the weight of the point falls on us far more heavily
when stated after twenty-five verses describing perhaps Judah's
finest hour.[17] Wrath is consuming and coming and certain.

But Josiah already knew all this. Huldah's prophecy
(22:16-17, 20) had made that clear. Yet he pressed on in fidelity
to the covenant, in commitment (vv. 1-3), sacrament (vv. 21-23),
and worship (v. 24). But why? Would it make any eventual
difference? Would it last? Would it save the nation? Would it
cool God's wrath? No, to all these. But Josiah's is a faithfulness
that does not confuse obedience with pragmatism and so
pushes on, not because it will change anything but simply
because God demands it. Obedience without incentives is likely
genuine. DeGraaf says it well:

> Josiah knew that the judgment upon Judah was sure to come, but
> he wanted to press ahead with the reformation of Judah anyway.
> In this he showed a diligence unmatched by any king before or
> after him. He did not declare that there was no point in reformation
> since it could not save Judah anyway. He wanted to go ahead with

---

[17]Verse 27 forms quite a contrast to the promise of 19:32-34. There Yahweh decides
to save in the face of all perils that we might safely trust; here in 23:27 Yahweh rejects
what he has chosen—in spite of its religious conformity (cf. Jer. 3:6-10)—that we might
never presume.

the reformation solely for the sake of the honor and righteousness of the Lord. The Lord has a right to be served, even if our service does not bring about our salvation.[18]

Josiah's 'nevertheless' obedience conjures up Jesus' defense of Mary of Bethany. She stirs a furor of supposedly righteous indignation by pouring expensive ointment on Jesus' head. But Jesus commends her and says, among other things, 'She has done what she could' (Mark 14:8). One might say something similar of Josiah—and of any of the Lord's people who remain faithful with no relief in sight.

Tony Campolo tells of going to a funeral home to pay his respects to the family of an acquaintance. He ended up, quite by mistake, in the wrong parlor, which held the body of an elderly man whose widow was the only mourner present. This lady seemed so lonely Campolo decided to stay for the funeral. He even drove with her to the cemetery. After the graveside service, as he and the widow were driving off, Campolo admitted to her that he had not known her husband. 'I thought as much,' she said. 'I didn't recognize you. But it doesn't really matter.' Squeezing his arm so hard it hurt she confessed, 'You'll never, ever, know what this means to me.'[19]

That's not as far from Josiah as appears. Granted, in one sense it was a bumbling mistake. And yet, given his dilemma, he did what the situation demanded and what opportunity offered. He did what he could. And that was the pattern of Josiah's obedience. And it is the way of Josiah's spiritual descendants who, unlike the king, may not have the potential to sway a nation but who worship God faithfully and keep his commandments though it may not resolve personal problems, bring economic success, or relieve emotional distress.

The Unerring Word of Yahweh (23:15-20)
Before concluding we must go back and sneak a look at Josiah's desecration of worship centers in the former northern kingdom, especially in Bethel. There stood Jeroboam I's high place (see

[18]S. G. De Graaf, *Promise and Deliverance*, 4 vols. (St. Catharines, ON: Paideia, 1978), 2:390.
[19]Philip Yancey, *Where Is God When It Hurts?* (Grand Rapids: Zondervan, 1990), 177.

1 Kings 12:25-33). Josiah pulls it down, burns it, beats it to dust (v. 15) and defiles the altar by burning human bones on it (v. 16a)—to which our writer adds: 'in line with the word of Yahweh which the man of God had preached who had proclaimed these events' (v. 16b). He refers to that fascinating story in 1 Kings 13 of the man of God from Judah who interrupted Jeroboam's dedication service by preaching to the altar:

> Altar, altar, here's what Yahweh says: See! A son is going to be born to the house of David—Josiah his name—and he shall sacrifice upon you the priests of the high places who make offerings upon you, and they will burn human bones on you (1 Kings 13:2).

Here in 2 Kings 23:16 our writer is saying: 'Well, there you have it; Josiah exactly fulfilled that "Bethel prophecy" from 300 years ago.'[20] Yahweh's word never falls to the ground; it will infallibly come true.

This prophetic fulfillment packs a solid assurance. In the present context it bolsters Huldah's prophecy of 22:15-20. If Yahweh's word from 930 BC has come to pass, then surely his word through Huldah in 622 will as well. And if Yahweh's centuries' old prophecies come so clearly to pass, should we not count every syllable from God's mouth as unquestionably reliable?

---

[20]Some nitpickers may say, 'But 1 Kings 13:2 says Josiah will sacrifice on that altar "the priests of the high places" who made offerings there and 2 Kings 23:16 only speaks of burning human bones there.' Well, keep reading. Verse 19 reports that Josiah did to other high places throughout Samaria 'in line with all the works he had done in Bethel', which is spelled out in v. 20. For that reason the first verb form in v. 20 should be translated with a 'so that' since it is explicative of v. 19b: 'so that he *sacrificed all the priests of the high places* who were there upon the altars and burned human bones upon them.' That's what Josiah also did in Bethel, which precisely fulfills 1 Kings 13:2. What did that involve? I assume executing the priests then serving there (the Bethel shrine was apparently still functioning in Josiah's time, cf. 17:28) and burning their dead carcasses upon the altar. No, it's not nice, but it's faithful: read Deuteronomy 13. Josiah is here the executioner of Yahweh's covenant justice. Of course, many biblical scholars deny that 1 Kings 13:2 is a genuine prophecy. For them, Josiah's name was put in as a 'prophecy after the event' or as a much later addition. They would hold that 1 Kings 13:2 was really spun off or concocted in light of the 2 Kings 23:15-18 event (so we have phony prophecy, not predictive prophecy). Some (like John Gray) would say that there may have been an original prophetic denunciation in 1 Kings 13:2 but they just don't know what it was. Does the church owe them thanks for this profound confusion? Whether there is genuine predictive prophecy is not so much a matter of evidence but of world view. Many scholars operate from an anti-supernaturalist bias which regards predictive prophecy as impossible. Theirs is not the Shepherd's voice—why should the church pay any attention?

Let me add, however, that the prophecy of Josiah's purging work carries the promise of still more. In 1 Kings 13:2 he is called 'a son to be born to the house of David'. De Graaf picks up the cue:

> The son of David's house had come as an avenger of the Lord's rights, which had been violated. One day David's great Son will also bring judgment. Then the claims of the Lord's covenant will be fully restored.[21]

What we see in Josiah signals that there is something more to come.

In September 1864 General Grant traveled out to the Shenandoah Valley to confer with his subordinate Phil Sheridan. He wanted General Sheridan to go back on the offensive against Jubal Early's Confederate troops. Grant and Sheridan paced back and forth in a field near Sheridan's headquarters discussing the matter, its logistics and timing. A sergeant was lounging against a rail fence within watching distance. When a buddy came near, the sergeant jerked his thumb at the duo and announced, 'That's Grant.' And then, somewhat reflectively, he added: 'I hate to see that old cuss around. When that old cuss is around there's sure to be a big fight on hand.'[22]

Grant was always the sign of something more—of war to be exact. And Josiah is like that. He signals that there is another Son of David to come who will do Josiah-work among the people of God, refining, purifying, avenging (Mal. 3:1-6)—and dividing (Matt. 3:12). Even now one can see this Second Josiah in action, purging his church, as a glance at Revelation 2–3 makes clear.

The wrap-up of Josiah's reign (vv. 28-30) makes sad anti-climactical reading, especially his death in needless battle with the Egyptians. But these sad verses are merely a harbinger of what is to come—Josiah's end foreshadows Judah's. Here's where it stands:

[21]S. G. De Graaf, *Promise and Deliverance*, 2:391.
[22]Bruce Catton, *Grant Takes Command* (Boston: Little, Brown & Co., 1969), 362-63.

Judgment has been announced. It is now simply a matter of timing. At this juncture in Judean history, strangely enough, Judah finds herself with yet another righteous king—a second Moses to match her second David (Hezekiah). Josiah is a king long-awaited (1 Kings. 13:2). He is the best of all kings, but he is a king come too late.[23]

---

[23]Provan, *1 and 2 Kings*, 270.

29

Rush to Ruin
(2 Kings 23:31–25:26)

There's no good way to do it. You see, you are a man and you have skinned your leg or gotten a cut on it and had to slap a band-aid over the affected area. But the time has come to remove the band-aid—hence your quandary. Like many men, you likely have hairy legs. And now you've two options. You can very slowly and deliberately peel off the band-aid, feeling the pain as it pulls every hair attached to it, and prolong the agony. Or, you can grab the edge of the band-aid very firmly and with a lightning-like jerk remove it in one pain-inclusive flash and be done with it. Had the writer of Kings known band-aids, I'm confident he would've chosen the latter course. At least he did here in this two-chapter-plus section. He's telling us the story of Judah after Josiah's death in 609 BC and one gets the distinct impression that he *wants to hurry*. He covers the reigns of four kings over 22 years (they fall into a double three-months, eleven-years pattern, 23:31, 36; 24:8, 18) in rapid nuts-and-bolts style. It's like what he did in 15:8-31 when he barreled through the last kings of the northern kingdom. So here he doesn't want to dawdle over the story of Judah after Josiah's death; he wants to get it over with. His message is simple: in twenty-two years Jerusalem was toast.

Though our writer for the most part flies over these years, he must include kings and dates and sieges in the process and, because of this, a bare-bones chronology is necessary so we can keep our bearings as we follow his story (it is on the following page).

327

Chronology

Jehoahaz (23:31), 609 BC

Jehoiakim (23:36), 609-598 BC

> Battle of Carchemish (cf. 24:7), 605
> Deportation No. 1 (cf. Dan. 1:1-4)
> Jehoiakim rebels (24:1), 601 (?)

Jehoiachin (24:8), 597 BC

> Deportation No. 2 (24:10-16; cf. Ezek. 1:1-3)

Zedekiah (24:18), 597-587 BC

> Zedekiah rebels (24:20), after 593 (cf. Jer. 51:59)
> Babylonian siege (25:1-2), 589
> Jerusalem falls (25:3-10), 587
> Deportation No. 3 (25:11-12)[1]

Now let's hear the writer's story. He is saying that 'Judah is history' and our exposition will spell out what sort of history we find here.

A Boring History
Well, it is. It's the old drip…drip: four times we read 'He did evil in Yahweh's eyes' (23:32, 37; 24:9, 19). Nothing bracing or refreshing here, just the same stale stuff. None of the trembling

---

[1]Several notes: First, at the Battle of Carchemish (cf. Jer. 46) in 605 Crown Prince Nebuchadnezzar and the Babylonians surprised Pharaoh Necho and the Egyptian army and drove them all the way to Hamath (ca. 140 miles SW), where Babylon inflicted a still more crushing defeat on Egypt. For all practical purposes, Egypt was now confined to her Nile ghetto (2 Kings 24:7). Secondly, in 601 Babylon attacked Egypt, both sides suffered heavy losses, and Nebuchadnezzar returned home to refurbish his army—a turn of events which may have tempted Jehoiakim to rebel. Third, we don't know when Zedekiah rebelled against Babylon but likely after 593 since in that year Zedekiah had to go to Babylon, probably to reaffirm his loyalty. Fourth, there's a debate over whether Jerusalem fell in July 587 or 586. The edge goes to 587; see Rodger C. Young, 'When Did Jerusalem Fall?,' *Journal of the Evangelical Theological Society* 47/1 (2004): 21-38. For concise survey of 605-587, see John Bright, *A History of Israel*, 3rd ed. (Philadelphia: Westminster, 1981), 326-31.

faith of a Hezekiah or enthusiastic obedience of a Josiah that gives spice and flavor and drama to kingdom life. I suppose some would contend that Jehoahaz and Jehoiachin with their three-month reigns had little opportunity to create interest. That's debatable, but let's admit that Jehoiakim and Zedekiah are the main culprits.

I can't get interested in writing their biographies. Briefly, it may be that Jehoiakim (23:34-24:5) had little option about his 'new tax' program (23:35)—Necho had to be paid somehow. But Jehoiakim had a swanky palatial residence built for himself and refused to pay the builders (Jer. 22:13-19), brazenly burned the scroll of Jeremiah's prophecy piece-by-piece in the grate (Jer. 36:1-26), and had no scruples about pursuing and liquidating faithful prophets who opposed him (Jer. 26:20-23). He was anti-Yahweh to the core. Zedekiah (24:18-25:7), on the other hand, didn't have enough backbone to be that way. He was as floppy as Jehoiakim was rigid. Zedekiah was the proverbial politician who doesn't know what he thinks until he reads the morning papers and checks the latest polls. Take a quick read through Jeremiah 37–38 to see Zedekiah in living indecisive color. He reminds me of a cartoon from a few years ago. It may have been one of Gary Larson's. There was a fence with an entrance in it and a sign above the entrance: Boneless Chicken Ranch. And all around were chickens flopped on the ground, none of them (obviously) standing, since they were boneless. That was Zedekiah—he was not only chicken but boneless to boot. So whether vicious wickedness (Jehoiakim) or spineless wickedness (Zedekiah) sat on Judah's throne in her last days made no essential difference. 'He did evil.' And we yawn together.

Sometimes people think parts of the Bible are so boring—like this section of Kings. But it's not the writer's fault! When will we realize that though there is always a bite to holiness and a spice to uprightness evil is sheer tedium? It's like watching a football (American, with the oblong ball) game with your team losing 52-0. You pass the time at the concession stand or in conversations with friends simply to pass the time and avoid the pain. Who can really blame pastors who might look at this text and exclaim, 'How am I going to preach this stuff?'

In one sense their instinct is right. How can the Bible be exciting when it must tell of such tediously wicked men? Actually, only holiness stirs and only godliness fascinates.

A Doomed History (24:1-4, 13, 20)

Judah was past hope. Our writer has already made this point repeatedly, so I won't labor the matter here. However, we ought to note his description of that doom in this passage.

He says it is a *faithful* doom. That is, Judah's end was a fulfillment of Yahweh's word and in bringing an end to Judah Yahweh was being faithful to that word. It may seem a negative faithfulness but it *is* faithfulness nevertheless. Yahweh is a faithful God even when he destroys. One sees this in 24:2: Yahweh sent out Chaldean, Aramaean, Moabite, and Ammonite raiders against Judah to 'destroy it in line with the word of Yahweh which he had spoken by the hand of his servants the prophets'. The reference, of course, is to 21:10-15 and 23:26-27. Yes, the historians may be right—these raiders in 24:2 may have been egged on by Nebuchadnezzar; it may have been inconvenient for him to squash Jehoiakim after Babylon got beaten up so badly on the Egyptian frontier in 601. The raiders may have been his interim solution to Jehoiakim's asinine rebellion. But our writer-theologian has the real scoop on the matter and Nebuchadnezzar doesn't really figure in it—*Yahweh* sent those raiders to destroy Judah and fulfill his word. One meets the same emphasis in 24:13: Nebuchadnezzar rifles the temple and royal treasures and hacks up the gold vessels Solomon had made 'just as Yahweh had spoken'. The writer refers to 20:17.

He says it is an *irreversible* doom. He has, as noted, already hammered this point home but does so here with a frightening twist:

> Surely at the mouth [lit.] of Yahweh it happened in Judah to remove (them) from his presence, because of the sins of Manasseh, in line with all he had done—and also (because) of the innocent blood he shed, so that he filled Jerusalem with innocent blood. And Yahweh did not want to forgive (vv. 3-4).

That last line does not mean that Yahweh did not want to forgive but might relent anyway. It means, as most versions have it, that he was unwilling to forgive, would not forgive. But I have translated it as I have to highlight the stark surprise we should feel. Here is the God of Exodus 34:6-7 and of Psalm 103:10 and he *does not want to forgive*. It is a frightening statement about a frightening God. What can be more frightful than when forgiveness is not even an option?

He says it is a *compounded* doom. The connection of 24:20 with its context is tricky, as is its translation. It seems to begin with a causal particle:[2] 'For because of Yahweh's anger it happened in Jerusalem and in Judah to the point that he threw them out from his presence.' That's a wooden translation. To what does 'it' refer? Keil may well be right that 'it' refers to verses 18 and 19, to Zedekiah's doing evil or to the fact that such a wishy-washy but God-resisting man as Zedekiah became king. He quotes Sebastian Schmid (ca. 1680): 'Not that it was of God that Zedekiah was wicked, but that Zedekiah, a man…simple, dependent upon counsellors, yet at the same time despising the word of God and impenitent (2 Chron. xxxvi.12, 13), became king, so as to be the cause of Jerusalem's destruction.'[3] In short, Zedekiah himself was part of Yahweh's wrath against Judah, his instrument for working their ruin. The leaders Yahweh gives a nation may be part of his judgment upon that nation. And in Judah's case this only makes a certain doom doubly certain.

So Judah's is a doomed history. Why should we be surprised? I'm reminded of an incident William Shirer relates. Sometime in 1952 he was waiting in the NBC studios with some of the network's radio personnel. They were awaiting a man who was supposed to interview Shirer about the latest book he had written. They were going to record the interview and broadcast it on Saturday of that week. Half an hour passed. They began telephoning for the absentee interviewer. Finally reached him at home. He told them that he had not come to do the interview for the simple reason that NBC had fired him the week before![4] That seems reasonable. Why should they be surprised? That is the situation in Judah. After Manasseh who could be surprised over a ravaged nation with an unforgiving God?

---

[2]Though it could be emphatic: 'Indeed…'

[3]C. F. Keil, *The Books of the Kings*, Biblical Commentary on the Old Testament (1876; reprint ed.,, Grand Rapids: Eerdmans, 1965), 510.

[4]William L. Shirer, *A Native's Return: 1945-1988*, vol. 3 of *20ᵗʰ Century Journey* (Boston: Little, Brown and Co., 1990), 195.

A Sad History (24:8-16; 25:8-17)

There is a pall that lies over the text, a gloom the writer wants you to feel. One senses it first in his record of Jehoiachin's fleeting tenure. Jehoiachin reigned just long enough to hand over Jerusalem to Nebuchadnezzar in 597 BC (24:8-12). It was the only sane thing to do. But then, in 24:14-16, the writer piles up his 'exile' words—five uses of the root *glh* in three verses: Nebuchadnezzar 'led off into exile all Jerusalem' (v. 14a); there were 'ten thousand exiles' (v. 14b); so 'he exiled Jehoiachin to Babylon' (v. 15a); the king's mother, wives, officials, and leading men Nebuchadnezzar 'brought as exiles from Jerusalem to Babylon' (v. 15b); then he brought apparently another tally of folks, including artisans, 'as exiles to Babylon' (v. 16).[5] That is the sadness of 597 BC—exile. The cream of Judah carted off to Babylon. Here the sadness centers on *what they left*.

But the writer also squeezes sadness out of the 587 BC situation in 25:8-17. About a month after the Babylonians broke open the city and captured the fleeing Zedekiah, Nebuzaradan, one of Nebuchadnezzar's underlings, arrives to supervise the demolition. They burn down the temple and Jerusalem's residences and pull down the city wall (25:9-10). Then, as if simply reporting the burning of the temple was utterly inadequate, our writer dwells in some—should we say 'loving'?—detail on the articles and utensils the Babylonians pilfered from the temple (25:14-15). Nor did they cart off merely the portable items: they hacked up Jachin and Boaz, the two bronze pillars that stood in front of the temple, as well as that 11,000 gallon bronze 'sea', and carried it all off (25:13, 16). Our writer couldn't quite stand it—he had to describe for us those marvelous bronze pillars (25:17; Jer. 52:21-23 goes into even more detail).[6] In the 587 fiasco he stresses the pillaging and destruction of the temple, the place where Yahweh delights to anchor his presence and hear the prayers of his people (1 Kings 8:29-30). Now it's a smoking ruin. Here the sadness centers on *what they lost*.[7]

---

[5]No one I know of knows just how to understand the tallies given in verses 14 and 16. Does verse 14 give an approximate number and verse 16 a more exact one? No one really knows. And how to explain the 3,023 in Jeremiah 52:28? Were these folks from the countryside rather than the city?

[6]On the bronze pillars and sea, see my *The Wisdom and the Folly: An Exposition of the Book of First Kings* (Ross-shire: Christian Focus, 2002), 73-77. First Kings 7:16 and Jeremiah 52:22 give the height of each pillar's 'capital' as five cubits; here in 25:17 it is three cubits—I don't know the reason for the discrepancy.

I think (I can't prove it beyond doubt) the writer wants to leave an emotional impression on his readers. I think he wants to make them sad. The situation is, I suppose, like a hurricane. A coastal city in our day will generally know in advance of the devastating force the approaching hurricane packs and almost the precise moment it will hit. Evacuations have already been completed and the storm strikes. But when folks go back to survey the damage they are appalled. Homes may be leveled or blasted and drenched beyond repair, trees uprooted, personal treasures blown miles away and forever lost. One knew it was coming, knew its power, knew its danger, yet still looks in horror at its devastation. So with the end of Judah. Yahweh's prophets had clearly proclaimed it, said how irreversible it was and how appalling it would be. Yet when one stands watching the exiles dragging themselves off and wall-less ruins smoking, sadness sinks into one's spirit like never before. I think the writer wanted to do that. For a reason. Sadness is sometimes the first step toward repentance (2 Cor. 7:8-11). Desolation may stir a prodigal's heart.

A Stupid History (24:1, 20; 25:22-26)

At least three distinct acts of stupidity parade themselves in the story of Judah's downfall. Two of these are the revolts of Jehoiakim (24:1) and Zedekiah (24:20), the third is Ishmael's assassination of Gedaliah (25:22-26).

We cannot be sure precisely when Jehoiakim and Zedekiah rebelled. As noted, Jehoiakim likely did so about 601 when Nebuchadnezzar had to return to Babylon to lick his wounds and refit his army. A good dose of reality would have saved him. Babylon had pushed Egypt off the playing board of history (24:7), marooning her down in her own corner of the world. Egypt could lend him no viable assistance. To rebel was suicide.

And Zedekiah's mind changed with the wind. After reading Jeremiah's prophecy (especially chs. 37–39) one wonders if Zedekiah ever had a conviction about anything. Perhaps he and a majority of his advisors actually thought Pharaoh Hophra would come to Judah's aid. But Egypt was all mouth and hot

[7]Cf. Paul R. House, *1, 2 Kings*, New American Commentary (Nashville: Broadman & Holman, 1995), 398.

air. Hophra apparently sent some kind of force to meet the Babylonians (Jer. 37:5-11) but it was quickly driven back and the Babylonians resumed their stranglehold on Jerusalem. Zedekiah was not merely befuddled—he was brainless.

One might imagine that stupidity had gone up in Jerusalem's smoke or had plodded off to Babylon with the exiles. But no, folly remained in Judah. A sort of provisional government was set up over the conquered territory under the governorship of Gedaliah.[8] After reading 25:22-24 one has the impression that matters in Judah have almost reached a degree of sanity again. Four military leaders with their respective contingents have come to Gedaliah's headquarters at Mizpah (about eight miles northwest of Jerusalem). Gedaliah assured them that they could live safely under the aegis of the Babylonians (25:24). Perhaps those left in Judah could enjoy a little breathing space and establish some coherence in their lives.

But no! Ishmael son of Nethaniah and his executioners butcher Gedaliah and all the Jews and Babylonians residing at Mizpah (25:25).[9] The others in Judah, fearing Babylonian reprisals, hightailed it to Egypt (25:26). One wonders why Ishmael did what he did. True, he was of the 'royal seed,' and yes, he had the support of Baalis the 'king' of the Ammonites (Jer. 40:13-14), but no one in his right mind would imagine that a revolt against Babylon could be successful at this time. Hence I agree with Cogan and Tadmor that Ishmael simply had a vendetta against those he viewed as 'collaborators' and thought that his trail of blood would make a 'statement'.[10] And so we have Jehoiakim, Zedekiah, and Ishmael, these three—the three stooges of Judah.

Barbara Tuchman in *The March of Folly* argues that 'folly is a child of power' and that 'the power to command frequently

---

[8]Gedaliah's father Ahikam had intervened to save the prophet Jeremiah's life (Jer. 26:24) and was one of King Josiah's delegation to Huldah the prophetess (2 Kings 22:14).

[9]We can't be sure of the timing. If the 'seventh' month of 25:25 is in the same year as the 'fifth' month of 25:8, then this occurred within two months of Jerusalem's destruction. In any case, Gedaliah's regime was brief.

[10]M. Cogan and H. Tadmor, *II Kings*, Anchor Bible (Garden City, NY: Doubleday, 1988), 327; for a contrary view, see Robert L. Cohn, *2 Kings*, Berit Olam (Collegeville, MN: Liturgical, 2000), 171. See Jeremiah 40:1-43:7 for much more detail surrounding these events.

causes failure to think'.[11] Her thesis is often confirmed, whether by two-bit rulers and warlords of rump states like Judah or by the power-mongers of the most hairy-chested regimes. I found it interesting that Hitler's physical condition began to deteriorate after 1942. Hitler had had the flu, and his physician, Theodor Morell, had given him some injections. Afterward Hitler's left eye began to tear and numbness arose in his left leg then moved to his left hand. In 1944 an eye, ear, nose and throat specialist was examining Hitler. He found out that for two years Dr. Morell had been relieving Hitler's chronic pains with 'Dr. Koester's Antigas Pills'. These contained strychnine and belladonna. The pills were given to Hitler's personal servants who shelled them out to the Fuhrer whenever he felt the need for them. The specialist reported his findings to Dr. Karl Brandt, Hitler's primary surgeon. Brandt told Hitler that he was being slowly poisoned. For this Brandt was relieved from his position.[12] I suppose the good news for the world was that the quack Morell was consistently poisoning Hitler to death. But perhaps the surprising thing is that Hitler didn't have the sense to accept a reputable specialist's word about it. Power and stupidity seem such congenial bedfellows. And they certainly were in the closing years of Judah's existence. It was as if her rulers and petty chieftains operated in a trance of senselessness, a sort of 'dumb-and-dumber' mode. One wonders if it is not a God-imposed stupidity intended to rush a nation into the fury of his judgment.

[11]Barbara Tuchman, *The March of Folly* (New York: Alfred A. Knopf, 1984), 32.
[12]John Toland, *The Last 100 Days* (New York: Random House, 1965), 12.

30

A Whisper of Hope?
(2 Kings 25:27-30)

George Smathers ran against Claude D. Pepper, an incumbent Democratic senator, in the Florida primary election of 1950. Smathers defeated Pepper in that election. His victory was partially attributed to some smear tactics Smathers' campaign managers used in their election pitches. One of these stated:

> Are you aware that Claude Pepper is known all over Washington as a shameless extrovert? Not only that, but this man is reliably reported to practice nepotism with his sister-in-law, and he has a sister who was once a thespian in wicked New York. Worst of all, it is an established fact that Mr. Pepper, before his marriage, habitually practiced celibacy.[1]

One despairs over the intelligence level of any electorate that might find such stuff convincing. Nevertheless one has to admit that it *sounds* bad. But a moment's thought –and maybe a glance at the dictionary–tells you that it says far more about New York than about Mr. Pepper. It sounds bad but it's not.

That is something like what we meet in 2 Kings 25:27-30 — only the opposite slant. In this concluding clip we hear of Jehoiachin, no longer a teenage king but eligible for seniors' discounts, being restored to a measure of freedom and favor while in captivity in Babylon. But in principle the problem

---

[1]Paul F. Boller, Jr., *Congressional Anecdotes* (New York: Oxford, 1991), 131.

is similar with the anti-Pepper propaganda. Here, however, it sounds good; but is it? Or is our thinking that Jehoiachin's exaltation is a positive omen simply our naïve, initial, non-reflective impression? Perhaps, if we look closely, these last four verses of Kings are really non-committal or even negative. Yes, there's a debate with—you guessed it—three views.

Some think that verses 27-30 carry a primarily negative message. The Davidic descendant Jehoiachin is treated as the puppet figure he is; his eating at a pagan overlord's table is a picture of his total dependency, expressing the final historical demise of the Davidic monarchy. Hence 'the portrait of Jehoiachin comes before us with a hopeless finality that the plaintive "all the days of his life" (2 Kings 25:30) serves only to underscore'.[2] Others see a primarily positive picture here:

> But it is also possible that this is more than an historical note. It may be a *careful and intentional theological assertion* in which the deep and undeniable hope of Israel is reasserted. On that basis, it is argued that the royal promises to David and all the deep hopes of Israel ride on this desolate man. The paragraph is added to show that even Babylon has not crushed Judah's future, because the future lies beyond the grasp of Babylon in the safe hands of God. This little paragraph of hope structurally then off-sets the long, massive narrative of judgment and destruction.[3]

Still others regard both of these views as wide of the mark, the negative for being too negative and the positive for being too positive. Rather we must follow a more 'chastened' track: the clip is not totally pessimistic but does not hold out hope

---

[2] So W. J. Dumbrell, *Covenant and Creation* (Nashville: Thomas Nelson, 1984), 162. See also John Gray, *I & II Kings*, Old Testament Library, 2nd ed. (Philadelphia: Westminster, 1970), 39-40, 773; and Richard Nelson, *First and Second Kings*, Interpretation (Louisville: John Knox, 1987), 265-67, who says, 'the limited improvement of Jehoiachin's lot is a foretaste of the gray future which the captive nation faces' (p. 267). However, Nelson sees a gleam of grace in the 'wild card' of God's promise to David (pp. 268-69).

[3] Walter Brueggemann, *2 Kings*, Knox Preaching Guides (Atlanta: John Knox, 1982), 100-101 (emphasis his). I am not sure Brueggemann is entirely convinced of this view; cf. his *1 & 2 Kings*, Smyth & Helwys Bible Commentary (Macon, GA: Smyth and Helwys, 2000), 606. For other 'positive' partisans, see Terence E. Fretheim, *First and Second Kings*, Westminster Bible Companion (Louisville: Westminster/John Knox, 1999), 224-25; Iain W. Provan, 'The Messiah in the Books of Kings,' in *The Lord's Anointed*, ed. Philip E. Satterthwaite, Richard S. Hess, and Gordon J. Wenham (Grand Rapids: Baker, 1995), 67-85; see also the commentaries of C. F. Keil and Matthew Henry, who read this text positively long before it became a matter of debate.

for a restoration of the Davidic kings, nor even of a return to the land; instead it presages 'a more tolerable future for all vanquished Judeans'; it is a hope 'not to be despised' and yet 'not to be exaggerated';[4] it functions as an 'implicit call to repent' and only implies 'the possibility of a future'.[5]

Now where do we go from here? What are we to make of this welter of opinion and argument? We will deal with what the text says and then with what it implies.

What does the text say?

Evil-merodach of our text is Amel-Marduk ('Man of Marduk') in Akkadian. He succeeded his father Nebuchadnezzar in 562, reigned two years, and according to Berossus, was assassinated and replaced by his brother-in-law Neriglissar.[6] It was in his accession year that Evil-merodach released Jehoiachin (v. 27b), but the precise date is given in the full formula of 27a (thirty-seventh year of Jehoiachin's exile, the twelfth month, the twenty-seventh day).

This date formula in verse 27a is one of several in 2 Kings 25: (1) In the ninth year of Zedekiah's reign, the tenth day of the tenth month (v. 1), Nebuchadnezzar and troops besiege Jerusalem; (2) verse 3 places the exhaustion of food supplies and apparently the Babylonian breach of the city on the ninth day of the fourth month (see Jer. 39:2) in the eleventh year of Zedekiah (see v. 2); (3) since Jerusalem had fallen verse 8 ties its date to the reign of Nebuchadnezzar—his nineteenth year, fifth month, seventh day, when Nebuzaradan torched temple and city (vv. 9-10); (4) verse 25 offers only the seventh month in its date—presumably the one after the fifth month of verse 8, though we cannot be sure; in any case, this date marked Ishmael's mass murder at Mizpah (vv. 25-26); then (5) we meet our date in verse 27a, which pegs the new benefits Jehoiachin

---

[4]Donald F. Murray, 'Of All the Years the Hopes—Or Fears? Jehoiachin in Babylon (2 Kings 25:27-30),' *Journal of Biblical Literature* 120/2 (2001): 245-65; quote from p. 265.

[5]J. Gordon McConville, *Grace in the End: A Study in Deuteronomic Theology* (Grand Rapids: Zondervan, 1993), 89-90, 138 (quotes from p. 89); see also his 'Narrative and Meaning in the Books of Kings,' *Biblica* 70 (1989): 31-49. In the history of this debate Martin Noth was long a key proponent of the negative view, Gerhard von Rad of the positive, and H. W. Wolff of the 'repentance' or 'in-between' view.

[6]Ronald H. Sack, 'Evil-merodach,' ABD, 2:679.

received. Now I do not want to assume what has not yet been supported, but it is interesting to note that the first four 'datings' all lead to negative and destructive actions, whereas the last (v. 27) leads to what seems to be a positive one.[7] The writer apparently intends to set off his last segment as a contrast to all that precedes in 2 Kings 25.

Let us survey the rest of the text. First, in his accession year Evil-merodach 'lifted up the head of Jehoiachin king of Judah from the prison house' (v. 27b). Whether or not one thinks that is a positive datum in the grand scheme of Judah's future, it is yet itself a positive item. Of course, Joseph has shown us that 'lifting up the head' can be a double-edged sword: it can mean Pharaoh restores you to your position (Gen. 40:13) or that he lifts your head from your shoulders and hangs you (Gen. 40:19)! But the latter option is a sort of twist on what is admittedly a way of expressing restoration (Ps. 3:3). How severe Jehoiachin's confinement was we do not know, but at any rate he was released from it.

Second, Evil-merodach 'spoke good things with him' (v. 28a). This at least means that the king spoke kindly (e.g., NRSV, NIV) with his vassal. Some would draw attention to the connections of 'good' (Heb., *tōb*) with covenant and would argue that the terminology implies Evil-merodach initiated a covenant or treaty with Jehoiachin.[8] At the very least it is an indication of favor.

Third, Jehoiachin was elevated to a new position (v. 28b), with the new clothes appropriate for it (v. 29a). We should not miss the fact that this was a signal honor for Jehoiachin—among all the vassal kings in Babylon Evil-merodach assigned first place to Jehoiachin.[9] If some point out that he is still a pensioner at a pagan court, at the very least he is the premier pensioner.

Fourth, the text highlights Jehoiachin's ongoing privileges and provision (vv. 29b-30). Jehoiachin not only ate at the king's table but received regular food allowances for himself and his household. The so-called 'Jehoiachin Tablets' from Babylon

---

[7]I found D. F. Murray, 'Of All the Years the Hopes,' 248-50, very useful on this scheme of dates in 2 Kings 25 but simply cannot see how he then sees verses 27-30 as the last in 'a series of devastating events for Judah'.

[8]Since this was done in Evil-merodach's accession year, it may have been part of a Babylonian amnesty program with which Mesopotamian kings sometimes inaugurated their reigns. On this, see Robert P. Gordon, NIDOTTE, 2:356.

[9]K. D. Fricke, *Das zweite Buch von den Königen*, Die Botschaft des alten Testaments (Stuttgart: Calwer, 1972), 364.

corroborate Jehoiachin's exile there and itemize the food allotments he received during Nebuchadnezzar's regime.[10] He seems to have received all this with additional perks under Evil-merodach. Verses 27-30 highlight his new freedom and favor, his new position and provision. Not only so, but he is—significantly—called 'king of Judah' twice in verse 27.[11]

What does the text suggest?
What the text says runs in a positive vein. However, one can see that someone could still look at these verses and say, 'Why, yes, Jehoiachin received favorable treatment, but he's still an underling at a pagan court and—besides—why should the fortunes of Jehoiachin himself suggest anything about hope for Judah?' So in this section I want to set down some additional indications that verses 27-30 are meant as a subtle word of hope.

First, I think our section is meant to function as a deliberate contrast to the bleak episodes in its preceding context. I wonder (and I can do no more than this—I can't *prove* this) if this Jehoiachin section isn't intended as the opposite number of the Zedekiah section in verses 1-7. There is no escape for the hapless Zedekiah—he is captured, carted off to Riblah, and sentenced. Before his very eyes every one of his sons is executed. That slaughter is his last visible memory; his eyes are 'put out' and, as if the blind man is still a threat, he is clamped with fetters and carried off. Jehoiachin's treatment here is markedly different. Is that deliberate?

But there is a closer contrast: the Jehoiachin restoration (vv. 27-30) is meant to stand as a positive scenario over against the Gedaliah fiasco of verses 22-26. Bähr sums it up well:

> The two brief narratives [vv. 22-26 and 27-30] by which the author closes his work are not mere appendages to the history, but the proper epilogue to the words: "So Judah was carried away out of their land" [v. 21b].[12]

---

[10]See D. Winton Thomas, ed., *Documents from Old Testament Times* (New York: Harper & Row, 1958), 84-86 (trans. by W. J. Martin); and John M. Berridge, 'Jehoiachin,' ABD, 3:662-63. On '*ăruḥâ*' as food allowance, see R. H. O'Connell, NIDOTTE, 1:513.

[11]Fricke, *Das zweite Buch von den Königen,* 365.

[12]K. C. W. F. Bähr, *The Books of the Kings,* Lange's Commentary on the Holy Scriptures, in vol. 3, *Samuel-Kings* (1868; reprint ed.,, Grand Rapids: Zondervan, 1960), 301. Note: I treated verses 22-26 in the previous chapter because that section continued the theme of Judean stupidity. That, however, does not negate Bähr's point that, literarily, verses 22-26 and 27-30 function as contrasting parts of an epilogue.

I think this is a cogent way to look at the end of the book. Ishmael's sheer malice and harebrained stupidity along with the survivors' flight to Egypt (vv. 25-26) dash any hopes of a viable life and rump regime in Judah. It is telling that this group's 'final exile finds them back in a "pre-exodus" place' and yet 'Jehoiachin lives on in Babylon, from which the next exodus will take place'.[13] Jehoiachin's treatment in verses 27-30 may seem a very pastel hope but it is quite a turn-around when viewed through the Zedekiah and Ishmael disasters.

Secondly, consider the writer's mere selection of this piece. Fricke points out that this addendum with which the writer closes his book deals with an event that occurs twenty-six years later than his previously reported events (i.e., Jehoiachin's restoration comes ca. 561 BC, twenty-six years after 587). Clearly, Fricke infers, our writer must credit this event (= vv. 27-30) with great significance.[14] Why tack on something from twenty-six years down the time-line unless one thought it had special importance? Some might still say that he simply wanted to pound home a negative point: the exiled king is still in Babylon. But if he wanted to stress the negative, why didn't he simply stop with verse 26? How better than that to show how utterly discombobulated Judah was?

Thirdly, we must consider theology. I think verses 27-30 point not merely to a general hope about the survival of the people but to a focused hope about the line of David. More 'nuanced' scholars will raise eyebrows. But I think the writer probably had a reason for twice dubbing Jehoiachin 'king of Judah' in verse 27. And even when Yahweh was ready to rip the Davidic kingdom apart, he clearly told Jeroboam, 'I will afflict the seed of David on account of this—*only not all the days*' (1 Kings 11:39). It seems to me a text like that stands behind a passage like this. Or one could simply say that Yahweh's 2 Samuel 7 word is not something either Babylon or apostate Judah can falsify.[15] It seems to me then that biblical theology would lead us to see a ray of hope in this kindness done to the exiled Davidic king.

---

[13]Fretheim, *First and Second Kings*, 224.

[14]Fricke, *Das zweite Buch von den Königen*, 363.

[15]Please see my *2 Samuel: Out of Every Adversity* (Ross-shire: Christian Focus, 1999), 77-80, on the indefectibility of Yahweh's covenant with David.

Though I have taken a 'positive' view here I must acknowledge that the hope is put subtly in these verses. This is not a dogmatic oracle of a preacher but the suggestive narrative of a writer. Nevertheless, as has been said before, sometimes subtle insinuations can be mighty encouragements.

Anne Moody was a college student who was active in the civil rights movement in Mississippi in the 1960s. At one time part of the civil rights strategy involved sending half a dozen black students to 'white' churches at morning service time. Sometimes policemen were waiting along with the ushers. It was common to be turned away. But there was one Episcopal church they entered, where two ushers asked if they would sign the guest list before they ushered them to their seats. Moody describes her reaction:

> I stood there for a good five minutes before I was able to compose myself. I had never prayed with white people in a white church before. We signed the guest list and were then escorted to two seats behind the other two girls in our team. We had all gotten in. The church service was completed without one incident. It was as normal as any church service. However, it was by no means normal to me. I was sitting there thinking any moment God would strike the life out of me. I recognized some of the whites, sitting around me in that church. If they were praying to the same God I was, then even God, I thought, was against me.

In spite of this, she went on to say:

> When the services were over the minister invited us to visit again. He said it as if he meant it, and I began to have a little hope.[16]

It was only the fact that a church didn't turn her away, only the freedom to sit, if she wanted, in a worship service with whites, only the convincing earnestness of a minister inviting her back. Not all that much. 'But I began to have a little hope.'

That is the impact Jehoiachin's fortunes should have on the people of God. They should begin to have a little hope. Nor would it prove unfounded, for Matthew, in that marvelous

---

[16]Anne Moody, *Coming of Age in Mississippi* (New York: Dell, 1968), 285.

'Christmas sermon' at the outset of his gospel, takes us on through those dismal years after Jehoiachin. Matthew 1:12-16 picks up the story where 2 Kings 25 leaves off. And who would think that any sure hope from God could be hidden under this failed, dilapidated, and captive people? At this point (= Matt. 1:12) Israel has lost the land (the Abraham promise) and the kingship (the David promise). As for the tone of the times in Matthew 1:12-16, well, read Haggai, Nehemiah, and Malachi. Judah stays under foreign domination; life is hard. In those books the earth is mostly brown, the sky is gray, the leaves are pale, the wind is cold. But precisely in this time, this darkest, bleakest segment of Israel's history, the Messiah is given (v. 16)! It was when this people was trampled, beaten down, and teetering between faith and compromise, that the Sun of righteousness began to blaze. It is not your righteousness but Yahweh's stubbornness that brings redemption. The God of power and fury turns from his fury in Jehoiachin's Descendant. And we should have more than a little hope.

Other books of Interest
from
Christian Focus Publications

THE
WISDOM
AND THE
FOLLY

An Exposition of the Book of First Kings

DALE RALPH DAVIS

The Wisdom and the Folly

An Exposition of the Book of First Kings

Dale Ralph Davis

'The range of scholarship is extraordinary (is there any learned book or paper on First Kings that this writer has not winkled out?), His humour and humanity, plus a priceless American-style turn of phrase, add relish to the dish. Here is a safe and strong pair of hands to guide new, and older, readers through the treasure – and the uninspiring bits – of First Kings.'

Dick Lucas

'Robust – that's the word …a robust understanding, defence, explanation and application of First Kings as the Word of God. Here is no "First Kings in my own words" – the boring, fruitless fate of most commentaries on Bible History – but a delicious feast of truth, proof that the ancients were right to call the historians "prophets".'

Alec Motyer

'…this exposition enables the contemporary reader to breathe the air of 1 Kings, re-live its challenges, and above all, to encounter personally the God who speaks and acts throughout its pages. This is a book to unsettle spiritual complacency and challenge us to a deep integrity in our relationship with the living God.'

David Jackman

ISBN 1-85792-703-6

FOCUS · ON · THE · BIBLE

I SAMUEL

LOOKING ON THE HEART

'The best expository commentary I have read in years.'
Eric Alexander

DALE RALPH DAVIS

1 Samuel

Looking on the Heart

Dale Ralph Davis

Dale Ralph Davis has developed a reputation as someone who is able to communicate the meaning of biblical texts with a freshness that does not compromise the content. That he has managed to do this is an achievement in itself, that he has managed it in a popular commentary is exciting!

Comments about Ralph Davis' commentaries in this series

'Ideas pop out everywhere, even in the most unlikely places. New insights abound.'

Richard A. Bodey

'an excellent... crisp, lively... exposition'

Bibliotheca Sacra

'the most practical expository work that this reviewer has ever encountered'

Southwestern Journal of Theology

'Dr. Davis has a great sense of fun. He must often have his class or his congregation in stitches!'

Christian Arena

'presents historical and theological material in a way that can only excite the expositor.'

Warren Wiersbe

'a great feast of biblical truth made so digestible, garnished with so many apt illustrations.'

Alec Motyer

ISBN 1-8592-516-5

Romans

The Revelation of God's Righteousness

'Paul's epistle to the Romans may possibly be the most influential letter ever written.' **Dale Leschert**

Paul Barnett

Romans

The Revelation of God's Righteousness

Paul Barnett

'*Paul Barnett's refreshing commentary on the Letter to the Romans is marked by warmth, clarity, careful exegesis of the text, and a fine grasp of the historical circumstances surrounding this letter. Throughout his exposition Dr Barnett sensitively applies the apostle's profound, yet much-needed, message to our own context. I warmly commend this clear exposition of the apostle Paul's gospel.*'

Peter O'Brien

'*Paul Barnett combines a thorough going exegesis which is sane and helpful, as well as lucid and well argued, with a pastor's heart and a good eye for application. This is a brilliant commentary on a key book, which I warmly and wholeheartedly recommend. Every preacher and lay reader should have it and read it!*'

Wallace Benn

'*Distinguished New Testament historian and pastor, Bishop Paul Barnett, has given us a clearly written commentary on Romans which, while critically conversant with the present debate over the new perspective, is clear and accessible to preachers and Bible teachers. The deft hand of a scholar preacher is everywhere evident in the neat organization, precision, lucid explanative and warmth of this most helpful work.*'

R. Kent Hughes

Paul Barnett is retired Bishop of North Sydney, Senior Fellow in the Ancient History Documentary Research Centre, Macquarie University, Teaching Fellow at Regent College, Vancouver and Faculty Member Moore Theological College Sydney.

ISBN 1-85792-727-3

Christian Focus Publications
publishes books for all ages

Our mission statement –
STAYING FAITHFUL
In dependence upon God we seek to help make His infallible
Word, the Bible, relevant. Our aim is to ensure that the Lord
Jesus Christ is presented as the only hope to obtain forgive-
ness of sin, live a useful life and look forward to heaven with
Him.

REACHING OUT
Christ's last command requires us to reach out to our world
with His gospel. We seek to help fulfill that by publishing
books that point people towards Jesus and help them develop
a Christ-like maturity. We aim to equip all levels of readers for
life, work, ministry and mission.
Books in our adult range are published in three imprints.
  Christian Focus contains popular works including biographies, commentaries, basic doctrine and Christian living.
  Our children's books are also published in this imprint.
  Mentor focuses on books written at a level suitable for Bible College and seminary students, pastors, and other serious readers. The imprint includes commentaries, doctrinal
  studies, examination of current issues and church history.
  Christian Heritage contains classic writings from the past.

Christian Focus Publications, Ltd
Geanies House, Fearn,
Ross-shire, IV20 1TW, Scotland, United Kingdom
info@christianfocus.com

For details of our titles visit us on our website
www.christianfocus.com